AMERICAN EDUCATION

THE TASK AND THE TEACHER

p 186

AMERICAN EDUCATION

THE TASK AND THE TEACHER

John H. Johansen
Northern Illinois University

Harold W. Collins
Northern Illinois University

James A. Johnson
Northern Illinois University

Frank Carley
Formerly of Miami-Dade College

WM. C. BROWN COMPANY PUBLISHERS
Dubuque, Iowa

Printed in the United States of America

To Our Children

Table of Contents

Section II THE ORGANIZATION AND ADMINISTRATION OF PUBLIC EDUCATION IN THE UNITED STATES

Section III THE LEARNING PROCESS

Credits

301, *upper right*; 302; 304, *upper left*; 321, *upper right*; 324, *upper*; 328

198; 205, *lower right and left*; 265 — Courtesy of Eastman Kodak Company

66; 69; 70; 72; 73; 74; 75; 78; 79; 241; 242; 243; 244; 261, *lower left* — Courtesy of History of Education Research Center, Northern Illinois University, DeKalb, Illinois.

xix; 46; 159; 202, *lower left and right*; 203; 204; 206, *upper right and left*; 207; 208; 233; 236; 254, *lower left* — Courtesy of Minnesota Mining and Manufacturing Co. (3M) New York, New York. 3M Company Photo.

52; 53, *lower*; 55, *lower right* — Courtesy of Naperville Central High School, Naperville, Illinois.

23; 35; 57; 89; 158; 161; 165; 170; 184; 185; 186; 188; 205, *upper left and right*; 219; 220; 222; 223; 239; 240; 257; 260; 268; 269; 270; 271; 272; 282; 291; 292; 294; 295, *upper*; 299; 300; 306; 314; 316; 317; 318; 319; 320; 324, *lower*; 327 — Courtesy of Northern Illinois University, DeKalb, Illinois.

206, *lower*; 209, *lower*; 210, *upper right*; 230; 237; 238; 254, *upper right*; 301, *lower*; 304, *lower right* — Courtesy of RCA, Camden, New Jersey.

231; 252; 375; 380 — Courtesy of Triton College, Northlake, Illinois.

List of Figures

xiii

Preface

This textbook seeks to introduce the reader to the profession of teaching. It is a relevant text for use in introductory undergraduate education courses and is particularly pertinent for students who might be considering entering teaching and other allied educational careers, both professional and para-professional. Special emphasis is given to the importance, development, roles, opportunities, rewards and frustrations of teaching.

American Education: The Task and the Teacher presents an overview of the roles that education has played in the past, and the expectations that both society and individuals hold for it today. It considers the American educational enterprise in terms of its problems, possibilities, and potentialities. Discussions of patterns of school organization, elements of control and the basics of school financing are included. The characteristics of learners and the curricula provided for the many different kinds of learners are considered in the light of emerging and innovative methods of instruction, including the use of recent technological advances and multi-media resources. The history of educational thought, practice, and persistent issues is treated as it relates to the contemporary scene.

Illustrative materials, pictorial and graphic, are used along with quotations and examples to assist the reader in identifying with the content. While clarity and brevity were considered to be of prime importance, bibliographic information is provided to enable the reader to pursue his interests in greater depth. Discussion questions and suggested learning activities are presented with each chapter. At the end of each chapter a brief and pertinent selected article is presented to enhance the concepts discussed within that chapter.

Valuable contributions were made to this book by Marvin Alexander, College of San Mateo in California, and Norman L. Mc-Cumsey, Northern Iowa University. Special recognition is given to Nita Collins for her efforts in preparing the manuscript.

JOHN H. JOHANSEN
HAROLD W. COLLINS
JAMES A. JOHNSON

AMERICAN EDUCATION

EDUCATION

THE TASK AND THE TEACHER

The Role of Education in the United States

In this section the authors have chosen to view education in terms of the expectations of societies and individuals. Chapters one and two approach the topic from a contemporary viewpoint, while chapter three examines expectations of education as they have related to our history.

The American society is a reflection of our representative democratic form of government. As such it professes to the ideal precepts of a democracy. The basis of these ideals is freedom: freedom of expression, freedom of opportunity, and the freedom of people to determine their own destinies. A high premium is placed on the worth of the individual and his opportunities for education. A major function of education in a democracy is to develop individuals to their fullest capacities so that they in turn may contribute to the achievement of the ideals of a democratic society.

The societal expectations for education are many and varied. Among these expectations two consistent desires can be recognized: the perpetuation of certain knowledge elements of our culture, and the refinement of our actual ways of living to cause them to become more congruent with our ideals. The latter of these goals gives rise to expectations for the schools in resolving some of our social problems.

Individual expectations for education are also many and varied. Every American in his own individual way has ideas of what he wants the schools to do for him and for his children. These expectations are expressed and our school programs reveal these expressions. Individual voices join to form societal choruses to be heard by those who are charged with directing education. While the size and complexities of our society make it increasingly difficult for an individual to be heard, our form of government and our educational systems are committed to the protection of the right of individuals to be heard.

Historically, expectations for education have changed as our nation has developed. Generally, our educational system has responded to the demands of individuals and to the demands of society. In the future the needs of individuals and of society are not likely to be met by schools that take merely a reflective or responsive posture. The schools must assume a leadership role.

CHAPTER 1

Societal Expectations for Education

American society is pluralistic. It contains many diverse groups within the larger group: young and old, liberal and conservative, black and white, atheists and believers, urbanites and farmers, union members and nonunion members, have and have-nots, and many more. Each of these sub-societies has purposes. Their purposes are sometimes in harmony with the majority of the members of the larger American society and sometimes in discord. The purposes of the overall American society, plus those of its subgroups, give rise to societal or group expectations for education.

The American Scene

Many Americans famous in our history have stated their views on the relationship of education to our overall democratic society:

Above all things, I hope the education of the common people will be attended to; convinced that on their good sense we may rely with the most security for the preservation of a due degree of liberty.

Thomas Jefferson

Of all the work that is done or that can be done for our country, the greatest is that of educating the body, the mind, and above all the character, giving spiritual and moral training to those who in a few years are themselves to decide the destinies of the nation.

Theodore Roosevelt

Without popular education, moreover, no government which rests upon popular action can long endure.

Woodrow Wilson

The common school is the greatest discovery ever made by man. It is supereminent in its universality and in the timeliness of the aid it proffers. The common school can train . . . children in the elements of all good knowledge and of virtue.
Jails and prisons are the complement of schools; so many less you have of the latter, so many more you must have of the former.

Horace Mann

More recently others have said:

The human mind is our fundamental resource. . . . The Federal government's responsibility in this area has been established since the earliest days of the Republic—it is time now to act decisively to fulfill that responsibility for the sixties.

John F. Kennedy

1

Because our schools help shape the mind and character of our youth, the strength or weakness of our educational system today will go far to determine the strength or weakness of our national wisdom and our national morality tomorrow. That is why it is essential to our nation that we have good schools. And their quality depends on all of us.

Dwight D. Eisenhower

When I look at American education, I do not see schools, but young Americans who deserve the chance to make a life for themselves and ensure the progress of their country. If we fail in this, no success we have is worth the keeping, but I say to you that we will not fail.

Richard M. Nixon

The previous quotations were directed generally to the relationship between education and the survival and welfare of the overall American society. Other Americans not so famous also have thoughts and expectations about what schools should be doing for society. If one could tune in on their thoughts as he walked the streets and visited in the meeting halls throughout the nation, he would very likely hear some of the following ideas expressed:

Our schools must first of all teach children to be devoted and loyal to their country. Young people have to learn to respect the Constitution and the flag of the best country in the world. Kids got it good in this country and they better appreciate it—they might have to fight for this land someday.

Better help me and some of my kind git jobs. We helped build this place. And it ain't that we don' wanna work, it ain't that we is just plain lazy—it is that we needs to learn how to do somethin' so we can get good jobs, you know, man, *good* jobs, not just sweepin', cleanin' and pickin'. And somethin' else, the schools they better quit sayin' my kids cain't learn and teach 'em.

The best thing the school can do for society is to teach youngsters all the knowledge they can and then help them learn how to think with it. The more a young person knows the better prepared he is to live in this competitive world—and therefore, probably the better able to serve this society and help solve its problems. That makes sense to me—apply brain power, not babble power, and remember we'll always have problems. Kids need good, solid, fundamental college preparatory training. They also need to learn a few more social graces—many of them are crude. I don't go for this long haired "hippie" stuff.

The difference between right and wrong, that's what the schools should teach. All the technical knowledge and cultural appreciation in the world isn't going to help us nearly so much as it could so long as we have killing, stealing, looting, rioting, and all that goes with it going on. In addition to the customary three "r's" we need respect and religion. For this country to survive, children have to learn respect for other people, respect for rule by law and respect for our Creator. Really, I don't see what's so wrong about religion in the public schools—after all, this is a religious country—and it might help teach about right and wrong. Those who don't want it can ignore it.

These statements reflect further the pluralistic nature of American society, and also the many and varied expectations its members have for education. Citizens do recognize the relationship between societies and their schools. The first statement expressed a concern for developing loyalty to the United States along with an appreciation for its history and heritage. Schools were envisioned as playing a major role in causing the young to love their country and to be ready to defend what it stands for from those who would destroy it either from without or from within. Another statement recognized the relationship between education and jobs, and the relationship between jobs and freedom from poverty. Education was seen as a means for men to improve themselves, to loosen their shackles, and to determine their destinies. It was further emphasized that the schools must serve all children from all the classes of society and cause them to learn. The failure of a child to learn in school appeared in the previously quoted statement as a failure of the school to teach the child. It was indicated that schools need to align their teaching to the needs of their constituent society. Still another statement reiterated the relationship between knowledgeable individuals and effective citizenship. Great faith was evidenced in the educated to use rational methods to resolve their social problems. Morality and law and order were the theme of the last statement cited, as schools were viewed as having an obligation supplementary to the home in developing the character of its students.

What does the American society expect from its schools? The answers, if itemized, would result in an infinite list. Most of the items on the list, however, could be classified under two major headings: (1) the transmission of culture, and (2) resources for assisting in the resolution of social problems. These two tasks require the mustering of major talents and resources, for both tasks are highly complex. Cultures are diverse, and the social problems of the United States are many and varied.

Transmission of Culture

Culture may be defined as the ways of living that societies have evolved or developed as their members have encountered and interacted with their environment. As such it includes knowledge, beliefs, arts, morals, values, laws, languages, tools, insti-

tutions, and ideas. Every individual is cultured—that is, he has a way of living; however, rarely, if ever, would any individual know the complete culture of his society. For example, while most citizens of the United States enjoy and use plumbing facilities they do not have the specialized knowledge of plumbers. Nor do most citizens have a complete knowledge of medicine, yet they benefit from its advanced state in our culture. Individuals learn the culture of their societies from infancy; much of it they gain from imitation and by osmosis. With maturity, individuals consciously or unconsciously choose for their purposes that which they value from the larger culture.

> Culture is a human production, and man differs from animals because he creates culture, and because he transmits what he has learned and what he has created from one generation to the next.
>
> Robert J. Havighurst

The United States, because of its multiethnic origins, contains many subcultures. Most large cities have neighborhoods which reflect immigrant cultures. These neighborhoods feature the foods, arts, and handicrafts of the ancestoral backgrounds of the inhabitants.

Frequently, the neighborhood residents sponsor festivals featuring facets of their ethnic culture. Cultural elements with a distinct uniqueness also develop in geographic regions of our nation, and in the rural, suburban, and urban demographic groups. From these fertile milieus, which have been accumulating, adulterating, and altering for the past three and one half centuries, Americans seek to identify the uniqueness of their total culture.

Schools in our society have been given the responsibility of transmitting culture. They are expected by the citizenry to accomplish this task. What shall they transmit? While a clear and specific answer to this question cannot be given, history has provided some guidelines.

There is little question that the schools are expected to transmit the knowledge element of culture. Historically in our early colonies this meant to teach the young to read, write, and cipher using the Bible as the basic textbook. As the colonies grew and became a nation and the Westward movement began, knowledge came to include vocational skills necessary for our growth. During these periods the secondary schools came into existence, partly in recognition of the added knowledge necessary to foster the development of our growing nation. Today, one need only look at the curriculum of a modern secondary school to realize that knowledge has become an increasingly comprehensive term. It still represents reading, writing, and ciphering; it also represents social studies, biological and physical science, agriculture, home economics, industrial education, languages, business, art, and a multitude of other specialties ranging from automobile body repair to contract bridge.

The "knowledge explosion" has caused many educators to seriously consider what knowledge the school should transmit. It is obvious that in the amount of time customarily dedicated to formal schooling, only a small portion of the total knowledge that man now possesses can be passed on to the young. If one could conceptualize knowledge as being of a material nature such as

Learning to read is considered a basic cultural necessity.

books, and then try to imagine the size of a mountain it would make, the immensity of the task can be partly realized. Selectivity is necessary as decisions are made regarding which portions of the total knowledge available are to be transmitted by the schools. Americans seem to have said: first of all, let us make certain that each individual is required to learn the knowledge which is necessary for his survival in our society; secondly, let us permit each individual to determine what he wants to learn which will assist him and perhaps incidentally advance our society; and thirdly, let us plan and hope that in the process, skills will be mastered to foster and enhance the development of more knowledge to the betterment of our way of life. So certain parts of the "mountain" are parcelled out to all young people, after which they can select some more if they so desire, while hopefully and simultaneously the mountain gets larger and larger.

Knowledge transmission, through the American school system, has undoubtedly contributed to the relatively high leadership position of the United States in materialistic manifestations of cultural accomplishments. Our standard of living is closely related to the United States' commitment to knowledge for all citizens through a public education. Level of education is definitely a fourth variable in the economic formula of land, labor, and capital.

Active involvement in citizenship education.

Citizenship education through social studies.

A second traditionally accepted responsibility of the schools in terms of cultural transmission is that of citizenship education. The schools are expected to, and do, make efforts to cause children to appreciate and understand our system of government. An educated citizenry is not only one that has knowledge, but one that is composed of individuals who will use this knowledge to foster an effective scheme of government, of, by, and for the people. In addition to formal instruction in our schools, youngsters also learn about good citizenship by participating in various forms of student government simulating our local, state, and national systems. Student councils, mock elections, and student government days are examples of these activities. While specific societal expectations for citizenship education will vary, perhaps from blind indoctrination to the advocation of laissez faire behavior, the most common position of the schools has been that of causing mature students to analyze critically and then to participate in improving our system.

Our overall society has prescribed democratic ideals; ideals toward which our society is striving, and which the schools are expected to exemplify, practice, and teach. A democratic society places a high premium on the worth of the individual. In 1960, the President's Commission on National Goals, in reporting on the domestic goals of our society stated:

The status of the individual must remain our primary concern. All our institutions—political, social, and economic—must further enhance the dignity of the citizen, promote the maximum development of his capabilities, stimulate their responsible exercise, and widen the range of effectiveness of opportunities for individual choice.[1]

Closely related to the importance of the individual is the commitment to equality—on this subject the Commission reported:

Vestiges of religious prejudice, handicaps to women, and, most important, discrimination on the basis of race must be recognized as morally wrong, economically wasteful, and in many respects dangerous. In this decade we must sharply lower these last stubborn barriers.[2]

It is important to note that the major responsibility for achieving the societal goal of equality, particularly in reference to the elimination of racial discrimination, has been placed on the schools. The U.S. Supreme Court in their 1954 *Brown v. Board of Education of Topeka* decision marked the beginning of an era of efforts to eliminate racial segregation.

In terms of the democratic process, which is the core of citizenship training, the Commission said, "To preserve and perfect the democratic process in the United States is therefore a primary goal in this as in every decade."[3] In elaboration of this point the Commission continued:

Democracy gives reality to our striving for equality. It is the expression of individual self-respect; it clears the way for individual initiative, exercise of responsibility, and use of varied talents. It is basic to the peaceful adjustment of differences of opinion.[4]

In citizenship education, the schools are expected to bring about a congruency between the American ideals and real life circumstances. Part of the dissension apparent in high schools and colleges today can be

1. *Goals for Americans: The Report of the President's Commission on National Goals*, p. 3.
2. *Ibid.*, pp. 3–4.
3. *Ibid.*, p. 4.
4. *Ibid.*, p. 5.

attributed to this lack of congruency. Students seem to be saying, "Your actions speak so loudly that I can't hear your words." They accuse the older generation of professing peace and practicing war, espousing equality of opportunity and perpetuating inequality, and advocating participation in political and school decision-making while at the same time castigating those who would dare raise a dissenting voice. Some students seem to have lost faith in the American system, advocating its destruction, while still others strive to work from within to improve it. Schools today, particularly at the levels of secondary and higher education, in response to student dissent and protest, are having to change their traditional ways of participatory student citizenship education.

While American society in general recognizes the necessity of, and subscribes rather unanimously to, the transmission of knowledge and training for citizenship in our schools, the unanimity begins to fragment as subcultural elements are considered. The influence of community subcultures can be observed as local schools decide what they shall teach. The increase of Afro-American studies in many urban schools is indicative of this phenomenon.

Pluralism, Democracy, and Values

As has been indicated, America is a pluralistic society consisting of many different subsocieties. This results not only from our multi-ethnic origin, but also from our emphasis on the protection and enhancement of individual freedoms, as specified in the United States Constitution and as practiced in our daily life. Thus, the democratic form of government fosters pluralism. Gans has

suggested that American democracy needs to be modernized to accommodate itself to pluralism.

I believe that the time has come to modernize American democracy and adapt it to the needs of a pluralistic society; in short, to create a pluralistic democracy. A pluralistic form of democracy would not do away with majority rule, but would require systems of proposing and disposing which take the needs of minorities into consideration, so that when majority rule has serious negative consequences, outvoted minorities would be able to achieve their most important demands, and not be forced to accept tokenism, or resort to despair or disruption.
Pluralistic democracy would allow the innumerable minorities of which America is made up to live together and share the country's resources more equitably, with full recognition of their various diversities. Legislation and appropriations would be based on the principle of 'live and let live,' with different programs of action for different groups whenever consensus is impossible. Groups of minorities could still coalesce into a majority, but other minorities would be able to choose their own ways of using public power and funds without being punished for it by a majority.[5]

The fostering of pluralism encourages the perpetuation and development of many different value systems. What are values? Phenix has recognized two distinct meanings of the term *values:* ". . . a value is anything which a person or persons actually approve, desire, affirm, or expect themselves to obtain, preserve, or assist. According to the second meaning, a value is anything which *ought to be* approved, desired, and so forth, whether or not any given person or persons in fact do adopt these positive attitudes

5. Herbert J. Gans, "We Won't End the Urban Crisis Until We End 'Majority Rule,'" *The New York Times Magazine*, Section 6, Col. 4–5, p. 24, 3 August 1969. © The New York Times Co. Used by permission.

toward it."[6] Schools must be concerned with both definitions—they operate in "what is" and are expected to create "what ought to be," and have some difficulty being certain of the values in either case. The United States Constitution has set forth some values, and a body of case law seeks to define them. What of issues not so clearly defined? What, for example, are the value preferences of different groups of people regarding honesty, cleanliness, manners, loyalty, sexual morality, and punctuality? As one reflects upon this problem it becomes clear that people cherish different viewpoints. Whose viewpoints should be perpetuated? When must individual freedom be sacrificed to the needs of society? Are there absolute values that must be accepted and adhered to by all for the success and vitality of our society? Or, are values relative in nature depending upon circumstances?

The following excerpt from a recent article by Joseph Junell is pertinent to the aforementioned questions.[7]

. . . My own experience as an observer in hundreds of classrooms has convinced me that while teachers often profess to be dealing with values, they are seldom sure of what they are teaching or to what purpose. The judgment is not mine alone. Theodore Brameld, the noted Boston University educator and philosopher, has conceded on at least one occasion that ". . . our schools and colleges, by and large, are neither consistent nor clear about the values they are obliged to instill in the young. . . . Insofar as American education has tended to regard its chief business as that of conveying information and training in skills, it has tended to store its values, so to speak, in the educational attic. . . ."[8]

Even more damaging is the evidence from the studies on the changing values of the new teacher completed within the past 10 years. Brief excerpts from two surveys of the literature are worthy of review. The first of these, by the psychologist Jacob W. Getzels, reports the findings from four major studies conducted by the University of Chicago. According to Getzels, they reveal an unmistakable drift among college students (teachers included) from a traditional, hard-nosed value orientation to a shifting, quixotic pattern which social scientists have come to call the "emergent values." "The goal of behavior is not personal rectitude but group consensus, not originality but adjustment." Great importance has been placed on "an overriding value of sociability and frictionless interpersonal relations" in which "the hard-working self-determined Horatio Alger hero is giving way to the affable young man in the gray flannel suit." Taking the place of "Puritan morality or . . . moral commitment, as a value, there are relativistic moral attitudes without strong personal commitments. Absolutes in right and wrong are questionable. In a sense, morality has become a statistical, rather than an ethical, concept; morality is what the group thinks is moral."[9]

The second survey, by W. W. Charters, Jr., corroborates most of Getzels' findings,

6. Philip H. Phenix, "Values in the Emerging American Civilization," *Teachers College Record* 61(1960):356.

7. Joseph S. Junell, "Can Our Schools Teach Moral Commitment?" *Phi Delta Kappan* 50(1969):445–446.

8. Theodore Brameld, *Cultural Foundations of Education*. New York: Harper & Brothers, 1957, p. 13.

9. From Jacob W. Getzels' chapter, "The Acquisition of Values in School and Society," in *The High School in a New Era*, edited by Francis S. Chase and Harold A. Anderson, pp. 152–155. Chicago: University of Chicago Press, 1958.

but its principal virtue lies in a summary of the work of George Spindler, the Stanford anthropologist. Unlike Getzels, Spindler worked in the realm of hypothesis. Vast industrial expansion, he reasoned, plus two global wars and a turbulent social history, had all but eroded the traditional values of a former agrarian society. The last citadel of moral respectability, the work-success ethic and the hard-line traditional value system, was to be found in the middle and lower middle classes. It is from here that is drawn the vast majority of America's teachers.

The influence of teacher training institutions, however, is clearly in the direction of emergent values. The result has been to create "ambivalence" and "vacillation" among some young teachers and to drive others to the extremes of rigid "authoritarianism" on the one hand, or to the "groupthink" cult of social adjustment on the other. A third teacher, whom Spindler calls the adaptive teacher, follows a pattern similar to those described but in far less severe form.

To date I know of no research which would prove that Spindler's teachers do indeed follow these patterns of behavior. However, Charters does cite a number of studies to show that the new teacher reflects "such emergent values as sociability, a relativistic moral attitude, consideration of others, conformity to the group, and a hedonistic present-time orientation."[10] Moreover, there can be no doubt of the influence exerted by teacher training institutions and their new cult of "scientific inquiry."

It is my personal belief that teachers are less committed to relativism per se than they are to the system which engenders it. A philosophy which regards hierarchy and permanence as questionable virtues logically points to the application of empiricism in value teaching. Thus when you suggest to this young teacher that scientific methods are by no means a cure-all for society's ailments or that there is need to pass on to future generations a body of fixed values, he will smile indulgently and ask: "Whose values? Yours or mine?" This is tantamount to saying, of course, that the importance of any particular value is largely a matter of personal preference and that what is one man's meat may well be another man's poison. Nor are models for this kind of logic found wanting in schools of education. For example, James P. Shaver of Utah State University argues that in a democratic, pluralistic society, where value conflict is inevitable, each defendant's claim in a clash of values must be given equal consideration. To illustrate this interesting point of view I quote from his survey on the scientific method of value teaching entitled "Reflective Thinking, Values, and Social Studies Textbooks":

> In the dispute over racial segregation, the Negro's claims for integration are supported by our commitment to brotherhood, the equality of opportunity, and to equal protection of the law. By the same token, however, the segregationist's position has been defended in terms of freedom of association, of property rights, and even of the right to local control in such matters. Each of these is also an important American value.[11]

Yet to accuse the new teacher of this kind of relativistic thinking simply draws a shrug of the shoulders and a complacent reply:

10. From the chapter by W. W. Charters, Jr., entitled "The Social Background of Teaching," in *Handbook of Research on Teaching*, edited by N. L. Gage, pp. 727–730. Chicago: Rand McNally & Co., 1963.
11. James P. Shaver, "Reflective Thinking, Values, and Social Studies Textbooks," *School Review*, Autumn, 1965, p. 327.

"You use one set of criteria for making value judgments; I use another. You fall back on traditional models and personal feelings. I examine past experience and all the possible consequences. Only then do I make up my mind. Yours is largely a conditioned reflex; mine a reasoned act. It's the only kind of response I accept as valid from my students."

"But isn't it possible," you argue, "just possible, for a value judgment to stand independent of the consequences—come hell or high water?"

"You mean the hang-tough values? What are they? Look, my friend, I use moral data in making judgments too. I love my parents, my wife, and my children. I am truly my brother's keeper. But this doesn't mean that I shouldn't put a value to the same kind of test as any other idea or judge its merits by the evidence."

"Can you always trust your evidence?"

And so the conversation comes to a close.

"Far more than my emotions."

This may be something of an exaggeration of the new teacher's philosophic outlook, but it is not entirely so. In comparing the educational practices of East and West, Clarence Faust, for one, has remarked on our increasing propensity to "refer questions of the truth of opinions and theories to the consequences of holding them, or at least to view propositions so attested as more substantial and valuable than those otherwise established."[12] Its implied methodology (that scientific methods are the way of all truth) is part and parcel of a great rash of inquiry-type programs in the social sciences now proliferating throughout America under the stimulus provided by Bruner, Fenton, and others. Surely, its flavor of pragmatist ethics, à la John Dewey and his distinguished colleagues, Sidney Hook,

Abraham Edel, Max Otto, and others, is unmistakable. All is marked, by this calloused view of any distinction between an idea and a value, by an irresolvable conflict between moral prescription and choice, and—what is perhaps its most prenicious feature—the Deweyan thesis that truth is operational, that effects rather than causes are its chief determinants.

Bertrand Russell, who agreed with John Dewey on most things, could not agree with him on this. He felt that switching the basis of truth from past events (causes), which cannot be manipulated or controlled, to future events (effects), which can be, gave to collective man the notion of unprecedented freedom and power he had no right to assume. In such "cosmic impiety" Russell sensed a danger that could lead to "vast social disaster."[13]

Although my thesis is far less cosmic in scope than Russell's, I nonetheless see in this linking of truth about values to the consequences of holding them a sinister influence upon value teaching no less disastrous in its effects. It is logical to assume, for example, that where consequences become the sole arbiters of truth, guiding principles occupy a very uneasy position in the affairs of men. Such, in fact, is the very spirit which pervades the method called "valuing" (in contradistinction to value teaching), a popular catchword now on the lips of every educator. Simply stated, it is the method of assigning value to ideas and beliefs after an inquiry-type examination of them has

12. Clarence H. Faust, "Theory and Practice of Education in the United States," in *Humanism and Education in East and West.* Paris: A UNESCO Publication, 1953, p. 82.
13. Bertrand Russell, *A History of Western Philosophy.* New York: Simon & Schuster, Inc., 1945, pp. 826–828.

proven them deserving of it. Touted as a scientific breakthrough in creating a responsible morality, it embraces most if not all the techniques known to science: observing, comparing, summarizing, classifying, coding, imagining, interpreting, criticizing, looking for assumptions, collecting and organizing data, hypothesizing, applying facts and principles, exploring alternatives, making decisions, designing projects, etc.

The list is indeed a mouthful, but there is far more involved. Under this formidable battery of techniques all values of feeling and belief connected to some crucial issue are subjected to a pitiless spotlight of inquiry. No value which does not represent knowledge—that is to say, some proof of its own merits—is admissible. Values of pure feeling are suspect or soon become so for want of evidence. If, as some philosophers suggest, matters of true feeling fall outside the purview of science, so much the worse for feeling; everything is grist to the mill. A value such as compassion, for instance, in an investigation of socialized medicine, would have a rough time of it, if indeed students had temerity enough to bring it into the discussion at all.

Within such an arena, then, scientific intellectualism provides the framework for decision making. Morality is seldom established; it is always being "discovered." Children are never set moral boundaries within which they may work out problems by whatever powers of mind have been vouchsafed them, but beyond which they may not venture. All is placed on the auction block, including the bargaining rules. Pitirim Sorokin, who is sometimes prone to be carried away by his own rhetoric, was not without justification when he said: "We live in an age in which no value, from God to private property, is universally accepted. There is no norm, from the Ten Commandments to contractual rules and those of etiquette, that is universally binding. . . . What one person or group affirms, another denies; what one pressure group extols, another vilifies. . . . Hence the mental, moral, religious, social, economic and political anarchy that pervades our life and culture. . . ."[14]

The ultimate result cannot but cast serious doubt on any notion that decisions about matters in which value is involved should—indeed must—reflect a hierarchy of moral absolutes, or at least what one anthropologist has defined as "conditioned" or "moving" absolutes.[15] In the absence of these we can only assume that moral choice is unlimited and that once we are taught the art of listening to the voice of reason, our faculties of intellect will take charge of that part of man which still separates him from the angels: namely, his secret compulsions, his haunting dreams of power and position, his most deeply rooted psychological barriers to truth. Could former President Truman, if faced with incontestable proof, bring himself to admit that his decision on Hiroshima was a terrible misjudgment? Would President Johnson bow to overwhelming evidence of tragic miscarriage in Vietnam? I wonder. Powerful men with far greater intellectual perspicacity, whom history has proved wrong, have gone to their graves proclaiming the strategic accuracy of their decisions. In fact, they could not do otherwise, for the act of losing face is often self-destructive beyond limits that humans can bear.

14. Pitirim A. Sorokin, *The Reconstruction of Humanity.* Boston: The Beacon Press, 1948, p. 104.
15. Clyde Kluckhohn, *Culture and Behavior.* New York: The Macmillan Co., 1964, p. 277.

This conspicuous lack of any fixed signposts for the guidance of behavior is not without parallel in the classroom. Several years ago when Buddhist priests in Vietnam protested U.S. intervention by self-immolation, I watched senior students in a contemporary problems class formulate opinions, unchallenged by the teacher, that this kind of zeal is a species of fanaticism. The notion of such behavior as being essentially a moral problem, resolvable only in terms of moral absolutes, simply did not enter into the discussion. It could not; it would have been inundated by a mountain of intellectual considerations—political, economic, and social —which dominated the discussion.

More interesting was my observation of a debating panel made up of bright youngsters who had been arbitrarily assigned the task of defending the position of the conscientious objector. It was obvious from the start that these students felt uncomfortable with their role, trending to equate pacifism with cowardice and disloyalty. It was also clear that no one had taken the trouble to point out to them that pacifism, in the tradition of the Christian martyrs, Gandhi, King, and others, can demand a courage as painful and difficult to maintain as that of a soldier on the battlefront. When, as generally happens in these cases, the whole argument was reduced to the ultimate test of the pacifist's belief—his severely limited choice of personal annihilation in preference to the destruction of another life—the entire concept was put down as somehow weird and irrational. The absence of any framework of real moral fiber had rendered this discussion an interesting though perfectly harmless intellectual exercise for both teacher and students.

Prescriptive morality is certainly a dubious virtue into which moral relativism often leads class discussion. There is now a movement afoot to bring down into the primary grades the fruits of reflective thought. *Scholastic Magazine,* for example, which prints reading matter for millions of school children throughout America, last year provided its readers with carefully researched and balanced arguments, pro and contra, on the Vietnamese conflict. Some schools incorporated this material into their teaching of the Minnesota Plan, a major social science project developed by the University of Minnesota, whose professed "behavioral goals" include among others the learner who "respects the rights of others" and who "values human dignity."[16]

Such is the subtle nature of hypocrisy that few of us who practice it are aware that we are doing so. One secondary teacher I know, who could not equate the teaching of dignity for all humans with what was happening in Vietnam, collected pictures of Vietnamese children, all victims of the war. Lacerated and maimed, their flesh seared by napalm, they stared out from his bulletin board with tragic, pain-filled eyes. Class reaction was mixed; there was morbid curiosity, shock, and complaints of a "gruesome sense of humor." Nevertheless, every time the subject of Vietnam came up for discussion he admonished his class: "First, let's take a long hard look at those pictures, then we'll talk." As I watched I was strongly reminded of Ivan Karamazov's (from *The Brothers Karamazov*) tortuous search for an

16. Edith West and William Gardner, "The Role of the Social Studies in Developing Values," Background Paper No. 11, *Social Studies Curriculum Development Center,* University of Minnesota, p. 15.

answer to the evil of men's senseless cruelties. "But the children, Alyosha!" was the one question he kept hammering out again and again to his younger brother, who was training for the priesthood. "They haven't yet tasted of the apple. What about the children?"

It was to be expected that this young teacher, a rare gift to the profession, would be asked one day to answer the complaints of a parent who felt that his "political opinions" were dangerously prejudicial. On the second day he came up before his principal; the third day his bulletin board was down; and on the fourth day he was again safely teaching reflective techniques.

The fact remains that most children come to the classroom with essentially humane attitudes. If such were not the case, this writing could have no purpose, for it has been shown rather conclusively by researchers such as Anna Freud, Spitz, Goldfarb, and Bowlby, that the time from birth to age five or six is more crucial to attitude formation than all the years thereafter.[17] But for this average child, as Gordon Allport puts it, "the foundations of character were established by the age of three or five, only in the sense that he is now *free to become;* he is not retarded; he is well launched on the course of continuous and unimpeded growth."[18]

This simple fact poses a question of grave import. What happens in an atmosphere in which primary attitudes and values are dealt with all of a piece, the trivial along with the significant,[19] where choice is given free reign so long as it is based on consequential proof, where fixed guideposts and boundaries are either suspect or treated with no more reverence than ideas? This is certainly not to infer that moral prescriptions are mandates from heaven. For my part, I am willing to accept the social scientist's view—Ashley Montagu's for one—that value arises out of the most satisfactory relationship between human needs and environmental conditions and that this involves choice.[20] By the same token, choice without value does not constitute morality; it is opportunism pure and simple. Choice takes on moral essence only when it transcends biology and acquires in doing so an arbitrary element that is at once inflexible and static in its demands. (Value conflicts are exceptions, to be sure, but even so choice is still painfully limited.) In making us behave as we do, it commits us to *total responsibility.*

The very process by which this happens dictates no less arbitrarily the only methods by which it can be taught. Here it is helpful to return briefly to Mr. Getzels for one of his insights. Learning values, he informs us, is quite a different thing from learning the capitals of states or the multiplication table. Values are not so much learned as they are "interiorized" through intimate and complex processes of *identification,* in which a child strives to integrate and stablilize his own self-image by becoming "as one" with other persons—parents, older siblings, friends, teachers. The process is carried on

17. See John Bowlby's summary of these investigations entitled *Maternal Care and Mental Health.* Geneva: World Health Organization, Monograph Series No. 2, 1951.

18. Gordon W. Allport, *Becoming.* New Haven: Yale University Press, 1965, p. 33.

19. I have noticed that even Bishop Pike, a leading voice for the new morality, does not escape this vice.

20. Ashley Montagu, *The Direction of Human Development.* New York: Harper & Brothers, 1955, p. 153.

for the most part unconsciously, on a level of feeling and emotion, and seldom if ever intellectualized. During the while the child assumes not only "the outward manners and expressive movements of his 'significant figures' but attempts also to incorporate their values and attitudes."

In this way, Getzels feels, the school "can acquire an eminence second only to the home perhaps—an eminence that it certainly does not have now. . . . The teachers become, or at least can become, significant figures for the child." Far more meaningful than what a child is told to do is the teacher "model" placed before him to which he can attach importance. In short, "One cannot so much *teach* values as *offer appropriate models for identification.*"[21]

If Getzels' "significant figures" mean anything at all, it is that espousing values outweighs considerably the teacher's ability to reflect upon them. No less important is the fact that identification occurs also through fantasy, or, to use the literary term, through vicarious experience. It is curious that social scientists are just now beginning to learn through experimentation what men of letters have known intuitively for centuries. "Some evidence indicates," Gordon Allport tells us in his book *The Nature of Prejudice,* "that films, novels, dramas may be effective, presumably because they induce identification. . . . If this finding stands up in future research, we shall be confronted with an interesting possibility. . . . Perhaps in the future we shall decide that intercultural programs should *start* [italics Allport's] with fiction, drama, and films, and move gradually into more realistic methods of training."[22] In elementary social studies, now so heavily overshadowed by the mystique of concept building, inquiry learning, and the addition of new disciplines, a frontal attack on the emotions has enormous implications for children who are "free to become." I have supported this view elsewhere in my writings and am firmly convinced of its great potential.

But such an assessment, I am aware, points irrevocably to a major reconstruction in the social studies program for children. I see no other way. This subject at all levels has been for too long conceived and taught in a moral vacuum; in the elementary grades the materialistic bias and poverty of social and moral ideas are established facts. Yet if science has told us anything at all about small children, it is that the "crucial period" in a child's life is a very precious thing. John Bowlby places its discovery "Among the most significant developments in psychiatry during the past quarter of a century. . . ."[23] Unlike the period for other kinds of learning, which ends only with death, its time grows fleeting and must be nurtured in its own way if it is not to become irretrievably lost. For never again will this child identify so keenly with the vicissitudes of his significant figures and groups. Never will he feel so intensely their despair at injustice, brutality, and intolerance, nor accept so uncritically their own shining virtues. Horatio Alger may have given his countless readers a version of the American success story as phony as a three-dollar bill, but I, for one, am still unable to disembarrass myself completely of the idea that industry, like cleanliness, is next to Godliness. The curious thing is that the characters and events have long since faded from memory.

21. Getzels, *op. cit.,* p. 160.
22. Gordon W. Allport, *The Nature of Prejudice.* Reading, Mass.: Addison-Wesley Publishing Co., Inc., 1954, p. 488.
23. Bowlby, *op. cit.,* p. 11.

In practical terms I envision a social and moral drama of conflict, a goodly portion of which would deal with the unsung protagonists of history. I have experimented briefly with this form in my own writings for children, though not with results necessarily acceptable to book publishers. It would mean of course that the white world, from the sixteenth century onward, would emerge something less than perfect. But no matter. It is the unique idea involved here that counts—a phenomenon commonly known in literary circles as the story of the underdog, whose powers are as strange as those which lurk in Freud's world of the unconscious. Harking back to the time of tribal fires and the teller of tales, it is as ancient as man himself.

Indeed, the phenomenon could bear some relationship to a current and fascinating theory that moral behavior is philogenetically evolved. According to the ethologist Konrad Lorenz, a leading exponent of this view, ritual among many lower animals is an instinctive behavioral adaptation for disarming the more explosive instinct of aggression, both of which are imperative to survival. Man shares the same aggressive instinct, claims Lorenz, and moral behavior represents merely a higher evolutionary step—though a very complex one—above animal ritual, designed to serve the same purpose.[24] True or not, it is entirely possible that the kind of vicarious experience we have been discussing is an important—perhaps the *most* important—means of achieving this higher moral expression; that children who are deprived of its more controlled forms suffer measurable psychic damage by seeking it through dangerous patterns of fantasy.

Whatever the case may be, if such an emphasis on my part indicates a kind of perverse blindness to the virtues of scientific intellectualism, well and good. I am far less concerned that our children learn to create new values in a changing world than I am about their ability to safeguard and perpetuate a few of what Sir Herbert Read has called the great simplicities which touch the deepest springs in human relationships. At the same time, I do not see how they can serve mankind except as a great hierarchy of universals whose demands upon all alike are exacting and immutable. It is significant that the late Clyde Kluckhohn, a noted anthropologist who spent the greater part of his productive years describing the incredible diversity which marks human culture, should have written near the end of his life: ". . . all talk of an eventual peaceful and orderly world is but pious cant or sentimental fantasy unless there are, in fact, some simple but powerful things in which all men can believe, some codes or canons that have or can obtain universal acceptance. . . ."[25] It is upon our commitment to these and the successful teaching of them that all civilizations, if they are to survive, must ultimately rest.

While Junell decried the modern trend away from traditional or absolute values, Hunt in the following excerpt defends a form of relativism.[26]

The thesis of this article is that the prevailing view of the young today favors what might be referred to as situational morality.

24. Konrad Lorenz, *On Aggression*. New York: Bantam Books, 1967.
25. Clyde Kluckhohn, *Culture and Behavior*. New York: The Macmillan Co., 1964, pp. 286, 287.
26. Maurice P. Hunt, "Some Views on Situational Morality," *Phi Delta Kappan* 50(1969):452–455. Used with permission.

(The terms morality and ethics, for purposes of this article, will be used interchangeably.) Situational morality is a form of relativism as applied to social relations. The concept will be defined more precisely as I proceed.

I do not intend this article as an extensive, documented treatment of historical background and present situation. It is offered as the studied opinion of one social observer who happens to have a major interest in this field.

It appears that most sociologists, anthropologists, social psychologists, theologians, philosophers, and other social observers feel there is a serious moral crisis in this and other countries as of the late 1960's. If this analysis is correct, it would seem that we are reliving many other periods of history when cultures which once were viable have shown signs of falling apart. Many of these cultures have disintegrated, with new cultures arising to glue the society together again. On the other hand, false alarms seem to have been common (Spengler's *Decline of the West,* perhaps?).

The present moral crisis is often described as an outcome of a clash between absolutistic and relativistic values. I am of the opinion that this is an oversimplification. Absolutists tell us that the value crisis is a result of our losing sight of time-honored Truths (the capital "T" is deliberate). It is argued that after relegating the eternal verities to the trash heap, we drift in one of two directions: toward 1) a state of valuelessness—that is, trying to live without settled or coherent values, or 2) a tendency to pursue "false" values—or, at best, values of minor worth. Among currently accepted values regarded as dubious or dangerous are use of alcohol, wearing miniskirts, gambling, use

of drugs for pleasure, wearing beards and long hair among males, and the like.

In contrast, relativists worry about the value crisis primarily in terms of whether or not people in general will find it possible to cast aside absolutistic values and adopt relativistic values *soon enough* to bring ethical thinking in tune with the demands of modern industrialized culture. According to this view, if the young develop a relativistic orientation soon enough, industrialized culture will survive. Not only will it survive, but there is a likelihood that its fundamental orientation will be democratic and progressive in the sense that life will gradually improve for most persons—particularly the oppressed minorities.

My contention is that the time is long past when we could maintain as guides to living any kind of value system based upon absolutes—whether the absolutes are derived from God or Nature. Absolutistic thought characterized the nineteenth and earlier centuries, whereas the twentieth century becomes increasingly dominated by some kind of relativistic view. Our young are committed to relativistic thinking—to the point where it seems to them the only way to think which gears with the knowledge given us by science and technology about human life and the nature of the universe.

Probably it has always been too late to "turn back" from relativistic thinking. When man first began to reflect scientifically (i.e., to experiment by testing hypotheses with evidence), which probably dates from his appearance as a species, he was already on the road toward the eventual "scientizing" of entire cultures. Looking back, it would almost seem that relativistic thinking was predestined for *Homo sapiens;* the combination of a large endowment of cerebral cortex with hands and a bodily structure adapted to land could, over the long run, probably lead nowhere else except toward an experimental frame of mind. (Pity or envy the bottle-nosed dolphin as you wish; his brain may be as good or better than man's but his body isn't constructed right!)

There are still many persons reluctant to admit that this is an age of relativism. Pope Paul, for example, seems convinced that, without absolutes, organized religion and all human culture will collapse. Protestant fundamentalists share the view. The same is true of those naturalistic thinkers who feel that moral law is derived from some sort of absolute Natural Law.

To me, therefore, the moral crisis no longer can be described in terms of a contest between an absolutistic world view and a relativistic world view. This mode of description may have been valid before Einstein published his first paper on the special theory of relativity (1905), but now it is hopelessly inappropriate. We will cease tilting with windmills as soon as we recognize that the moral crisis of 1969 can be described only in terms of a contest between different versions of relativism. It is now a question of relativism$_1$ vs. relativism$_2$ vs. relativism$_3$ vs. all other modes of relativistic thought now extant.

My opinion is that a crisis in values really does exist and that unless it is at least partially resolved we can expect to see a rise in the level of cultural disorganization and ever more signs of serious cultural disintegration. Signs of cultural disorganization and disintegration already abound. They are likely to become much more threatening before they abate.

Present cultural disorganization is primarily a product of value conflicts. These value conflicts tend to take two conspicuous forms (although I do not rule out other forms). These two forms of conflict are induced by 1) abortive attempts to retain or reinstate values supported by absolutes, and 2), of much more importance, vacillation with respect to which of various relativistic views to adopt. The first type of conflict will pass with time because absolutistic thinking appears doomed, whether we take action in its behalf or against it. But while such conflicts are with us, they may cause a great deal of disturbance and undoubtedly should not be ignored. The second type of conflict is more difficult to handle because it requires us to make more subtle distinctions, to know more about man and his world, and it may be with us for a very long time. In short, it demands a lot of intellectual sophistication on the part of teachers and students to handle the kind of moral conflict most characteristic of the present culture of the young—that is, which kind of relativism to commit oneself to.

Before proceeding further in this analysis, it is essential that we look at the assumptions common to the various relativistic views concerning morality which are now competing with one another, because all of them do share certain fundamental premises. It appears to this writer that the following list, although not intended as exhaustive, is a somewhat close approximation of what all relativists believe.

1. Moral or ethical rules are invented—not discovered—by man; they are not derived from natural or divine law.

2. As such, they are not necessarily universal or eternal; they may vary widely from culture to culture. This is not the same position as "cultural relativism"—which re-

gards any moral value as good if it conforms with the cultural norm in which it exists.

3. Moral or ethical rules can be expected to change over the course of time. What is true in one situation will be false in another because moral truth does not "stay put." However, change is not necessarily or even desirably rapid.

4. Moral rules vary according to situation, provided we define situation as a "field" of psychological forces whose basic datum is the interaction of a person with his psychological environment. That is, a person interacts with a perceived (not to be confused with physical) environment and out of such interaction forms concepts and principles which guide moral behavior at that time. (The domination of a specific psychological *situation* in governing moral choice is why we use the term "situational ethics.")

5. Like many other kinds of human commitment, ethical principles, even though relativistic, may be cherished with great intensity—enough to "die for"—to use a trite but direct expression.

Although the foregoing five assumptions are perhaps enough to give readers a sense of what is taken for granted by relativistic moralists, they leave much unsaid. What I now wish to dwell on briefly is differences between the moral structures which can be built on fundamental premises such as these.

There is, for example, a line of thinking which stems from cultural relativism. Cultural relativism not only emphasizes strongly the almost infinitely broad sweep of moral beliefs as we range from one culture to another, but tends usually to take a neutral stance with respect to their worth. This is like saying "A culture is a culture is a

culture . . ." ad infinitum—which is to say one should refrain from making value judgments about the comparative worth of cultural norms. A problem inherent in this position is that to maintain it consistently one has to say that the culture of Hitler's Germany could be considered no worse—or better—than the culture of Churchill's England.

Another version of moral relativism can be derived from a line of thought usually associated with the pragmatism of William James. Although the interpretation is simplistic, the statement goes like this: "Anything is good if it works." Taken directly and without qualification, this is purely and simply a morality of expediency. We see it in operation every day in all kinds of places —used-car lots, deliberations of Congress, the machinations of the big business-military amalgam, and the like.

Then there is the kind of moral relativism embodied in Riesman's concept of the "other directed person." The other directed person keeps his psychological radar alerted to what the group with whom he identifies is doing. He then does his best to do the same. He tries to fit in, to conform. If he can do so, then he is doing the "right" thing. Adults become alarmed because this seems such an obvious trait among youth; but how often does one see an adult attend Easter church services wearing blue jeans? Conformity for many persons may be a useful hedge against psychological insecurity but it is hardly the basis for building a constructively moral civilization.

Another approach to morality which I see as particularly rife among my students is the "live-and-let-live" idea. When verbalized, it goes something like this: "I have my standards and X has his; I don't agree with X's standards but he has as much right to his as I have to mine. Whatever he thinks is right for him, *is* right for him." This makes of morality a series of individual, personalized decisions but is anti-social in the sense that each individual is granted warrant by every other individual to do whatever he chooses. To a large degree, group concerns are ruled out.

To me, the above examples of relativistic morality all seem inadequate. They have a negative quality; they appear to lack the ingredients for making positive and defensible moral choices. Our young deserve at the very least an understanding of other possible alternatives. A useful morality can defend certain moral choices as being better than others on grounds more substantial than present cultural norms, sheer expediency, group conformity, or letting each person be his own arbiter.

The approach proposed here is not represented as original; it is probably quite old. One begins by saying that an adequate situational morality is a "morality of consequences." But carrying it only this far is to offer nothing better than what has been described. What kind of consequences, to whom, and over what time span? When can it be said with at least some degree of confidence that one set of consequences is truly better than another?

It seems to me that a relativist can be consistent with his major premises and still be rather positive about what he recommends. Human experience has been a highly valuable testing ground of values. Are there not some which have stood well the test of time? (This is not the same as saying that such ideas are derived from God or Na-ture.) Human inventions, whether in the realm of moral ideas or in our ability to predict a chemical reaction, do undergo continuous tests of experience.

Whether we should take such experience seriously depends on various factors. Probably the test of time is relevant, provided the value under question has been debated for a long time. For example, the question of the relative merits of peaceful, non-coerced resolution of interpersonal conflict and forced, authoritarian, and violent resolution of such conflict has been before the human race for thousands of years. Today, most persons who are reasonably well educated and reasonably sane seem to opt for peace. We are all too well aware of the outcomes of violence; we should not have had to have our Vietnam experience to clinch the case for peace.

And does not the experience of the human race speak rather strongly for reason—for the use of careful reflection in the solution of problems? Our historical experience suggests that man has been, and may continue to be, unreasonable much more of the time than he is reasonable. But what man has been, what he is now, or what he may be in the foreseeable future, does not constitute a valid argument for advocating irrationality as a way of life.

In the case of values which are now emerging, man's past experience may not provide adequate tests. The use of drugs to induce pleasurable sensations seems as old as the human race. Yet the particular manner and purpose of their use may change drastically, as may the available scientific evidence concerning their effects. The use of marijuana by substantial proportions of students is a new phenomenon—at least in the context in which it now occurs. We now have some scientific evidence—lacking in the past—concerning its effects.

In the case of any newly emerging value, we have to judge its merits as best we can on the basis of all that we can find out about its consequences for good or ill. And we can hardly afford to take a short view. Moral values should be judged in terms of consequences to future generations as well as our own, since we have a responsibility to them too. On this ground, to cite one example, parents who have enough children to produce net gains in the size of population would seem highly immoral, since the population explosion may well be the most dangerous problem facing mankind. . . .

———————

While Junell and Hunt have presented different points of view, particularly in reference to the source of values, they both in fact advocated the necessity of establishing and perpetuating values for the continuation of a desired kind of society. Havighurst has suggested that the following, which he considers to be values of an urban, industrial, democratic society, and *not* social class values, must be taught by the American schools:

Punctuality, orderliness, conformity to group norms, desire for a work career based on skill and knowledge, desire for a stable family life, inhibition of aggressive impulses, rational approach to a problem situation, enjoyment of study, and desire for freedom of self and others.[27]

The task of the schools in doing their part in educating youth for citizenship in pluralistic urban America is both complex and immense.

The School and its Relationship to Social Problems

The United States has many unresolved problems both foreign and domestic; problems that affect groups and individuals; problems that individuals expect society to help them solve. In many cases these problems are so complex an individual may feel helpless as he faces them. The days of the American pioneer resolutely and quite individually making his way in his environment are fast fading. Today, man's destiny is strongly interdependent on that of others; his basic necessities of life, such as food, shelter, and clothing, are difficult to create by himself. The American citizen today exists in a complicated environmental system over which he as an individual has very little control. Therefore, his individual problems become social problems which require the organized efforts of society to solve. Schools as agencies of society are looked to as one resource for solving these problems. Let us briefly examine some of these problems.

Race Relationships

A rather persistent major social problem throughout history that has received increased attention in the United States the last decade has been that of race relations. In 1954 the United States Supreme Court in *Brown v. Board of Education of Topeka* reversed prior decisions supporting the separate but equal doctrine, and said that separate but equal facilities in education were

27. Robert J. Havighurst, "Overcoming Value Differences," *The Inner-City Classroom: Teacher Behaviors,* ed. by Robert D. Strom, pp. 47–48. Columbus, Ohio: Charles E. Merrill Books, Inc., 1966.

A form of integration in the classroom. School integration has been interpreted as including an integrated faculty, an integrated student body, and a faculty-student combination form of integration.

Physical integration in the classroom is one beginning step in achieving social integration wherein hopefully members of each group accept and respect members of the other group.

inherently unequal. The Court based its reasoning on the idea that while schools may be equally excellent educationally, with highly qualified staff members and superior facilities, they will differ because of the composition of the student population. This difference, if based on racial segregation, will have an adverse effect upon black students. Since the *Brown* decision, some progress has been made in integrating schools in both the South and the North. School segregation in the North has been most often termed as *de facto* segregation. This type of segregation is considered to be of the fact and not "deliberate," resulting primarily from neighborhood residence patterns and neighborhood schools. The *Brown* decision made *de jure* or "deliberate" segregation illegal. The legal status of de facto segregation is still in question. Courts have ruled that attendance center (neighborhood school) lines are illegal if drawn in such a way to promote segregation *(Taylor v. Board of Education in New Rochelle, New York).* They have also ruled that de facto segregation in and of itself is not illegal. The issue becomes further complicated when an entire school population of a district or city becomes predominantly black. In these circumstances, arrangements involving complex legal problems would have to be made to transport students from one school district to another, and in some instances from one state to another. Some plans involving voluntary exchange of students to foster integration have been made. Other programs which attempt to resolve the problem of segregated schools have included bussing, open enrollment, redistricting, creation of educational parks, and consolidation. Bussing plans involve the transportation of students, both white and black, from one school to another in order to bring about racial balance. Theoretically, open enrollment basically permits students to enroll in any school of their choice. Redistricting involves the redrawing of school attendance boundary lines to facilitate racial balance. Consolidation plans are designed to merge smaller school districts into larger ones, and thus permit a more desirable racial balance. Educational parks represent an attempt to group elementary and secondary school facilities in planned locations so that the pupils who attend come from a wide area, thus avoiding segregation that results

James Farmer, Assistant Secretary, Health, Education and Welfare.

from neighborhood schools. Recent complication to the resolution of the problem has been a growing tendency for black separatism, in which black leaders have opposed integration as strongly and vociferously as white segregationists have.

Kenneth Clark, a psychologist who provided the NAACP with much of the social scientific data upon which the Supreme Court's decision in *Brown v. Board of Education of Topeka* was based, has recently written an article reflecting on that decision and its many ramifications, both direct and subtle. His comments are reproduced here in their entirety.[28]

The history of civil rights litigation in state and federal courts up to the *Brown* decision of 1954 can be understood in terms of a basic struggle, dating back to the *Dred Scott* decision of 1857, to determine the social and judicial perception of the Negro, to determine how the Negro is to be perceived and treated in relation to the treatment of other human beings within the framework of American democracy.

The underlying problem was that the Negro was regarded as semi-human or in some subtle way as subhuman; and as not only different, but different and inferior. The common denominator of *Dred Scott, Plessy vs. Ferguson,* and almost all related court decisions up to *Brown* was that the Negro in some way was special and inherently unworthy of the rights white American citizens would be expected to have without question and without litigation. Indeed, the fact that the Negro was required to persist in seeking judicial determination of his rights was, in itself, indicative of the basic racist reality of the society of which he was a part.

Therefore, the May 31, 1955, implementing decision of the Supreme Court in *Brown,* which enunciated a policy of guidance to the states for carrying out the *Brown* mandate to desegregate public schools "with all deliberate speed," was a conscious effort to make fundamental social change less disruptive. The court, in seeking to facilitate a rational and orderly transition from a system of segregation to one of nonsegregated schools, asked that such criteria as "local conditions" be considered. It was clear that in this decision the court was stepping outside the limited role of determining the constitutionality of segregation and was assuming the more complex role of establishing guidelines for administrative and social change.

Some observers interpreted this decision —with some justification—as the court's accepting the gradualist approach as means for effective desegregation. In retrospect, the "deliberate speed" formula seems a serious error to many, including Supreme Court Justice Hugo Black, who criticized the court in a 1968 statement. In practice it seems to have led to more rather than to less disruption. Here, court reliance on social science evidence would have been useful, for students of social change have observed that prompt, decisive action on the part of recognized authorities usually results in less anxiety and less resistance in cases where the public is opposed to the action than does a more hesitant and gradual procedure. It is similar to the effect of quickly pulling off adhesive tape—the pain is sharper but briefer, and hence more tolerable.

---

28. Kenneth B. Clark, "Fifteen Years of Deliberate Speed," *Saturday Review,* 20 December 1969, pp. 59–61, 70. Copyright Saturday Review, Inc., 1969. Used by permission.

The essential questions faced by the Supreme Court were not questions of legal precedent, historical in nature, but questions relating to the social consequences of legally imposed segregation. Without such evidence, the court could only speculate about the probable damage caused by the violation of Constitutional rights implicit in segregated education. The social scientists testified concerning the damage inherent in the total pattern of segregation on the human personality. On the basis of their testimony, the court held that separate educational facilities are inherently unequal by virtue of being separate. By providing such evidence, the social scientists made it possible to avoid the need to obtain proof of individual damage, and to avoid assessment of the equality of facilities in each individual school situation. The assumption of inequality could now be made wherever segregation existed.

However, in doing so, the court, which appeared to rely on the findings of social scientists in the 1954 decision, rejected the findings in handing down the 1955 implementation decision. An empirical study of various forms and techniques of desegregation suggested that the gradual approach to desegregation did not increase its chances of success or effectiveness. The findings further suggested that forthright, direct desegregation within the minimum time required for the necessary administrative changes tended to facilitate the process. Gradualism or any form of ambiguity and equivocation on the part of those with the power of decision was interpreted by the segregationists as indecision, provided them with the basis for increasing resistance, and gave them time to organize, intensify, and prolong their opposition. The pattern of massive resistance and sporadic, violent opposition to desegregation occurred after the 1955 decision. There is no evidence that a more direct, specific, and concrete implementation decree would have resulted in any more tension, procrastination, or evasion than the seemingly rational, statesmanlike deliberate speed decision of the court. It does not seem likely that the pace of public school desegregation could have been slower.

The results of "all deliberate speed" have been ironic and tragic. In the South, where, admittedly, American racism was most violent, primitive, and deeply rooted, progress could be substantial and still leave a racist society fundamentally untouched. After *Brown,* a number of Southern states developed and tested strategies of resistance to the court decision. Massive resistance of interposition was resorted to in defiance of the court, and the degree of integration in elementary and secondary schools has been minimal. Nevertheless, the South has accepted or initiated more overt changes than the North. In fact, the South can look at the North with a certain ironic condescension in terms of the acceptance of rapid change toward a non-racist society.

The North, for its part, did not think the *Brown* decision applied to its schools. The North had joined earlier in the Negro reaction against Southern resistance to change. Now it became clear that racism was also virulent in the North, all the more insidious for its having been long unrecognized. Even Negroes had not consciously acknowledged the depth of racism inherent in Northern society. And when the North discovered its racism, it tended to provide justification for it. In addition, in the academic community, it began to be clear in the 1960s that apparently sophisticated and compassionate theories used to explain slow Negro student performance might themselves be tainted with racist condescension. Some of the theories of "cultural deprivation," "the disadvantaged," and the like, popular in educational circles and in high governmental spheres until recently and in fact still prevalent, were backed for the most part by inconclusive and fragmentary research and much speculation. The eagerness with which such theories were greeted was itself a subtly racist symptom.

The cultural deprivation theory rejects explanations of inherent racial or biological inferiority, and asserts that the total pattern of racial prejudice, discrimination, and segregation found in a racist society blocks the capacity of school personnel to teach minority group children with the same observable efficiency as that given other children. These children may, therefore, be expected to remain academically retarded no matter how well they are taught. Among the specific barriers emphasized by different writers in varying degrees are: environmentally determined sensory deficiencies; withdrawn or hyperactive behavior; low attention span; peculiar or bizarre language patterns; lack of verbal stimulation; absence of father or stable male figure in the home; and lack of books in the home.

In spite of the fact that these factors have dominated the literature and have been frequently repeated and generally accepted as explanations of the academic retardation of lower status children, they have not been verified as causal factors through any precise and systematic research reported in the published literature. The evidence, or indeed lack of evidence, suggests, therefore, that this concept has gained acceptance through intuition, general impressions, and repetition.

Nevertheless, cultural deprivation theorists have not only provided the public school educational establishment with a respectable rationalization for maintaining the status quo of educational inefficiency for low status children, but the related technology of this theory—compensatory or educational enrichment programs—appears to provide the basis for inherent contradictions in its premises and assumptions.

An uncritical acceptance of this theory and explanation seems to be contradicted by:

1) the concretely demonstrated psychological fact of the normal curve in the distribution of human intellectual potential, personality characteristics, motivation, and other personal characteristics believed to be related to academic performance;

2) the modifiableness of human beings;

3) the fact that normal human beings who are taught, motivated to learn, expected to learn, and provided with conditions conducive to learning, will learn up to or near the limits of their capacity.

Furthermore, the cultural deprivation theories are clear violations of the law of parsimony, since they seek more complex explanations without determining that simpler explanations are not adequate. Cultural deprivation theories appear to by-pass more direct and specific educational variables such as quality of teaching and supervision, acceptance or rejection of the students by teachers, and educational methods and facilities.

Given the history of educational rejection of Negro children, it would seem obvious to one trained in the methods of science that much more direct variables would have to be held constant and checked out with more precision and more sensitive instruments than the Coleman report [*Equality of Edu-*

cational Opportunity, by James Coleman] does before one could resort to the more elaborate, ambiguous, and seemingly uncontrollable catchall variable of cultural deprivation. In this regard it is significant that the literature, while eloquent and repetitive in its expansion of the cultural deprivation hypothesis, is almost totally silent on discussions or research that seek to determine the relationship between subtle or flagrant rejection of a child by his teachers because of race, color, economic status and family income, and the level of his academic performance. These social, psychological, and educational variables seem worthy of a serious attention and research that they have not as yet received.

Theories of cultural deprivation are often regarded as liberal, because they posit environmental inadequacy rather than genetic inferiority, and because they are often used to support demands for integration. The problem with this approach, exemplified by the Coleman report, is that it concludes that the environmentally caused characteristics of white children are the positive component of integrated schools, and that Negro children educationally gain primarily from association with white children.

Further research is necessary to determine whether correlation and causal factors have been confused in this important study. But perhaps most important, it is necessary to study the majority white school as a total unit as compared to the majority Negro school, to determine what happens in the school itself *because* white children are present. Sensitive instruments must be sought to measure teacher and administrative expectations, counseling attitudes, quality of curriculum, and the like, but beyond the assessment of these individual factors it is necessary to evaluate the total

pattern of advantage or deprivation.

On the basis of years of observation and research of ghetto education, I would advance the proposition that one would find a significantly high correlation between a pattern of deprivation and ghetto schools, and a pattern of advantage and white urban and suburban schools. It is not the presence of the white child per se that leads to higher achievement for the Negro child who associates with him in class; it is the quality of the education provided because the white child is there that makes the difference, or so I believe the empirical evidence indicates. To argue, without irrefutable proof, that this is not the case is to lend support to a racially defined environmental theory of academic achievement that is no less callous in its consequences than a genetic theory of racial inferiority would be.

Perhaps the most ironic development since the 1954 *Brown* decision, however, has not been the continuation of white racism in the South, nor the acknowledgment of the more subtle white racism of the North, but the emergence and growth of black racism. In 1954, when the *Brown* decision was handed down, desegregation and integration were the priority of the civil rights movement and Negroes generally. Fifteen years later, many militants have proclaimed the death of the civil rights movement and have denied the value of integration itself, and specifically have questioned the significance of the *Brown* decision and the truth of the social science findings on which it rested. One must thus look at the decision and its social science foundation from a new perspective, and inquire whether these charges are justified.

During the period since 1954, black nationalism has experienced a sharp rise in support from young Negro militants and from many whites. This represents in some forms the continuation of the nationalism of the Garvey movement of the 1920s, identifiable in degree by the black nationalism of Malcolm X. In other, and more serious, manifestations it has gained support among Negro students and youth. The seeming common denomination of both is the repudiation of integration and the apparent repudiation of the struggle for desegregation, the rejection of the *Brown* decision, and the implicit rejection of the whole rationale and psychological approach to the meaning of racism. This would logically include a denial of the social science explanation of the inevitability of inferiority in segregated systems, on which the *Brown* decision depended.

Under the guise of assuming a positive identity, black nationalism has adopted an imitation of white racism with its hallowing of race, its attempt to make a virtue out of color, its racist mystique. This rationale argues that the detrimental consequences of a biracial society are neutralized or transformed into positive consequences by virtue of the fact that Negroes themselves are now asserting the value of racism. This argument would give primary weight to voluntarism, that is, that racism would lead to affirmative not negative results if it were voluntarily accepted or sought by the previous victims, as it was voluntarily maintained by the oppressors. The character of racism would depend on the attitude one had toward it; it would have no objective reality of its own.

The paranoia of racism, whether imposed or sought, must rest on insecurity. It is the verification of the psychological interpretation of the negative consequences of segregation. Racism does produce doubts and insecurities in the victims as well as in the perpetrators. It increases hostility and aggression and self-hatred.

The Lorelei quest for identity through racism is based on superstition. Despite the verbal transformation from self-contempt to apparent pride, the conditions of injustice remain. We are asked to obscure them by the rhetorical posturing of pride. In a strikingly similar analogy, it is psychologically obvious that any man who proclaims how irresistible and potent and virile he is must have deep doubts about it. He would clearly be regarded as preoccupied with sexual anxiety. Such self-pretense conceals—or attempts to conceal—deep, poignant, and tragic insecurity. Given the fact that the realities of racism in America have not changed, that the Negro is still condemned to segregated schools, to segregated and deteriorated residential areas, and to an economic role that is not competitive with the white society, the cult of blackness must be recognized as what it is—a ritualized denial of anguished despair and resentment of the failure of society to meet its promises.

Separatism is an attempt to create verbal realities as substitutes for social, political, and economic realities. It is another and intense symptom of the psychological damage a racist society inflicts on its victims.

A specific indication of the damage of separatism is that the victims internalize racism. Some forms of black separatism involve genuine and deep self-destructive, suicidal dynamics. They reflect the most cruel, barbaric, tragic, dehumanizing consequences of white oppression—the wish of the oppressed to die—and in dying to destroy others in a similar predicament. The white racists who so damage their fellow human beings must be prepared to face the same judgment the Nazis, who sent millions to death camps, must face.

Responding to a button reading "Being Black Is Not Enough," some Negroes have said, "Well, being white has always been enough." But if one looks at the moral decay, the instability, and the unresolved problems of white society, one perceives that being white is not enough, that it is effective only in terms of self-aggrandizement and at the expense of exploitation of those who are not white. Its success depends on victimization, for racism is not only subjective, it also demands an object. Positive racism has the necessary obverse of rejection of all those who do not happen to meet the chosen racial criteria.

So, rather than refute the social science assumptions that led to the *Brown* decision, the present cult of black separatism intensely verifies it. Black separatism can be seen as a "sour-grapes-and-sweet-lemon" reaction against the failure of the society to implement and enforce the findings of *Brown.*

The vocal, well-publicized, well-endowed cult has to be understood for what it is, for otherwise it can be cynically manipulated and used by white racists who are now the often silent allies of the separatists. The rationale of the sophisticated white intellectual who endorses black separatism in his university, his church, his political party, his academic or professional society, while continuing to live in a restricted suburb and continuing to support the institutional relegation of Negroes to inferior status, must be seen by Negroes for what it is: an attempt to handle racial antiviolence, to deal with guilt.

The basic standard for such understanding is that which functioned in the *Brown* decision, namely that racism and segregation are a reflection of superstition, institutionalized untruth, cruelty, and injustice, and that race is irrelevant as a criterion for preference or rejection. The poignant tragedy is that the society is using the victimized groups as the agent for the perpetuation of irreconcilable injustice and racial irrelevance. Any white or black intellectual who denies this must be more comfortable with superstition and rationalization. One cannot deal with the reorganization of society on a nonracial basis by intensifying racist symptoms.

Nor can one build a solid pride on the quicksands of emotion, anger, rage, hatred —no matter how justifiable. Genuine pride —the pride that makes life worth the struggle with some hope of serenity—must come from solid personal achievement, from sensitivity and concern and respect for one's fellow man, from compassion and willingness to struggle to give some substance to one's own life by trying to help others live with confidence in the possibility of positives. Pride, like humility, is destroyed by one's insistence that he possesses it.

Racism in any form is dangerous, but particularly, as is now true among many whites and Negroes, when it is intellectually supported. Such supporters often fail to follow the implication of their rhetoric to its logical conclusion: that, if segregation and separatism are desirable and good as a phase and as a means, they are even more to be desired as ends in themselves.

All the implications of the *Brown* decision and all the social science arguments in its support point to the inherent dangers of racism. The latest surge toward self-imposed separatism is the greatest verification of all. I read into the separatist movement among Negroes a more severe symptom than those described in *Brown*. It convinces me even more persuasively that we must redouble our efforts to obliterate racism, whatever its manifestations, wherever it appears.

———————

In addition to the *Brown* decision, Title IV of the 1964 Civil Rights Act specifies that racial discrimination must end in all programs receiving federal financial assistance in order to qualify for future aid. This additional legislative aid provided incentive power to bring about further integration. Between 1954 and 1964 integration moved at a very slow pace in the South. Since the passage of the Civil Rights Act of 1964 it has proceeded more rapidly. In 1964, only about one percent of the Negro pupils in the South attended integrated schools; by 1969, the percentage of Negro pupils attending integrated schools had risen to approximately twenty percent. It is important to note that in interpreting these percentages an integrated school is considered to be one that Negroes attend in which a majority of the pupils in attendance are white.[29]

The Civil Rights Act of 1964 resulted in the Department of Health, Education and Welfare being charged with the responsibility of enforcing those portions of the Act that pertained to education. Various guidelines and timetables were established. The original guidelines came out in April, 1965, and called for integration of all grades by the fall of 1967. They were subsequently revised and in the latest revision, the fall of 1969 was established as the deadline for compliance. In the summer of 1969, HEW indicated that there would be a slight easing of desegregation guidelines in the most troublesome districts of the South. This announcement was followed by a flurry of various kinds of announcements and pronouncements. The most significant end product of the activity was that the U.S. Supreme Court on October 29, 1969, ruled that the Constitution no longer allows "all deliberate speed" as a standard for desegregation. The decision called for integration immediately in all school districts, and struck down the Nixon administration's late summer policy decision to delay desegregation in thirty-three Mississippi school districts.

Desegregation thrusts are also being made toward the North. The Justice Department has filed a desegregation suit against the Madison County School District in Illinois. It has also accused the Chicago Board of Education of maintaining and perpetuating faculty segregation.

It should be recognized that race problems in the United States have multiple causations and that the efforts to promote integration, while concentrated heavily on the schools, cannot be completely resolved by the schools. The resolution of racial issues resides in the attitudes of citizens, both black and white. While these attitudes are formulated under strong influences within the home and within peer group associations of the child, the school can and must continue to be a strong influence on the attitudes developed by the pupils. Legal progress toward resolving segregation is summarized in the following excerpts from *U.S. News and World Report*.[30]

29. "The Progress of School Desegregation in the South," *U.S. News and World Report* 19 May 66 (1969):51.
30. "Gains in Negro Rights," *U.S. News and World Report* 66(1969):51–53. Used with permission.

THE RULES AGAINST SEGREGATION
As Ordered by Courts and Congress

SCHOOLS

1954—Supreme Court held racial segregation in public schools to be unconstitutional, but set no deadline for desegregation.

1955—Supreme Court ordered lower courts to require desegregation of schools "with all deliberate speed."

1958—In Little Rock, Ark., case, Supreme Court held its rulings "can neither be nullified openly and directly" by State officials "nor nullified indirectly by them through evasive schemes for segregation."

1963—Student-transfer plans applied on a racial basis were invalidated by the Supreme Court.

1964—Ordering Prince Edward County, Va., to reopen its public schools—closed in 1959—Supreme Court held one district cannot close its public schools to escape integration while other schools in the State remain open.

1964—Congress passed a Civil Rights Act providing for a ban on federal aid to school districts practicing racial discrimination. This speeded desegregation in South.

1965—Supreme Court abandoned its 1955 rule of "all deliberate speed" and declared "delays in desegregating school systems are no longer tolerable."

1968—"Freedom of choice" plans widely used in the South—letting pupils choose their schools—were held by Supreme Court to be inadequate unless they actually desegregate schools.

De Facto Segregation

Supreme Court has never ruled directly whether an all-Negro or nearly all-Negro school is illegal if its racial makeup results solely from its location in a Negro neighborhood. This is the so-called de facto segregation that exists widely in the North.

Federal courts have held, however, that even in Northern States which had no segregation by law, racial separation in schools is illegal if it results from official actions or policies that are racially discriminatory.

Congress has forbidden withholding of federal aid to force the bussing of pupils or the closing of schools to overcome racial imbalance in school enrollments.

PUBLIC ACCOMMODATIONS

1964—Civil Rights Act barred discrimination on racial grounds in privately owned public accommodations such as restaurants, hotels, motels, theaters and sports arenas; authorized suits by Attorney General to break up a pattern of practice of such discrimination.

VOTING

1957—Civil Rights Act empowered Federal Government through the Attorney General to seek court injunctions against deprivation of voting rights.

1960—Congress authorized federal judges to appoint referees to help Negroes register and vote, provided criminal penalties for bombing, bomb threats or mob action aimed at obstructing court orders.

1960—Supreme Court upheld both 1957 and 1960 voting laws, also threw out an Alabama act gerrymandering the Negro vote in Tuskegee.

1964—Civil Rights Act barred unequal application of requirements for registration of voters, required literacy tests be in writing.

1965—Voting Rights Act suspended literacy tests in States where less than half the voting-age population was registered, authorized Attorney General to send federal examiners to supervise voter registration, barred new State regulations unless approved by federal court.

1966—Ruled poll tax unconstitutional as qualification for voting.

TRANSPORTATION

1946—State law requiring racial separation of passengers on interstate motor carriers was invalidated by Supreme Court as an unconstitutional burden on interstate commerce.

1950—Segregation on interstate railways was held by Supreme Court to violate the Interstate Commerce Act.

1956—In Montgomery, Ala., case, Supreme Court ruled racial segregation on local buses violates the Fourteenth Amendment.

1960—Segregation in bus stations used by interstate passengers was ruled by Supreme Court to violate Interstate Commerce Act.

1962—Any form of segregation required by a State in interstate or intrastate transportation facilities was held illegal by Supreme Court.

HOUSING

1948—Supreme Court ruled that courts cannot be used to enforce restrictive covenants by which homeowners agree not to sell to Negroes.

1953—No damages can be recovered from one who violates such a restrictive covenant, Supreme Court held.

1967—Supreme Court invalidated a California constitutional amendment declaring a property owner has a right to sell to whomever he pleases.

1968—Open Housing Act of Congress prohibited racial discrimination in sale or rental of about 80 per cent of all the nation's housing.

1968—Supreme Court interpreted an 1866 federal law as banning racial discrimination in sale or rental of any property.

MARRIAGE

1967—Supreme Court ruled States cannot ban interracial marriages.

PUBLIC FACILITIES

A series of federal-court rulings barred racial discrimination in such tax-supported public facilities as hospitals, libraries, parks, pools, beaches and golf courses.

1964—Civil Rights Act authorized the filing of suits by the Justice Department in order to enforce desegregation of public facilities.

EMPLOYMENT

1941—President Roosevelt, by executive order, barred racial discrimination by employers holding defense contracts. This ban has been expanded by succeeding Presidents until it now applies to all companies that hold federal contracts.

1964—Civil Rights Act outlawed racial discrimination by employers of 25 or more workers, by employment agencies or by labor unions. The 1964 legislation also established an Equal Employment Opportunity Commission to investigate charges of discrimination.

Poor People In America

Another domestic social problem which is intimately related to education is that of poverty. While the United States is one of the richest nations on earth in terms of material wealth, some of its people suffer from extreme poverty. The Social Security Administration defines poverty as an annual income of less than $3335 for a non-farm family of four.[31] Using this measuring stick, in 1967 there were 26 million persons in the United States—13 per cent of the nation's population—with incomes below the poverty level. Of these, 17.8 million were white (69 per cent), and 8.1 million were Negro (31 per cent). Of the total number of whites and Negroes in the nation, about 10.3 per cent of the nation's whites and 37.5 per cent of its Negroes were poor under the Social Security definition.[32] In 1967 about one-half (51%) of the poor population lived in metropolitan areas.[33] In 1966, 17.9% of the children under 18 were poor.[34]

Many more statistics could be cited to further delineate the problem; however, let it suffice to conclude that poverty in America is a very serious problem; that while poverty affects both whites and non-whites, the problem percentage-wise is much more serious for non-whites; that it is widely dis-

31. "Who Are The Poor," *NEA Research Bulletin,* May 1969, 47:35.
32. *Ibid.*
33. *Ibid.,* p. 36.
34. *Ibid.,* p. 38.

tributed throughout both metropolitan and farm areas, but 14% of the population of the central city is poor and is densely concentrated in racially segregated areas; and that with the exception of the suburban area, approximately one of every four children is being reared under conditions of poverty.

How does the poverty problem relate to education? Children of poverty, sometimes inaccurately labeled as "culturally deprived" or "disadvantaged," simply do not possess at the time of entrance into school as many of the skills needed for success in school as those children who have not been impoverished. This is caused by combinations of many factors, among them physical debilitation, lack of intellectual stimulation, different cultural background, negative self-concept, and many more factors related to their environmental background. Further, and perhaps more significantly, many schools have not developed the kinds of programs necessary to enable these students to succeed. As a result, their poverty background is reinforced by failure in school. Many teachers, either having been of the middle class originally or having become a

Substandard housing is a reflection of unemployment and poverty.

part of the middle class due to upward social mobility, have difficulty in relating to and therefore teaching impoverished children. The schools then have the task of adjusting their programs, changing their techniques, doing their very best to enable their students to obtain the skills necessary to compete favorably in our society. The federal government has recognized this task, and is endeavoring to help. Title I, in particular, of the Elementary and Secondary Act of 1965 provides funds to state education agencies specifically for the purpose of improving education programs for the poor. Under Title I, local school districts design programs, ranging from those providing physical necessities such as eyeglasses and shoes to those providing counselors and remedial reading specialists to supplement their existing programs. Funds are allocated on the basis of the number of poor families in a school district. Other federal programs such as Head Start, National Teacher Corps, and Upward Bound are also aimed at improving the opportunities of the poor.

Unemployment

Closely related to poverty is unemployment and underemployment; that is, individuals working at jobs who are qualified for better jobs. It has been estimated that today there are about two million unemployed and about ten million underemployed, 6.5 million of whom work full time and earn less than the annual poverty wage. Approximately 500,000 of the unemployed are "hard-core" unemployed who lack the basic education necessary to secure and hold a job.[35] Daniel P. Moynihan, now urban advisor to President Nixon, has expressed the importance of employment quite poignantly:

The principal measure of progress toward equality will be that of employment. It is the primary source of individual or group identity. In America what you do is what you are: to do nothing is to be nothing; to do little is to be little. The equations are implacable and blunt, and ruthlessly public . . .[36]

In relating to the Negro American he continued:

For the Negro American, [employment] is already and will continue to be the master problem. It is the measure of white bona fides. It is the measure of Negro competence, and also of the competence of American society. Most importantly, the linkage between problems of employment and the range of social pathology that afflicts the Negro community is unmistakable. Employment not only controls the present for the Negro American, but in a most profound way, it is creating the future as well.[37]

Do the schools have a societal role to fill in solving the problem of unemployment and underemployment? They certainly do, from basic reading and writing skills to vocational and technical training programs for adults. Efforts are being made in these directions in high schools through day and night programs, technical and trade schools, and community colleges. Again though, the schools cannot completely resolve the problem; they can, as one agency of society, however, make a major contribution.

Violence

A fourth issue, contributed to by problems of race relationships, poverty, and un-

35. *Report of the National Advisory Commission on Civil Disorders*, p. 414.
36. *Ibid.*, p. 252.
37. *Ibid.*, p. 252.

"The foundation of our society is a respect for and an observance of law and order.... We need to make respect for law and order the first priority in our national life, for the rule of law is paramount to this nation's continued existence."

J. Edgar Hoover

employment, is that of violence and crime. Civil disorders have increased, ranging from riots to campus takeovers to student protests in high schools, reaching the point where the schools are closed. Does this problem have relevance to education? It most certainly does. Contributory causes of riots in the cities are racial difficulties, poverty, and unemployment. Former President Johnson, in an address to the nation on July 27, 1967, in referring to riots and violence, said:

. . . The only genuine, long-range solution for what has happened lies in an attack—mounted at every level—upon the conditions that breed despair and violence. All of us know what those conditions are: ignorance, discrimination, slums, poverty, disease, not enough jobs. We should attack these conditions—not because we are frightened by conflict, but because we are fired by conscience. We should attack them because there is simply no other way to achieve a decent and orderly society in America . . .

Schools cannot ignore these issues. They must attack with the peaceful weapons of education to solve them.

While the causes of campus violence are being researched, and no single cause stands out boldly among the rest, it is apparent that social unrest in society is reflected in its collegiate institutions. Students are calling for greater degrees of participation in determining their destinies. They want a vote, or at least a strong voice, in curriculum decision-making and the hiring and firing of faculty. At the very least they are defining a new role for college students in a participatory democracy.

While social problems other than race relations—or stated more broadly, intergroup conflict, poverty, unemployment, and violence—exist and are related to the schools, these particular problems stand out as being illustrative of the most urgent in this decade. It should be recognized that these problems are those of an urban industrial society and have grown in intensity as people have moved from farms and small towns to cities. The degree of interrelatedness of the social problems, one to another, each and all to the schools, further demonstrates the complexity of devising solutions.

The Role of the School: Transmit—Respond—Lead

What should be the posture of the school in American society? Historically, and into the present, schools have been responsible for the transmission of culture. In this role, as has been indicated, they have assumed a passive and reflective posture. What society deems has been the "good" of the past and is worth preserving, even if not utilitarian or relevant, was presented to children in school for their use and for posterity. In many schools today, transmission is still the primary goal. However, schools have also added another role, a different posture: that of *responding*. As society changes, and needs are recognized in society that can be fulfilled by the school, the school responds or adjusts to these needs. For example, as computers were developed and operators were needed, the schools began to train the specialists necessary. Much of the schools' reactions to social problems fall into the response posture. As poverty was recognized as a problem, and children came to school hungry, the schools fed them. A third posture is possible, that of *leading*. In this posture the schools would strive to achieve the ideal society as it has been envisioned. In this role, the school acts as an agent of change for society, attempting to mold and shape it to desired ends. While schools did not serve as the initiator, they have been placed in a position of leadership in building an integrated society. It appears that they may be increasingly called upon to take the leadership role. Schools assume all three postures (transmit, respond, lead) in their various responsibilities. The blend of these postures changes as societal expectations change.

Commitments in Education: Universality—Equality— Liberation—Excellence

Four definite commitments have been in evidence in the development of education in the United States. These four, universality, equality, liberation, and excellence, are most intimately related to our society and culture. *Universality* refers to the basic idea that every child should have a good common school education. Our forefathers recognized the importance of education to the survival of the concept of democratic living, and as states were formed, they placed in their constitutions the provision for a free common school education. This provision was most often accompanied by specific legislation requiring compulsory school attendance through a specified age. The age requirements varied, but ordinarily they were set to make certain that the child received an elementary education through approximately the eighth grade. This commitment for all practical purposes has been achieved and it has contributed greatly to the strength of our nation. Today, there is strong evidence of a commitment to universality in education beyond the common school; proportionately more and more students attend secondary schools, community

colleges, colleges, universities, and various continuing education programs. Secondary education became legal (in a sense) in the famous *Kalamazoo Case* in 1872 when the Supreme Court of Michigan recognized the right of a community to tax itself for secondary schools. Communities now tax themselves directly for community colleges. America has done reasonably well in accomplishing its commitment to a common school education for all.

In terms of *equality* we have espoused equal opportunity. While legal strides have been made, realistically assessed, the goal has not been achieved. It is still quite apparent, for example, that the wealth of a local area has much to do with opportunity. States have tried to eliminate these disparaging differences with state aid formulas designed to equalize at least a minimum amount of expenditure per child for education. Differences among the wealth of the states further compounds the national problem. As has been mentioned earlier, the residential living patterns also compound the issue, as the poor live with the poor, blacks with other blacks, and middle class persons with other middle class persons. This type of segregated education by race, and by criteria other than race (by social class, for example), deprives all youth of the richness of our culture and of the knowledge that they need, knowledge which can be gained by interaction with others. Social interaction which can be accomplished in schools seems necessary to help solve some of our major social problems. As a nation, we have much distance to travel before our commitment to equality has been met.

Liberation, closely related to equality, refers to the opportunity for individuals in our society to better themselves. While this requires individual motivation, it also requires a society that not only permits but encourages and facilitates personal advancement. Education is seen as a great liberator; the skills learned in school can help an individual to rise above his environment. The second generation of a family should, if we are meeting this commitment, do better than the first. This kind of development should continue. There is no question that it has for many people; but for others, such as those in many minority groups, or those in poverty, society has slowed down, blocked, and even trapped their progress. The situations of many of the poor have been perpetuated by our society, perhaps unconsciously; but nevertheless, it has happened. Education can provide the opportunity for liberation. We must, however, examine our educational system to make certain that it is providing opportunities rather than inhibiting them. To accomplish equality, changes will have to be made in much that is done in education. Herein lies an opportunity for schools to play the leadership role; they can in fact help change and mold society. They must, however, convince those who finance the schools, the American citizens, of the worthiness of their cause and their suggested solutions.

Excellence adds another dimension. In addition to providing basic education and basic opportunity for all, our future strength lies in using our human resources so that each individual can develop his unique talents to the fullest. At this task, to which we are committed, we have barely begun. To accomplish this excellence our instructional procedures must be modified; we need to do a better job of tailoring in order to suit our students. Again, herein lies a chance for schools to lead, to utilize their resources to the fullest and to gain more resources.

QUESTIONS FOR DISCUSSION

1. What elements of the culture of the United States are particularly essential to the survival of representative democracy as a form of government?
2. What values should the school transmit as being representative of our culture?
3. Should the schools be used as agents of planned social change?
4. What provisions, if any, should be made for the schools to transmit the cultural elements of local ethnic subgroups?
5. Which of the many social problems facing the United States do you consider to be the most serious? What role can the school play to help resolve this problem?

SUPPLEMENTARY LEARNING ACTIVITIES

1. Gather and analyze demographic and sociological data in the area of the institution that you attend, looking specifically for cultural diversity.
2. Devise a questionnaire designed to secure societal expectations for schools and use it to interview individuals selected in a random fashion.
3. Invite persons of different cultural backgrounds and different socio-economic classes to your class to gain their perceptions of American education.
4. Invite authorities from various social service agencies in your area to learn what they perceive the functions of schools to be in relationship to the social problems with which they are concerned.
5. Arrange for interviews with practicing front line school social workers, both those who work in cities and in rural areas, to gain their perceptions of the role that schools can play in solving social problems.

SELECTED REFERENCES

Baltzell, E. Degby. *The Protestant Establishment*. New York: Random House, Inc., 1964.

Bayles, Ernest E., and Bruce L. Hood. *Growth of American Educational Thought and Practice*. New York: Harper & Row, Publishers, 1966.

Bruebacher, John S. *A History of the Problems of Education*. 2nd ed. New York: McGraw-Hill Book Co., 1965.

Butts, Freeman R., and Laurence Cremin. *A History of Education in American Culture*. New York: Holt, Rinehart, and Winston, Inc., 1953.

Callahan, Raymond F. *An Introduction to Education in American Society*. New York: Alfred A. Knopf, Inc., 1965.

Clark, Kenneth B. *Dark Ghetto: Dilemma of Social Power*. New York: Anti-Defamation League, 1965.

Corwin, Ronald G. *A Sociology of Education*. New York: Appleton-Century-Crofts, Inc., 1965.

Counts, George S. *Education and American Civilization*. New York: Bureau of Publications, Teachers College, Columbia University, 1952.

Goals for Americans: The Report of the President's Commission on National Goals. Englewood Cliffs, N.J.: Prentice-Hall, Inc., 1960.

Goslin, David A. *The School in Contemporary Society*. Chicago: Scott, Foresman and Co., 1965.

Hartford, Ellis Ford. *Education in These United States*. New York: The Macmillan Co., 1964.

Havighurst, Robert J., and Bernice L. Neugarten. *Society and Education*. 3rd ed. Boston: Allyn & Bacon, Inc., 1967.

Landes, Ruth. *Culture in American Education*. New York: John Wiley & Sons, Inc., 1965.

Linton, Ralph. *Tree of Culture*. New York: Alfred A. Knopf, Inc., 1955.

McLendon, Jonathon C. *Social Foundations of Education*. New York: The Macmillan Co., 1966.

Myrdal, Gunnar. *An American Dilemma: The Negro Problem and Modern Democracy*. rev. ed. New York: Harper & Row, Publishers, 1944.

Pounds, Ralph L., and James R. Bryner. *The School in American Society*. New York: The Macmillan Co., 1967.

Report of the National Advisory Commission on Civil Disorders. New York: Bantam Books, 1968.

Strom, Robert D. *The Inner-City Classroom: Teacher Behavior*. Columbus, Ohio: Charles E. Merrill Books, Inc., 1966.

Westby-Gibson, Dorothy. *Social Perspectives on Education*. New York: John Wiley & Sons, Inc., 1965.

Public Schools:
The Myth of the Melting Pot

Colin Greer

It is fashionable these days to point to the decline of the public school, as if there were a time in some golden past when the schools really served all of the people all of the time. Legend tells of the Little Red Schoolhouse that made equal opportunity available to children of every economic and social class, and, a little later in the nation's history, functioned as the primary instrument of the melting pot that offered poor immigrant children access to the fullness of American life. Today the schools are criticized for their failure to provide equality of opportunity to poor black children. The charge is true, but it is by no means the whole truth, nor is it new. The public schools have always failed the lower classes—both white and black. Current educational problems stem not from the fact that the schools have changed, but from the fact that they continue to do precisely the job they have always done.

What we are witnessing, in our current panic over urban education, is no more than an escalation of the criticisms made by school reformers since the turn of the century. The many innovations introduced over the past fifty years have made it easier for school systems to handle the huge numbers of students brought into the schools by compulsory attendance legislation and a job market requiring increasingly sophisticated talents, but they have not changed the basic function of the schools as the primary selector of the winners and losers in society.

The very fact that we can look with pride at more and more students going on to secondary and higher education reveals a system that with increasing efficiency benefits some and denies others in the bosom of its material prosperity. Public schooling cannot be understood, nor the current problems manifest in it, apart from a consideration of the predominant influence of social and economic class. For at least the last eighty years, socio-economic class, as signified by employment rates and levels, has determined scholastic achievement, as measured by dropout and failure rates.

From 1890, at least, the schools failed to perform according to their own as well as the popular definition of their role. In virtually every study undertaken since that of Chicago schools made in 1898, more children have failed in school than have succeeded, both in absolute and in relative numbers. The educators who collaborated on the Chicago study found an exceedingly high incidence of poor school performance. They were quick to look to foreign birth as an explanation, but immigrants spawned Americans and still, with each passing dec-

* Colin Greer, "Public Schools: The Myth of the Melting Pot," *Saturday Review,* 15 November 1969, pp. 84–86. © Saturday Review, Inc., 1969. Used by permission.

ade, no more than 60 per cent of Chicago's public school pupils were recorded at "normal age" (grade level); the rest were either "overage" (one to two years behind), or "retarded" (three to five years behind). In Boston, Chicago, Detroit, Philadelphia, Pittsburgh, New York, and Minneapolis, failure rates were so high that in no one of these systems did the so-called normal group exceed 60 per cent, while in several instances it fell even lower—to 49 per cent in Pittsburgh, and to 35 per cent in Minneapolis.

The truth is that the mobility of white lower classes was never as rapid nor as sure as it has become traditional to think. The 1920 census, for example, showed that even the favored English and Welsh migrants found half their number tied to the terrifying vulnerability of unskilled labor occupations. Americans of English stock (dominating national language, customs, and institutions) had 40 per cent of their number working in coal mines and cotton factories.

And what of the school in all this? Clearly, according to the same body of data, a close relationship obtained between various group designations (native-born with and without foreign parents, and foreign-born), which revealed that levels of school retention in any given group coincided with that group's adult employment rate. Dropout rates for all groups, including the Negro, were in direct proportion to rates of adult unemployment. Further, the high degree of school achievement among Jews, which has confirmed our expectation of public schools, did not mean success for all Jews. Otherwise, why the remedial classes and dropout panic in several of the schools on New York's Lower East Side with as much as 99 per cent "Hebrew" registration?

Where the family was poor enough to take in boarders to cover rental costs, and desperate enough to join the city's welfare roles, then delinquency, prostitution, and child-labor were as much the burden of Jewish families, for whom such characteristics were real if not typical.

With rising industrial unemployment and an expanded technological economy, the school-leaving age increased so that the problem of caring for all grades of ability on the elementary school level escalated to the high school level. Vocational instruction programs were an inevitable corollary to the academic program and quickly became a symbol of the schools' stratification role. Today, the junior college serves as the junior high school had served earlier, operating to a large extent as an extension of secondary education, with back-seat status justified by the democratic rationale of monumental numbers to be catered to.

The pattern of school failure has been perennially uniform, but concern for it was by no means as great as the concern on the part of educators to get more pupils into school. In 1917, and again in 1925, federal compulsory education legislation put added strength behind various state actions to this effect. Compulsory school-leaving age moved from twelve to fourteen and then to sixteen, but always with the proviso that the two years at the top were dispensable for those who either achieved a minimal grade proficiency determined by the classroom teacher or, more importantly, could prove that they had a job to go to.

In 1919 Chicago gave 10,000 such work permits, in 1930 only 987. Between 1924 and 1930 the allocation of work permits in a number of cities was reduced by more than two-thirds. The school had not suddenly become essential to mobility, but a shrinking unskilled job market required fewer men less early, and so the schools were expected to fill the gap.

The assumption that extended schooling promotes greater academic achievement of social mobility is, however, entirely fallacious. School performance seems consistently dependent upon the socio-economic position of the pupil's family. For example, of high school graduates who rank in the top fifth in ability among their classmates, those whose parents are in the top socio-economic status quartile are five times more likely to enter graduate or professional schools than those of comparable ability whose parents fall in the bottom quartile. Similarly, while American males born after 1900 spend more years in school than their nineteenth-century predecessors, federal and other estimates indicate no concomitant redistribution of economic and social rewards.

The factory, the union, the political machine were agents of mobility and Americanization before the school. Local stability for an ethnic group preceded its entry into the more prosperous reaches of society. The establishment of an ethnic middle class was basic to entry onto a wider middle-class stage via public education. It was the nation's demand for manpower that set the tone for assimilation, and the place of any one group on the economic ladder depended more on the degree to which the culture of the former homeland coincided with the values most highly prized in the culture of the new host society. Jews, Scandinavians, and Greeks, for example, were already practiced in the arts of self-employment, individual ambition, and the Puritan ethic with its corollary Gospel of Wealth. For the Catholic peoples, the Irish and Italians, padrone and party-boss authority seemed to go hand in hand with their being classified as dull, unambitious, and generally of low intelligence by urban teachers from the earliest days of heavy immigration. Bootstraps were not classroom resources.

The school failure problem was generally tucked away in xenophobic concern for expressions of loyalty and the management problems of running an "efficient" system. And efficiency was measured by the success schools enjoyed in getting more youngsters into the classroom, almost never by academic success or lack of it. "The ratio of the number of children in school to the number in the community who ought legally to be in attendance" was the measure, and academic success was by no means a necessary concomitant.

But if students were to stay in school longer, then the public school structure had to be stretched "by facilitating the progress" of those who were locked hitherto into repeating their grades. As surveyists in Chicago remarked, "vanishing opportunities of employment" meant that the time had come for "curricular offerings based on ability and purpose."

Once intelligence tests were considered "a measure of potential"—and this was precisely how surveyists, school supervisory personnel, and professors of education viewed IQ tests—it was a short step to the realization that the broadened base of high school admissions meant that academic work in the nation's high schools had to be reorganized. Very soon, it was observed, too, that the amount of academic work had been considerably reduced because there were so many more students who previously had not gone beyond the fifth grade. One survey team described them as "the boys and girls of secondary age who show little promise of being able to engage profitably in the activities commonly carried out by pupils of normal or superior ability."

Commitment to more and more schooling, beginning at kindergarten now (although only one in four of the eligible could go as yet) and continuing as long as possible, did nothing to modify the record of poor school performance. Compulsory attendance at higher levels only pushed failure rates into the upper grades throughout the 1920s and 1930s in such cities as Chicago, Boston, New York, Philadelphia, Detroit, and Washington, D.C.

Chicago noted a 65 per cent increase among the "underprivileged" between 1924 and 1931. Elementary school backwardness stood at 61.4 per cent, but 41 per cent of all those entering ninth grade were seriously behind, too; in tenth grade the figure was 32 per cent. Apart from such factors as pupil "feeble-mindedness" as an explanation, there were school difficulties to blame, too. Overcrowding in Detroit, where 13,000 were in half-day sessions and 60 per cent in school were "inadequately housed" in 1925; in Philadelphia, Cleveland, and New York the same overcrowding, unsanitary conditions, and serious financial problems prevailed.

On a scale of nine semesters, Philadelphia high schools lost 65 per cent of incoming students at the end of the first semester, lost another 32 per cent at the end of the fourth and were down to 19 per cent of the total in the final semester. In one instance, of a 339-pupil sample established for survey purposes, only ninety-one survived two years. Federal data on schools published in 1937 showed clearly the nationwide "cumula-tive elimination of pupils in school." While 1,750,000 American youngsters entered grade nine, 86.7 per cent were still in school one year later; by grade eleven, only 72 per cent were left, and finally 56 per cent were graduated. Separate data for New York City showed just over 40 per cent of ninth-grade classes graduating. In the late 1940s, George Strayer recorded the same old story in Washington, D.C., New York City, and Boston. Fifty per cent of Boston's ninth graders failed to graduate; in New York the figure was up to more than 55 per cent. In James Coleman's assessment of *Equal Educational Opportunity* in the nation (1966), in the Havighurst study in Chicago (1964), and in the Passow report in Washington, D.C. (1967), the narrative remains staggeringly unchanged.

The Negro, the individual farthest down, has epitomized the inexorable relationship of success and failure, inside and outside the school. The link between permanent unemployment or chronic underemployment and educational failure is black now, but blacks have inherited a whirlwind no less familiar to them than to lower-class whites. Employment conditions were most severe when it came to the Negro, and school failure rates were at once more glaring and more poignant. But, in effect, the public schools served Negro children as they served the vast majority of others; in Chicago, Philadelphia, Detroit, and New York, that has been the problem since 1890.

But if white lower classes have been vulnerable to the economic market place, the Negro, who worked sporadically and as a reserve force, was constantly a victim. If school success or failure had little meaning in the economic market place for whites, it bore no relevance whatever for blacks. As a result, Negro school failure was quickly isolated as a separate problem early in the twentieth century. When, in the 1940s, Negroes finally entered the lower levels of industrial employment from which they had been excluded, those levels had already become a shrinking sector of the economy, and the massive numbers of school dropouts had no place to go. And so it remained appropriate—even inevitable—to consider Negro school performance as a separate question. But the truth is that academic effort has never been relevant to the place of the poor in society.

In 1931, George Strayer, with a lifetime of school evaluations behind him, looked back on progress in public education over the twenty-five preceding years. Most clear in his assessment of that progress was that not only were the top 10 per cent (in terms of IQ scores) in high school, but that 50 per cent of all eligible students from nursery school through college were involved in formal education. That more of the nation's youngsters were in school was the point of his argument, but still more needed to be put there. He acknowledged that very high failure rates were "still characteristic" of the majority of school systems. That was not a high priority problem, however, but a job "we may certainly hope to accomplish within the next twenty-five years."

The fact is that we haven't, and we haven't precisely because the objectives and priorities of the first twenty-five years of the twentieth century have gone unexamined. Paul Mort, a school surveyist sensitive to the growing alienation of urban community groups from public schools in the 1940s, blamed both the alienation and school failure rates on the historic rigidity of the system, its patent failure to consider or to plan

for modification for future needs, and the firefighting assumptions that offered more and more of the same, making progress in education no more than the "expansion and extension of the commonplace." The capacity for future innovation and modification has been assumed, because the contradiction between public school pretensions and the measure of its achievement has been entirely disregarded. Consequently, we have no valid education philosophy on which to build differently. And things are unlikely to be much different until we have first exposed our illusions, and finally addressed the problems whose symptoms we fervently wish would go away.

If the assumptions on which public education was founded have gone unexamined, the problem is now compounded by rising aspirations. We could afford failure in the schools as long as the economy had room for unskilled workers and as long as the lower classes accepted without protest what appeared to be their inevitable place. Now, however, there are practically no jobs left for the unskilled, and even if there were, the black lower class no longer is willing to accept only that kind of opportunity—not in a society in which real wealth is increasing so fast.

What this means, in effect, is that in a variety of different ways we have increased our demands on the schools. Thirty years ago the purpose of public education was culturally defined as little more than baby-sitting for all the children. Now, neither corporations, government, suburban parents, nor the black community are willing to accept the school as a mere custodian. Its purpose has been redefined by society: Not only must it serve all children, but it must graduate them all with salable skills.

We criticize the schools and look for change in the present distribution of costs and benefits; we are aware that other social institutions educate, and we have been aware for a long time of the selective nature of public education, but we nevertheless accept the notion that public schools are an assumed asset in the regeneration of society. We have adopted a history based on men and events chosen from the history of democratic ideas in education, while we ignore other men, whom we have labeled anti-intellectual. David Crockett and Horace Greeley, for example, leveled scornful tirades against the creation of elite institutions that served an emerging meritocracy. The land and money, they said, might instead have contributed to a real experiment in universal public education, to make public education truly public in its services, not merely in its uses. Schools have been public only in the sense that what happens in them is typical of what happens outside.

Having assumed the salutary past of the school, we have engaged in discussion and debate over the present efficacy of schools with no question but that schools must be; they are generic to the American landscape. These assumptions preclude debate and scholarly inquiry as to why we maintain schools and what we can reasonably expect of them. Until we can question the validity of these assumptions, we cannot begin to achieve the social restoration of which we speak so eloquently, but for which there is little precedent. We can only continue to generate rationalizations across a variety of disciplines for a national commitment to an ideology that claims simply, but erroneously, that the public schools have always done what they are now expected to do The truth is they never have.

CHAPTER 2

Individual Expectations for Education

Greeting his pupils, the master asked:
 What would you learn of me?
And the reply came:
 How shall we care for our bodies?
 How shall we rear our children?
 How shall we work together?
 How shall we live with our fellowmen?
 How shall we play?
 For what ends shall we live? ...
And the teacher pondered these words, and sorrow was in his heart, for his own learning touched not these things.

Chapman and Counts[1]

Nearly a half century has passed since Chapman and Counts submitted the above dialogue, which illustrates individual learning needs and desires for other than "book larnin'". How well have we done in meeting such individual learning needs? Daily newspapers yield indications that these learning needs have not as yet been satisfactorily met. During the decade of the sixties, the criticism of irrelevance was leveled against existing operations of the schools. It seems likely that today's pupils would respond to

the master's question in much the same way as pupils responded a half century ago.

One challenge for today's teacher in assisting his pupils in finding individual answers to such questions is in keeping abreast of the times. Teachers can ill afford a "generation gap" identity and pupils can ill afford to be taught by teachers who do not possess relevant knowledge, outlooks and attitudes. Consider just one of the pupils' questions—How shall we rear our children? During the last half century the answers to that question have been dealt with primarily within the home. Since the family unit served as the general environment within which to raise children, the schools were not expected to be deeply involved with the question of rearing children. It has been suggested that recent social changes—including more women in the work force, fewer numbers of relatives living in the household, and greater geographic mobility of families—have combined to make the family a less effective agent within which

1. J. Crosby Chapman and George S. Counts, *Principles of Education,* p. ii.

to raise children.[2] These changes in the family are directly related to changes in the ways children are raised today. However, many teachers obtained their knowledge and attitudes regarding the rearing of children within the traditional family setting. Therefore, some teachers are still likely to feel that the family should be the agent for providing child-rearing knowledge. But, *if* the family setting today is truly a less effective agent in rearing children than when our teachers were raised, then such teachers are likely to have difficulty accepting contemporary attitudes regarding the basic question—How shall we rear our children?

During the past half-century the schools have adjusted in many ways to the shift of many former family responsibilities on the school. Teachers have inherited many of the responsibilities formerly reserved for the home. Today's schools and teachers are very much expected to be involved with various responsibilities related to rearing children. A very significant aspect of the operations of the schools deals with pupil personnel services, including health and dental care, sex education, guidance, discipline, manners and codes of dress. Educators are now questioning—Where does all this end? Who decides what the limits are? What are or should be the actual responsibilities of the teacher in this regard?

At this point it seems of particular importance to note that the questions posed regarding the nature and extent of pupil personnel services seem to elicit answers which will lend themselves to the processes the schools should use to meet *group* goals. However, the essence of the schools' efforts perhaps ought to be determined by the *needs of individuals* outside of groups. By high school age, many of today's pupils are sophisticated enough to be able to determine their own unique needs and the schools should be flexible enough to meet individual needs regarding things other than subject matter. Perhaps the most relevant questions are those which ask the individual what it is *he* desires or needs assistance with as related to his health, his sex education, his guidance, or his manners.

Many other persistent needs exist which pupils expect their education to satisfy whatever the societal setting. Thus, the task of the teacher regarding education and the individual becomes that of constantly examining individual expectations and applying knowledge gained from his own education and experience toward the fulfillment of his pupils' personal expectations.

Parental and Pupil Expectations

Expectations of education have become American tradition being passed along so that both parents and pupils expect the schools to satisfy a wide variety of individual needs. When parents and pupils have been asked "What are the most important reasons for going to school?" their responses concur, for the most part, with the major societal expectations of the schools as previously discussed. For example, pupils of all ages are quick to suggest that intellectual development is the highest expectation within their educational experiences even though some may not be mature enough to express their desires in this fashion. Likewise, individuals expect the schools to provide meaningful school experiences with regard to citizenship, personality, vocational training, recreation and health. Parents

2. James S. Coleman, "Social Change: Impact on the Adolescent," pp. 11–18.

from all segments of society generally influence their children to believe that education is the main ingredient for being a successful person and for being an effective individual within the societal setting.

Participation as a Citizen

An individual's attitudinal development is considerably influenced by his environment, including the influences of various societal institutions. In turn, an individual's attitudes and values influence his behavior. However, each individual is ultimately privately responsible for determining what his citizenship behavior shall be. He elects to vote or not, to violently protest or not, to accept normative standards or not. Not withstanding these many influences upon an individual, as a participatory citizen the individual eventually stands alone and practices the act of citizenship in his unique way.

Does the display of the American flag in the classroom mean much to the students of today?

One of the functions ascribed to the public schools has been that of helping students become "good citizens." Parents, board of education members, school administrators, teachers and legislators have given much attention to citizenship as a dimension of an individual's education. Most states have laws which direct the schools to engage in specific teaching tasks aimed at developing citizenship. For example, an Illinois law states that every public school teacher shall teach the pupils honesty, kindness, justice and moral courage for the purpose of lessening crime and raising the standard of good citizenship (sections 12–27, School Code of Illinois, 1965). Implied in this law is that honesty, kindness, justice and moral courage are criteria for lessening crime and, therefore, contribute to the promotion of good citizenship. Terms such as honesty, kindness, justice and moral courage are not only difficult to define, but are also difficult to teach within the school setting. In spite of such difficulties, schools (that is, teachers) are expected to accept the challenge of providing individual pupils with learning experiences which will help each of them to develop alternatives for solving the moral problems of life. The schools are also expected to help cause youth to understand the desirableness of being kind and just individuals even if some adults they know are unkind and unjust. Individual moral courage, while an admirable attribute of character, and important to citizenship, is difficult to attain in a formalized school setting.

Teaching as related to these aspects of good citizenship draws heavily from an idealistic premise that charges teachers to serve as models in their manner of participation as citizens. Likewise, this idealistic approach also draws heavily upon the character analysis of great citizens past and present. The risk of this latter kind of teaching is that the "gospel" becomes Pollyannish and at times unreal. One aspect of the teaching task is to enlarge upon the dimensions of this idealism and "tell it like it is" so that the students have several alternatives to model, choose from, or modify for their own personal life style.

Since the early 1930's the American public schools have also been charged with the responsibility for developing other aspects of citizenship. American patriotism, the principles of representative government as enunciated in the American Declaration of Independence, and the Constitution of the United States of America have been emphasized in citizenship training. For many years, teachers have taught that each good citizen should demonstrate his patriotism by serving his country in peace as well as in war, by respecting the United States flag and by voting in elections. A kind of nationalistic idealism was assumed when good citizenship was taught in this manner. This form of idealism seemingly held true in an era when our society was closer knit, less complex and agrarian oriented. Thus, many living Americans coming from this heritage continue to operate from such a basis of idealism, not being cognizant of the conflicts resulting from the impersonal, complex, and multi-group influences of the contemporary, urban, pluralistic, machine oriented society. Herein lies one of the causes of the generation gap. Our young people tend to utilize bold dramatic methods in their desire to be heard whereas older people believe the way to be heard is through more traditional "good ol' days" procedures. However, today when an individual pursues the traditional channels of expression he is frequently overwhelmed by the massiveness and complexity of our contemporary society. With all of our technological sophistication, communication problems are still manifest among us. A small voice is practically unheard and a letter to an elected governmental representative is likely to be of minor importance in and of itself. Thus, an increasing number of young people seem to find it necessary to pool their efforts for the purposes of being heard. Consequently, a tension climate has developed between the active, impulsive, "tell it like it is," *now* oriented young citizens and their dramatic ways of communicating, and the less active, deliberate, "it was good enough for me," traditionally oriented older citizens. All are involved in a kind of trial and error re-examination of the dimensions of good individual citizenship. Obviously, each individual must ultimately make his choice as to what kind of citizen he is to be.

Personality

Individuals are unique with regard to personality. While it may be that, particularly between siblings, certain characteristics of personalities are similar, no two personalities are exactly alike. One's personality is considered to be the habitual patterns and qualities of behavior as expressed by physical and mental activities and attitudes, and also the distinctive individual qualities of a person considered collectively.

Many differing experiences affect the personality development of an individual. Since the experiences of life vary among individuals, it follows that personalities also differ among individuals. Behavioral scientists have observed that, in addition to the influences of heredity, similar personality characteristics in individuals are related to the similarities of life experiences of the individuals. In essence, this line of reasoning assumes that personality characteristics are learned from experience. Thus, particularly with peers, school experiences do in fact contribute to the development of one's personality. An individual's peer group identity and his experiences with the peer group are strong influences on his personality development. Therefore, it appears to be a reason-

able expectation of parents that schools should provide experiences that will enhance the personality development of their children. As pupils mature, they become increasingly aware of many dimensions of their own personality and often select activities and courses which they believe will help develop their personality.

Biological qualities such as age, sex, stature and pigmentation also influence one's personality. Various ethnic and racial groups influence the behavior patterns of their young through the sharing of similar experiences. Characteristics of an individual's personality are in part reflections of the individual's age group, sex group and racial group. An individual's behavior is partially adjusted to the forces of these biological qualities impinging upon him.

In summary, an individual's behavior is affected by the total impact of his life's ex-

Activities and personality development—Is there a relationship?

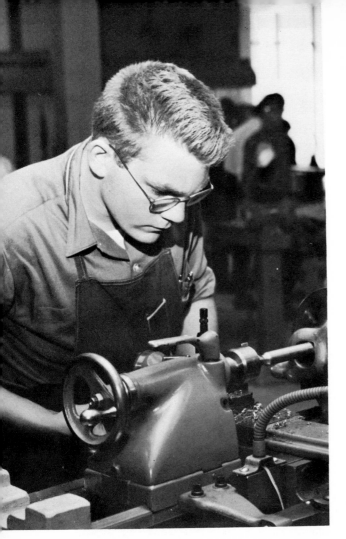

A salable skill such as being able to operate industrial machinery is a common expectation for schools.

All youth need to develop salable skills and those understandings and attitudes that make the worker an intelligent and productive participant in economic life.

Education Policies Commission
Education for all American Youth
(Washington, D.C.: National
Education Association, 1944), p. 26.

periences. Heredity and environment interact to make each individual a distinct and unique person.

Vocational Education

"While general education may be defined as those curricular experiences designed for all citizens in a democratic society, vocational education is concerned with those curricular experiences necessary for proficiency in a specific vocation. Obviously, general education is the foundation for any vocation."[3] As an individual progresses through school he needs assistance in deciding how much general education is required to provide himself with an adequate foundation for a selected vocation. A part of such decision-making is the universal expectation of education which suggests that the more education you have, the better job you can obtain. Since this is a generalized expectation, it says very little about the question—"What kind of education is needed to assure one of a better job?"

As is suggested in the next chapter, the schools of colonial America were generally not expected to deal with vocational subjects. The reading and writing expectations were not considered as the general education bases upon which to build for vocational education, but rather were considered as the bases for spiritual salvation.

As the societal and individual expectations of the schools increased, vocational education slowly came into the curriculum. The so-called comprehensive high school is unique to America and has gained considerable reputation as an excellent secondary educational prototype. The term "compre-

3. Daniel Tanner, *Schools for Youth*, p. 353.

The demand for technicians continues to rise.

Typing is a very valuable skill.

Girls and drafting?? Why not?

hensive" implies that both general education and vocational education be provided in order to meet the *individual* needs of the pupils. With both the general education and vocational education curricula provided, high school students are able to pursue a common general curriculum, vocational subjects and a wide range of school activities to satisfy their own individual interests and vocational plans.

Vocational education as a concerted public movement did not gain momentum in the United States until after World War I. It is true that there were several federal acts, such as the Morrill Act of 1862, which provided for certain aspects of vocational education prior to the close of World War I. During World War I, the nation's need for technically trained manpower was the primary thrust for the passage of the Smith-Hughes Act of 1917. From that time to the present there has been an increasing amount of federal and state legislation providing funds for vocational education. Since vocational education is more expensive than the traditional academic subjects, and since most of our schools continue to give most attention to the academic subjects, additional funds must continue to be provided to operate effective vocational programs. The curriculum of the comprehensive high school can be expected to contain programs of vocational education which have essentials as follows:

1. The program is directly related to employment opportunities, determined by school officials in cooperation with occupationally concerned and content individuals and groups.
2. The content of courses is confirmed or changed by periodic analyses of the

occupations for which the training is being given.

3. The courses for a specific occupation are set up and maintained with the advice and cooperation of the various occupational groups concerned.

4. The facilities and equipment used in instruction are comparable to those found in the particular occupation.

5. The conditions under which instruction is given duplicate as nearly as possible desirable conditions in the occupation itself and at the same time provide effective learning situations.

6. The length of teaching periods and total hours of instruction are determined by the requirements of the occupation and the needs of the students.

7. Training in a particular occupation is carried to the point of developing marketable skills, abilities, understandings, attitudes, work habits, and appreciations sufficient to enable the trainee to get and hold a job in that occupation.

8. Day and evening classes are scheduled at hours and during seasons convenient to enrollees.

9. Instruction is offered only to persons who need, desire, and can profit from it occupationally.

10. The teachers are competent in the occupation for which they are giving instruction and possess adequate professional qualifications for teaching.

11. Vocational guidance, including effective follow-up of all students who finish or drop out of a course, is an integral and continuing part of the program.

12. Continuous research is an integral part of the program.[4]

For an individual to eventually become a productive member of our society, he must be prepared to engage in a specific vocation. Therefore, at some point in one's educational development, even for the college-bound student, exposure to and involvement with some aspect of a vocational education program is a desirable prerequisite to entering the world of work. One of the contributing factors to the unemployable status of many of our youth is that large numbers of them leave school without having acquired a salable vocational skill. Pupils (and parents) are often so convinced of the panacea notion ascribed to education that many pupils who ought to be acquiring a salable vocational skill pursue college bound curricula instead. A challenge to the schools and to teachers in meeting individual expectations is to increase the vocational education opportunities and communicate the nature of such opportunities to the students prior to their leaving school. When this is accomplished, fewer of our students will be entering the world of work poorly prepared.

Recreation

As an educational concept, recreation is particularly concerned with the after work hours activities. Such recreational pursuits should be enjoyable to an individual as well as constructive for the individual. Recreational activities are primarily those engaged in during one's leisure time. The historic

4. Office of Education, *Public Vocational Education Programs.* Washington, D.C.: U.S. Department of Health, Education, and Welfare, April 1960, pp. 2–3.

School dances are a part of the social recreation program of the school.

leisure time activities is increasing due to the impact of advanced technology and research in the field of work. Man is living longer, working less, and has more leisure time with the prognosis that this pattern will continue well into the future of society. In addition, American incomes have been rising and are predicted to continue rising, barring an economic depression. Americans with increased leisure time, along with increased income, seek more and more recreational pursuits.

In order to satisfy the growing recreation need among individuals, adequate recreation programs must continue to be developed and sponsored by the several agencies of local, state, and federal governments. In addition, volunteer and private organizations such as the Boy Scouts, Girl Scouts, Y.M.C.A., Y.W.C.A. and industry sponsor recreational programs. In many communi-

traces of mankind indicate that individuals within the various civilizations throughout our world have always participated in music, games, sports, painting and other recreational activities. During the last century in the United States there has been a steady progression of park site puchases, developments of state and national parks and lakes, formations of camping clubs, gun clubs, fishing clubs, as well as immense growth in the manufacturing of recreational materials. Recreation continues to grow as a means of satisfying certain basic human needs.

Various statistics cite the recreation need. For example, the average life span is continually increasing. The average length of life in 1885 was 40 years; in 1950 it was 70 years; predicted for 2000 is 75 years. While man's average life span is being extended due to the impact of advanced technology and research in the field of medicine, the percentage of man's total lifetime spent in

Individual learning activities are an important part of the school program, and can be influential in determining future recreational activities.

ties the schools cooperate with local governments in providing recreational activities. Recreation programs which effectively satisfy such objectives will do much to satisfy the recreation need for individuals in our American society.

Recreation and the School

What can individuals expect of the schools in terms of recreation? Throughout the history of education in the United States there have been conflicting philosophies regarding the curricular offerings of the school. Some proponents of general education restrict the roll of the school to the academic subject disciplines, and argue that our schools should erase the so-called "frills," including recreation programs. A comprehensive curricular approach suggests that the recreation program should be an integral part of the over-all school program. Presently, most of the schools in the United States are actively engaged in recreation. Also, school buildings are being used and school personnel are contributing more and more to community recreation programs. The elements of school recreation programs are drawn from many departments within the school. While the physical education department plays a vital role with various activities involving sports and games, it is a misconception to believe that the physical education departments can provide all that is needed in an all-inclusive recreation program. In addition to sports and games activities, other activities in the school recreation program include music activities, dance, arts and crafts, dramatics, outdoor

5. Charles A. Bucher, *Foundations of Physical Education*, pp. 238–239.

activities and hobby clubs. In again stressing the emphasis of the worth of the program to the individual pupil, it follows that recreational programs consisting solely of group activities are less than satisfactory. It is highly probable that the recreational offerings of the school may be the only opportunities many students will have to learn to satisfy their own personal recreational needs.

Health

In 1918 the Commission on Reorganization of Secondary Education set forth the Seven Cardinal Principles of Education. The first principle listed was *health*. Since that time other committees, commissions and groups have reiterated the health objective as a function of the schools. Outcomes expected from the school health program include development of health knowledge, the development of desirable health attitudes, a development of desirable health practices, and development of health and safety skills.[5]

Hot lunch programs enhance good health.

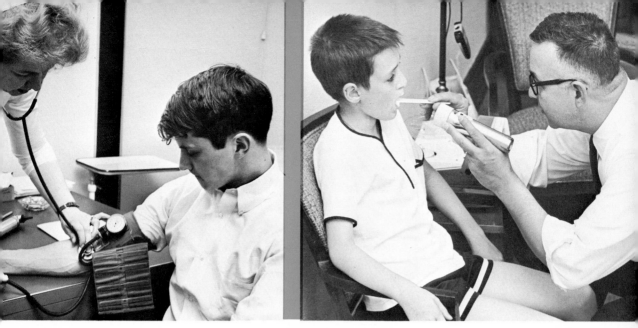

Health is also the business of the school.

Since health education is really everybody's business, and since every state has compulsory school attendance laws, it seems reasonable to expect that the schools educate for health. However, the public health agencies are also charged with the responsibility for health education and services within cities, states, and the nation. Initially the public health agencies, under the supervision of medical personnel, appeared to be the more competent agency for meeting public health needs. With increasing expectations of the schools to provide for all of one's education, health education in the schools has greatly expanded. At the present time, some schools have very adequate health programs including facilities and well qualified personnel. Other schools provide only minimal, if any, health services.

There does not seem to be a simple solution to this controversy as to where the responsibility lies for school health. Probably the answer to this problem will vary according to the community. The solution would seem to depend upon how each community can best meet the health needs of the people who inhabit its particular geographical limits. The type of administrative setup that most fully meets the health needs and makes for greater progress should be the one that is adopted. Vested interests should not be considered, and the health interests of the *consumer* should be the primary concern. Health is everybody's business and everyone should strive for the best health program possible in his community, state, nation, and world.[6]

Modern schools and teachers are somewhat responsive to the individual needs and expectations of pupils. They must become *more* responsive. Various formal and informal school activities and programs are felt to contribute to the development of desirable citizenship behaviors and personality traits. Vocational education programs help foster the development of salable skills. Dimensions of social poise and physical development are both enhanced through recreation programs. Also, the basic health needs are checked and administered to through the expanding health programs of our schools.

6. *NEA Research Bulletin,* December 1966, 44: 107. Used with permission.

QUESTIONS FOR DISCUSSION

1. Identify specific ways in which the schools engage in citizenship education. Can you think of better ways? Identify them.
2. State some ways in which personalities are developed. Also state some ways in which the schools influence personality development.
3. List the advantages and disadvantages of the specialized high school compared to the comprehensive high school.
4. In what ways are the goals of the interscholastic athletic programs incompatible with the goals of the recreation programs? What should be the relationship of these goals?
5. Discuss the school's responsibility for health services.

SUPPLEMENTARY LEARNING ACTIVITIES

1. Poll selected samples of students and parents to determine their respective views regarding the school's role with citizenship education. Compare the two views.
2. Invite a school psychologist to class to discuss personality development. Give attention to the role of the school.
3. Conduct a telephone survey of various employers to determine their views regarding the school's role in vocational education.
4. Survey the total community recreation program. In what ways could the schools and the local government cooperate to improve the community program?
5. Visit the public health office in your community for the purpose of seeking relevant information regarding public health

services. What is the budget? Where does the money come from?

SELECTED REFERENCES

Archambault, Reginald, ed. *Dewey on Education.* New York: Random House, Inc., 1966.

Benson, Charles S. *The Cheerful Prospect: A Statement on the Future of American Education.* Boston: Houghton Mifflin Co., 1965.

Bucher, Charles A. *Foundations of Physical Education.* St. Louis: The C. V. Mosby Co., 1968.

Chapman, J. Crosby, and George S. Counts. *Principles of Education.* Boston: Houghton Mifflin Co., 1924.

Coleman, James S. "Social Change: Impact on the Adolescent." *Bulletin of the National Association of Secondary Principals* 49(1965): 11–18.

Corey, Fay L. *Values of Future Teachers.* New York: Teachers College Press, 1955.

Cremin, Lawrence A. *The Genius of American Education.* Pittsburgh: University of Pittsburgh Press, 1965.

Dewey, John. *Democracy and Education.* New York: The Macmillan Co., 1916.

Educational Policies Commission. *Education for All American Youth: A Further Look.* Washington, D.C.: National Education Association, 1952.

Edwards, Newton, and H. G. Richey. *The School in the American Social Order.* Boston: Houghton Mifflin Co., 1963.

Erickson, Erik H., ed. *Youth: Change and Challenge.* New York: Basic Books, Publishers, Inc., 1963.

Goodman, Paul. *Compulsory Mis-Education and the Community of Scholars.* New York: Random House, Inc., 1964.

Henry, David D. *What Priority for Education?* Champaign: University of Illinois Press, 1961.

Holt, John. *How Children Fail.* New York: Pitman Publishing Corp., 1964.

Lee, Gordon C. *Education and Democratic Ideals.* New York: Harcourt, Brace and World, Inc., 1965.

Morris, Van Cleve, et al. *Becoming an Educator.* Boston: Houghton Mifflin Co., 1963.

Stember, Charles Herbert. *Education and Attitude Change.* New York: Institute of Human Relations Press, 1961.

Tanner, Daniel. *Schools for Youth.* New York: The Macmillan Co., 1965.

Thayer, V. T. *Formative Ideas in American Education.* New York: Dodd, Mead and Co., 1965.

Wiggin, Gladys A. *Education and Nationalism.* New York: McGraw-Hill Book Co., 1962.

Area
Vocational Schools

Michael Russo

Just outside Clarkston, Georgia, a few miles from Atlanta, sits a $1.4 million dollar complex of buildings that is shaping the future and changing the past for some 1,500 people each year.

Every day of the school year 600 students from a six-county area pour into the four huge buildings—floor space to equal three football fields—to receive education in an extremely wide range of vocational subjects. With the training they are getting they are assured of a good job after graduation.

In the evening the flat expanses of glass blaze with light as some 850 adults attend classes designed to retrain them for new occupations. Victims of technological change or a poor start in education, these people are changing their past and, like their teen-age counterparts who go to school during the day, building for the future.

The massive complex of buildings is the DeKalb Area Technical School, just one of 331 area vocational schools built or under construction in 41 States with the aid of Federal funds.

Vocational high schools have been very much a part of the American scene for decades. By the middle of this century, good vocational high schools existed in many parts of the country. Some of them, however, were restricted in their facilities, operating funds, and curriculum offerings. Since the close of World War II many of the tools and techniques of industry, to which

most vocational schools were geared, have become obsolete. And an ever-growing army of young people and adults have needed up-to-date technological training and retraining to meet the constantly changing needs of industry.

The Vocational Education Act of 1963 is helping to solve some of the problems created by these circumstances and conditions. Under this act, Federal grants to States are available for construction of vocational-technical facilities to cover up to 50 percent of the costs.

Funds allocated to the States can be used to "improve, maintain, and extend" the facilities of existing vocational schools or to build new area vocational schools in other geographic areas.

The term, "area," describes schools which provide training for workers in the industries of a defined geographic area. The act defines four types of area vocational schools:

1. A specialized high school used exclusively or almost so to provide full-time vocational education in preparation for full-time work in industry—

2. A department of a high school used exclusively or principally to provide training in at least five different occupational fields to those available for full-time study prior to their entering the labor market—

---

* Michael Russo, "Area Vocational Schools," *American Education*, June 1966, pp. 15–18.

3. A technical or vocational school providing vocational education predominantly to persons who have completed or left school and who are able to study on a full-time basis before going to work—

4. A department or division of a junior college, community college, or university providing vocational education in at least five different occupational fields, under the supervision of the State board, and leading to immediate employment but not toward a baccalaureate degree.

The DeKalb Area Technical School in Georgia is a fine example of what the Congress had in mind. Established jointly by the DeKalb County Board of Education and the Georgia Department of Education, this school offers courses in twenty occupational fields and covers the chief vocational interests of a six-county area.

DeKalb offers courses in data processing and in electrical, electronic, chemical, and mechanical technology. If a student is interested in office occupations he may choose accounting, punchcard accounting, secretarial science, or clerical studies. For the aspiring tradesman DeKalb offers appliance repair, auto mechanics, drafting, electrical construction, machine-shop operations, radio and television servicing, welding, refrigeration, practical nursing, and medical assistant training.

That's the DeKalb vocational menu. But how is the instruction served? Thirty-four full-time and forty-eight part-time instructors form the faculty. DeKalb operates with separate day and night staffs, though eight of the day staff also teach six hours in the evening.

The physical layout of DeKalb consists of fourteen classrooms (too few already), a mechanical-technical section containing nine machine shops, and an automotive and diesel area containing four major shops. Four laboratories are set aside for electrical/electronics training, including a separate one for radio-television.

At this writing more than $80 million has been expended in Federal funds by the States for area vocational educational facilities to serve all age groups with programs below the professional level.

The plant also includes three chemistry labs, one physics lab, five office occupation labs (including data processing), and five for health occupation studies. All courses share four drafting rooms.

DeKalb operates a closed-circuit TV system, provides a library reference section for each of the major curriculum divisions, and operates a clinic for remedial reading. These up-to-date instructional facilities are typical of many area vocational schools.

Naturally, technical curriculums of area vocational high schools vary from community to community. For example, in Staples, Minnesota—a center for manufacture of heavy earth-moving machinery and farm equipment—the emphasis in vocational training is just where it belongs, on the operation and maintenance of heavy machinery. Young men learn the "innards" of bulldozers, cranes, and plows. The graduates of the Staples school get good jobs in local plants or in the construction trades.

But an area vocational school is not an unchanging technological mechanism. It anticipates changes in the industries of the area. Moving to meet new local demands requires school administrators to anticipate rather than to react later to new facts of life in area industry. Schools must plan, therefore, with a degree of built-in flexibility.

Flexibility is the big feature of the large Atlanta Area Vocational School now under construction. Total flexibility. Except for corridors and a few necessarily fixed units, almost everything under the roof will be movable. There will be numerous electrical outlets to supply enough power for any conceivable need. With so many mobile walls, the Atlanta Area Vocational School will be something of a quick change artist.

The school has additional functional features. For instance, the auto shop and other heavy equipment areas that need access to roads and the outdoors are placed on the periphery of the buildings, with adjacent apron spaces for outside work.

This Atlanta school will have an attractive and pleasant appearance. Service areas have been planned and landscaped so that they are hidden from view. Though the school has ample parking, the landscaped parking lots will add to rather than detract from the dignity of the building.

The architectural plan has provided two interior courts open to the sky. Artistic landscaping and lighting will complete the courtyard decor. Students will have not only a place to take a breather, but also an airy passageway from one classroom to another.

Many area vocational schools operate year round with both day and night classes. In fact there was no other solution for the community of Milwaukee. Here at the Vocational-Technical and Adult School the answer had to be classes twelve months a year and virtually a twenty-two-hour-a-day operation for nine months a year. Summer enrollment is open only to post high school vocational students.

According to George Parkinson, director of the school, there were about 22,000 students enrolled in day and night programs this fall, and there will be a cumulative enrollment of about 38,000 students by the end of the year. The student body is not only large, but also cosmopolitan, with students from all over Wisconsin, other States, and several foreign countries. The school is free to residents of Milwaukee but charges a fee to those living outside the city.

The Vocational-Technical and Adult School has five separate divisions:

1. The continuation program with 874 students is primarily for dropouts and is held during the day.

2. The Adult High School with students aged 18 to 65 operates during the day with 312 students and in the evening with 876.

3. The Apprentice School with 949 students operates for indentured apprentices who attend classes one day a week.

4. The Institute of Technology features courses at the junior college level and awards associate degrees to its graduates. It operates both during the day and in the evening with a total enrollment of more than 8,000.

5. The Adult School has the largest number of students, 3,000 during the day and 12,553 at night, and offers courses under the Manpower Development and Training Act as well as under the Vocational Education Act.

The Milwaukee school conducts some 60 different programs encompassing approximately 1,200 courses. In fact, almost any vocation not requiring a degree can be learned there.

What about basic education subjects taught in area vocational schools? These are no less important to the student taking technical training than to the college preparatory student. Courses in reading, mathematics, science, and the like are important in learning a trade, and are given along with specialized training. A person's ability to keep pace with new developments in his line of work is directly tied to his proficiency in these fundamental subjects.

It is as important for the vocational student to discover his particular occupational niche as it is for the college-bound student to discover his academic potential. Vocational students are tested for aptitudes and abilities and counseled to assist them in preparing for the right career choices. Thus, the personal needs of the students and the needs of the community are satisfied at the same time.

Qualified students, well planned vocational curriculums, adaptable and attractive buildings, and an eye on the demands of industry—all these contribute toward a successful attack on the problems of supplying trained workers and filling the needs of an area's labor market.

During many visits around the country it has become apparent to me that there are a few distinctive features that mark the truly well-planned area vocational school. If I were to list them, I think I would include the following:

The shops and laboratories of the ideal school should be developed around an occupational cluster, partitioned with acoustically treated removable walls. Rooms on both sides of a conventional corridor might well be modified to achieve fuller use of these corridors and still not overlook traffic patterns or safety codes and regulations. Sometimes a corridor can become part of a larger related unit. It has been found that lining corridors with lockers is not the best utilization of space. Lockers could be installed in a cross-sectional corridor unit with doors going to the outside; this would minimize traffic and leave the larger corridors to be used for individual study carrels. To avoid confusion, locker rooms, dressing

rooms, and showers for use of evening students should be separated from those for use of day-school students.

Laboratories should be adaptable to changes which may be brought on by technical advances in science and industry. The mechanical and electrical services of these laboratories should be planned so that when new automated equipment is added to the school's facilities it can be installed at a minimum cost.

On shop layouts machines should be grouped so that they may be used by single-skill classes as well as multi-occupational classes. Space for storage of materials, tools, and projects should be planned. The possibilities of incorporating into the school system a large central storage unit, which could also be used as a teaching station, should be considered.

One of the most neglected of all elements in vocational schools has been the library. Small specialty reference libraries are no longer enough. There should be a large central library which will serve all the people in the community as a vocational-technical education resource center. These libraries should be properly staffed, and shelves should be fully stocked with the latest reference books and periodicals.

Great demands are placed on the use of lecture halls in an area vocational school. Sometimes a classroom-sized lecture hall is adequate but often—particularly for evening and night classes—large ones are needed. These should offer all students an unobstructed view. A round, stadium-type room is often advisable. They should be designed not only for lectures and visual aids but also for heavy track systems and turnstile floor areas for use of equipment. The ideal lecture hall, therefore, should become a truly educational unit, one which can be divided into a number of smaller rooms but still be used as a large hall when needed.

Thoughtful vocational educators everywhere are enthusiastic about installing built-in equipment, creating facilities for film demonstrations, providing closed-circuit TV systems, and varying the size and shape of classrooms and lecture halls. The word in contemporary vocational schooling is "modular." The well-planned school is one that can change with the times, one in which a room or facility can be added or eliminated without upheaval.

Since area vocational schools must train all who qualify, the school buildings should be designed to include features to accommodate physically handicapped students.

A ramp, rather than stairs, and a larger entrance door, perhaps electronically controlled, should be planned. Other special facilities that are needed include interior ramps with grab bars conveniently located, round hand railings in corridors and stairways, and slant-type stairs with lipless risers no higher than six inches.

Cafeterias should be planned to serve two, three, or more meals a day. This not only will help meet the needs of many students with small incomes but also will provide food services for those who come directly from their jobs.

Public transportation and parking facilities need to be well planned. Many persons are discouraged from taking advantage of the educational programs which are available because these facilities are not adequately provided. The new Atlanta-Fulton County Area Vocational School, for instance, will have a paved, well-lighted parking area for 1,600 cars.

This brief description doesn't say it all by any means. But the points I have mentioned have proved to be very successful. The Office has prepared a detailed guide for educators who need information about establishing an area vocational school. This illustrated brochure, entitled *Basic Planning Guide for Vocational and Technical Education Facilities* (OE-80040; price 20¢) may be obtained from Superintendant of Documents, U.S. Government Printing Office, Washington, D.C., 20402.

Expenditures of Federal, State, and local funds for vocational education have grown phenomenally in the last 20 years. In 1945 approximately $66 million was spent for vocational education, compared to more than $588 million in 1965. It is significant that the amount States and local school districts spent was three times what the Federal Government contributed. Federal funds for vocational education totaled $146 million compared to $175 million in State funds and more than $266 million in local funds.

Enrollment in vocational classes more than doubled in that 20-year period. In 1945 there were slightly over 2,000,000 students enrolled in vocational education compared with 5,395,000 in 1965. Since enactment of the Vocational Education Act of 1963 the number of students participating has increased by 1,178,000 or more than 20 percent.

Projections of the U.S. office of Education indicate that 364 new area vocational schools will be built in the coming fiscal year with the aid of Federal funds. This number is greater than the total number of such schools built in the three years since the Vocational Education Act of 1963 was passed. Area vocational schools are fast becoming a vital part of the Nation's educational system.

CHAPTER 3

Our Educational Past in Perspective

Many changes have taken place in American education since the first schools were established in this country. In this chapter, we shall take a brief look at some of these changes that have taken place in the history of American education.

As someone once said, history permits us to climb to a high place and look back over the road that we have traveled. Once we can see this road clearly, we can avoid some of the mistakes that we have made before. By the same token, we can capitalize upon the successes in our educational past. Then too, a knowledge of the history of education permits a teacher to appreciate the proud heritage that American educators possess. Let us proceed then with a brief look at the history of American education—the task and the teacher.

Educational Expectations in Colonial America

Of course, when the colonists arrived at Jamestown in 1607, they brought their ideas concerning education with them. Earlier in this book, it was pointed out that Americans today have various expectations of the public schools. Just as contemporary Americans have certain expectations of the present day educational system, so were there certain educational expectations in colonial America. Colonial America was divided roughly into three geographical areas—the Northern Colonies in the New England area, the Middle Colonies centered in New York, and the Southern Colonies located in the Virginia area. The colonists in each of these three areas had somewhat different expectations of the schools that existed in their respective areas. A New England Puritan, expressing his expectations in contemporary language might have said:

I expect two things from our schools here in the Northern Colonies. First, my children must learn to read so they can understand the Bible. Secondly, the schools must teach my boys Latin and Greek so that if they wish to go on to college they will be qualified to do so.

This interest in education in the Northern Colonies coupled with the fact that most of the colonists in that area were of similar religious convictions led to the early establishment of public schools in that area. In fact,

A colonial battledore, a variation of the horn-book printed on heavy paper and folded like an envelope.

The earliest known illustration of a secondary school in America. This is the Boston Latin Grammar School founded in 1635. This illustration comes from an old pictorial map of Boston made about 1748, just before this school building was torn down. This was probably not the original building which housed the Boston Latin Grammar School.

A colonial hornbook from which children learned the ABC's. It consisted of a heavy sheet of paper tacked to a piece of wood and covered with a thin sheet of cow's horn.

by 1635, only fifteen years after Boston had been settled, a Latin Grammar School was established in that area. Grammar schools had existed in Europe for many years prior to their appearance in colonial America. As their name implies, the Latin Grammar Schools included instruction in the classical languages of Latin and Greek. Such instruction was considered to be absolutely essential for the very few colonial boys who went on to a university. The school boys—for only boys were admitted—who attended the Latin Grammar School spend most of their time memorizing and then reciting what they had learned to the schoolmaster.

> And ye shall know the truth, and the truth shall make you free.
>
> Gospel of John (8:32)

Recalling his experiences as a Latin Grammar School student, one graduate recalled:

At ten years of age I committed to memory many rules of syntax, the meaning of which I had no notion of, although I could apply them in a mechanical way. The rule for the ablative absolute, for instance—"A noun and a participle are put in the ablative, called absolute, to denote the time, cause or concomitant of an action, or the condition on which it depends"—I could rattle off whenever I encountered a sample of that construction, but it was several years after I learnt the rule that I arrived at even the faintest conception of what it meant. The learning by heart of the grammar then preceded rather than accompanied as now exercises in translation and composition.

The educational expectations of a typical colonist from the Middle Colonies can be illustrated by the following statement that could have been made by a parent living in that area at that time:

Since there are many different religions represented here in the Middle Colonies, I want my children to attend a parochial school where they will not only learn to read and write, but also where they will receive instruction in my particular religion.

These Middle Colonies are sometimes referred to as the "colonial melting pot" due to the fact that they were settled by people of many different nationalities and religions. These divergent backgrounds made it difficult for the Middle colonists to agree upon the curriculum for a public school system, and therefore each religious group established its own parochial school system. It is interesting to note that many of these same educational problems that were found in colonial America still exist today. For instance, there are still many divergent groups in the American society, so that we may still be considered a melting pot (or if you prefer to use more recent popular terminology, a vegetable stew).

Yet another example of an educational problem that has persisted since colonial times is that dealing with parochial education. Just as the Middle colonists did, a number of religious groups still feel the need to maintain their own parochial school systems.

> For wisdom is better than rubies; and all things that may be desired are not to be compared with it.
>
> Proverbs (8:11)

The Southern Colonies consisted of large plantations and relatively few towns. This meant that two rather distinct classes of people—a few wealthy plantation owners, and a mass of poor black slaves and white indentured servants who worked on the plantations—lived in the Southern Colonies. This also meant that people lived far apart in the Southern Colonies. If we could turn back the clock to colonial days, we would probably hear a Southern plantation owner explain his educational expectations something like this:

Let me say first of all that we don't really need a public school system here in the Southern Colonies because, in the first place, the plantation workers do not need any education at all, and in the second place, the children of us plantation owners live so far apart that it would be impractical to have a central public school for all of them to attend. For these reasons, we do not have and do not need a public school system. I hire a tutor to live here on my plantation and teach my children. When my boys get old enough I'll send them back to Europe to attend a university.

The only education available to the poorer people in the Southern Colonies was that provided by individual parents for their children and that provided by certain missionary groups interested in teaching young people to read the Bible. A boy from a poor family who wished to learn a trade would receive his practical education by serving an apprenticeship with a master craftsman who was already in that line of work.

Early School Laws

The first law passed in colonial America dealing with education was passed in Massachusetts in 1642. This law, requiring parents to educate their children, reads as follows:

This Court, taking into consideration the great neglect of many parents and masters in training up their children in learning, and labor, and other implyments which may be proffitable

to the common wealth, do hereupon order and decree, that in every towne ye chosen men appointed for managing prudentiall affaires of the same shall henceforth stand charged with the care of the redresse of this evil, so as they shalbee sufficiently punished by fines for the neglect thereof, upon presentment of the grand jury, or other information or complaint in any Court within this jurisdiction. And for this end they, or the greater number of them, shall have power to take account from time to time of all parents and masters, and of their children, concerning their calling and implyment of their children, especially of their ability to read and understand the principles of religion and the capitall lawes of this country, and to impose fines upon such as shall refuse to render such account to them when they shall be required; and they shall have power, with consent of any Court or the magistrate, to put forth apprentices the children of such as they shall [find] not to be able and fitt to imploy and bring them up.

In 1647, yet another law dealing with education was passed in Massachusetts. This law, which has come to be known as the "Old Deluder Act," required towns of certain size to establish schools. This law stated:

It being one chiefe project of that old deluder, Satan, to keepe men from the knowledge of the Scriptures, as in former times by keeping them in an unknown tongue, so in these latter times by persuading from the use of tongues, that so at least the true sence and meaning of the originall might be clouded by false glosses of saint seeming deceivers, that learning may not be buried in the grave of our fathers in church and commonwealth, the Lord assisting our endeavors,—

It is therefore ordered that every township in this jurisdiction, after the Lord hath increased their number to 50 householders, shall then forthwith appoint one within their towne to teach all such children as shall resort to him to write and reade, whose wages shall be paid either by the parents or masters of such children, or by the inhabitants in general, . . . and it is further ordered that where any towne shall

A photograph of the title page and board back of the oldest known edition (1727) of the New England Primer. It was the most widely used textbook in colonial America.

The contents of the New England Primer reflected the religious emphasis of education in colonial America.

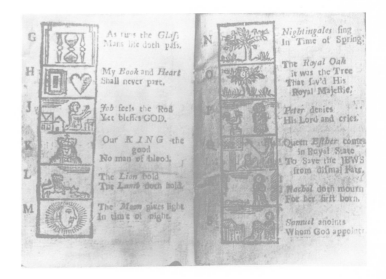

The Seal of the Society for the Propagation of the Gospel in Foreign Parts. This society, which was the missionary society of the Church of England, was responsible for the support of most of the charity schools in the English colonies during the 18th Century. The society also furnished books for churches and school libraries. This seal shows their conception of education and their attitude toward Indians.

increase to the number of 100 families or house-holders they shall set up a grammar schoole, the Master thereof being able to instruct youth so farr as they shall be fitted for the University, provided that if any town neglect the perform-ance hereof above one year, that every such town shall pay five pounds to the next school till they shall perform this order.

In addition to the passage of these laws, further proof of the colonists' early interest in education can be found in the following agreement signed by a number of the citizens living in Roxbury in 1645:

Whereas, the Inhabitantes of Roxburie, in consideration of their relligeous care of posteritie, have taken into consideration how necessarie the education of theire children in Literature will be to fitt them for public service, both in Churche and Commonwealth, in succeeding ages. They therefore unanimously have consented and agreed to erect a free schoole in the said town of Roxburie, and to allow twenty pounds per annum to the schoolemaster, to bee raised out of the messuages and part of the lands of the severall donors (Inhabitantes of said Towne) in severall proportions as hereafter followeth under their hands. And for the well ordering thereof they have chosen and elected some Feoffees who shall have power to putt in or remove the Schoolemaster, to see to the well ordering of the schoole and schollars, to receive and pay the said twenty pounds per annum to the Schoolemaster and to dispose of any other gifte or giftes which hereafter may or shall be given for the advancement of learning and education of children ...

Our First College

In 1636, only sixteen years after the settlement of Boston, the first college was established in colonial America. This school was named "Harvard College" after the man who helped to finance the school's humble beginning. The conditions surrounding the establishment of Harvard, and the school's philosophy and curriculum are explained in the following document, written in 1643 and entitled *New England's First Fruits,* which is partially reproduced here:

In Respect of the Colledge, and the Proceedings of "Learning" Therein: 1. After God had carried us safe to New England, and wee had builded our houses, provided necessaries for our livelihood, rear'd convenient places for God's worship, and setled the Civill Government: One of the next things we longed for, and looked after was to advance Learning and perpetuate it to Posterity; dreading to leave an illiterate Ministery to the Churches, when our present Ministers shall lie in the Dust. And as wee were thinking and consulting how to effect this great Work; it pleased God to stir up the heart of one Mr. Harvard (a godly Gentleman, and a lover of Learning, there living amongst us) to give the onehalfe of his Estate (it being in all about 1700.l.) towards the erecting of a Colledge: and all his Library: after him another gave 300.l. others after them cast in more, and the publique hand of the State added the rest: the Colledge was, by common consent, appointed to be at Cambridge, (a place very pleasant and accommodate) and is called (according to the name of the first founder) Harvard Colledge.

The Edifice is very faire and comely within and without, having in it a spacious Hall; (where they daily meet at Commons, Lectures and Exercises), and a large Library with some

Harvard College buildings constructed in 1675, 1699, and 1720. These buildings were dormitories. Most of the instruction took place in the homes or offices of the president and tutors.

Bookes to it, the gifts of diverse of our friends, their Chambers and studies also fitted for, and possessed by the Students, and all other roomes of Office necessary and convenient, with all needfull Offices thereto belonging: And by the side of the Colledge a faire Grammer Schoole, for the training up of young Schollars, and fitting them for Academicall Learning, that still as they are judged ripe, they may be received into the Colledge of this Schoole: Master Corlet is the Mr., who hath very well approved himselfe for his abilities, dexterity and painfulnesse in teaching and education of the youth under him.

Over the Colledge is master Dunster placed, as President, a learned conscionable and industrious man, who hath so trained up his Pupils in the tongues and Arts, and so seasoned them with the principles of Divinity and Christianity, that we have to our great comfort, (and in truth) beyond our hopes, beheld this progresse in Learning and godlinesse also; the former of these hath appeared in their publique declamations in Latine and Greeke, and Disputations Logicall and Philosophicall, which they have wonted (besides their ordinary Exercises in the Colledge-Hall) in the audience of the Magistrates, Ministers, and other Schollars, for the probation of their growth in Learning, upon set dayes, constantly once every moneth to make and uphold: The latter hath been manifested in sundry of them, by the savoury breathings of their Spirits in their godly conversation. Insomuch that we are confident, if these early blossomes may be cherished and warmed with the influence of the friends of Learning, and lovers of this pious worke, they will by the help of God, come to happy maturity in a short itme.

Ofer the Colledge are twelve Overseers chosen by the generall Court, six of them are of the Magistrates, the other six of the Ministers, who are to promote the best good of it and (having a power of influence into all persons in it) are to see that every one be diligent and proficient in his proper place.

Further insight into the nature of Harvard College may be found in the following entrance requirements published in 1642:

When any scholar is able to read Tully, or such like classical Latine author *extempore*, and make and speak true Latin in Verse and Prose, and decline perfectly the paradigms of nounes and verbes in the Greek tongue, then may he be admitted into the college, nor shall any claim admission before such qualifications.

Harvard was the only colonial college for nearly sixty years until William and Mary was established in 1693. Other colleges which were established early in our history included Yale (1701), Princeton (1746), King's College (1754), College of Philadelphia (1755), Brown (1764), Dartmouth (1769), and Queen's College (1770).

The Latin Grammar School was the only form of secondary school found in the colonies until the early 1700's, at which time a few private secondary schools were established. These schools were established out of a need for a more practical form of secondary education than the existing Latin Grammar Schools provided. Insight into the nature of these early private secondary schools can be gained from the following newspaper ad, which was published in the October–November, 1723, edition of the *American Weekly Mercury* of Philadelphia:

There is a school in New York, in the Broad Street, near the Exchange where Mr. John Walton, late of Yale-Colledge, teacheth Reading, Writing, Arethmatick, whole Numbers and Fractions, Vulgar and Decimal, the Mariners Art, Plain and Mercators Way; also Geometry, Surveying, the Latin tongue, and Greek and Hebrew Grammers, Ethicks, Rhetorick, Logick, Natural Philosophy and Metaphysicks, all or any of them for a Reasonable Price. The School from the first of October till the first of March will be tended in the Evening. If any Gentleman in the Country are disposed to send their sons to the said School, if they apply themselves to the Master he will immediately procure suitable Entertainment for them, very cheap. Also if any Young Gentleman of the City will please to come in the evening and make some Tryal of the Liberal Arts, they may have opportunity of Learning the same things which are commonly taught in Colledges.

In 1751 Benjamin Franklin opened a secondary school in Philadelphia which he called an academy. The curriculum in Franklin's Academy included practical training in areas such as surveying, navigation, and printing, as well as courses in English, geography, history, logic, rhetoric, Latin and Greek.

Franklin's Academy served a real need as the colonies developed a greater need for technically trained citizens. Other academies were quickly established and this type of school flourished for approximately one hundred years. These academies were private schools and many of them admitted girls as well as boys.

The New Nation and Its Educational Needs

One of the great problems facing the United States, after winning her independence from England, was that of welding

A picture of the academy and charitable school of Philadelphia founded by Benjamin Franklin in 1751. It is the first institution in America, so far as present records show, to bear the title of academy. Later on it developed into the University of Pennsylvania.

her people, who had come from many diverse political and religious convictions, into a nation of informed voters. This meant that all citizens should be able to read so that they could keep informed on the issues the country faced. This interest in education found in the new nation was manifested in a number of different ways; for instance, groups of citizens created petitions for better schools. An example of such a petition is the following, which was submitted in 1799 to the General Assembly of Rhode Island:

A PETITION FOR FREE SCHOOL. *To the Honorable General Assembly of the State of Rhode Island and Providence Plantations, to be holden at Greenwich, on the last Monday of February,* A.D. *1799:*
The Memorial and Petition of the Providence Association of Mechanics and Manufacturers respectfully presents—

That the means of education which are enjoyed in this state are very inadequate to a purpose so highly important . . . we at the same time solicit this Honorable Assembly to make legal provision for the establishment of free schools sufficient to educate all the children in the several towns throughout the state. . . .

Yet another indication of the new national need for, and interest in, education is the following comment made by Thomas Jefferson in 1816:

If a nation expects to be ignorant and free in a state of civilization, it expects what never was and never will be . . . There is no safe deposit but with the people themselves; nor can they be safe with them without information.

Despite this new interest in education, the school of the early 1800's was very humble and inadequate. An excellent description of an 1810 New England school is contained in the following reflection of a teacher who taught in this school:

(A) The school building: The school house stood near the center of the district, at the junction of four roads, so near the usual track of carriages that a large stone was set up at the end of the building to defend it from injury. Except in the dry season the ground was wet, and the soil by no means firm. The spot was particularly exposed to the bleak winds of winter; nor were there any shade trees to shelter the children from the scorching rays of the summer's sun, as they were cut down many years ago. Neither was there any such thing as an outhouse of any kind, not even a wooden shed.

The size of the building was 22 x 20 feet. From the floor to the ceiling it was 7 feet. The chimney and entry took up about four feet at one end, leaving the schoolroom itself 18 x 20 feet. Around these sides of the room were connected desks, arranged so that when the pupils were sitting at them their faces were towards the instructor and their backs toward the wall. Attached to the sides of the desks nearest to the instructor were benches for small pupils. The instructor's desk and chair occupied the center. On this desk were stationed a rod, or ferule; sometimes both. These, with books, writings, inkstands, rules, and plummets, with a fire shovel, and a pair of tongs (often broken), were the principal furniture.

The windows were five in number, of twelve panes each. They were situated so low in the walls as to give full opportunity to the pupils to see every traveller as he passed, and to be easily seen. The places of the broken panes were usually supplied with hats, during school hours. A depression in the chimney, on one side of the entry, furnished a place of deposit for about half of the hats, and the spare clothes of the boys; the rest were left on the floor, often to be trampled upon. The girls generally carried their bonnets, etc., into the schoolroom. The floor and ceiling were level, and the walls were plastered.

The room was warmed by a large and deep fire place. So large was it, and so efficacious in warming the room otherwise, that I have seen about one-eighth of a cord of good wood burning in it at a time. In severe weather it was estimated that the amount usually consumed was not far from a cord a week. . . .

> Experience keeps a dear school, but fools will learn in no other.
>
> Benjamin Franklin

The school was not infrequently broken up for a day or two for want of wood. The instructor or pupils were sometimes, however, compelled to cut or saw it to prevent the closing of the school. The wood was left in the road near the house, so that it often was buried in the snow, or wet with rain. At the best, it was usually burnt green. The fires were to be kindled about half an hour before the time of beginning the school. Often, the scholar, whose lot it was, neglected to build it. In consequence of this, the house was frequently cold and uncomfortable about half of the forenoon, when, the fire being very large, the excess of heat became equally distressing. Frequently, too, we were annoyed by smoke. The greatest amount of suffering, however, arose from excessive heat, particularly at the close of the day. The pupils being in a free perspiration when they left, were very liable to take cold.

The town and church schools of the early colonial period were supplemented by the dame school. In fact, it was a common requirement for that period that children know how to read before entering a town school. Hence, the necessity of these dame schools, which taught the children the alphabet, possibly the catechism and the rudiments of reading.

The ventilation of the schoolroom was as much neglected as its temperature; and its cleanliness, more perhaps than either. There were no arrangements for cleaning feet at the door, or for washing floors, windows, etc. In the summer the floor was washed, perhaps once in two or three weeks.

(B) The Instructors: The winter school usually opened about the first week of December, and continued from twelve to sixteen weeks. The summer term commenced about the first of May. Formerly this was also continued about three or four months, but within ten years the term has been lengthened usually to twenty weeks. Males have been uniformly employed in winter, and females in summer.

The instructors have usually been changed every season, but sometimes they have been continued two successive summers or winters. A strong prejudice has always existed against employing the same instructor more than once or twice in the same district. This prejudice has yielded in one instance, so far that an instructor who had taught two successive winters, twenty-five years before, was employed another season. I have not been able to ascertain the number of instructors who have been engaged in the school during the last thirty years, but I can distinctly recollect thirty-seven. Many of them, both males and females, were from sixteen to eighteen years of age, and a few, over twenty-one.

Good moral character, and a thorough knowledge of the common branches, formerly were considered as indispensable qualifications in an instructor. The instructors were chiefly selected from the most respectable families in town. But for fifteen or twenty years, these things have not been so much regarded. They have indeed been deemed desirable; but the most common method now seems to be to ascertain, as near as possible, the dividend for that season from the public treasury, and then fix upon a teacher who will take charge of the school, three or four months, for this money. He must indeed be able to obtain a license from the Board of Visitors; but this has become nearly a matter of course, provided he can spell, read, and write. In general, the candidate is some favorite or relative of the District Committee. It gives me great pleasure, however, to say that the moral character of almost every instructor, so far as I know, has been unexceptional.

Instructors have usually boarded in the families of the pupils. Their compensation has varied from seven to eleven dollars a month for males; and from sixty-two and a half cents to one dollar a week for females. Within the past ten years, however, the price of instruction has rarely been

Plan of the University of Virginia drawn by Thomas Jefferson in early 19th Century. The University was opened in 1825. This plan represents a radical modification of the semi-monastic conception of college life held by the earlier colonial colleges. The building facing in the main court is for lectures and recitations; those flanking it are professors' houses; the smaller buildings are dormitories.

less than nine dollars in the former case, and seventy-five cents in the latter. In the few instances in which instructors have furnished their own board the compensation has been about the same, it being assumed that they could work at some employment of their own enough to pay their board, especially the females.

(C) The Instruction: Two of the Board of Visitors usually visit the winter schools twice during the term. In the summer, their visits are often omitted. These visits usually occupy from one hour to an hour and a half. They are spent merely in hearing a few hurried lessons, and in making some remarks, general in their character. Formerly, it was customary to examine the pupils in some approved Catechism, but this practice has been omitted for twenty years.

The parents seldom visit the school, except by special invitation. The greater number pay very little attention to it at all. There are, however, a few who are gradually awakening to the importance of good instruction; but there are also a few who oppose everything which is suggested as, at the least, useless; and are scarcely willing their children should be governed in the school.

The school books have been about the same for thirty years. Webster's Spelling Book, the American Preceptor, and the New Testament, have been the principal books used. Before the appearance of the American Preceptor, Dwight's Geography was used as a reading book. A few of the Introduction to the American Orator were introduced about twelve years since, and, more recently, Jack Halyard.

Until within a few years, no studies have been permitted in the day school but spelling, reading, and writing. Arithmetic was taught by a few instructors, one or two evenings in a week, but, in spite of the most determined opposition, arithmetic is now permitted in the day school, and a few pupils study geography.

The Development of the Common School

The national interest in education during the late eighteenth and early nineteenth century culminated in a movement to es-

A portrait of Horace Mann—the father of the common school.

tablish free public schools—or common schools, as they were then called—for all children. The man who led this fight for common schools was Horace Mann (1796–1859). Horace Mann became the first secretary (a position we now call the state superintendent of schools) of the Massachusetts state board of education in 1837. In that position, Mann was able to do a good deal to promote the common school cause. Each year, Mann wrote an annual report of his work as the secretary of the state board of education. His twelfth annual report included the following statement about the importance of the common school:

Without undervaluing any other human agency, it may be safely affirmed that the common school, improved and energized as it can easily be, may become the most effective and benignant of all the forces of civilization. Two reasons sustain this position. In the first place, there is a universality in its operation, which can be affirmed of no other institution whatever. If

administered in the spirit of justice and concilia-
tion, all the rising generation may be brought
within the circle of its reformatory and elevating
influences. And, in the second place, the materials upon which it operates are so pliant and
ductile as to be susceptible of assuming a
greater variety of forms than any other earthly
work of the Creator. The inflexibility and rug-
gedness of the oak, when compared with the
lithe sapling or the tender germ, are but feeble
emblems to typify the docility of childhood
when contrasted with the obduracy and intrac-
tableness of man. It is these inherent advantages
of the common school, which, in our own state,
have produced results so striking, from a system
so imperfect, and an administration so feeble.
In teaching the blind and the deaf and dumb,
in kindling the latent spark of intelligence that
lurks in an idiot's mind, and in the more holy
work of reforming abandoned and outcast children, education has proved what it can do by
glorious experiments. These wonders it has done
in its infancy, and with the lights of a limited
experience; but when its faculties shall be fully
developed, when it shall be trained to wield its
mighty energies for the protection of society
against the giant vices which now invade and
torment it—against intemperance, avarice, war,
slavery, bigotry, the woes of want, and the
wickedness of waste,—then there will not be a
height to which these enemies of the race can
escape which it will not scale.

Through his work as secretary to the Massachusetts state board of education, his
speaking, and his writing—including his annual reports such as the one just quoted—
Horace Mann deserves much of the credit
for helping to establish the common school
system in the United States. So much so, in
fact, that he is now remembered as the "father of the common school."

Yet another of the many men who did
much to help promote education in the
United States during the mid-nineteenth
century was Henry Barnard (1811–1900).
Barnard served as the secretary of the state

board of education in Connecticut and then
in Rhode Island. Barnard was a prolific
writer and his writings were very influential
in helping to sell the need for better education. He edited and published the *American
Journal of Education* which represented a
gigantic compilation of information about
education. In 1867 Henry Barnard became
the first United States Commissioner of
Education.

Due to the work of Horace Mann, Henry
Barnard, and many other men of foresight
who saw the value—indeed, the essential-
ness—of a common education for all citizens
if the new democratic society was to endure, a system of common schools was
firmly established in the United States during the last half of the nineteenth century.
Massachusetts, the state that led the way in
many facets of education, passed the first
compulsory school attendance law in 1852.
Other states eventually passed similar laws
so that by 1900, thirty-two states required
compulsory school attendance.

The Development of
the Public High Schools

It was mentioned earlier in this chapter
that the Latin Grammar School was the first
form of secondary school that existed in this
country. It was also mentioned that the
Academy eventually replaced the Latin
Grammar School as the dominant secondary
school in the United States.

In 1821, a new form of secondary school,
one unique to the United States, was established at Boston, Massachusetts. This new
secondary school was called the "English
Classical School" but three years later in
1824 its name was changed to the "English
High School."

The curriculum of this new English High School emphasized mathematics, social studies, science and English. The first high schools were for boys between the ages of twelve and fifteen, but later on girls were also admitted.

About 1900, the high school replaced the academy as the dominant type of secondary school in this country, and, needless to say, remains so today. Figure 3.1 shows, in graphic form, the historical development of secondary schools in the United States.

Teacher Education

As the United States developed a need for better schools and better education, it was inevitable that the subject of better trained teachers should also receive atten-

tion. Citizens of the United States were slow to realize that good education required good teachers. Up until the mid-1800's teachers had, for the most part, been very poorly prepared for their work. A teacher's job was not considered very important and commanded very little prestige. In fact, advertisements which appeared in a Philadelphia newspaper during colonial times and which are reproduced on page 78 show that even indentured servants were sold as school teachers.

Since education had a strong religious motive in the colonies, the schools were often conducted in the church by the minister. When the job got too big for the minister to handle by himself, a layman would be hired to teach the school. Oftentimes, in addition

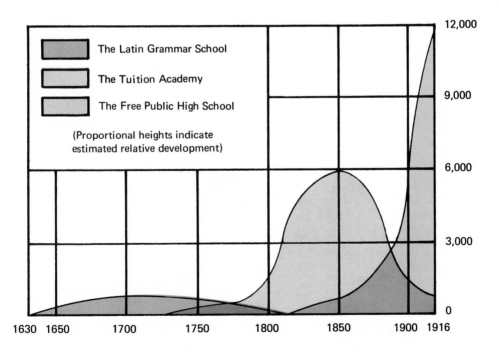

Figure 3.1. The Historical Development of Secondary Schools in the United States.

Source: E. P. Cubberley, *The History of Education.* Boston: Houghton Mifflin, 1920, p. 699. Used by permission.

To Be DISPOSED of,

A Likely Servant Mans Time for 4 Years who is very well Qualified for a Clerk or to teach a School, he Reads, Writes, underſtands Arithmetick and Accompts very well, Enquire of the Printer hereof.

Lately improted from Antigua and to be Sold by Edward Jones in Iſacc Norris's Alley. A PARCEL of likely Negro Women & Girls from thirteen to one and twenty Years of age, and have all had the Small-Pox.

To Be SOLD, TWO verly likely Negroe Boys, Enquire of Capt. Benjamin Chriſtian, at his Houſe in Arch-Street. Alſo a Quantity of very good Lime-juice to be Sold cheap.

An advertisement in a 1735 issue of the Pennsylvania Gazette showing an indentured servant for sale as a school master. The lower two ads show Negro slaves for sale.

to teaching the school, the teacher would be required "to act as court messenger, to serve summonses, to conduct certain ceremonial services at the church, to lead the Sunday choir, to ring the bell for public worship, to dig the graves, and to perform other occasional duties."

Some boys became teachers by serving as an apprentice to a schoolmaster. This method of learning the art of teaching was quite logical since the apprenticeship was a well established way of learning trades in that day. The following record of such an apprenticeship agreement was recorded in the courts of New York City in 1772:

This Indenture witnesseth that John Campbel Son of Robert Campbel of the City of New York with the Consent of his father and mother hath put himself and by these presents doth Voluntarily put and bind himself Apprentice to George Brownell of the Same City Schoolmaster to learn the Art Trade or Mystery—for and during the term of ten years . . . And the said George Brownell Doth hereby Covenent and Promise to teach and Instruct or Cause the said Apprentice to be taught and Instructed in the Art Trade or Calling of a Schoolmaster by the best way or means he or his wife may or can.

Benjamin Franklin, in proposing the establishment of his academy, claimed that:

a number of the poorer sort [of academy graduates] will be hereby qualified to act as Schoolmasters in the Country, to teach children Reading, Writing, Arithmetic, and the Grammar of their Mother Tongue, and being of good morals and known character, may be recommended from the Academy to Country Schools for that purpose; the Country suffering at present very much for want of good Schoolmasters, and obliged frequently to employ in their Schools, vicious imported Servants, or concealed Papists, who by their bad Examples and Instructions often deprave the Morals and corrupt the Principles of the children under their Care.

It is interesting to note that Franklin suggested that the "poorer" graduates of his academy would make good teachers. This wording indicates again the low esteem of teachers at that time.

The first formal teacher training institution in the United States was a private normal school established in 1823 at Concord, Vermont. This school was established by the Rev. Samuel Hall and was called the Columbian School. Some insight into the nature of Hall's school can be obtained from the following advertisement which appeared in the May 20, 1823 edition of the North Star newspaper:

COLUMBIAN SCHOOL, CONCORD, VT.

The second term will commence on the third Tuesday (17th day) of June next. The School will be under the direction, and will be principally instructed by the Rev. Mr. Hall.

Books used in the school must be uniform. Hence, arrangements are made so that they may be obtained at either of the stores in town. Branches taught, if required, are the following: Reading, Spelling, Defining, Geography (ancient and modern), History, Grammar, Rhetoric, Composition, Arithmetic, Construction of Maps, Theoretical Surveying, Astronomy, Natural Philosophy, Chemistry (without experiments), Logic, Moral Philosophy, Mental Philosophy, and General Criticism.

It is wished to have the languages excluded. This will not, however, be strictly adhered to.

TERMS: For Common School studies, $2. per term of 12 weeks. Other branches from $2.50 to $4.

It is intended to have instruction particularly thorough, and hence an additional instructor will be employed, when the School amounts to more than 20. Board obtained near the School room, on reasonable terms.

Application may be made to Mr. Lyman F. Dewey, Mr. John Barnet, or Mr. Hall.

Concord, Vt. May 14, 1823.

This ad points out that the curriculum in Hall's normal school included "Mental Philosophy," which was the forerunner of educational psychology, and "General Criticism" (presumably of the student's practice teaching).

> To be a schoolmaster is next to being a king. Do you count it a mean employment to imbue the minds of your fellow citizens in their earnest years with the best literature and with the love of Christ, and to return them to their country honest and virtuous men? In the opinion of fools, it is a humble task, but in fact it is the noblest of occupations. Even among the heathen it was always a noble thing to deserve well of the state, and no one serves it better than the molders of raw boys.
>
> Erasmus

The first high school in the United States, established in 1821 at Boston. This was the counterpart of the Latin Grammar School. The term high school was not applied to it until the school had existed for several years. It was first called an English Classical School.

The first public tax-supported teacher training school in this country was the Lexington Normal School located in Lexington, Massachusetts. This school was opened in 1839. Horace Mann, as secretary of the state board of education, was very influential in the establishment of this state normal school. The curriculum in the Lexington Normal School, and other similar state normal schools which were quickly established, was patterned after similar schools that had existed in Europe since the late 1600's. These early normal schools offered a two year program designed to prepare its students, many of whom had not attended a secondary school, to teach elementary school. The normal schools eventually developed four year programs and, during the 1920's, changed their names to "State Teachers' Colleges." Then later, during the 1950's, many of these institutions expanded their curricula to include liberal arts and changed their names to "State Colleges." During the last decade, many of these same institutions that started as two year normal schools have begun offering graduate work, including doctoral programs, and have changed their names to "State Universities."

It was not until about 1900 that states began passing teacher certification laws which regulated the amount and type of training that a person must have to become a teacher. Prior to the passage of these laws, anyone could legally teach school.

In summary, this chapter has pointed out a number of important concepts concerning the history of education in the United States. These concepts include the following:

1. The educational program in Colonial America was largely transplanted from Europe.

2. The colonists attempted to make educational provisions almost as soon as they set foot on the new world.

3. The motive for providing education in Colonial America was almost entirely religious in nature.

4. Education has played an important role in the development of the United States, from 1607 when the first colonists settled at Jamestown to the present.

5. Many of the educational problems of Colonial America have persisted to the present time.

6. The last of these concepts is that the role of education in the United States has increased in importance down through the ages; so that today education has a larger and more important role to play in our country than ever before.

As chapters 1 and 2 have pointed out, our total society and individuals within our society have come to expect a great deal from our contemporary school system. Our educational system has become extremely large and complex in its effort to meet these societal and individual expectations. In the remaining sections of this book we will explore a number of facets of this enormous, complex educational system.

QUESTIONS FOR DISCUSSION

1. Briefly trace the history of elementary education in the United States, mentioning only the highlights.

2. What were the basic differences in the early educational programs that developed in the Northern Colonies, Middle Colonies, and Southern Colonies?

3. Briefly describe the function and curriculum of the Latin Grammar School.
4. Trace the historical development of secondary education in the United States.
5. What basic changes have taken place in teacher education in the history of the United States?

SUPPLEMENTARY LEARNING ACTIVITIES

1. Develop a creative project centered around some aspect of the history of American education. (Examples: a one act drama, a history of education game, or a multi-media presentation.)
2. Write a paper on the contributions to education of Horace Mann, Henry Barnard, or Samuel Hall.
3. Seek out and interview an elderly retired teacher about the nature of his teacher training, and also about his first teaching position. You may wish to tape record the interview.
4. Attempt to locate some artifact related to the history of education (an old textbook, slate, teaching aid, or school records) and, using library references, write a paper about the artifact.
5. Invite an elderly person to your class to informally discuss "education in the good old days."

SELECTED REFERENCES

Aiken, W. M. *The Story of the Eight Year Study*. New York: Harper and Brothers, 1942.

Bailyn, Bernard. *Education in the Forming of American Society*. Chapel Hill, N.C.: University of North Carolina Press, 1960 (pp. 3–47).

Boorstin, Daniel. *The Americans: The Colonial Experience*. New York: Random House, Inc., 1958 (chapters 24–26).

Brubacher, John S. *A History of the Problems of Education*. New York: McGraw-Hill Book Co., 1947.

Butts, R. F. *Cultural History of Western Education*. New York: McGraw-Hill Book Co., 1947.

Butts, R. F., and Lawrence A. Cremin. *A History of Education in American Culture*. New York: Holt, Rinehart & Winston, 1953 (chapters 1–2).

Cole, Luella. *Education from Socrates to Montessori*. New York: Rinehart and Co., 1950.

Counts, George S. *Dare the Schools Build a New Social Order?* New York: The John Day Co., 1932.

Cremin, Lawrence A. *The Transformation of the School*. New York: Alfred A. Knopf, 1961 (chapter 2).

Curtis, S. J., and M. E. A. Boultwood. *Short History of Educational Ideas*. London: University Tutorial Press, Ltd., 1951.

Dewey, John. *Democracy and Education*. New York: The Macmillan Co., 1916 (chapters XI, XII).

———. *Experience and Education*. New York: The Macmillan Co., 1938 (chapters I–III, VII).

Drake, William E. *The American School in Transition*. Englewood Cliffs, N.J.: Prentice-Hall, 1955 (chapters III, IV).

Good, H. G. *History of Western Education*. New York: The Macmillan Co., 1947.

Gross, Carl H., and Charles C. Chandler. *The History of American Education Through Readings*. Boston: D. C. Heath & Co., 1964 (Part II).

Meyer, Adolph E. *The Development of Education in the Twentieth Century*. 2nd ed. New York: Prentice-Hall, Inc., 1949.

Parrington, Vernon Louis. *Main Currents in American Thought*. Vol. I. *The Colonial Mind*. New York: Harcourt, Brace & Co., 1927 (chapters I–IV).

Spencer, Herbert. *Essays on Education*. New York: E. P. Dutton & Co., 1910 (chapter I).

Thayer, V. T. *The Role of the School in American Society*. New York: Dodd, Mead & Co., 1960 (chapters I–V).

Thut, I. N. *The Story of Education*. New York: McGraw-Hill Book Co., 1957.

Three Hundred Years
at a Glance

U.S. Office of Education

THE BEGINNINGS

"I thank God there are no free schools, and I hope we shall not have them these hundred years; for learning has brought disobedience and heresy and sects into the world," said Governor Berkeley of Virginia. He echoed a popular attitude of his day, 1670.

Free public education was not easily won. In 1647 the Puritan fathers in Massachusetts passed two unprecedented laws: Each town of 50 or more houses was to appoint a teacher of reading and writing and to provide wages for the teacher. Each town of 100 or more houses was to provide a grammar school (roughly corresponding to our high school) to prepare students for university.

But it was more than 100 years before the colonists really began to comply with these laws. In general, the educational institutions of the New World resembled those of the Old in that they perpetuated distinctions of social and economic class. The Puritans, for example, established Latin grammar schools for the upper classes and apprentice programs for the lower. Their feeling was that the loftier forms of learning ought to be restricted to the children of the fortunate.

Today the United States provides more education in more variety for more of its citizens than any other nation in history.

Only 200 years ago, however, more than nine out of ten youngsters had no school at all. And those who did go to school usually had to content themselves with the slim educational offerings of "Colonial dame schools," run by women of modest education for modest compensation. . . .

IN THE NEW NATION

In 1767, no more than one of every fifty Johnny Aldens went on to Latin school or higher education.

During the next half-century, schools and colleges multiplied rapidly. Despite the testimony of the newspapers of those years (they opposed free public education) and the tax records (most showed little or no financial support for public schools), Americans were hungry for learning. It was quite common for townsmen to build a school with their own hands, chip in to hire a teacher, and then design a course of instruction for their children.

This is how the "common" or public elementary schools were established; this is how the district system came into being. A loose collection of educational atoms—of autonomous, small educational jurisdictions rather than an organized system in any lit-

* U.S. Office of Education, "Three Hundred Years At A Glance," *American Education*, March, 1967, pp. 7–13.

eral sense—the district system was based on the smallest possible administrative unit: one school, one teacher, and the local board to supervise. In any case, this was the beginning of the distinctively American public school arrangement, born in New England and spreading across the Nation.

The early Americans supported education not so much because they considered it a desirable end in itself, but because they believed it would further the interests of religion. The Massachusetts law of 1647 which required every town to establish a school came from a feeling of the settlers that it was "one of the chief projects of Satan to keep men from a knowledge of the Scriptures."

During the 19th century, however, secular control began to replace the basically religious orientation of school sponsorship and supervision. This was the "Age of the Academy" in American education, a period that saw the rapid establishment of private schools offering to young men commercial and preprofessional training, and to young women instruction in the fine arts and social graces. By 1850, there were 6,000 such institutions educating more than a quarter of a million students . . . some on the elementary level, most on the secondary, and a few offering college and university work.

Young ladies had no place to go after their academy training until 1838, when Oberlin in Ohio became the first college to admit female students.

Though the first public high schools were established during this period, the Nation was still a long way from having a public school system free to all. Some States provided a free elementary education to the children of paupers, but even the most enlightened required parents who were not absolutely destitute to pay "rate bills"—in effect, tuition fees—for their schoolage children.

Such States as Massachusetts, which enacted statutes requiring general tax support for free public education, rarely enforced the law. The rich continued to argue that taxation for public education was deprivation of private property without just cause.

Thus public education was still a tentative and shaky enterprise. School terms were limited to two or three months a year, teachers had no professional training (nor was there any place to get it), and the equipment in most schools consisted of little more than a wood stove, a bench for the pupil, and a rod for the teacher. . . .

GROWING PAINS

The United States had 800 newspapers in 1830 and 1,400 a decade later. Even so, almost one quarter of the adult population admitted to illiteracy in the 1840 census.

Johnny Lowell's school of the 1830's was supported with tax funds, but the concept of free public education was still new enough and radical enough to provoke continuing and bitter debate throughout the country. "I hope," wrote one Southern reader to his newspaper, "that you do not conceive it at all necessary that everybody should be able to read, write, and cipher!" On the other side of the argument, a leading Philadelphia editor of the 1830's complained that as matters then stood, "The peasant must labor in order that the rich might cultivate their mind."

The proponents of free education were struggling to overcome the impression that public schools were fit only for paupers. And there were other sources of criticism.

The wealthy attacked public schooling on the ground that it promoted socialism; clergymen attacked the idea because, they said, it advanced atheism.

During the 1830's and 1840's, Horace Mann and Henry Barnard began crusading for educational reform in New England. "The common school," Barnard told the Connecticut legislature, "should no longer be regarded as common because it is cheap or inferior, but common as the light and air because its blessings are open to all." Mann called education "the balance wheel of the social machinery. . . . It does better than to disarm the poor of their hostility toward the rich; it prevents being poor."

The influence of such pioneers was strengthened in 1857, with the establishment of the National Education Association. Apart from signaling the development of American teaching from a rather haphazard occupation to a profession, the NEA also gave school personnel the strength of unity in pressing for better educational practices.

By 1870, the views of these and other advocates of public schooling were beginning to win out. Every State had eliminated tuition fees for its public schools; the principle of compulsory tax support for public education had gained widespread acceptance. To the notion that every citizen should be required to help finance public schools was added a new proposal: every child should be required to attend elementary school. Within 50 years, Americans would accept this revolutionary proposal and would extend public support to high schools. Gradually we were developing a form of public education that offered every youngster—whatever the circumstances of his birth—a chance for an academic education, rather than reserving it for the children of the wealthy.

Changes in our political and social attitudes toward education, as well as the strength of our growing economy, paved the way for educational expansion and improvement. The Morrill Land Grant Act of 1862 —signed by President Lincoln two years after his predecessor vetoed it as unconstitutional—donated six million acres of Federal land to the States to endow colleges of agricultural and mechanical arts.

This period also brought to the fore educational philosophers such as John Dewey, Francis Parker, William Tawes, and Thomas Elliot. Many of the theories they advanced still influence our classrooms. . . .

SCHOOL FOR ALL

In the little red brick buildings of the cities, in the white frame schoolhouses of the countryside, American education was blossoming. The first Office of Education survey in 1870 showed that only 57 percent of school-age children were attending public school; by 1937, more than 83 percent were enrolled.

Other comparisons of those years suggest the rate at which American education was changing from a privilege for the few to a program for the masses. In 1870, the average youngster attended school only 78 days a year; by 1937, he went to school nearly 150 days a year. In 1870, the annual school expenditure per child was $15.55; by 1937, it was more than six times as much. In 1870, only 9,000 people received college or university degrees; in 1937, more than 180,000 degrees were awarded. In 1870, only two percent of our youth earned high school diplomas; by 1937, 45 percent did.

High schools, confined largely to the cities and a few wealthy rural areas in the latter part of the 19th century, had become a recognized part of American life throughout the Nation by 1937. The university, which existed in name only in 1880, was now a reality: 24,000 people received advanced professional degrees in 1937. Extension courses were beginning to carry the opportunity for college study out into communities where there were no higher educational institutions. Junior colleges, born at the turn of the century, were multiplying rapidly: from 46 in 1917 to 453 in 1937. Their enrollments leaped from 4,500 to 122,000.

Only two States had compulsory attendance laws in 1867, when the U.S. Office of Education was established; by 1918, all the States did. Between 1910 and 1940, the number of high school students rose from one million to seven million, even though the number of high school-age youngsters increased only 35 percent in that period. Kindergartens, introduced in St. Louis just before the Civil War, were by now an acknowledged rung on the educational ladder.

School programs were changing, too. The old exclusiveness and narrowly classical emphasis of the upper schools were giving way to a new curriculum designed to prepare students for the world of work and the business of living. The American comprehensive high school, encompassing both liberal and vocational, college-preparatory and terminal programs, was evolving.

The founding of the American Federation of Teachers in 1916 reflected this change in philosophy. An affiliate of the American Federation of Labor, the AFT was a new form of teachers' organization— a merging of professional orientation toward educational needs with the militance characteristic of labor unions.

The Federal Government, which had not produced a major piece of educational legislation since the Morrill Land Grant Act of the Civil War period, passed the Smith-Hughes Act in 1917. This act gave the States funds to establish vocational education programs for high school youngsters, and to train teachers and buy equipment for the broader new curriculum.

The United States was undergoing major economic and social changes. After having sustained its worst war to date, the Nation was now undergoing a catastrophic depression. "The Crash" and the social havoc that followed seemed to generate a national social conscience. Minority groups—Negroes, Mexican-Americans, Indians, Orientals— who had in the past been largely ignored by public educational institutions, were brought under the blanket of universal public education. Hundreds of special schools were established to care for children who were blind, deaf, or mentally defective. Prisons began to offer educational programs, child labor laws were enacted, and the Federal Government began to send surplus food for school lunches into the hardest-hit States.

IN OUR TIME

Just as the United States began to struggle out of the worst depression in its history, the Nation entered its second major international conflict. The astonishingly high draft rejection rate for illiteracy proved— to our dismay and surprise—that a high school diploma was no guarantee of intellectual attainment or academic achievement: young men from some regions of the country scored consistently higher on military entrance examinations than did draftees from other regions.

Further, increasing mobility of Americans after World War II made the disparities in educational quality a national problem. The dropout from Peoria might become the military reject in New York City, the illiterate from Boston a welfare burden in Los Angeles. Increasingly sophisticated thinking about such educational problems as these led most States to require more years of education, to establish broader curricula, and to set up tougher standards for teacher certification.

Yet, it was difficult to maintain high standards in the face of the postwar "baby boom." At the very time that educators were seeking to emphasize quality of schooling, they were forced to provide schooling in more quantity than ever before. Moreover, colleges and universities found the G.I. Bill a mixed blessing: it showered them with billions of dollars in unexpected tuition fees at the same time that the influx of veterans required expansions of staff and facilities.

This tension between quality and quantity significantly altered American education because—along with two other developments—it sharply increased the Federal Government's influence in education. The other two developments were the national alarm caused by the Russians' orbiting of Sputnik and the sudden transformation of American Negroes from docility into a vocal, militant group demanding the justice promised them for 100 years.

Sputnik frightened Americans; they were shaken by the prospect that the Soviet Union had bested the United States in space exploration. The resulting hue and cry produced the National Defense Education Act of 1958, which was designed initially to improve the teaching of science and mathematics in our schools and colleges, as well as to increase the number of graduates in the technological disciplines.

Selma—at this point more a symbol of the civil rights movement than the name of a single town—directed the attention of the Nation to the inferior status of American Negroes, and to the inferior education that helped keep them at the bottom of the national ladder. For the first time, Americans were forced to examine the proposition that it would take more than the stroke of Abraham Lincoln's pen to strike from American Negroes the shackles that bound them to poverty of purse and spirit.

Since 1963, Congress has enacted 24 major pieces of legislation for education—more than in all the preceding 97 years put together. These laws, ranging in scope from the Elementary and Secondary Education Act of 1965 to the Higher Education Act of the same year, touch every aspect of education from preschool to postgraduate. They span the sociological distance between the bread-and-butter welfare projects of the 1930's and Project Head Start of the 1960's. They help meet the pressing educational needs of the times—construction costs, student aid, library resources, vocational training, research and demonstration.

But, in this seventh decade of the 20th century, the American school is still trying to bridge the gulf between the intellectual elite and the functional illiterate. Education, which brought us into the atomic age, has yet to rescue some of our citizens from a near-medieval helplessness in the face of a world which they neither made nor understand. For too many of our children, Batman—the pop-art farce of the decade— remains the most accessible cultural experience.

Still, we've made much progress: the average American today has completed 12 years of school; one generation ago, the average was eight years. Enrollments beyond high school have tripled in the years since World War II, due in large part to the expansion of programs in junior colleges, state universities, and technical institutes and to the increase in scholarship aid available to students. In 1946 about one of five Americans aged 18 to 21 continued his education after high school; today almost one of every two (45.6 percent) does. Additionally, millions of adults attend classes of one sort or another, so the expression "cradle to the grave" more accurately describes an educational phenomenon than an economic concept. Taking account of weaknesses along with strengths, it is hard to beat the best American schools today. . . .

The Organization
and Administration
of Public Education
in the United States

This section of the book is devoted to the ways that schools in the United States are organized, controlled, and financed. Each of these functions of the educational enterprise has evolved as the nation has developed. Patterns of organization, control, and finance reflect rather directly the needs and expectations of society.

The patterns of organization for public education in the early days of the nation were not complicated. Our society was basically an agrarian one with a widely scattered population. Men were concerned with conquering the frontier. One room schools for grades one through eight were built in the rural areas, while the multi-graded common school developed in towns and cities. Private universities were also established in the very early days. As the frontier was developed, and as the nation began to change to an industrial and urban way of life, the needs of the nation changed and so did its patterns for the organization of education. Today we have public education from the nursery school level through the university along with many other forms of adult education. Each of these levels has purposes and programs which have their roots in the needs of society and the expectations of people.

The control of education in the United States is both unique and complicated. It is unique because of its decentralization. Local people have more to say about education in the United States than in most other nations of the world. It is complicated because it involves at least three and sometimes four levels of government. The legal responsibility for education in the United States rests with state government; however, the actual operation of schools is delegated to local government. At the same time the federal government is interested in the enterprise. Again, as our society has changed from agrarian to industrial and as our population has become increasingly mobile, the patterns of control of education have changed. The trend has been toward greater direct control of education at the state level, and a greater interest shown in education, particularly in the area of civil rights and other national problems (such as poverty) by the

federal government. New patterns of control are emerging.

The financing of education has changed from an almost complete local effort to where, in most states, the local contribution is currently about fifty percent. The state and federal government make up the remainder of the costs. The property tax provides most of the revenue at the local level, sales and income taxes at the state level, and the income tax at the federal level. State contributions to school financing have tended to equalize the amount of money spent per pupil in a state. Federal monies have been directed toward specific projects at specific times in our history.

As society changes, the methods of organizing, controlling, and financing education are also likely to change. Frequently the institutions of society lag in making the necessary accommodations to society. It should be remembered that institutions are created to serve society, and therefore should be changed by society when necessary.

CHAPTER 4

Organization for Learning

As was indicated in Section I, formal programs of education evolve from the needs and expectations of societies and individuals. As our colonial settlements grew and developed, the colonists recognized that some of their desires for the education of their children could be better met by organizing children in groups and assigning specific adults from the communities to serve as teachers. Thus began the formal organizational patterns for education in the United States. They began with a basic idea of efficiency; it was felt that one adult could teach a group of children, and in so doing permit other adults to pursue other important duties. As the population began to grow and people began to cluster in communities, other principles of organization emerged—for example, the grouping of children by age so that one teacher could concentrate his efforts in teaching specific content in the most appropriate way to a particular age group. Later the principalship and superintendency emerged as specialties needed to effectively conduct the educational program in an organized fashion. While there is still disagreement regarding the *best* or-

ganization for learning, particularly for the individual child, it is nevertheless quite clear that American education was organized on at least two basic principles: (1) division of labor; that is, let some adults teach while others engage in other productive work, and (2) classification of students by age or common developmental levels. Organization for learning in the United States, while it has become increasingly refined, still reflects these two basic principles.

Purposes and Programs

Today four general divisions of vertical progression in educational organization are clearly recognized: pre-elementary, elementary, secondary, and higher education. Within these levels, many subdivisions exist. Figure 4.1 illustrates the overall status of educational organization as it exists today.

At each of the levels certain goals and purposes are expected to be accomplished. A sequential program is envisioned based primarily on developing maturity and content complexity. One pertinent general observation that can be made about content is

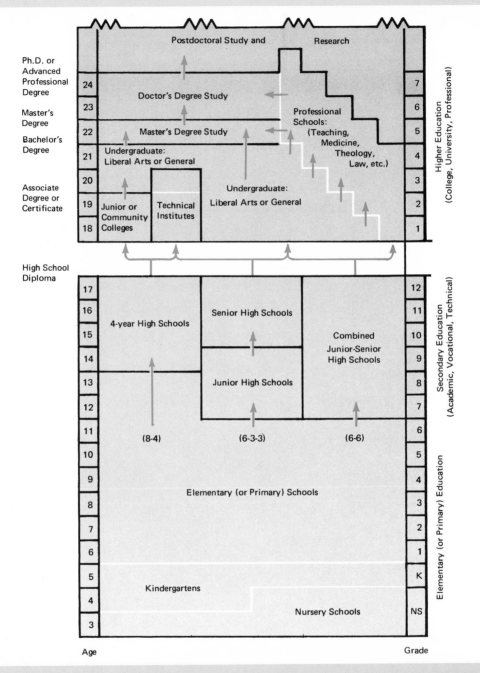

Figure 4.1. The Structure of Education in the United States.

Source: Kenneth A. Simon, and W. Vance Grant, *Digest of Educational Statistics 1966.* Washington, D.C.: U.S. Government Printing Office, 1966, p. xii.

that as the vertical progression proceeds from pre-elementary to higher education the overall educational programs contain less general education and become increasingly specialized. Figure 4.2 illustrates this idea. General education is that portion which concerns itself with the development of

> No other people ever demanded so much of education as have the Americans. None other was ever served so well by its schools and educators.
>
> Henry Steele Commager

concerns itself with the development of basic skills and common understandings. These include:

1. Communication arts: speech, language usage, reading, writing, listening, discussing, and spelling.
2. Computational skills and quantitative thinking: arithmetic, reasoning, and problem solving.
3. Social and group living: history, geography, government, community living, human relations, citizenship, value building, character building and sensitivity to problems of group living.
4. Science: understanding of scientific phenomena and natural law, the use of methods of science in problem solving, understanding the world.
5. Aesthetic development: music, art and handicrafts.
6. Health: knowledge of the body, nutrition and health habits.
7. Recreation: play, physical education and handicrafts.[1]

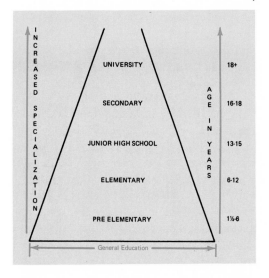

Figure 4.2. The Decrease in Time Allotted to General Education as Related to Vertical Progression.

Specialized education represents that part of the program, generally elective, wherein an individual student pursues a specialty. For example, Johnny Jones and his parents may decide at the end of the eighth grade that the only general education that Johnny will take in the future is that which is required by law, and that his program in secondary education will be vocational with his eventual goal that of becoming an automotive mechanic. At the same time, Ray Noble and his parents may decide that Ray will continue to higher education and therefore take a specific college preparatory curriculum in high school. Ray may eventually decide to become a lawyer and then will specialize further at the university level. Ann Smith may decide to pur-

1. Galen J. Saylor and William M. Alexander, *Curriculum Planning*. New York: Rinehart and Co., 1954, p. 356. Used by permission.

sue the college preparatory curriculum in secondary school and if she so desires and is financially able, could pursue liberal arts in higher education, and in so doing specialize almost completely in general education. It is significant to note that the choice of specialization in the United States is that of the individual student and his parents, and not that of the government or society. To be sure, various state laws do prescribe general education requirements and societal and economic conditions often limit the available occupational choices, but basically the choice is the individual's, limited only by his particular talents, ambitions, and financial circumstances. In general today, elementary and secondary education is assured for all regardless of their individual financial resources. Higher education in the form of tax-supported community colleges has increased its availability to all. The trend in the United States today is toward making more and more education available for academically able students at lowered costs to the individual.

The remainder of this chapter presents brief descriptions of the organization and purposes of each of the major levels of education. Community colleges and adult education programs are discussed separately because of their increasing popularity in the contemporary American scene.

Pre-elementary

Basically, pre-elementary education consists of two divisions, nursery school and kindergarten. Nursery schools generally include children from the ages of 18 months to four years, whereas kindergartens generally accept children between the ages of 4 years to six years.

The first nursery school in the United States was opened in 1826, in the model community established by Robert Owen in New Harmony, Indiana; however it was not until 1919 that the first public nursery school was established. The concept of nursery school education has gained only slow acceptance. Public nursery schools seemed to have gained their greatest impetus in the depression era. Recently, through the war on poverty, nursery school education is again being stimulated. Operation Headstart, operating under the Office of Economic Opportunity, is illustrative of this trend. The number of day care centers is also increasing, resulting in part from the increased numbers of working mothers. While many day care centers admittedly do not represent the epitome of nursery schools, they do in fact represent a form of early childhood education which is carried on outside of the home and family. A recent article by Harold Shane succinctly points out the major reasons for increased interest in early childhood education.[2]

A major contemporary development in education—one which seems certain to influence public schools in the 1970's—is the widespread reawakening of interest in the very young child. It is important at this juncture for educational leadership to be aware of some of the factors and events which have led to this new concern for early childhood. In particular, thought needs to be given to the practices and policies which will be introduced, studied, and evaluated as a downward extension of the public schools occurs in the coming decade.

2. Harold G. Shane, "The Renaissance of Early Childhood Education," *Phi Delta Kappan* 50(1969): 369, 412–413. Used by permission.

A Long History

For centuries great educators such as Comenius, Pestalozzi, Froebel, Basedow, and Montessori intuitively sensed the importance of children's experiences before the age of six. Also, during the past 40 years, nursery and pre-school specialists have made a strong case for the guidance of boys' and girls' early learning. Rose Alschuler, James Hymes, and Laura Zirbes are representative of the many contemporary figures who, beginning in the 1920's, made important contributions to pre-school practice.

Sometimes this was accomplished through research, but more often through reasoned conjectures based upon empirical study and personal insight.

In years past, children were, of course, also made the object of quite careful medical and psychological research. For example, the writings of Arnold Gesell and Frances Ilg provided useful longitudinal child-growth data. Willard Olson and Robert Havighurst, respectively, made "orga-

---

... If our schools are to serve as positive agencies for the maintenance of a "free" society, they must be concerned today with "society" as well as with the "child," with "subject matter" as well as with "method" with "product" as well as with human "freedom," and with social and moral "ends" as well as with classroom "procedures" and educational "means" ...

John L. Childs

---

nismic age" and "developmental tasks" standard pedagogical phrases, while Jean Piaget for a quarter century has been respected for his developmental-cognitive studies.

But despite enthusiastic supporters and a substantial literature before 1960, no priority and frequently little heed was given by the public schools or the general community to the development of programs for children in the four-year span beginning at two and extending through age five. True, the Lanham Act expediently provided money for the care of children of working mothers during World War II, and some districts began to offer kindergarten programs for two or three hours a day. But for the most part, the importance of early childhood was honored more by words than by actions in the schools. Even today in many states considerable parental pressures (or tuition) is required before kindergarten programs are launched for four-year-olds. In wide areas there are no kindergartens at all.

Let us now look at the confluence of events and circumstances that have led to the present renaissance of interest, which holds promise for the long delayed provision for education of two-to-five-year-olds.

Factors in Renaissance

The renaissance of interest in the very young has been stimulated by many things. An inventory of some of these elements and events follows.

Political decisions. To be both blunt and succinct, it seems rather obvious that policies and "politics" at the federal level have had a distinct bearing on the funding of educational programs begun prior to the kindergarten level. By the earlier Sixties it was becoming clear that there was much social dynamite in the ghettos of the city and in Appalachia-type rural slums. One of a number of ways of postponing or precluding explosions was providing educational programs for the children of the poor.

Current social commentaries. Recent attention-capturing books that focus on the complex challenges and appalling conditions of ghetto education have helped to convince many citizens of the importance of an early, problem-preventive approach to educating our children of poverty. Although they vary appreciably in quality and insight, this genre of book includes such titles as *Education and Ecstacy, Our Children Are Dying, Death at an Early Age, How Children Fail,* and *The Way It 'Spozed To Be.*

The great national concern which has developed for the problems of rural areas and the inner city has quickened interest in the young child and lent support to providing for education of the culturally different.[3] Educators have begun to point out that it is short-sighted and wasteful to have so-called compensatory education in elementary and secondary schools to repair damage done to boys and girls before they enter kindergarten or the primary school.

Head Start. Operation Head Start, as part of the war on poverty, is both a result of the new recognition for the importance of children's early experiences and a cause of the current awareness of these early years.[4]

Environmental mediation. One important influence in developing programs for very young children is the concept of environmental mediation—the idea that during the child's early life wholesome forms of intervention in his milieu can help him become

more effective in his transactions and interactions with others. While a sentimental interest in improving the environment of children has existed for centuries, the concept of a deliberate, planned intervention is, for practical purposes, a phenomenon of the Sixties.

Creating intelligence. Closely related to the point above is the accumulating evidence suggesting that the young child's intelligence is modifiable, that we can in effect "create" what we measure as an I.Q. The old "ages and stages" concept simply does not correspond with new information about childhood, the ways in which children learn, and the ways in which they develop. Benjamin Bloom, Ira Gordon,[5] and J. McVicker Hunt[6] are among writers who stress the significance of a facilitating environment for the optimal development of children and emphasize the importance of children's early years. Research done by David Krech[7] with infrahuman subjects strongly suggests that glia (memory) cells,

3. The January, 1969, *Kappan* contains a number of provocative and relevant articles on the inner city and segregation. Also cf. Edward T. Hall's article [*Phi Delta Kappan* 50(1969):] 379–80.

4. For a succinct assessment see Keith Osborn, "Project Head Start," *Educational Leadership,* November, 1965.

5. Cf. Ira Gordon's article [*Phi Delta Kappan* 50 (1969):] 375–78.

6. The following references are helpful: Benjamin S. Bloom, *Stability and Change in Human Characteristics.* New York: John Wiley & Sons, Inc., 1964; Ira J. Gordon, "New Conceptions of Children's Learning and Development," in *Learning and Mental Health in the School.* Washington, D.C.: Association for Supervision and Curriculum, 1966, pp. 49–73; and J. McVicker Hunt, *Intelligence and Experience.* New York: The Ronald Press, 1961.

7. David Krech, "The Chemistry of Learning," *Saturday Review,* January 20, 1968, p. 48–50. Also cf. Krech's article [*Phi Delta Kappan* 50(1969):] 370–74.

brain size, and the blood supplied to the cerebral hemispheres actually can be increased by intervening in the milieu to create stimulating surroundings. His article is especially provocative in that it implies that we may have been losing out on the best years of the learner's life by postponing his in-school education—until the ripe old age of six.

Psychoneurobiochemeducation. The rapidly developing field which Krech has called "psychoneurobiochemeducation" has implications for early contacts with children. Specialists in certain disciplines such as biochemistry have conducted experiments with both subhuman and human subjects that are beginning to demonstrate the use of drugs (such as pipradol, or magnesium pemoline) in influencing mind, mood, and memory. While pharmacies and surgical suites operated by boards of education seem unlikely to dominate our schools, there is reason to believe that very early school contacts for children having personality and learning problems may permit chemical therapy to reclaim these boys and girls who would otherwise become liabilities to society.

Experiments in early learning. Experiments in early learning, although not unique to the present decade, have fueled discussions and provided relevant—and sometimes disputed—data to the process of creating education policies which will govern school practices in the 1970's.[8] O. K. Moore's[9] inquiries into responsive environments, Dolores Durkin's[10] exploration of pre-school reading instruction, and Bereiter and Engelmann's[11] controversial work on early academic learning through predominantly oral methods at the University of Illinois as they attempted early cognitive training are illustrative of contemporary projects.

Improved understanding of subcultures and group membership. Cultural anthropologists such as Edward T. Hall[12] have begun to point out the implications of membership in a given U.S. subculture. Accumulating evidence suggests that it is during the first four or five years of life that many personal behaviors—in language, attitude, values, even ways of learning—begin to take on the form they will retain for a lifetime. We now spend billions for remedial work, for penal and mental institutions, and for belated compensatory or supportive education necessitated, in a number of instances, because schools have not had early contacts with the children who will become their clientele.

The early influences of social class. Research by Jerome Kagan[13] has begun to suggest that social class membership—closely related to subculture group membership—begins permanently to influence personality, for better or worse, by the age of five or before.

8. Cf. Bernard Spodek's article [*Phi Delta Kappan* 50(1969):] 394–96.

9. O. K. Moore, "Autolectic Responsive Environments for Learning," in *The Revolution in the Schools*, edited by Ronald Gross and Judith Murphy, pp. 184–219. New York: Harcourt, Brace and World, 1964.

10. Dolores Durkin, *Children Who Read Early*. New York: Teachers College Press, Teachers College, Columbia University, 1966.

11. Carl Bereiter and Siegfried Englemann, *Teaching Disadvantaged Children in the Preschool*. Englewood Cliffs, N.J.: Prentice-Hall, Inc., 1966.

12. Cf. Edward T. Hall, *The Silent Language* (1959) and *The Hidden Dimension* (1966), both published by Doubleday & Co., Inc., New York.

13. Jerome Kagan, "The Many Faces of Response," *Psychology Today*, January, 1968, pp. 60–65.

Ethnicity as a mediating factor. Gerald Lesser[14] and his associates convincingly state, as a result of several replicated studies, that ethnicity (i.e., ethnic, subculture group membership) apparently causes children to learn in different ways.

Language development. For years now, Basil Bernstein's[15] work, which demonstrates that social class and one's linguistic characteristics are intimately related, has been widely accepted. The research cited, as well as analogous studies, which space precludes listing, are beginning to form a mosaic of data suggesting that these years of early childhood are more critical than any other stage of human development. In other words, if society, through its educational planning, does not vigorously begin to foster facilitating environments for very young children, it may be too late or immensely expensive to remove the psychological scar tissue that has long since formed on the personalities of certain young children before they enter school at the age of six.

Educational technology. A number of other elements have made educators more acutely interested in the initial years of childhood.[16] Improved technology has produced "talking" typewriters, "talking" books, and other teaching aids that can be used by boys and girls of three and four if they are in a school setting where they are available. Also, the progress made in developing Stage III computers promises to provide equipment that can be used in four- and five-year-old kindergartens.

Mass media: the phantom curriculum. The "phantom curriculum" to which mass media daily expose the child also has a bearing on early childhood education. By the time the child is enrolled in kindergarten or the primary school, he has an ill-assorted but important array of information.[17] There are those who not only contend that the massive sensory input of mass media is making children educable sooner, they also contend that the schools have a responsibility to help children at an early age acquire more coherent input. The problems here have been widely recognized, although much remains to be done in coping with them.

The rediscovery of Montessori, Piaget, and Vygotsky. While it is difficult to determine whether it is a cause or a result of the renaissance in early childhood education, the rediscovery of the work of Montessori, Piaget, and Vygotsky certainly has helped to enliven the instructional scene. These distinguished persons focused their work on aspects of methods, cognition, human development, and language growth at age five or below.

A decline in the elementary school population. Finally, a small group of prescient educational leaders, persons who are of a pragmatic turn of mind, are casting a speculative eye on the two- to five-year-old group because of the widespread use of the "pill." In view of the drop in the U.S. birth rate in the last few years, there will be an inevitable decline in the gross elementary school population by 1975. One way of utilizing

14. Cf. the article by Fort, Watts, and Lesser [*Phi Delta Kappan* 50(1969):386–388]. Also cf. Susan S. Stodolsky and Gerald Lesser, "Learning Patterns in the Disadvantaged," *Harvard Educational Review,* Fall, 1967, pp. 546–93.

15. Basil Bernstein, "Language and Social Class," *British Journal of Sociology,* November, 1960, pp. 271–76.

16. Cf. article by Meierhenry and Stepp [*Phi Delta Kappan* 50(1969):409–411].

17. John McCulkin, "A Schoolman's Guide to Marshall McLuhan," *Saturday Review,* March 18, 1967.

the staff and the space that are likely to become available will be to extend the school's responsibility downward. . . .

Nursery schools can be categorized by their form of financial support: public or governmental, private, and parochial. Nursery schools that serve as a downward extension of the local public elementary schools and are supported by local district tax monies are very rare. However, the impetus being provided by the federal government to develop pre-school programs for children of poverty, accompanied by research findings which indicate the significance of early childhood experiences to later intellectual development, may very well cause more local school systems to extend their public school education to include the nursery school group. While Headstart did not have the dramatic effect that was anticipated, it did have an effect, and perhaps the experience served to point out that greater effectiveness could have been achieved with children younger than four years of age. While public schools hesitate for a variety of reasons—primarily financial, coupled with public reluctance—to embrace the nursery school children into their system, private and parochial nursery schools will continue to function, fulfilling the needs of those who want this service and can afford to pay for it or who happen to be fortunate enough to have philanthropic facilities available.

18. Richard M. Brandt, "Readiness for Kindergarten," *Kindergarten Education*. Washington, D.C.: Department of Elementary-Kindergarten-Nursery Education, National Education Association, 1968, pp. 14–21.

Kindergartens have received greater public acceptance than nursery schools. The first permanent public school kindergarten in the United States was established as a part of the St. Louis, Missouri public school system in 1873. Since then public school kindergartens have grown slowly but steadily. In 1940 approximately 595,000 pupils were enrolled in kindergarten; by 1967 kindergarten enrollment had climbed to 2,414,-000. During the same period first grade enrollment rose from approximately three to four million. The U.S. Bureau of Census reports that in 1950, 51.7 per cent of the five year olds were enrolled in school; by 1966 this percentage had increased to 72.8 per cent.

Kindergartens and nursery schools have similar goals. Major efforts are made to (1) develop body skills, (2) develop skills in interpersonal relationships, (3) enhance the development of a positive self concept, (4) develop both oral and written language skills, and (5) enhance intellectual concept development.[18] In addition to these developmental tasks, which incidentally are applicable at all levels of education, the pre-

Developing body skills is an important goal in early childhood education.

elementary curriculum content includes mathematics, science, social science, humanities, health, and physical education. The uniqueness of pre-elementary education resides in the selection of appropriate content and materials, and the use of appropriate methodology for very young children. Pre-elementary programs are extremely flexible; the key principle is to learn by doing; that is, to gain enriching experiences without the encumbrance of accomplishing specific content, and in so "doing" learn to work and play effectively with others.

Elementary children pursue reading skills.

Elementary

The elementary schools have been the backbone of American education. Historically they are referred to as common schools, and traditionally under the graded organization they contained grades one through eight. As was indicated in chapter 3, elementary schools were organized in the colonies, and the "Old Deluder Act" passed in Massachusetts required towns to establish and maintain schools. While Massachusetts had the first compulsory school attendance law in 1852, Pennsylvania, in 1834, became the first state to provide a program of free public schools. The phrase "public schools" as used in the early days of the nation is practically synonymous with the term elementary schools today. Horace Mann, known as the "father of the common schools" was most influential in spreading the concept of the importance of a common school education for all citizens of a democracy. An elementary school education was at one time considered to be the terminus in formal education in America, now it is more truly only the end of one of our most basic steps.

The traditional elementary school organization contained grades one through eight. Frequently these grades were envisioned within the structure as consisting of three levels: (1) *primary,* containing grades one through three, (2) *intermediate,* containing grades four through six, and (3) *upper,* containing grades seven and eight. After the completion of the traditional eight grades in the elementary school the student entered a four year high school. This traditional plan (8-4) dominated the organizational scene up and through the early 20th century. In fact, in 1920, 83 per cent of the public secondary school enrollment was in four year high schools.

Modifications have been made in this plan. In 1910, the first junior high schools were established. They included the upper grades of the elementary schools, and in some instances, if legal district organization permitted, they included the first year of the four year high school. This was the beginning of the 6-3-3 plan. By 1960, only 18 per cent of the total secondary school enrollment was in four year high schools, leaving 82 per cent to be located in other reorganized systems. Twenty-five per cent of the enrollment was in separate junior high schools. Under the 6-3-3 plan elementary education is thought of as including only the first six grades.

Another modification of a more recent vintage is the grouping of grades five through eight and referring to that grouping as a middle school. With this arrangement the ninth grade is considered as a part of a four year senior high school. A school system using the middle school organization is referred to as having the 4-4-4 plan. In addition to the 8-4, 6-3-3, 4-4-4, other plans are also used including 6-6, 7-2-3, and 8-2-2. There are a number of reasons for these various plans, some of the reasons directly related to the goals of instruction, others being only tangential. Let us examine briefly the goals of elementary education as they relate to the organizational patterns.

The goals of the elementary schools, particularly through grades six, are the goals of general education stated earlier in this chapter. Many of these goals are subject matter content-oriented and can be sequentially developed. In arithmetic for example, the child counts before he adds, and adds before he multiplies. This reasoning is sound and the graded organization is in part based on this rationale. However, other goals of general education such as those dealing with interpersonal relationships, group living, and socialization are more closely related to the personal-social needs of learners. It is from these personal-social needs of learners, resulting from their developing maturity, that different organizational patterns have emerged. It reflects an effort again to group students, and again by age, but based on developmental personal-social needs of the members of an age group other than the purely academic content-oriented function of the school.

The junior high school student, for example, is a young adolescent. Thirteen-year-old seventh or eighth graders in terms of personal and social development were rec-

Many modern elementary schools have gymnasiums.

ognized as having significantly different needs than those of the pre-adolescent ten- or eleven-year-olds. This recognition suggested a separate organization for these age youngsters with somewhat different goals and procedures. A unique feature of most junior high schools recognizing these differences is that of exploratory education. The student is introduced to a variety of specialized educational areas. He may be given the opportunity to explore course work in business, agriculture, home economics, and various trades, plus being given counseling regarding his interests and abilities for further academic pursuits. The junior high school is looked upon organizationally as including the group of youngsters between childhood or pre-adolescence and the recognized adolescent of the senior high school. Tangentially, many junior high schools came into existence to facilitate school building housing problems. In very practical terms, many junior high schools are converted senior high school buildings. As such, new high schools could be constructed, the old high school put to good use, and pupil housing pressures reduced at the elementary school level. Unfortunately, sometimes this type of growth has admittedly produced a distinct junior high building and a distinct organizational structure, but *not* a distinct or unique educational program for young adolescents.

The middle school represents a recent effort to bridge the gap between childhood and adolescence. The junior high school, while designed for this purpose, has tended to become high school oriented. Perhaps the knowledge explosion and the concomitant increased knowledge expectations for younger children, along with increasing social maturity at a lower chronological age, have in part precipitated this development.

Nevertheless, many educators feel that today a fifth or sixth through eighth grade grouping can more suitably meet the needs of the ten- to fourteen-year-old population than can either the elementary or junior high school grouping. A middle school teacher in Philadelphia is supportive of this viewpoint.[19]

The term "middle school" has suddenly become fashionable in educational jargon. It has been used rather freely to describe various grade combinations—5 through 8, 6 through 9, 6 through 8, 4 through 7, and even, usurping the range sacred to junior high school, 7 through 9. Many of us, however, feel that the middle school is not dependent upon grade combinations but is really a completely new approach to the education of young people between the primary and the high school years. Grade combinations are much less important than the focus and spirit of the whole operation.

My not very original theory is that the early years of a youngster's schooling should be devoted to making the tools of living and learning familiar to him. He needs to learn the basics—reading, writing, and arithmetic—and to have the experiences that lead to social learning. In the late school years, he needs to gain the specialized and basic knowledges that will be vital to his career and to his whole adult life. The experiences of the years between—the middle school years—must be uniquely and individually tailored to each individual so that the tools may become the skills he needs in order to realize his full potential, and the fifth year

19. Mildred T. Wilson, "What About the Middle School?" *Today's Education* 58(1969):52–54. Used with permission.

is none too early for these tailored experiences to begin.

We at Conwell Middle Magnet School have had the opportunity of developing a school that offers such experiences. The school, which draws from all sections of Philadelphia, is completely ungraded. When students apply for admission we screen them carefully in order to determine their present skills and attitudes. We use this information to guide us in planning each student's program so that it will provide the sort of initial support important to his development.

We believe that young people during these in-between years are very different from those in any other period and also that they differ from each other to a greater degree than do members of any other group. At this stage, erratic physical and emotional growth patterns are usual and have definite effects on learning. During these years, when attitudes are formed, uncertainty as to abilities and values often keeps a young person off-balance, ill-equipped to profit from the traditional structured group learning process. The school's first responsibility seems to be to create a climate where it is possible and satisfying for each student to develop his own potential.

At Conwell, we have gone about this in many ways. Naturally, staff is of primary importance; not only must teachers measure up scholastically; they must also be able to see each student as an individual and really want to help him to make the most of himself.

The members of the staff must learn to work together in various team combinations. They must be willing to learn to give up the center of the stage and use their talents as directors and managers of learning experiences—to set the stage, even present the script, and then get out of the way and let the student learn.

The fundamental administrative unit at Conwell is the cross-discipline team made up of five teachers and about 180 students. These five teachers and two others from the labs each serve as adviser for a group of about 25 students, and the team is collectively responsible for the appropriateness of every student's program. We have four such teams, with an overlap of year levels in each one.

Every student on the roster is assigned a large block of "team time." The roster indicates lab assignments as well. (The term *lab* is used to designate any time assigned outside the team program, and covers physical education, art, science lab, business lab, journalism, TV production, foreign languages, various music offerings, the learning laboratory, and any other individually prescribed activity.)

The teachers in the teams are specialists in the basics—social studies, mathematics, science, and the communicating skills—and have complete autonomy within the team assignments over how each student's time is used. The scheduled daily team meetings make immediate adjustments possible as required.

Since it is more important for students to learn a skill thoroughly than to meet with a teacher a given number of times a week, the whole range of organizing for learning is at the disposal of the team teachers. This can result in teachers' having a realistic amount of time for planning and working.

As a school, we have focused our attention on six major areas for development—personal responsibility, learning strategy, critical thinking, creative thinking, effective social behavior, and effective communication. Our goal is to provide students with an environment where it is almost natural for every youngster to develop to the highest degree of which he is capable.

The general atmosphere of the school is friendly and busy. Visitors often remark that the many students moving about all seem to be going somewhere to do something. No demonstration classes are conducted, but visitors are free, after an orientation tour (often student-led), to spend time anywhere that particularly interests them. In the team rooms, they see various combinations of youngsters operating with or without teacher guidance and usually a sizable number working with some of the machinery designed to spread the influence of a good teacher and bring out independence in the student.

In the classrooms, teachers are available for consultation, but they hold back to give the student a chance to discover for himself or to learn from his errors if he's working on a specific skill. Teachers watch how a particular youngster goes about learning and plan his future course according to his specific needs and not on the basis of "what all twelve-year-olds require." Conwell students display a professionalism that is certainly not to be expected in the light of their ages, the broad range of their measured potential, their achievement records, their economic and social backgrounds, and their general behavior history.

Our experience indicates that middle school doesn't depend on grade range or team teaching or any specific administrative method. We have found that getting the youngster at fifth year instead of at the seventh is good because it gives us a head start on thwarting the potential dropout, and we

have found teaming important because more of us get close to every youngster and our pooled caring leads to understanding and confidence—students feel safe and important.

We have found that by relating the general curriculums to actual essentials for surviving in the society at a basic level and adding however much an individual student can master confidently, we can cut to a minimum passed-over subject matter and poorly learned skills. We hope to send off each student secure in the knowledge that he can learn, that he knows how to go about learning, and most of all, with a feeling that learning is really worthwhile. That will beat out mere Carnegie units anytime!

A professor of educational administration takes a different viewpoint.[20]

No one professionally active in education has to be told that all American education, public and private, is troubled today. But early adolescent education has been troubled almost since its inception.

Now, some educators say that junior high schools of grades 7-9 are on the way out; middle schools of grades 5-8 are on the way in. These people frequently claim that everything that has gone wrong in junior high schools can be made right in the 5-8 middle school.

Things have gone wrong in junior high schools, but every learning objective, every innovation which is proposed for the 5-8 middle school—team teaching, modular flexible scheduling, nongradedness, com-

20. Samuel H. Popper, "What About the Middle School?" *Today's Education* 58(1969):52–54. Used by permission.

puter terminals, talking typewriters, independent study—can be actualized in the 7-9 structure without compromising its institutional integrity. Indeed, I believe that the middle school composed of grades 5-8 is an institutional corruption. It is at once corruptive of early adolescent education and of childhood education in the elementary school.

The established institution for early adolescent education has been in a consistent state of growth since its beginning about 60 years ago, despite having been called "tramp steamer of the educational fleet," "stepchild of public education," "a school without teachers," and "a stepping-stone organization." Obviously, something in the cultural environment of American society is responsible for this growth. What is the something that generates such a powerful pressure on the school system that even an admittedly malfunctioning junior high school organization is better than none at all?

As I see it, the "something" is the need for an educational organization specially designed to meet the developmental requirements of early adolescence, the most difficult period of all human growth.

Kindergarten is the boot camp of formal education. Family and school join in an effort to introduce society's very young to the importance of achievement and the rewards of performance. By means of gold stars, appointment to the honored position of monitor, and other bonuses, pupils soon learn that a system of differential rewards for different levels of effort and achievement is a classroom norm.

When pupils reach high school, performance pressures intensify. Scholastic standing, college boards, and such things as competitions sponsored by industry and government are the visible evidence of this.

Elementary and high school students are, for the most part, physiologically and psychologically capable of satisfying school and family expectations. But in between, in early adolescence, a physiological revolution begins. Pupils, heretofore well-composed, encounter difficulty in conforming to performance expectations. At this point, they need the special school organization we traditionally called "junior high school."

Ideally, this special school organization is oriented to the pupil as a human being as well as to the pupil as a learner of cognitive skills. The learning of cognitive skills is not overlooked, but during this time of physiological and emotional stresses and strains, the pupil is granted a psychosocial moratorium from those cultural disciplines that school, as a socializing agent of society and as a social system, imposes.

Few disagree with the concept that early adolescents need a special unit of school organization in which they are to be exempted temporarily from the achievement and performance pressures of our society—an organization in which they can survive the turbulence of an "ego resynthesis" (a reference to Erik Erikson) without embarrassment and fear of failure. Disagreement arises, however, over what age brackets constitute early adolescence.

Advocates of the grades 5–8 middle school claim that the onset of adolescence has shifted downward because of a changed climate, improved diet, sharply modified social relations, and a host of other natural and cultural influences. However, during nearly six months of reading the research literature in reproductive physiology at the medical library of the University of Minnesota, I have found no substantive evidence in support of this claim. On the contrary, a 1968 publication of the Committee on Adolescence of the Group for the Advancement of Psychiatry is supportive of both general and specialized literature bracketing the early adolescent period as about age 12 to 15—the age bracket that has been institutionalized in American early adolescent education from the beginning.

Of course, more extensive research might lead to a different conclusion. To end argument, could we not ask specialists in reproductive physiology to determine the age for us? If their studies conclusively showed that the onset of adolescence has been accelerated since 1910, lowering the age brackets served by early adolescent education would be justified. Otherwise, to adopt the grades 5–8 middle school structure would be to ignore the raison d'être of this special kind of school. It would compromise the institutional integrity of the organization.

In my opinion, the ills that beset schools for early adolescents do not arise because of the ages of the pupils they enroll but because the schools seldom succeed in offering the special kind of education young adolescents need.

Anthropologist Margaret Mead sets the special case of early adolescent education in a revealing perspective when she notes that in our type of culture, early adolescents need ". . . freedom from pressure—freedom from choosing their careers, freedom from being told that if they don't pass this exam or that exam they won't ever get anywhere." She concludes, "The junior high school was set up to protect young adolescents."

For the most part, however, the junior high is not fulfilling its protective mission. In my research material, I have junior high report cards indicating a grade of D- in physical education, a C- in home economics. On a trial basis, Yale University has discarded the traditional grading system, but anyone who suggests that a junior high school teacher or principal follow this lead is usually made to feel like a thief separating a blind man from his guide dog. These educators agree, in principle, that junior high schools exist to satisfy the needs of early adolescents, but they go right on calculating grade-point averages to the last decimal point and otherwise turn their junior high school into a pressure-cooker microcosm of society.

The crux of the problem, it seems to me, is a failure to have special preparation programs for those preparing to teach early adolescents. Today, most junior high school teachers are trained in so-called programs of secondary education that are geared to prepare high school teachers.

Schools of education differentiate preparation for other units of public school organization. Why can't they do the same thing for early adolescent education?

Figure 4.3 points out what educators expect the middle school to do as well as what many educators perceive that the junior high school is doing.

Tangentially, again the middle school came into being in many instances to solve school building and population problems. Further, and perhaps more significantly, it has been seen as a means to eliminate de facto racial segregation. It represents a compromise between the neighborhood school and total integration. The middle school can serve a larger area and, therefore, potentially achieve a better racial bal-

A middle school program is designed to recognize the uniqueness of the growth stage spanning the transition from childhood to adolescence.

The junior high has evolved into exactly what the name implies—*junior* high school.

MIDDLE SCHOOL EMPHASIZES—	JUNIOR HIGH SCHOOL EMPHASIZES—
. . a child-centered program	. . a subject-centered program
. . learning how to learn	. . learning a body of information
. . creative exploration	. . mastery of concepts and skills
. . belief in oneself	. . competition with others
. . student self-direction, under expert guidance	. . adherence to the teacher-made lesson plan
. . student responsibility for learning	. . teacher responsibility for student learning
. . student independence	. . teacher control
. . flexible scheduling	. . the six-period day
. . student planning in scheduling	. . the principal-made schedule
. . variable group sizes	. . standard classrooms
. . team teaching	. . one teacher for a class
. . a self-pacing approach, with students learning at different rates	. . a textbook approach, with all students on the same page at the same time.

A middle school program is designed to foster the intellectual, social, and emotional growth of children without snatching their childhood from them.

Figure 4.3. Differences Between Middle Schools and Junior High Schools.

Source: Educational Research Service Circular, *Middle Schools In Action,* Washington, D.C.: American Association of School Administrators, 1969, p. 17. Used with permission.

ance within its boundaries. The middle school concept is still too new to assess either its effectiveness or acceptance as an organizational pattern.

It is important to point out again that organizational patterns are related to goals, but they are also related to physical facilities and in the case of the middle school to social problems. It is further pertinent to note that in order to achieve efficiency in educating masses, the American system of education has attempted to group pupils by age and by developmental characteristics.

While these efforts have resulted in admirable accomplishments the public schools still have not resolved organizationally the nagging persistent problem of individualizing instruction. Each student is an unique individual who develops and learns at his own rate. Can a program of universal education designed to serve the masses of elementary school children be organized to suit each and every individual? Can each student be made to feel important? Can his individual expectations be met? These are some of the challenges facing educators today, not only at the elementary school level, but at all levels.

Secondary

Secondary education began in the early colonies with the establishment of the first Latin grammar school in Boston in 1635. Its purposes were reflective of the expectations of the people. It was to prepare students for college—colleges in those days were predominantly concerned with preparing clergymen—and clergymen could in turn help the people achieve their goal of salvation. The Latin grammar school was eventually replaced by the tuition academy, the first of which was established by Ben Franklin in Philadelphia. Franklin is accredited with broadening the base of secondary education. His academy included students who did not intend to go on to college as well as those who did. He recognized that our developing nation needed men trained in commerce and surveying, for example, as well as theology and the classics. The concept of the academy grew and flourished, reaching its greatest heights in the middle of the 19th century. It met in part the societal needs of a developing nation. It was semipublic in nature and supported chiefly by tuition and donations. The academies were gradually replaced by the free public high school, the first of which was established in Boston in 1821. This high school, called the English Classical High School, was for boys only— a high school for girls was established in Boston in 1826. The first coeducational high school was established in Chicago in 1856. Perhaps the biggest boost to free public secondary education, however, was the decision of the Supreme Court of Michigan in 1872 which established the legality of communities to tax themselves for the support of public high schools. The American secondary school over a span of three centuries has developed from a privately supported college preparatory institution for a few elite to a publicly supported comprehensive institution available to most American youth. The Bureau of Census reported that in 1966 93.7 per cent of the youths ages 14–17 were enrolled in school either public or private. It is further interesting to note that the U.S. Office of Education reported that the high school graduates in 1967–68 represented 77.6 per cent of the class that entered the ninth grade in 1964–65. No other nation in the world can match this record. While the record is admirable, American secondary education still does not live up to the ideal expectations held for it.

In a report prepared for the Association for Supervision and Curriculum Development, Wiles and Patterson identified the following American democratic commitments for the education of adolescents.[21]

1. Universal education should be provided for all youth through the high school years.
2. The educational system should enable youth to secure the type of experiences which develop the personal, social, and vocational competencies needed in our society.
3. Various community agencies should be available to serve the educational needs of youth.

21. Kimball Wiles, and Franklin Patterson, *The High School We Need.* Washington, D.C.: Association for Supervision and Curriculum Development, National Education Association, 1959, pp. 2–4, 23. Used with permission.

A student commons area. Winona Senior High School, Winona, Minnesota.

4. A suitable program should be provided by the secondary school for all youth through the legal authority of the community.
5. Each youth should be free to select his vocational goals and pursue an educational program leading to these goals.

Have we met these commitments? Can they be met? Universality, a commitment of no small magnitude, has almost been achieved. In regard to the other four however, serious questions can be raised. Wiles and Patterson pose these questions:[22]

Do boys and girls gain mental health, the clarity of purpose, the self-reliance, the values and the problem solving skills that are needed for them to be effective individuals? Do they achieve the social insight, the empathy, the cooperative attitude, the democratic commitments that will help them live with others in our society? Do they come to possess the skills and knowledge that will enable them to support themselves and contribute to the economic development of the nation?

The answers to the questions will vary dependent upon the experience and perspective of the respondent; however, it would be an unusual individual who could respond strongly and affirmatively to all these queries.

The organization of secondary education in the United States today is related to the previously stated commitments. Secondary education includes the broad spectrum in the graded classification of grades 7–14. The lower portion of the spectrum includes the junior high while the higher portion is represented by community colleges. The middle portion including either grades 9–12 or grades 10–12 describes the senior high school. Let us consider briefly the senior high school.

The ideal senior high school is a comprehensive school. By comprehensive it is meant that (1) its pupil population is diverse, representing different cultures and

22. *Ibid.*, p. 3.

socio-economic groups, and (2) its curricular offerings present a balance of general and specialized education along with sufficient guidance services and elective courses so that a student may pursue the program of his choice. If its program is functioning effectively, students should become increasingly different in their achievement; that is, higher ability students should become increasingly superior in their attainments as compared to the less able students. This principle should be equally applicable in both the college preparatory, vocational, and general curricula students. The comprehensive high school should also permit a student to elect courses of his choice in any of the curricula. In other words, a college preparatory student would not be restricted from taking a beginning course in typewriting. While ideally students should become increasingly different in their pursuits of specialized education, the comprehensive

Vocational education in Quincy Vocational-Technical School, Quincy, Massachusetts.

Quincy Vocational-Technical School, Quincy, Massachusetts.

high school also should cause them to become increasingly alike in such things as their social insight, their attitudinal commitments toward democratic principles, and their empathy for others. Are our high schools accomplishing these goals? Can we have comprehensive high schools in this country when demographically, for example, the poor live with the poor, the rich with rich, and the black with black? Can students learn to live with others when they only interact with their own kind in schools? Is the comprehensive high school a realistically attainable organizational goal? Can a high school in a rural area with a total pupil population of less than four hundred pupils be comprehensive? The answers to these questions are being sought—they constitute part of the task of secondary education in America.

Community Colleges

The junior college or community college has emerged on the American scene in the last seventy years. The Joliet Junior College established in Joliet, Illinois in 1901, has the distinction of being the oldest extant public junior college; that is, of the public junior colleges founded in the late 1800's and early 1900's the Joliet Junior College survived and continues to operate as a junior college today. It is interesting to note that it was originally conceived as an extension of the high school and therefore considered as a part of secondary education and not higher education.[23] The organizational chart presented earlier in this chapter illustrates the junior college as being a part of higher education. Therein lies part of the dilemma of

23. James Thornton, Jr., *The Community Junior College,* p. 47.

> Colleges aren't strictly for geniuses. We can't afford to slam the door of opportunity in the faces of C-level high school seniors, who will help make our country's future. We must fight for our average students.
>
> Arthur S. Fleming

this sector of the American educational organization.

Perhaps it is most accurate to state that for some students the community college is truly an extension of secondary school; for others it is truly higher education, as they transfer to four year colleges or universities and graduate; for others it is terminal in specialized education and not an extension of high school, for they pursue goals not related to their previous secondary school ex-

Model of proposed Community College buildings, Joliet Community College.

perience. The confusion of classification in the educational hierarchy is normal for emerging institutions such as the community college and the junior high school. The community colleges as they now are organized and operated do have characteristics in common with both high schools and universities. This is as it should be, particularly if community colleges are truly going to become unique educational organizations dedicated to their purposes.

Thornton's research has identified six purposes:[24]

1. Occupational education of post-high school level,
2. General education for all categories of its students,
3. Transfer or pre-professional education,
4. Part-time education,
5. Community service,
6. The counseling and guidance of students.

In the light of the avowed purposes, it is easy to understand why it is difficult to classify the community college unequivocally as either secondary or higher education.

The community college in meeting its purposes, which reflect both individual and societal needs, has emerged as an unique and growing segment of American education. From their meager beginnings in the early 20th century the number of public junior colleges has grown to 503 institutions in 1965 which enrolled 1,152,086 students.[25] Further growth is predicted.

The community college provides for "at home" post-high school education. Students who cannot financially afford to pursue higher education elsewhere can start in the community college. Others can acquire necessary occupational skills. If an institution is truly a community college, it is responsive to the needs of the members of the community. It provides services for the people of the community. As such it fulfills the expectations of the people for education, expectations that either cannot or may not have been met by other institutions. Therein may reside the reason for its uniqueness and success.

Higher Education

Higher education, the capstone of American education, began in the early colonies with the establishment of Harvard College in 1636. It is significant to note that higher education began as a private endeavor. Today, approximately 63 per cent of the 2200 institutions of higher education are still under private control. Nevertheless, almost two-thirds of the students in higher education are enrolled in public institutions. The Morrill Act signed into law by President Lincoln was a tremendous boost to public higher education. This Act provided 30,000 acres to each state for each representative and senator then in Congress or when a state was admitted for the "endowment, maintenance and support of at least one college where the leading object shall be, without excluding other scientific and classical studies and including military tactics, to teach such branches of learning as are related to agriculture and mechanic arts."

Higher education is specialized education. Its purposes as delineated by the Educational Policies Commission are:[26]

24. *Ibid.*, p. 59.
25. *Ibid.*, p. 79.
26. Educational Policies Commission, *Higher Education in a Decade of Decision.* Washington, D.C.: National Education Association, 1957, pp. 6–10.

1. To provide opportunity for individual development of able people.
2. To transmit the cultural heritage.
3. To add to existing knowledge through research and creative activity.
4. To help translate learning into equipment for living and social advance.
5. To serve the public interest directly.

The organization of higher education is such that it facilitates the accomplishment of the purposes. Great responsibilities are placed upon the independent judgment of the students as they pursue their elected course of study; freedoms are provided for professors as they conduct their research; and both philanthropic and public monies are provided to sponsor research in the public interest.

The diversity of institutions both in kind and control contributes to meeting the purposes of higher education. The kinds of institutions include community colleges, technical colleges, liberal arts colleges, municipal colleges and universities, universities, land grant colleges and universities, and graduate and professional schools. Control differences include local, state, federal, sectarian, and non-sectarian private. This diversity permits a wide offering of specialized courses befitting the needs of individuals and society, and at the same time assures academic freedom and responsibility through an almost automatic system of checks and balances.

Adult Education

Adult education in its broadest sense includes any learning activity engaged in by an adult to promote his better living. In a more restricted sense it refers to programs of education formally organized by some educational agency for people beyond the compulsory school age who are not full-time students. In either case it is difficult to classify organizationally as it occurs at most levels of education.

The following purposes have been delineated:[27]

1. Americanization of immigrants from other lands.
2. Literacy and basic education for adults whose schooling was incomplete.
3. Modernization of education grown obsolete in a rapidly changing world.
4. Vocational rehabilitation necessitated by industrial and technological change.
5. Education for recreation and other use of increased leisure time.
6. Better understanding of man's larger and more complex social, economic, cultural, and political institutions.
7. Education for better citizenship and deeper international understanding.
8. Education for adjustment to problems of aging and retirement.
9. Knowledge essential for better health and family life.

These purposes not only are met at various levels of the educational hierarchy but they are also met by many diverse groups. Public schools and universities operate continuing educational programs, industries operate training programs for their employees, state and federal agencies sponsor training programs; private organizations such as correspondence schools or vocational schools, labor unions, clubs and organiza-

27. Chris A. DeYoung and Richard Wynn, *American Education*. New York: McGraw-Hill Book Co., p. 232. Used with permission.

tions, and formalized educational television groups offer opportunities for adults to develop or improve competencies.

While adult education occurred in many forms early in our history, the beginning of our organized movement occurred in 1926 with the formation of the American Association for Adult Education. This organization later merged with the Department of Adult Education of the National Education Association to form the Adult Education Association of the U.S.A. Much of the inspiration and support to organize adult education came from the Carnegie Corporation and its president, Frederick P. Keppel.

It has been reported by the National Association for Public School Adult Education that in 1965–66, 416,747 adults were enrolled in elementary level programs and 1,305,557 adults were enrolled in secondary programs. There were 22,495 elementary certificates awarded, 33,485 high school diplomas granted, and 77,818 equivalency certificates issued. The rapid changes in our society and the individual adjustments necessary to meet these needs are the basis for forecasting increasing growth in all forms of adult education in the future.

Reflections

The American pattern of educational organization has been relatively effective in providing mass education. Grouping individuals by developmental maturity, presenting content in sequential order, and recognizing the increasing independence of the student to make his own specialized choices as he progresses through the hierarchy, seem to be sound principles. The challenge today, however, is to develop methods of individualizing instruction within the group plan. Some efforts toward this will be discussed in chapter eight.

The role of private education in America was and still is an important role. We had private nursery schools, kindergartens, elementary schools, secondary schools, and colleges before any of them were accepted in the public domain. In a sense the expectations of a few people were met through private means, before they became the expectations of many and gained public acceptance. In this sense, private schools provide a seed bed for innovative activity.

As the organizational patterns of the past evolved from the needs and expectations of individuals and society, we can expect that the patterns of the future will arise from these same sources. Educators and citizens must be perceptive to recognize and delineate their goals, and then effective in designing patterns of organization to meet those goals. Teachers should not only expect change; they should be agents of change if change is indicated.

Questions for Discussion

1. How are the developmental tasks specified as kindergarten goals applicable to other levels in the organizational hierarchy?
2. Is individualized instruction possible in mass education as it exists in the United States today?
3. How can the organizational patterns of American education be utilized to aid in resolving some of America's social problems?
4. Can the personal-social needs of students be met in a graded organization?
5. In your judgment what is the most commonly used rationale for grouping stu-

dents for learning in contemporary America? Is it sound?

Supplementary Learning Activities

1. Visit a nursery school or kindergarten to specifically observe how the developmental goals are being accomplished.
2. Visit a middle school and a junior high school, looking for differences related to their purpose.
3. Invite a community college official to your class to discuss the relationship of the community college to the community.
4. Conduct a survey to determine the adult education opportunities available in your immediate area.
5. Interview citizens as to their attitudes regarding the role of the comprehensive secondary school in resolving social problems.

Selected References

Barker, Roger G., and Paul V. Gump. *Big School, Small School.* Stanford, California: Stanford University Press, 1964.

Bossing, Nelson L., and Roscoe V. Cramer. *The Junior High School.* Boston: Houghton Mifflin Co., 1965.

Brown, Frank B. *The Nongraded High School.* Englewood Cliffs, New Jersey: Prentice-Hall, Inc., 1963.

Conant, James B. *The American High School Today.* New York: McGraw-Hill Book Co., 1959.

———. *Slums and Suburbs.* New York: McGraw-Hill Book Co., 1961.

Department of Elementary School Principals. *Elementary School Organization.* Washington, D.C.: National Education Association, 1962.

Fields, Ralph R. *The Community College Movement.* New York: McGraw-Hill Book Co., 1962.

Frazier, Alexander, ed. *The New Elementary School.* Washington, D.C.: Association for Supervision and Curriculum Development, Department of Elementary School Principals, National Education Association, 1968.

Goodlad, J. L. "Individual Differences and Vertical Organization of the School." *Sixty-first Yearbook. National Society for the Study of Education.* Chicago: University of Chicago Press, 1962.

Knowles, Malcolm S. *The Adult Education Movement in the United States.* New York: Holt, Rinehart, & Winston, Inc., 1962.

Logan, Lillian M. *Teaching the Young Child.* Boston: Houghton Mifflin Co., 1960.

Mayer, Martin. *The Schools.* New York: Harper & Row Publishers, Inc., 1961.

McConnell, T. R. *A General Pattern for American Public Higher Education.* New York: McGraw-Hill Book Co., 1962.

Miller, Richard I. *Education In a Changing Society.* Washington, D.C.: National Education Association, 1963.

Moore, Elnora H. *Fives at School.* New York: G. P. Putnam's Sons, 1959.

Morphet, Edgar L., Roe L. Johns, and Theodore L. Reller. *Educational Organization and Administration.* Englewood Cliffs, N.J.: Prentice-Hall, Inc., 1967.

Popper, Samuel H. *The American Middle School: An Organizational Analysis.* Waltham, Mass.: Blaisdell Publishing Co., Division of Ginn and Co., 1967.

Thornton, James Jr. *The Community Junior College.* New York: John Wiley & Sons, 1966.

Wiles, Kimball. *The Changing Curriculum of the American High School.* Englewood Cliffs, N.J.: Prentice-Hall, Inc., 1965.

Wiles, Kimball and Franklin Patterson. *The High School We Need.* Washington, D.C.: Association for Supervision and Curriculum Development, National Education Association, 1959.

Junior College
Explosion

Edmund J. Gleazer, Jr.

Nothing that has happened in education in the past half century can surpass the recent flowering of the uniquely American junior college. Once, a young person who finished high school went on to a four-year college or went to work. A few joined street gangs. Today, however, there's another choice because education has a new dimension to help a student find his way into a career program in which he can succeed. Community and junior colleges are that new dimension.

This fall some 60 new two-year colleges opened—bringing the total to about 960. Expansion has been occurring at the rate of almost one a week for the past eight years, and it is likely to continue until most States have, like Florida and California, put community colleges within commuting range of nearly all their populations. Every State now has at least one junior college, and most urban areas have one or more.

Enrollments at these schools have increased at the rate of about 15 per cent each year since 1960 and will total nearly two million by the end of 1969. An average of about one-third of all students entering a higher education program start in a junior college. In some states the figure is much higher. In Florida, for example, 65 per cent of all college freshmen are enrolled in junior colleges, and in Illinois it's 45 per cent.

California, with its 85 junior colleges, enrolls an even higher percentage.

There are a number of reasons for the rapid development of the two-year college. There is a growing demand on the part of Americans for opportunity to get education beyond high school, and a general feeling that education can play a major part in raising the sights of men and women and improving their social conditions. Under Presidents Johnson and Kennedy, commissions made up of leaders from business, education, and government, and local civic-movers had begun to call for the provision of universal opportunity for at least two years of education beyond high school.

The community junior college, which had come on the scene early in the century but had moved neither very far nor very fast, seemed made-to-order for the job of extending and expanding opportunities for education beyond high school. Its low cost to students, proximity to those it was designed to serve, flexible admission arrangements, strong counseling services, and varied educational program seemed to suit the needs and the times.

Departing from conventional concepts of what constitutes college education, junior college planners focused on occupational

* Edmund J. Gleazer, Jr., "Junior College Explosion," *American Education* 5(1968): 12–13.

education courses as well as the traditional freshman and sophomore transfer program that prepares young people for pursuit of a four-year degree. They recognized that the world of work had become more sophisticated, that unskilled and even many skilled jobs were rapidly disappearing from the employment picture, replaced by new kinds of occupations that required special training, usually beyond high school. Thus, today the community colleges are offering scores of educational experiences to prepare men and women to enter occupations that are rewarding both in terms of earning potential and social standing.

The young person who does not wish to prepare for a professional career, but who has the interest and capability for semiprofessional and technical work, can choose from a number of program offerings. The cost to him will be minimal; he can live at home; and he can work part-time if need be. Moreover, there are many types of financial assistance programs open to him.

About one-third of all students enrolled in community colleges opt for the semiprofessional and technical education programs. These are generally clustered in three main groups: business-related—such as data processing, real estate sales, office skills of various types; industry-engineering-related —engineering assistance, missile technology, architectural drafting, aviation electronics, specifications writing; and paramedical and health-related—dental assistance, medical laboratory technology, nursing, and optical technology. These are only a few of the options.

A fourth group of programs is relatively new but growing rapidly. It is related to public service, and the most popular courses of study are probably law enforcement and fire protection. Some 200 community colleges now offer law enforcement programs, and in some places local police are required to take all or part of these courses. Other public service areas include social work and occupations in the field of city management.

In addition to formal programs in both occupational and transfer preparation, the community colleges are heavily engaged in community service work. The leaders of these institutions look upon them as community centers where people of all ages can come for recreational, social, and cultural activities. Swimming pools are open to the public at certain times, for example, and the auditoriums of the colleges are made available for meetings, concerts, and lectures. Short courses, workshops, and seminars are arranged for special interest groups.

Still another important effort of the community colleges is in the field of adult education. Evening programs often enroll as many as twice the number of students who are in the day programs, most of them working men and women who are upgrading themselves for better jobs, pursuing degrees, or just attending classes for the enjoyment of it. Here again, the community colleges are ideally suited for this kind of education because of their proximity to the people and their willingness to provide whatever educational experiences are required. Many community colleges publicly declare that they will develop courses upon request so long as there appears to be a reasonable need and interest—and they mean it.

Community colleges are also acutely aware that these times call for innovation and willingness to move swiftly into major social problem areas. Planners and directors of big-city colleges, for example, are making certain that there are enough campuses to serve all the people of their communities— including those who may live in blighted or ghetto areas. Chicago, Cleveland, Dallas, Denver, Honolulu, Los Angeles, Miami, New York, San Francisco, and Seattle are among the many urban areas that are putting community college opportunities within reach of all.

If there are any doubts about whether people take advantage of the offerings of the new community colleges, some recent statistics might help to erase them. When the first campus of the Tarrant County Junior College District opened in Fort Worth, some 4,000 students enrolled. Florida Junior College at Jacksonville opened with 2,500 students. Seattle Community College attracted 12,000 students the day it opened. Without the availability of these community colleges it is doubtful that more than a third of those enrolled would have continued their education.

Development of the community college dimension of American education has received impetus from the Federal Government. Most of the recently passed higher and vocational education bills have included support clearly earmarked for two-year colleges. The first major breakthrough came with the passage of the Higher Education Facilities Act of 1963, in which community or technical colleges were singled out for 22 percent of the construction funds for all undergraduate academic facilities. The proportion of allotments to junior colleges was increased in 1966 through amendments to the 1963 law which continued the facilities program. Under the amendments

the allotment was raised to 23 per cent in 1968 and to 24 per cent in 1969. Therefore, through the action of the 89th Congress in late 1966, nearly $500 million was authorized for public junior college construction alone for the period 1967–69.

Community and other junior colleges also have received support from such programs as the Allied Health Professions Act, the Vocational Education Act, the National Defense Education Act, the Higher Education Act, and the Education Professions Development Act.

Most public community colleges, of course, depend largely on local and state tax dollars for operations and construction. But the Federal support has helped many colleges to move more rapidly toward meeting important planning objectives in program and facilities development.

This is a happy story. But the very expansion and growth which makes it so have also generated some problems. How far and how fast can these junior colleges expand? How can they continue to broaden their offerings, increase their costs, and impose a greater financial burden on the citizens who are called upon to pay for public education? Financing must be considered a priority problem for the future.

Then there is the matter of faculty. Where do you find the necessary teachers? How do you prepare them for what most experts consider the "special" needs of junior college teaching? Estimates of the number of trained teachers needed during the next decade run into the tens of thousands.

Junior colleges are finding ways to upgrade and orient staff through workshops and training institutes. Some major universities offer further hope as they concentrate on developing graduate programs aimed especially at recruiting and preparing teachers for junior colleges. The Education Professions Development Act, with its promise of training institutes and other forms of assistance, will help. But the American Association of Junior Colleges considers staffing at the top of the list of problems that will face junior colleges in the future. The association, through a project aimed at recruiting and preparing teachers, is already beginning to do something about it. Through this new program, the association will be working with four-year colleges and universities as well as two-year institutions to plan recruiting and training of new junior college faculty members. Studies are also being conducted to determine possible sources for additional faculty members.

Community colleges suffer some of the same perplexities that are now confronting other institutions of higher education: student unrest, faculty protest, and dissention among minority or disadvantaged groups. But the community colleges have resolved many major problems in recent years, not the least of which was the lack of public acceptance, interest, and support during their early history. Their planners and leaders, undeterred by new problems, look forward to continued growth and expansion—and to providing an additional choice to America's young people.

CHAPTER 5

The Control of
American Education

The educational system of the United States is unique among the nations of the world. In terms of control, its most distinctive feature is decentralization. In other words, local governments have wide decision-making powers in terms of operating local school systems. Education in the United States is a legal function of state government; however, much of the authority of the separate states has been delegated to local government—more specifically, to local boards of education. The federal government also plays a role which can perhaps best be described as one of an interested party. As the educational system in the United States developed, the roles of the different levels of government have changed. While education still remains basically a local operation, the participation of state and federal governments has increased. The remainder of this chapter examines the current roles of the various levels of government as they relate to the control and operation of education today in the United States.

Federal Government

The federal government has become involved in education in four different, yet related, ways: (1) the application of the United States Constitution, (2) the function and operation of the United States Office of Education, (3) the direct operation of educational programs by various agencies of the federal government, and (4) the provision of federal aid in its various forms.

United States Constitution

The United States Constitution is the basic law of the land, and as such has had its effects on education. While no specific mention of education is made in the Constitution, the Tenth Amendment has been interpreted as implying that education is a

> "The powers not delegated to the United States by the Constitution, nor prohibited by it to the States, are reserved to the States respectively, or to the people."
>
> Tenth Amendment
> United States Constitution

function of the respective states. This interpretation in a sense resulted in the development of fifty different state systems of education. Further, it reinforced the type of educational decentralization that had begun to develop in colonial America. While the fifty states are markedly similar in their patterns of education, differences do exist. Examples of differences that exist include: (1) requirements for teacher certification, (2) provisions for financial aid, (3) regulations for compulsory attendance, and (4) provisions for teacher pension plans.

"Congress shall make no law respecting an establishment of religion or prohibiting the free exercises thereof; or abridge the freedom of speech or of the press; or the right of the people peaceably to assemble and to petition the government for redress of grievances."

First Amendment
United States Constitution

The First and Fourteenth Amendments have also had a definite impact on the administration of education in the United States. The First Amendment insures freedom of speech, religion, the press, and the right of petition. The Fourteenth Amendment provides for the protection of specified privileges of citizens. Based upon these amendments, the Supreme Court of the United States has made many decisions that have influenced the course of education in the United States.

Court Decisions

Court decisions based upon the First Amendment have been particularly influential in clarifying the relationship between religion and education. There have been a number of these decisions, and basically they can be classified into three groups: (1) those having to do with the rights of parents to educate their children in private schools, (2) those having to do with the use of public funds to support private education, and (3) those having to do with the teaching or practice of religion in the public schools.

An important case influential in determining the rights of parents to provide education for their children was the Oregon case. Briefly, in 1922 the legislature of Oregon passed a law requiring all children to attend public schools. The Supreme Court of the United States ruled that the law was unconstitutional (*Pierce v. Society of Sisters, 1925*). The reasoning of the Court was that such a law denied to parents the right to control the education of their children. This decision of the Supreme Court in addition

---

"No State shall make or enforce any law which shall abrogate the privileges or immunities of citizens of the United States; nor shall any state deprive any person of life, liberty, or property without due process of law; nor deny to any person within its jurisdiction the equal protection of the laws."

Fourteenth Amendment
United States Constitution

to establishing that private schools have a right to exist, and that pupils may meet the requirements of compulsory education by attending private schools, also established that a state may regulate all schools, public and private, and require the teaching of specific subjects. The Oregon decision reinforced an historical tradition of private and sectarian education in the United States and gave further impetus to the development of private schools. Thus, two systems of education, public and private, developed in the United States.

Cases having to do with the use of public funds to support private education are numerous. Prominent among them are the Cochran and the Everson cases. In *Cochran v. Louisiana State Board of Education,* 1930, the United States Supreme Court held that a Louisiana textbook statute that provided for furnishing textbooks purchased with tax-raised funds to private school pupils was valid. The ruling was technically based on the Fourteenth Amendment. In *Everson v. Board of Education* (1947), the United States Supreme Court held that tax-raised funds in a New Jersey school district could be used to reimburse parents for bus fares expended to transport their children to church schools. The decision of the Court in the Everson case was based on a five to four vote. These decisions permitting the use of public funds to provide transportation and textbooks for students attending private schools were based in the main on *child benefit theory,* the rationale being that the aid benefited the children and not the school or religion. Child benefit theory, while seemingly becoming an established phenomenon at the federal level, has not been unanimously accepted by the states.

Decisions by the highest courts in a number of states, among them Alaska, Wisconsin, Oklahoma, Delaware, and Oregon, have struck down enactments authorizing either transportation or textbooks for children attending denominational schools.

The matter of the use of public funds for private education is far from settled. Rising costs have made it increasingly difficult for nonpublic schools to survive. As nonpublic schools close, and their pupils enroll in public schools, the financial effort for public schools must be increased. Recent developments include passage of legislation in Pennsylvania, Connecticut, and Rhode Island providing payments to private schools for teaching secular subjects. These laws remain to be tested.

The matter of the practice of sectarian religion in public schools has been treated by the United States Supreme Court as recently as 1963. In that instance they ruled that the reading of the Bible and the recitation of the Lord's Prayer are religious ceremonies, and if done in public schools are in violation of the First and Fourteenth Amendments of the Constitution. The decision resulted from the appeals of two lower court decisions, one from Pennsylvania, *Schempp v. School District of Abington Township,* and the other from Maryland, *Murray v. Curlett.* These earlier decisions had held that reading the Bible and saying the Lord's Prayer were not illegal. In the McCollum case, *People of the State of Illinois ex rel. McCollum v. Board of Education of School District No. 71, Champaign, Illinois,* 1948, the Supreme Court ruled that release time for religious instruction, with voluntary pupil participation, but conducted on public school property, was a violation of the separation of church and state. In 1952 in *Zorach v. Clausen,* the Court upheld a New York statute which provided for release time for religious instruction off the school premises.

A most pertinent illustration of the use of the Fourteenth Amendment was the United States Supreme Court decision in the Brown case, *Brown v. Board of Education of Topeka,* 1954. The impact of this landmark decision repudiating the separate but equal doctrine is still being felt and reacted to. The judicial pronouncement in this case had legislative power added to it by the Civil Rights Act of 1964.

In addition to the First, Tenth, and Fourteenth Amendments to the United States Constitution, the Preamble to the Constitution has also had its effect on the development of education in the United States. The phrase "promote the general welfare," known as the *general welfare clause,* has been the basis for much of the federal support of education.

In summary, the United States Constitution, while it has been interpreted as delegating the function of education to the states, does contain within it protection for the rights of individuals which must not be violated in the operation of education by states and local districts. The general welfare clause permits the infusion of federal monies into education as seen fit by the Congress.

United States Office of Education

The United States Office of Education represents a formalized federal effort in education. It was originally established in 1867 as the Federal Department of Education. In

> "We the people of the United States in order to form a more perfect Union, establish justice, insure domestic tranquility, provide for the common defense, promote the general welfare, and secure the blessings of liberty to ourselves and our posterity, do ordain and establish the Constitution for the United States of America.
>
> Preamble
> United States Constitution

1953, after several changes of names, its title officially became the United States Office of Education, and it became part of the cabinet Department of Health, Education, and Welfare. The Commissioner of Education is appointed by the president with the advice and consent of the Senate. The Office collects and publishes information about all phases of education in the United States, engages in conducting and disseminating educational research, provides leadership, and administers much of the federal funding for education. From a meager and mild beginning, the U.S. Office of Education, particularly in the last few years, has grown to become a powerful and influential agency. It has even been suggested that a Secretary of Education in the president's cabinet is now needed and justified. The increasing strength of the United States Office of Education is viewed by some as a distinct trend away from the traditional pattern of decentralizing of educational authority in our nation. Other authorities are quick to point out that while its influence has grown, an examination of the record would reveal that federal control has not been increased. Nevertheless, it must be granted that the Office of Education has become a more powerful agency than it once was, and it must further be recognized that forces within our society (social, economic, and demographic), are such that in fact the resultant and concommitant problems cannot be resolved by local or state efforts. Thus, the role of the Office of Education has changed a great deal, and undoubtedly will continue to change.

The federal government has accepted responsibility and directly operates some educational institutions. The Congress provides funds for the operation of the school system of the District of Columbia. The Department of the Interior is responsible for the education of children of National Park Employees, and for outlying possessions, (Samoa), and trust territories (Caroline and Marshall Islands). The Bureau of Indian Affairs finances and manages schools on Indian reservations. The Department of Defense is responsible for the four military academies and also operates a school system for children of military personnel wherever they may be located. Further, the education given in the various training programs of the military services has made a tremendous contribution to the overall educational effort in our nation.

Federal Financial Support

Federal funding represents a fourth way in which the federal government has become involved in education. Figure 5.1 lists some selected illustrative federal acts which either directly or indirectly provided support for education.

1785	Ordinance of 1785
1787	Northwest Ordinance
1862	Morrill Land Grant Act
1887	Hatch Act
1914	Smith-Lever Agriculture Extension Act
1917	Smith-Hughes Vocational Act
1930	Civilian Conservation Corps
1933	Public Works Administration
1935	National Youth Administration
1935	Works Program Administration
1940	Vocational Education for National Defense Act
1941	Lanham Act
1944	G.I. Bill of Rights
1946	National School Lunch Act
1950	National Science Foundation
1954	Cooperative Research Program
1958	National Defense Education Act
1963	Manpower Development and Training Act
1964	Economic Opportunity Act
1965	Elementary and Secondary Education Act

Figure 5.1. Selected Federal Acts That Have Provided Funds for Education.

The list of federal acts presented in Figure 5.1, while by no means exhaustive, is illustrative. Some general observations can be made from an examination of the list. It is apparent that federal funding for education is not a new phenomenon. The 1785 and 1787 Northwest Ordinance Acts encouraged the establishment of education in the Northwest Territory. The Ordinance of 1785 required the reservation of the sixteenth section of each township for the maintenance of schools. Federal funding since this early beginning has increased steadily. It is also apparent that the funding has been categorical; that is, for a specific purpose.

Each of the acts listed had or has a purpose. Let it suffice for purposes of illustration to point out that (1) the Morrill Acts and the Hatch Act encouraged expanded agricultural, mechanical, and scientific education in institutions of higher education; (2) the Smith-Lever and Smith-Hughes Acts encouraged vocational education in secondary schools; (3) the CCC, PWA, NYA, WPA, while in the main designed to alleviate the economic depression of the 1930's, provided incidental aid to education and youth; (4) the NDEA Act specifically affirmed the feelings of Congress toward the importance of education for national defense; (5) the ESEA provided many thrusts, including efforts to meet the needs of children of poverty and to encourage research. The ESEA was somewhat unique in federal funding legislation in that it came as close to general aid as any federal legislation ever has, and it further provided the means whereby federal tax funds could be made available to private and church-related schools. In a sense it represented an infusion of the judicial child benefit theory attitudes into legislation.

A fourth observation that can be made is that federal funding originates and is administered through a number of federal agencies. For example, in addition to the Department of Health, Education and Welfare, funds are administered through the Departments of Agriculture, Defense, Housing and Urban Development, Labor, and Interior; and through agencies such as the Office of Economic Opportunity, Veteran's Administration, and the Peace Corps.

Federal Influence: Direct and Subtle

In summary, the federal government is an influential agent in American education. Its influence has been felt directly in terms of protecting individual rights as provided in the Constitution, attaining equality of opportunity for all, promoting general welfare in terms of domestic social and economic problems and national defense, and operating specific educational agencies. Its subtle effect is most strongly exerted through the financial incentives offered to stimulate specific programs.

State Government

Public education in the United States is a state function. States have recognized this function in their respective constitutions and have established laws directing the way in which it shall be conducted. Most states, the exceptions being Illinois and Wisconsin, have established state boards of education. The executive duties of administering education at the state level are primarily the responsibility of a state department or office of public instruction. These departments in the various states are headed by a chief executive officer, frequently called the state superintendent of public instruction or the chief state school officer. Let us examine briefly how each of these segments of control and operation at the state level influence education.

> "Religion, morality, and knowledge being necessary to good government and the happiness of mankind, schools and the means of education shall forever be encouraged."
>
> Northwest Ordinance, 1787

State Constitutions

The constitutional provisions of the states for education, while differing slightly in their precise wording, are markedly similar in their intent. An illustrative example is a statement in Section 2, Article VIII of the Constitution of the State of Michigan. It reads, "The Legislature shall maintain and support a system of free public elementary and secondary schools as defined by law. Each school district shall provide for the education of its pupils without discrimination as to religion, creed, race, color, or national origin." The various state constitutions are interpreted by state courts and legal counsel as conflicts arise. The decisions of state courts may be appealed to the United States Supreme Court. The United States Supreme Court will usually hear the case if in their judgment it is in the domain of the United States Constitution or federal law.

State Legislatures

The enabling legislation to conduct the educational enterprise is prepared by state legislatures. This legislation is usually classified and bound in a volume referred to as the *school code*. Legislation is both mandatory and permissive, therefore directing and guiding local school boards in their task of operating schools. The greater the tendency to enact permissive legislation, the greater amount of control is delegated to the local boards of education. State legislation is concerned with many aspects of education; for example, district organizational patterns, teacher certification and tenure regulations, financing of schools, attendance laws.

State legislatures, because of their im-portant and vital position in education, are the subject of much lobbying. In the realm of education the laws that they formulate deal with children and money, both of which are precious to most citizens. Influential lobbying groups may include: taxpayers' federations; patriotic groups; labor, business, and professional organizations; humane societies; and the various organizations concerned directly with education, such as state teachers' associations, school administrator associations, and school board associations.

State Boards of Education

State boards of education concerned with elementary and secondary education are now in operation in 48 of the 50 states. Illinois and Wisconsin are the exceptions; however, both Illinois and Wisconsin do have state boards for vocational education since this is a federal requirement in order to be eligible to receive federal funds for these activities.

Historically, the prototype of the modern day style of state boards of education was the board established in Massachusetts in 1837. It was the first state board with an appointed secretary in the person of Horace Mann. Henry Barnard, another pioneer educator, became the first secretary of the Connecticut State Board of Education, and later after serving in the same capacity in Rhode Island became the first United States Commissioner of Education.

The duties of state boards of education vary; however, in general they serve in a policy making capacity. In 1952 the National Council of Chief State School Officers recommended a specific list of responsibilities for state boards of education. This list-

1. Formulate policies and adopt such rules and regulations as are necessary to carry out the responsibilities assigned to it by the constitution and the statutes of the state.

2. Appoint and fix the salaries of the professional staff of the state department of education on the recommendation of the chief state school officer.

3. Establish standards for issuance and revocation of teacher certificates.

4. Establish standards for classifying, approving, and accrediting schools, both public and nonpublic.

5. Prescribe a uniform system for the gathering and reporting of educational data, for the keeping of adequate educational and finance records, and for the better evaluation of educational progress.

6. Submit an annual report to the governor and legislature covering the areas of action of the state board of education and the operations of the state department of education and to support education throughout the state.

7. Consider the educational needs of the state and recommend to the governor and the legislature such additional legislation or changes in existing legislation as it may deem desirable.

8. Interpret its own rules and regulations and upon appeal hear all controversies and disputes arising therefrom.

9. Publish the laws relating to education with notes and comments for the guidance of those charged with the educational responsibility.

10. Provide through the state department of education supervisory and consultative service and issue materials which would be helpful in the development of educational programs.

11. Accept and distribute in accord with law any monies, commodities, goods, and services which may be made available from the state or federal government or from other sources.

12. Designate the extent to which the board is empowered to exercise supervision over public and nonpublic colleges, universities, state institutions and public and nonpublic elementary and secondary schools in accord with the law and sound public policy on education.

Figure 5.2. Suggested Responsibilities for State Boards of Education.

Source: National Council of Chief State School Officers, *The State Department of Education*, Washington, D.C.: The Council, 1952, pp. 14–16. Used with permission.

ing is still appropriate; it is presented in Figure 5.2.

An examination of the recommended responsibilities of state boards of education reveals that in addition to a policy-making function, it is recommended that they serve in both regulatory and advisory capacities. Recommendations 2, 3, 4, and 5 are illustrative of regulatory activities, while 7 and 9 are distinctly advisory. The regulatory function of state school boards is of primary importance in achieving consistent operation of local schools, and the advisory function can be of particular importance to the legislature, especially in the light of lobbying pressures applied to the legislative decision-making process.

Membership on state boards is attained in three ways: either election by the people or their representatives, appointment by the governor, or ex officio by virtue of other office held. Figure 5.3 (page 130) provides this information for each state.

It is interesting to note the differences among states as to their preference in methods of selection. Iowa, New York, and Washington are somewhat unique in their elective procedures. In Iowa, conventions of delegates from areas within the state send nominations to the governor for his appointment; in New York the Board of Regents is elected by the legislature; and, in Washington the state board is elected by members of boards of directors of local school districts. Needless to say, there are advantages and disadvantages of both the elective and appointive procedures in selecting state school board members. The appointive procedure is considered by its proponents to be more efficient in that it is more likely to establish a harmonious relationship with the governor, and that it facilitates the placement of highly qualified persons who would not for various reasons seek election. The proponents of the elective procedures cite the "grass-roots" control feature, and the lesser likelihood of political manipulation. In either case, once members are selected, they usually have staggered terms to avoid a complete change in membership at any one time; they usually serve without pay, but with reimbursement for their expenses. Both of these provisions serve as safeguards from political patronage.

Chief State School Officers

The chief state school officer occupies an important position in the administration of education in his respective state. Usually he is the executive head of the state department of education, and as such through his staff provides leadership and supervisory service in addition to the customary clerical and regulatory functions of state departments of education. He presents his interpretation of educational needs to the governor, state board of education, and legislature. He frequently influences legislation, both directly and indirectly. While the provision for his duties vary from state to state, they are quite specifically delineated for him by a combination of the respective state constitution and school code. He also is likely to receive direction from the state board of education.

Information as to how chief state school officers are selected is presented in Figure 5.3. Currently, twenty-one state officers are elected by the people or their representatives, twenty-five are appointed by state boards of education, and four are appointed by the governor. The trend has been way from election and toward appointment, specifically appointment by the state board of education. Arguments advanced in favor of appointment include the notion that policy-making should be clearly differentiated from policy execution; that educational leadership should not depend so heavily on one elected official; and that a greater likelihood exists of recruiting and retaining qualified career personnel. Opponents to the appointment procedure claim mainly that the official selected under this system would not be responsible to the people. A major objection raised to gubernatorial ap-

State	Members of State Boards of Education			Chief State School Officers		
	Elected by People or Represent. of People	Appointed by Governor	Ex Officio	Elected by Popular Vote	Appointed by State Board of Education	Appointed by Governor
Alabama		x		x		
Alaska		x			x	
Arizona		x		x		
Arkansas		x			x	
California		x		x		
Colorado	x				x	
Connecticut		x			x	
Delaware		x			x	
Florida			x	x		
Georgia		x		x		
Hawaii	x				x	
Idaho		x		x		
Illinois				x		
	(No State Board)					
Indiana		x		x		
Iowa	x				x	
Kansas	x				x	
Kentucky		x		x		
Louisiana	x			x		
Maine		x			x	
Maryland		x			x	
Massachusetts		x			x	
Michigan	x				x	
Minnesota		x			x	
Mississippi			x	x		
Missouri		x			x	
Montana		x		x		
Nebraska	x				x	
Nevada	x				x	
New Hampshire		x			x	
New Jersey		x				x
New Mexico	x				x	
New York	x				x	
North Carolina		x		x		
North Dakota		x		x		
Ohio	x				x	
Oklahoma		x		x		
Oregon		x		x		
Pennsylvania		x				x
Rhode Island		x			x	
South Carolina	x			x		
South Dakota		x		x		
Tennessee		x				x
Texas	x				x	
Utah	x				x	
Vermont		x			x	
Virginia		x				x
Washington	x			x		
West Virginia		x			x	
Wisconsin				x		
	(No State Board)					
Wyoming		x		x		
Total	15	31	2	21	25	4

Figure 5.3. Methods of Selection of State School Board Members and Chief State School Officers.

Sources: Adapted from R. F. Will, *State Educational Structure and Organization*, U.S. Office of Education, O.E.-23038, Misc, no. 46, Washington, D.C. G.P.O. 1964, and data made available by Council of Chief State School Officers, NEA.

pointment is the danger of involvement in partisan politics. It is important to note that an elected state school officer is legally a state "official," while an appointed officer is an "employee." As a result of these differences, the working relationship of an elected official with the state board of education is not as likely to be clear and as cleanly defined as it is in instances where the chief state school officer is appointed by the state board of education, and therefore is clearly an employee.

State Departments of Education

The state departments of education, under the direction of the chief state school officer, carry out the activities of state government in education. A recent monograph has classified their activities into five categories: operational, regulatory, service, developmental, and public support and cooperation.[1] Until recent years, their activities have been largely operational and regulatory. Operational activities are those that have to do with the direct operation of schools such as those for the deaf or blind; regulatory activities center around the enforcement of state regulations for schools, such as making certain that only properly certified teachers are employed, and that buildings are safe. The service function has to do with helping local school districts. It includes the sharing of the knowledge and expertise of the state by providing consultant service, research information, or legal advice. Most states have improved their service activities in the past few years. Developmental activities have to do with planning in order to improve the state departments themselves so that they may further develop their capabilities. Public support

and cooperation activities involve communicating effectively with the people of the state, the legislature and governor, and other governmental bodies.[2]

While the traditional roles of state departments have emphasized the operational and regulatory functions, the problems of education today indicate that the state departments of education should play a stronger leadership function. Leadership can be accomplished with or without legislation. The federal government, through the Elementary and Secondary Act of 1965, Title V, provided money to be used by state departments of education for self study and strengthening.

Local School Districts

The most visible agency of control in education to both citizens and teachers is the local school district. The school district is controlled by a governing board made up of citizens residing in the geographical area that makes up the district.

Local school districts, while similar in their major purpose—that is, educating children—are widely different in their characteristics. In 1968, there were 20,440 districts in the United States having a total enrollment of approximately 45 million students in elementary and secondary schools.[3] These districts differ in many ways: geographical size; enrollment; geographical location, (urban, suburban, rural); socioeconomic composition; heterogeneity and

1. Roald F. Campbell, Gerald E. Stroufe, and Donald H. Layton, *Strengthening State Departments of Education*, p. 10.
2. *Ibid.*, pp. 10–15.
3. Richard H. Barr, and Betty J. Foster, *Fall 1968 Statistics of Public Schools*, p. 8.

homogeneity; wealth; type of organization, (K–8, 9–12, K–12); and many other ways. Most of the school districts in the United States are small in terms of enrollment. It has been estimated that forty-seven per cent of the districts enroll less than 299 pupils, and that this total enrollment makes up only about two per cent of the total national enrollment. Yet, only about one-half of one per cent of the districts have enrollments greater than 25,000, but these districts enroll about twenty-eight per cent of the total national enrollment.[4] The trend in school district organization has been to reduce the number of districts to obtain a more effective and efficient organization. The number of districts has been reduced from over 100,-000 in 1945 to the current 20,440. Such school reorganization is a slow but inevitable process. Along with consolidation the trend has also been to establish more districts that include both elementary and secondary education (K–12). Currently the great majority of pupils (over eighty-eight per cent) are in such districts.[5]

While the "putting together" or consolidation of smaller districts is being encouraged, problems have become apparent in very large city systems such as New York, Chicago and Los Angeles, that can be partly attributed to their immense enrollments. Communications in such districts can become distant and distorted. Patrons in such systems often express strong feelings that their districts are not responsive. They are calling for decentralization to enable them to gain some control over their neighborhood schools. Experimental efforts toward decentralization are being made in large urban areas such as New York, Chicago and Pittsburgh to meet these desires.

Local Control

Local control becomes a reality through the governing boards of local districts. They may make decisions within the power delegated to them by the state. Some of their powers include those to raise monies; obtain sites; build buildings; provide curricula; employ teachers and other personnel; and admit and assign pupils to schools. Local school boards must conform to mandatory statutes, and operate within powers delegated to them. It is within their power to enact local policies for education providing those policies do not violate existing state laws. Board members are local people. Ninety-five per cent of them in the United States are elected by popular vote, most frequently in special elections on a nonpartisan basis. The remaining five per cent are appointed.[6] Appointed boards occur most often in school districts enrolling over 25,-000 pupils.[7]

Local control is a characteristic that can be either advantageous or disadvantageous. The local school district, represented in personages by board members, often provides the closest relationship that many citizens have with a local form of government. This intimacy results not only from physical proximity, but also from the fact that schools deal with an extremely precious possession, the children of the people. Schools also frequently represent the agency which collects the largest amount of local tax monies. Fur-

4. Kenneth A. Simon and W. Vance Grant, *Digest of Educational Statistics*, p. 45.
5. Van Miller, *The Public Administration of American School Systems*, pp. 146–147.
6. *Ibid.*, p. 151–152.
7. Roald F. Campbell, Luvern L. Cunningham, and Roderick F. McPhee, *The Organization and Control of American Schools*, p. 165.

ther, education is viewed by more and more citizens as the most practical way to resolve social problems, particularly at the grass-roots level. There is little doubt that local control permits citizens to have their say in providing school programs that will be responsive to their local desires and needs. Conversely, local control also permits wide variances in educational opportunity. Local control historically has been conservative and provincial; each district's concern being for their own welfare without a strong regard for state or national problems. It can be argued, for example, that one factor, the mobility of our population, is sufficient reason to support greater centralization. Further, national domestic problems and our national defense require national policies and programs to be implemented in local schools. Social and economic trends in the last few years have resulted in a gradual erosion of local control of schools.

Federal-State-Local Interrelationships

The federal-state-local relationships of the past evolved as our country grew and developed. As our nation changed from basically a sparsely populated and agrarian society to an urban industrialized society, the nature of the federal-state-local relationship changed. While the states have been and still are the major source of legal control, the federal government has increased its influential and legal roles, particularly in efforts to assure constitutional rights and to respond to both foreign and domestic issues. The federal government's response to domestic problems which relate to education, such as poverty and segregation, and their tendency to attack such problems quite directly, rather than channel their efforts through state agencies, has at least in part caused state school officials to organize to have their views heard.[8] The Education Commission of the States was formed and currently has forty-one states and territories as members.[9] The stated purpose of the organization is to further a working relationship among state governors, legislators, and educators for the improvement of education. It is interesting to note that ECS is now playing a major role in national assessment, a project designed to assess educational achievement nationwide.[10] It has been suggested, however, that the *Education Commission of the States* represents a counterthrust toward more state-local direction of education.[11]

New federal-state-local relationships are emerging. Each level of government tends to look at the purposes of education from its own perspective: local school districts see their immediate local needs; states, the welfare of the state and its overall constituency; the federal government, its concern with equality, national security, and national domestic problems. While it is difficult to predict what the future relationships will be, it is clear that educational purposes and problems that are not resolved at the local level will likely be taken on by another level of government. The problems that we face seem to be of the magnitude that state

8. Roald F. Campbell, and Donald H. Layton, "Thrust and Counterthrust in Education Policy Making," *Phi Delta Kappan*, pp. 290–294.

9. Education Commission of the States. *Compact.* Vol. 3, No. 4.

10. Frank Womer, "ECS Takes Reins of National Assessment; Project Will Continue as Planned," *National Assessment of Educational Progress* 2 (1969):1.

11. *loc. cit.,* Campbell and Layton, pp. 290–294.

and federal involvements are necessary to resolve them. A new federal-state-local educational partnership is necessary and is emerging to forge solutions to problems of and related to education.

Teacher Power

As earlier portions of this chapter have indicated, public school control from a legal point of view is variously vested in federal, state, and local governments. This control, however, does not preclude the power of teachers through their organizations to exert considerable influence on the operations of schools. There was a time in our history when teachers for all practical purposes had little or no influence in determining the conditions of their employment, let alone have enough power to influence educational policies. In recent years, however, teachers have begun to exert their power through their professional organizations. Local teacher groups are affiliated with national organizations, namely the National Education Association with its one million plus membership, or the American Federation of Teachers, with its one hundred thousand plus membership located predominantly in urban centers. The topic of professional organizations and their roles in teacher power is considered in greater depth in chapter fourteen. Let it suffice to say at this point that today teachers do have power.

Teacher power is manifested at the local district level by the use of a local organization to press for negotiations. While the term negotiations has been defined in many ways, in terms of power it means a formalization of access procedures to the legally defined school power structure. Physically it results in a written document, called an

agreement, which most frequently spells out conditions of employment. The question of what is and what is not negotiable has not yet been clearly defined. It ranges from the broad definition of everything that affects a teacher, including curriculum, textbooks, in-service training, student teaching programs, and many other items to a narrow limitation considering just salaries. In some states the state legislature has clearly defined the subject matter for negotiation. In other states the issue is still wide open. Teacher groups have been extremely powerful in lobbying for and against various negotiation bills at the state level.

The power that teachers have gained, they have gained through organization. Their ultimate weapon has been a work stoppage or strike, which incidentally is not considered under the traditional judicial view as being legal. Nevertheless, the number of teacher strikes has steadily increased. It has been estimated that there have been 142 work stoppages by teachers since January, 1940, and that over 100 of these have occurred since 1964.[12]

The rise of teacher power should be accompanied by a corresponding rise in their responsibilities. Teachers have asked for, and in some cases demanded, a share in educational decision-making. In some cases these requests have been formalized, and in a sense legitimatized as a part of a negotiations agreement. In general teachers have expressed disagreement and resistance to the traditional flow of authority for decision making from the top down. They have been asking to be heard as citizens and as responsible, trained professionals. Their voices are being heard today. As they collectively

12. Stephen J. Knezevich, *Administration of Public Education,* pp. 369–370.

speak, they should be constantly aware of their responsibilities—responsibilities that they have as citizens and educators for the destinies of children and our society. If their actions and their use of power are perceived by many citizens as being irresponsible, it can be predicted that the power of the general public will be exerted as a counterthrust. The ultimate power for education in a democratic nation resides in the people.

QUESTIONS FOR DISCUSSION

1. What factors have caused the federal government to increase its participation in the educational enterprise?
2. Can education in the United States continue to be effective by continuing its long term tradition of local control? Provide a rationale for your answer.
3. What recommendations would you make in designing an organization at the level of state government to most effectively administer education?
4. Should members of local school boards be typically representative of the social composition of their respective communities? Why?
5. What role do you believe teachers should assume in fostering local educational improvements? How can they best use teacher power?

SUPPLEMENTARY LEARNING ACTIVITIES

1. Visit local school board meetings and report your observations to the class.
2. Invite members of the state legislature to your class to seek out their opinions on school legislation.
3. Examine copies of the school code for your state.
4. Invite persons from nonpublic schools to your class to seek out their opinions on the concept of the separation of church and state.
5. Invite officers from a local teachers' association to your class to seek out their opinions on teacher power.

SELECTED REFERENCES

American Association of School Administrators. *School District Organization.* Report of the AASA Commission on School District Reorganization. Washington, D.C.: The Association, 1958.

Barr, Richard H., and Betty J. Foster. *Fall 1968 Statistics of Public Schools.* Washington, D.C.: Superintendent of Documents, U.S. Government Printing Office, 1969.

Campbell, Roald F., and Donald H. Layton. "Thrust and Counterthrust in Education Policy Making." *Phi Delta Kappan* 49 (1968):290–294.

Campbell, Roald F., Luvern L. Cunningham, and Roderick F. McPhee. *The Organization and Control of American Schools.* Columbus, Ohio: Charles E. Merrill Publishing Co., 1965.

Campbell, Roald F., Gerald E. Stroufe, and Donald H. Layton. *Straightening State Departments of Education.* Chicago: Midwest Administration Center, University of Chicago Press, 1967.

Carlton, Patrick W. and Harold I. Goodwin. *The Collective Dilemma: Negotiations in Education.* Worthington, Ohio: Charles A. Jones Publishing Co., a division of Wadsworth Publishing Co., 1969.

Drury, Robert L. and Kenneth C. Ray. *Principles of School Law.* New York: Appleton-Century-Crofts, 1965.

Education Commission of the States. *Compact.* Vol. 3, No. 4, August 1969.

Elsbree, Willard S., Harold J. McNally, and Richard Wynn. *Elementary School Administration and Supervision.* New York: American Book Co., 1967.

Jones, James J., C. Jackson Salisbury, and Ralph L. Spencer. *Secondary School Administration.* New York: McGraw-Hill Book Co., 1969.

Knezevich, Stephen J. *Administration of Public Education.* 2nd ed. New York: Harper & Row, Publishers, 1969.

Lieberman, Myron. "Teacher Strikes: Acceptable Strategy?" *Phi Delta Kappan* 46(1965): 237–240.

Lieberman, Myron, and Michael H. Moskow. *Collective Negotiations for Teachers: An Approach to School Administration.* Chicago: Rand McNally and Co., 1966.

Miller, Van. *The Public Administration of American School Systems.* New York: The Macmillan Co., 1965.

National Council of Chief State School Officers. *The State Department of Education.* Washington, D.C.: The Council, 1952.

Nolte, Chester M. *An Introduction to School Administration: Selected Readings.* New York: The Macmillan Co., 1966.

Ostrander, Raymond H., and Ray C. Dethy. *A Values Approach to Educational Administration.* New York: American Book Co., 1968.

Reller, Theodore L., and Edgar L. Morphet. *Comparative Educational Administration.* Englewood Cliffs, N.J.: Prentice-Hall, Inc., 1962.

Simon, Kenneth A., and W. Vance Grant. *Digest of Educational Statistics, 1967.* Washington, D.C.: Superintendent of Documents, United States Government Printing Office, 1967.

Stinnett, T. M., Jack H. Kleinmann, and Martha L. Ware. *Professional Negotiation in Public Education.* New York: The Macmillan Co., 1966.

Education and the Renaissance
of State Government

James E. Allen

The case for the importance of state government, always a strong one, has been reinforced powerfully by the conditions and movements of our time. Objective and thoughtful analysis has made it increasingly clear that a nation as large and diverse as ours can not flourish either under the monolithic and inflexible governmental approach of excessive centralization or under the fragmented and provincial approach arising from too much control centered at the local level. The question, therefore, is not whether the state is important, but rather whether it can carry successfully the responsibilities that rest so clearly and urgently at this level of government.

With the philosophical concept of state government so strongly re-established and supported, concern for its continuing vitality now can be directed toward the practical matter of adjusting its machinery and its operation to the demands and dimensions of a rapidly changing era. These demands have generated three concepts of the role of state government which are and will be major factors in shaping the nature of the necessary adjustments.

The first of these concepts is that of a stronger state government in relation to its responsibilities to the people of the individual state. The second is that of the state as a liaison unit, bringing together greater Federal participation and growing local need in a balanced, orderly, and productive attack upon the problems of society. The third is that of state government recognizing our increasing unity as a nation and seeking to acknowledge the growing interdependence of the states through fuller, more realistic, and effective means of cooperation. As a major function of state government, education inevitably is affected by these concepts in terms of its structure, its organization, its operation, its financing—even of its aims and goals.

The demands that education now must seek to satisfy arise from a great variety of needs, problems, and new developments.

There are the pressures of rising expectations for education, of exploding knowledge, new advances in technology, and automation, of demands for justice for Negroes and other minority groups, of heightened demand for equality of opportunity, of dissatisfied teachers and parents seeking a more meaningful role in educational policy making, and of increasing Federal involvement in education. There are the problems of raising all our schools and colleges to a new level of quality, of redesigning and revitalizing our city school systems, of eliminating unnecessary school districts and reorganizing weak and ineffective districts, of

* James E. Allen, "Education and the Renaissance of State Government," *School and Society* 97 (1969): 148–151. Used by permission.

learning how to educate the poor and the seriously deprived, of eliminating racial isolation in schools and school districts, of updating the curriculum and keeping it up-to-date, of encouraging and helping teachers to keep abreast in scholarship and in technique, of opening opportunities for higher education for the disadvantaged, of bringing about reform and improvement in school administration and management, of financing sharply rising costs, and of developing better means of measuring the results of educational performance.

These pressures and problems, and others that could be cited, point to the nature and the scope of the educational action that is going to be required of the state. But it also is clear that if education, as one of the major functions of the state, is to play its proper part in the renaissance that must take place in state government generally, its decisions and actions also must reflect the three concepts which have emerged as major determinants of the character of state government in the future.

Reacting to these two influences, the role of the state in education is both changing in character and expanding in scope. For educator and political leader alike, this situation presents both obligation and opportunity. There must be a readiness to react, a willingness to innovate, to reform, to discard tradition where necessary, to be bold and daring, to consider new patterns of organization, and to enter into new relationships and to move decisively, with vision and imagination.

The leadership for the new role of the state in education obviously must be centered in state boards of education and in state education departments. It is essential, therefore, that these agencies be strong and

that whatever action necessary be taken to renew and reform in preparation for the higher level of leadership expected of them. For too long, weakness in the arrangements of the states for their governance of education has been tolerated, excused, ignored, and condoned. Weakness exists in varying degrees, of course, but complaints about the encroachment of the Federal government have a hollow ring indeed when measured against the undeniable default in too many instances of the exercise of state responsibility for education.

Pushed forward by a strong tide of increased expectation, educational advance will take place. If weak, the states surely will be engulfed, swept aside, for it will be impossible for them to accomplish what the people expect and society demands of education today. The kind of action, the types of programs that must be carried out by the state, demand strength and simply will be beyond the capabilities of state educational agencies that are not efficiently structured, adequately supported, suitably staffed, and realistically geared to the dimension of the educational task before us.

Fundamental to the educational task is the setting of goals. Here state boards of education and their administrative agencies must proceed with a clarity and a sharpness of definition that has not prevailed always in the past. Broadly generalized statements of goals will not satisfy the increasingly intense scrutiny of the public, of legislative bodies, hard-headed businessmen, and taxpayers. Vague statements of intention no longer will suffice, and support for education will be secured only by well-defined, precise presentations of goals that can be understood clearly and appraised accurately.

Also, there is no longer a willingness on the part of the public to wait for educational advance. The complacent kind of lethargy that once allowed a 50-year gap between the discovery of a new idea or practice and its widespread appearance in the schools has no place in a society that knows more and cares more about education than ever before. The development of our educational system must be planned carefully and tightly in such a way as to incorporate innovation quickly, to anticipate needs, and to be ready to meet them without the waste of hit-or-miss, stop-gap, hastily devised programs.

The concentration on education and the preoccupation with the pressures that are moving education today have brought forth a flood of new ideas and innovative practices. One of the main responsibilities of state educational agencies in a time of great urgency is, of course, to encourage and make provision for innovation. But even more, it is their responsibility to be prepared to guide the local educational agencies and to demonstrate, recommend, and help to disseminate those practices that hold greatest promise.

Central to the role of the state in education is the obligation to emphasize continually and insistently the goal of ever-higher quality. This obligation is two-fold; the state not only must encourage quality—and indeed not tolerate the existence of shoddiness in educational performance—but also must help to develop and to apply indicators of educational success. The degree of support that will be necessary to obtain the higher level of quality required of our times will depend more and more upon evaluation and accountability that can substantiate unequivocally successful performance.

The state's responsibility for education is to every child within its borders, no matter who he is, where he is, or what his condition or his needs may be. This responsibility has acquired a new sharpness of meaning and a new depth and breadth of dimension as society seeks more and more to make equality of opportunity a reality for all.

Local effort can do much to assure equality of opportunity, but many of the barriers that hinder the realization of this objective transcend the lines of locally constituted authority and must be the province of state action.

This has been demonstrated pointedly in the efforts that are being made to correct long-standing social and educational injustices. For example, the problem of the elimination of racial isolation in the schools can not be measured or attacked merely in terms of communities or local responsibility. Its effects are not confined so neatly, and its cure and prevention demand the combination of the full resources of community, region, and state. The broader view, the over-arching supervision of the state, are essential for the solution of a problem that in its insidious pervasiveness reaches out not only to handicap those directly affected in areas where the problem is acute, but to damage both moral and educational values in all areas. The same need for the exercise of state authority and for state supervision and guidance obtains in efforts to deal with the educational problems of those disadvantaged by poverty, social deprivation, and physical and mental handicaps.

It is becoming increasingly clear that one of the very practical and serious barriers to achievement of equality of educational opportunity is the outmoded structure of local school government. This affects not only efforts to eliminate segregation and to deal generally with the problems of disadvantagement, but acts to deny opportunity by fostering the continuance of small systems that do not have the resources to provide, especially at the secondary level, the full range of programs required for assuring equality of opportunity. It never must be forgotten that a local school district is a state agency of local jurisdiction. It exists to provide education of quality for all within its borders, and its success in this regard is the only justification for its continuing existence.

The planning for, and promotion of, the consolidation and reorganization of school districts is primarily a responsibility of the state, and state educational agencies are grievously delinquent if they do not provide a statewide plan and appropriate incentives to encourage action. If local action is not forthcoming, the state has the further responsibility of using its authority and resources to achieve the reorganization that will make possible the provision of full opportunity.

The whole question of equality of opportunity has its most dramatic focus in the plight of our city school systems. In a recent statement of policy and proposed action on urban education, the New York State Regents stated:

> The recent series of riots, boycotts and strikes have forced us to realize that no excuse can justify delay of a concerted effort to reform urban education. No task is more difficult or more essential; no issue forces us more seriously to adjust traditional policy and practice to new thought and action.

The states now must orient their services and their resources more strongly and intensively to the human needs of the inner-city. This is a matter of the greatest urgency, of the highest priority.

The proposals that the Regents have presented to the Governor and Legislature in New York for 1968 indicated, I believe, the kind of action that is required:

A. *Quality Incentive Grants* to the urban school districts which have the largest concentration of the "educationally poor." Half of the funds allocated to the urban districts would be available for school improvements throughout the district. The other half would be used specifically for projects in disadvantaged areas, in accordance with state approved plans, including the development and operation of day-long, year-round "community education centers," to serve persons of all ages.

B. *Urban Teacher Recruitment and Training* with emphasis upon seeking out and preparing talented personnel indigenous to disadvantaged areas for teaching in such areas. This program would include (1) internships in urban schools for college graduates; (2) pre-graduate internships for college students; (3) training of indigenous personnel for para-professional service; (4) special training in language skills for work with disadvantaged children.

C. *Planning Grants* for the development of long-range educational plans for central cities and their metropolitan areas and the support of demonstration projects that would test new educational arrangements within cities and between cities and suburbs.

The expansion and extension of state responsibility for education is indeed overwhelming and will tax to the utmost the capabilities and resources of state educational agencies. But education is so broad that both its needs and its effects are within the compass and concern of many other governmental and private agencies. Herein lies one of the richest and most promising resources for achieving educational goals, and state educational authorities must use this resource to the full in reaching out to establish new and creative relationships with these agencies. There has been a regrettable tendency in the past for state boards and state education departments to consider education as solely their province.

This kind of parochialism also has affected relationships among states and with the Federal government. It has no place in today's educational scene, for, just as many problems transcend local capabilities, so too are state capabilities transcended by the growing national character and emphasis of educational need. A sit-back or stand-off posture on the part of a state, a narrowly conceived states-rights attitude, will be detrimental not only to the national effort in education, but to state and local effort as well.

The Federal participation in the educational endeavor, which is a necessary and constructive development, can proceed in proper balance, facilitating rather than restricting freedom and creativity in our educational systems, and achieving maximum results only if the states wholeheartedly and purposefully assume their central role of liaison, guiding and directing Federal participation into channels which will yield significant benefits.

Equally detrimental will be a hesitation or a refusal on the part of states to enter into cooperative arrangements with other states that will combine and share experiences and provide a broader base for an attack on common educational problems. For this reason, I have given my full support to the Education Commission of the States, believing that this fledgling arrangement, with its coordination of political and educational

leadership, is one that holds great promise for the nurturing of a real renaissance of state power and effectiveness.

The state's role in education encompasses far more than I have been able to deal with in these remarks, but, even so limited, a survey seems to me to indicate that the states, in large measure, hold the key both to the pace and to the degree of educational progress that can be achieved in our nation.

Speaking to state school boards several years ago, I stated: "State boards of education stand today on the threshold of a great decision. Unless they take positive action soon, separately and cooperatively, to strengthen their role in the shaping of educational policies in America, they may be left with little to say and less to do about the vital function for which their respective states are constitutionally responsible." The pertinence of this warning has not diminished, and its message has application for general state government, as well as for education.

It is the health of our state governments that will determine our health as a nation. Strong, up-to-date state governments are the agencies most likely to be able to reduce the complexities of a nation so tremendous in size, so diverse in character, so enterprising in nature, and so dynamic in power, to manageable proportions that will continue to serve our cherished commitment to the individual and to encourage in our citizens a belief in their power to affect government that will engage them in the struggle to meet the needs of a changing world within the framework of our Federalistic form of government.

For the states, time is short. The potential is there. Steps have been taken to strengthen the states, to reinforce their powers of self-determination. But if these steps do not produce results, if the potential is not realized, if state power is not exercised, state government soon will find itself a very much weakened and an increasingly ineffective member of our three-way partnership of Federal-state-local government.

The three concepts that are shaping the search for greater vitality for the states constitute a foundation for optimism that the urgently needed renaissance in state government can and will take place. States stronger in relation to their responsibilities to their people, more effective as liaison agencies between Federal and local levels, and more active in interstate cooperation can realize their potential and carry out the ever-growing responsibilities that go along with the increasing importance of their strategic position in the structure of American government.

Massachusetts, like New York State, has a noble history as a state. Both have developed forms and institutions of government and education which have stood as landmarks through the years. But we can not rest on past laurels. A new era is upon us, calling for a new level of state leadership. May we, along with all the other states, have the courage and the determination necessary to provide that leadership.

CHAPTER 6

Financing the
Educational Enterprise

Education in the United States is big business. In 1966 there were nearly fifty million pupils enrolled in public and private elementary and secondary schools, over two million teachers employed to provide instruction for those students, and approximately twenty-six and one-half billion dollars spent for current operating expenditures to conduct the enterprise. It has been estimated that by 1976 there will be over fifty-two million pupils, over two and two-tenths million teachers, and current operating expenditures will exceed thirty-six billion dollars.[1] Another way to look at the magnitude of the enterprise is to recognize that in 1966 approximately one out of four persons in our population was enrolled in school, one out of sixteen white collar workers in the labor force was a teacher, and fifteen cents out of every tax dollar was expended for public education. It is also pertinent to note that in many communities the educational enterprise is the biggest business in the community.

Economics and Education

While it is true that our investment in education is a sizable amount, it is also true that among the nations of the world we are most able to support education. Figure 6.1 illustrates the per capita gross national product in United States dollars for the United States and other selected nations in 1965. The quotation presented from the AASA (page 144) reiterates our basic wealth and in a sense challenges our scale of priorities. It is interesting to note that in 1966, expenditures in the United States for the purchase and operation of automobiles were over twice that for public elementary and secondary education. Further, our expenditures for recreation and the sum of our expenditures for alcoholic beverages and tobacco were both about the same as our expenditures for education.[2]

While it approaches the impossible to estimate what proportion of the wealth of a nation *should* be allocated for education, it does seem clear that we in the United States are limited more by our willingness to pay than by our ability to pay. In other words, our task as a nation seems to be to delineate a hierarchy of values; that is, clearly spell

1. Kenneth A. Simon and Marie G. Fullam, *Projection of Educational Statistics to 1976–77.*
2. National Education Association, *What Everyone Should Know About Financing Our Schools*, p. 29.

out and place in rank order what we desire or what "ought to be." Once this is done we must commit monies to convert our words into action.

Education provides substantial economic returns for both society and individuals. At one time economists used a formula containing the elements of land, labor, and capital to estimate economic development. It soon became evident that another variable was exerting a significant influence. There is general agreement among economists that education is that significant variable. Using gross national product as an economic index, it can be shown that there is a positive relationship between gross national product and educational development. While this type of analysis is beset with some difficulties, such as comparable

United States	$3501
Canada	2451
Switzerland	2343
France	1910
West Germany	1900
United Kingdom	1817
Italy	1100
Japan	863
Mexico	455
Brazil	270
U.A.R. (Egypt)	160
India	101

Figure 6.1. Per Capita Gross National Product in U.S. Dollars for the United States and other Selected Nations, 1965.

Source: Adapted from National Education Association, *What Everyone Should Know About Financing Our Schools,* Washington, D.C.: National Education Association, 1968, p. 28.

Our economy has reached the opulent stage when it can provide the material needs of life and also support a wide range of services beyond these demands. The choice we must make, therefore, is whether education will rank high or low in our scale of priorities. The issue is not one of ability to finance an educational program consistent with the demands and responsibilities of this period. The nation has this ability. The issue is one of educational vision and of willingness to match this vision with appropriate fiscal action.

American Association of School Administrators
Financing Tomorrow's Schools.
National Education Association,
Washington, D.C.: 1960, p. 21.

data indices and the time lag associated with the contribution of education in terms of when the education was acquired and when its effects were realized, nevertheless the evidence does indicate the importance of education to economic development. Investment in education is an investment in the basic human resources of our society. A second benefit accrued to society from education is the training of skilled manpower. As the demand for unskilled labor decreases, and concomitantly the demand for skilled labor increases, education can fulfill the need to train the skilled manpower our society needs. In terms of individual economic returns, let it suffice to say that in our society the average income of families headed by high school graduates is almost double that of those who did not complete elementary school.[3]

3. *Ibid.,* p. 7.

Social development, closely intertwined with economic development, is also related to education. A basic premise undergirding our form of government is that informed citizens are necessary to our national survival. The skills necessary to be an informed citizen (such as literacy), and the skills necessary for problem solving are acquired through education. The values of society, or the ways of life that we cherish, are transmitted in part through our educational system.

Investment in education is an investment in society, both economically and socially. Education in a sense is the servant of society. Americans must continue to use education to foster the achievement of their ideals.

> There are obviously two educations. One should teach us how to make a living, and the other how to live.
>
> James Truslow Adams

> The whole people must take upon themselves the education of the whole people and must be willing to bear the expense of it.
>
> John Adams

Taxation

The monies used to finance the public educational enterprise today come largely from taxation. It has not always been so. In colonial America monies for schools were often obtained from lotteries and charitable contributions. Churches of the various denominations financed education for some. It was not unusual in the very early days of our nation for the patrons of the schools to provide services such as supplying wood, making building repairs, or boarding teachers in lieu of money.

Public support for education in this nation in terms of taxes was secured only after a long, hard battle. In the early 1800's the movement for free public schools gained impetus. Pennsylvania in 1834 became the first state to adopt free elementary education. In 1872, the village of Kalamazoo, Michigan voted to establish a public high school to be supported by taxation. A lawsuit was filed to test the legality of using taxation to provide a high school. The opinion of the State Supreme Court of Michigan was that the action was legal and constitutional. By the end of the nineteenth century, public schools were financed almost completely by local funds derived from local taxation.

Today money to support education comes from a variety of taxes collected by local, state and federal governments. These governments in turn distribute taxes to local school districts to operate their schools. The three major kinds of taxes used to provide revenue for schools are property taxes, sales or use taxes, and income taxes. In general, local governments use the property tax, state governments rely upon the sales tax—though they are increasingly using the income tax—and the federal government relies heavily upon the income tax.

It is pertinent to note the percentage of support for public elementary and secondary schools contributed by each level of government. In 1920–21, about 83.0 per cent of school revenues came from local governmental sources, 16.5 per cent from state sources, and about .3 per cent from federal sources.[4] Over the years this has changed with a marked increase in state support, and most recently in 1965, a definite increase in federal support. Figure 6.2 illustrates the per cent of revenue received from the three sources since 1957.

While Figure 6.2 provides data from an overall national viewpoint, an examination of the data from selected individual states reveals wide ranges from the national statistics. It should be remembered that education is a function of the state and therefore variability is to be expected. Figure 6.3 illustrates the estimated per cent of revenue by governmental source for public elementary and secondary schools in 1967–68 for selected states. The states are arranged in the table in a descending order in terms of local support (Fig. 6.3).

The variation in state financial support illustrated in Figure 6.3 represents primar-

State	Per Cent of Revenue		
	Local	State	Federal
Nebraska	87.5	3.9	8.5
Illinois	71.4	22.7	5.8
California	61.3	34.0	4.6
Maryland	52.0	39.8	8.3
Florida	44.3	43.7	12.0
Mississippi	31.6	50.2	18.2
Alaska	30.2	40.4	29.5
North Carolina	20.4	66.6	13.1
New Mexico	19.1	64.0	16.9
Hawaii	5.1	84.4	10.4

Figure 6.3. Estimated Per Cent of Revenue by Governmental Source for Public Elementary and Secondary Schools, 1967–68, for Selected States.

Source: Research Division, National Education Association, Rankings of the States, 1968 Research Report 1968-R1. Washington, D.C.: National Education Association, pp. 44–46.

ily a variation in general state aid. That is, state monies are provided to supplement the local education effort and for the most part are not "earmarked" or "tagged" for special purposes or programs. The variation in federal support in the main is a reflection of *categorical aid;* that is, specific aid for a specific purpose or to resolve a unique problem. For example, the Smith-Hughes Act provided a stimulus for vocational education; the National Defense Education Act of 1958 emphasized the enhancement of science, mathematics, foreign languages, and counseling services; the Elementary and Secondary Act of 1965 had as one important feature the provision of monies to assist school districts in providing programs for children of poverty. Other federal aid programs are designed to aid school districts that are affected by federally induced pop-

School Year	Federal	State	Local
1957–58	4.0%	39.4%	56.6%
1959–60	4.4	39.1	56.5
1961–62	4.3	38.7	56.9
1963–64	4.4	39.3	56.4
1965–66	7.9	39.1	53.0
1966–67*	7.9	39.1	53.0
1967–68*	8.0	39.3	52.7
1968–69*	7.3	40.7	52.0

* NEA Research Division Estimates.

Figure 6.2. Per Cent of Revenue Received from Federal, State, and Local Sources for Public Elementary and Secondary Schools.

Source: Committee on Educational Finance, National Education Association. *Financial Status of the Public Schools 1969.* Washington, D.C.: National Education Association, 1969, p. 60.

4. Stephen J. Knezevich, *Administration of Public Education*, p. 422.

ulation impaction such as may occur near a military installation or major federal research installation. Both state and federal aid are aimed at enhancing equality of opportunity, which is to be considered later in this chapter.

As was mentioned earlier, the local support for schools comes predominantly from the property tax. The property tax is one of the oldest forms of taxation, based on the premise that a measure of a man's property was a measure of his wealth. Property is most often considered in two categories, real estate and personal. Personal property may include such things as automobiles, furniture, machinery, livestock, jewelry, and less tangible items as stocks and bonds. The property tax was particularly appropriate for an agrarian economy.

The property tax, as with most forms of taxation, has both distinct advantages and disadvantages. Its major advantage is that it provides a regular and stable form of income. While it is perhaps not as sensitive to economic changes as the sales and income taxes, neither is it absolutely rigid. In fact, recent studies have indicated that it is quite elastic and responsive to economic growth.[5, 6] The stability of the property tax will likely cause it to continue to be the mainstay of local public school support.

A major disadvantage of the property tax has to do with establishing equality of assessment. In other words, parcels of property of equal value should be assessed at the same value. This is extremely difficult to accomplish. Wide variations exist within school districts, states, and the nation. A recent study indicated variation in assessment of residential property from 5.9 per cent of sale value in one state to 66.2 per cent in another.[7] Inequality of assessment causes the property tax to be an unfair tax.

The property tax is most generally thought of as a proportionate tax, that is, one that taxes according to ability to pay. However, inequality of assessment and the trend in an urban economy for wealth to be less related to real estate than it was in an agrarian economy have caused the tax to become somewhat regressive. Regressive taxes are those such as sales and use taxes that have a relatively greater impact on lower income groups.

State support for schools comes mainly from the sales tax and income tax. As of 1968, thirty-eight states had a personal income tax, forty-one had a corporate income tax, and forty-four had a general sales tax. Sales and income taxes are lucrative sources of state revenue. Both taxes are relatively easy to administer. The sales tax is collected bit by bit by the vendor and he is responsible for record keeping and remitting the tax to the state. The state income tax can be withheld from wages, hence facilitating collections. The sales tax is considered a *regressive tax* because all persons pay the sales tax at the same rate; therefore, persons in low income groups pay nearly as much tax for essentials as do those in high income groups. Income taxes are referred to as *progressive taxes* because they are frequently

5. John Shannon, "Property Taxation: Toward a More Equitable, Productive Revenue Source," *Trends in Financing Public Education.* Washington, D.C.: National Education Association, 1965, pp. 136–143.

6. U.S. Department of Commerce, Bureau of the Census, *Finances of School Districts,* 1962 Census of Governments, Vol. IV, No. 1. Washington, D.C.: Government Printing Office, 1963.

7. National Education Association, *What Everyone Should Know About Financing Our Schools,* p. 37.

scaled to the ability of the taxpayer to pay. Both state sales and income taxes are direct and certain, they are responsive to changes in the economy, and they can be regulated by the state legislature which is responsible for raising the money. It is interesting to note that in 1966, nationwide 58 per cent of all state revenue came from sales taxes, 21 per cent from income taxes, and 2.8 per cent from property taxes. The remainder came from licenses and miscellaneous taxes.

Federal support for schools comes from monies raised primarily from personal and corporate income taxes. These two taxes account for over eighty per cent of all tax collections by the federal government.

Equality of Opportunity

The opportunity for equal education is related to the financial ability of specific areas to pay for education. While wealth is not the only factor related to equality of opportunity, as was pointed out by the *Brown* decision, it certainly is an important one.

Children are educated in local school districts, which by and large, still produce nationwide about 52 per cent of the monies used for education. These monies are raised primarily with the property tax, and therefore are dependent upon the real estate wealth of the district. Wealthy districts, therefore, can provide more monies for education than poor districts with the same tax effort. Suppose, for example, that the total assessed valuation, that is, the value of all the property as determined by a tax assessor of a district, is $100,000,000 and that the district has 2000 pupils. This hypothetical district would have then an assessed valuation of $50,000 per pupil. A tax rate of $2 per $100 of assessed valuation would pro-

duce $1000 per pupil. By the same token if a neighboring district had an assessed evaluation of only $10,000 per pupil the same $2 per $100 rate would produce only $200 per pupil. With the same rate, or the same effort, one of these districts could spend $1000 per pupil while the other could spend only $200. In general, this results in children in wealthy districts being provided greater opportunities for education than children in poor districts.

Great differences can exist in wealth per pupil from school district to school district. Industrial developments can increase valuations in some districts, while at the same time neighboring districts may be largely residential with little valuation and large numbers of pupils. In the state of Illinois, for example, in a comparison of districts providing education for pupils K–12, the assessed valuation per pupil ranges from $4500 to $115,000.

States have recognized the disparaging differences in wealth among local districts and through state aid programs have attempted to provide financial equalization for educational purposes. This makes good sense, particularly since the state has the primary responsibility for education.

State aid can be classified by its use as being either general or categorical. General aid may be used by the recipient school district as it desires. Categorical aid is "earmarked" for specific purposes. Examples of categorical aid include monies for speech, driver education, vocational education, or transportation. Categorical aid is sometimes used as an incentive to encourage programs that are perceived as being needed.

General aid usually represents the states' efforts to equalize opportunity. The underlying premise is that each child, regardless of his place of residence or the wealth of the particular school district in which he lives, is entitled to receive essential basic educational opportunities. General aid is usually administered through some type of foundation program. The foundation concept involves the establishment of a per pupil dollar value which represents the desired foundation education in a state. The usual connotation of the word "foundation" is basic or minimum. Therefore, the foundation level is usually less than the actual per pupil expenditures. For example, the per pupil foundation level in Illinois in 1967–68 was $400; at the same time current operating expenditures per pupil were $621. A state in establishing a foundation level is in effect assuring that the amount of the per pupil foundation level will be expended for education for each pupil in the state. Foundation programs do encourage equality of opportunity from a financial viewpoint; however, it is pertinent to observe that they assure equalization only to a prescribed level. Districts can and do vary greatly in their expenditure per pupil.

The actual monies used to achieve the foundation level expenditures come from both state and local sources. Most often a minimum local tax rate is established, and the money this tax rate produces is subtracted from the foundation level with the remainder being paid by the state. The local tax rate will produce more money in a wealthy district than it will in a poor district. This concept is also a part of the equalization principle. Figure 6.4 presents a graphic representation of equalization and the foundation principle. It is important to note, however, that local districts can, and frequently do, spend more than the foundation level.

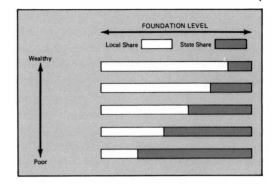

Figure 6.4. The Principle of Equalization as Related to the Foundation Level.

Differences in wealth exist among states just as they do among school districts within states. Since assessment practices vary from state to state it is difficult to use assessed valuation per pupil as an index to compare the wealth of states. A more accurate index is personal income per child. Figure 6.5 illustrates the variance in wealth among selected states.

State	Expenditures Per Pupil	Personal Income Per Child
New York	918	14,848
Connecticut	707	14,793
California	653	13,622
Wisconsin	611	11,033
United States	573	11,419
Illinois	572	13,927
New Mexico	512	7,785
Kentucky	438	8,514
Arkansas	398	7,769
Mississippi	339	6,162

Figure 6.5. Current Expenditures Per Pupil 1966–67 and Personal Income Per Child of School Age 5–17 in Selected States, 1966.

Source: Research Division, National Education Association, *Rankings of the States, 1968*, Research Report 1968-R-1. Washington, D.C.: National Education Association, pp. 31, 54.

Figure 6.5 also illustrates the wide variance in expenditure per pupil in the United States. New York's expenditure of $918 per pupil in 1966–67 was the highest, while Mississippi's expenditure of $339 was the lowest. The relationship between expenditure per pupil and personal income per child, while not perfect, does illustrate that high per pupil expenditures are directly associated with high personal income per child and that low per pupil expenditures are associated with low personal income per child. It is interesting to note that New Mexico and Mississippi, with relatively high state and federal aid (Figure 6.3), are still below the national average per pupil expenditure.

As was indicated previously in this chapter federal aid has increased. However, as was discussed in chapter five, the aid has been categorical. The Elementary and Secondary Act of 1965 with its emphasis toward improving educational opportunities for children of poverty, while categorical, came as close to general aid as any federal aid ever has. Greater federal support is necessary to bolster equality among states.

In summary, a first step in achieving equality of opportunity in education can be to equalize per pupil expenditures. Further, this equalization must represent a high level of support. Is it possible to equalize expenditures nationally when wide discrepancies exist in local and state wealth, and when at the same time nationally 52 per cent of the support for schools comes from local sources, 40.7 per cent from state sources, and 7.3 per cent from federal sources?

State and federal governments must provide a greater portion of support for schools if equality of opportunity is to be achieved. Both these levels of government can use the progressive income tax, the most fair tax, to gain access to funds. This is not to say that local support is not important. Local interest and initiative, unique to our system, should be expressed. Local financial contributions enhance the opportunity for local initiative. Nevertheless, the social and economic problems that prevail in our nation today, for which education can be a part of the solution, require more monies than can be raised locally. In a very pragmatic sense, it does not seem possible for local school districts, using only local resources, to resolve state and national problems.

Expectations and Expenses

Early in this chapter it was said that our expenditures for education were limited more by our willingness to pay than our ability to pay. Do we have the willingness to support our expectations for education? What are our national priorities? As a nation compared to other nations in the world we are wealthy. We do, however, have pockets of poverty. Parts of our nation are more able than others to support education. If as a *nation* we believe that education is important, and that education can help us achieve our national goals and professed ideals, than we must muster and utilize our financial resources accordingly.

QUESTIONS FOR DISCUSSION

1. What are the relationships between education and economic and social developments in a nation?
2. What are the three main kinds of taxes used to produce revenue for schools? Discuss each of these in terms of their productivity and fairness.

3. What factors in our society have caused the change in the educational support level provided by the three levels of government?
4. What have been some of the noticeable effects of both state and federal categorical aid in the public schools of your area?
5. Do you feel that nationwide equality of opportunity from a financial viewpoint can be achieved under our existing tax structure? Defend your position.

Supplementary Learning Activities

1. Collect and examine data related to the wealth of school districts in your immediate area or state.
2. Invite a county or township tax assessment official to your class to discuss the assessing process in your area.
3. Study and evaluate the foundation plan of state support for education in your state.
4. Conduct a survey to assess the feelings of citizens about various forms of taxation as they relate to the schools.
5. Interview members of the Board of Education in your immediate area to determine their opinions about financing of schools.

Selected References

American Association of School Administrators. *Education Is Good Business*. Washington, D.C.: American Association of School Administrators, 1966.

Benson, Charles S. *Perspectives on the Economics of Education*. Boston: Houghton Mifflin Co., 1963.

Burke, Arvid J. *Financing Public Schools in the United States*. New York: Harper & Row, Publishers, 1957.

Burkhead, Jesse. *Public School Finance: Economics and Politics*. Syracuse, New York: Syracuse University Press, 1964.

Campbell, Roald F., Luvern L. Cunningham, and Roderick F. McPhee. *The Organization and Control of American Schools*. Columbus, Ohio: Charles E. Merrill Publishing Co., 1965.

Coleman, James S. *Equality of Educational Opportunity*. Washington, D.C.: U.S. Department of Health, Education and Welfare, 1966.

Conant, James B. *Shaping Educational Policy*. New York: McGraw-Hill Book Co., 1964.

Gauerke, Warren E., and Jack R. Childress, eds. *The Theory and Practice of School Finance*. Skokie, Illinois: Rand McNally & Co., 1967.

Hill, Frederick W., and James W. Colmey. *School Business Administration in the Smaller Community*. Minneapolis: T. S. Denison and Co., Inc., 1964.

Innes, Jon T., Paul B. Jacobson, and Roland J. Pellegrin. *The Economic Returns to Education*. Eugene, Oregon: Center for Advanced Study of Educational Administration, University of Oregon, 1965.

Johns, Roe L., and Edgar L. Morphet. *Financing the Public Schools*. Englewood Cliffs, N.J.: Prentice-Hall, Inc., 1960.

———. *The Economics and Financing of Education, A Systems Approach*. 2nd ed. Englewood Cliffs, N.J.: Prentice-Hall, Inc., 1969.

Knezevich, Stephen J. *Administration of Public Education*. 2nd ed. New York: Harper & Row, Publishers, 1969.

Lindman, Erick L., ed. *The Federal Government and Public Schools*. Washington, D.C.: American Association of School Administrators, 1965.

Morphet, Edgar L., Roe L. Johns and Theodore L. Reller. *Educational Organization and Administration*. 2nd ed. Englewood Cliffs, N.J.: Prentice-Hall, Inc., 1967.

Mort, Paul R., Walter O. Reusser, and John W. Polley. *Public School Finance*. New York: McGraw-Hill, Inc., 1960.

National Education Association. *Rankings of the States 1968 Research Report, 1968–R1*. Washington, D.C.: National Education Association, 1968.

————. *What Everyone Should Know About Financing Our Schools.* Washington, D.C.: National Education Association, 1968.

Schultz, Theodore W. *The Economic Value of Education.* New York: Columbia University Press, 1963.

Simon, Kenneth A., and Marie G. Fullam. *Projections of Educational Statistics to 1976–77.* Washington, D.C.: Superintendent of Documents, United States Government Printing Office, 1968.

Accountability for Results:
A Basic Challenge to America's Schools

Leon M. Lessinger

Today, too many young Americans leave school without the tools of learning, an interest in learning, or any idea of the relationship of learning to jobs. It is a mocking challenge that so many of our children are not being reached today by the very institution charged with the primary responsibility for teaching them. A Committee for Economic Development report issued in the summer of 1968 summarizes the indictment: Many schools and school districts, handicapped by outmoded organization and a lack of research and development money, are not providing "the kind of education that produces rational, responsible, and effective citizens."

Now, the educational establishment—right down to the local level—is being asked ever more insistently to acount for the results of its programs. This fast-generating nationwide demand for accountability promises a major and long overdue redevelopment of the management of the present educational system, including an overhaul of its cottage-industry form of organization. Many believe this can be accomplished by making use of modern techniques currently employed in business and industry, some of which are already being used in the educational enterprise.

Before America's schools can productively manage the massive amount of money entrusted to them—and the even greater amount they need—they must be armed with better management capability. If education is going to be able to manage its budget properly, it must devise measurable relationships between dollars spent and results obtained. Education, like industry, requires a system of quality assurance. Anything less will shortchange our youth.

Sputniks and satellite cities, computers and confrontation politics, television and the technology of laborsaving devices—all have placed new and overwhelming demands on our educational system. Americans could say with the angel Gabriel of *Green Pastures*, that "everything nailed down is coming loose." How can we provide the kind of education that would assure full participation for all in this new complex technological society? How to prepare people to respond creatively to rapid-fire change all their lives while maintaining a personal identity that would give them and their society purpose and direction? How to do this when the body of knowledge has so exploded that it no longer can be stored in a single mind? How to do this when cybernetics is changing man's function? How to do this when the cost of old-fashioned education soars higher every year with little significant improvement?

* Leon Lessinger, "Accountability for Results: A Basic Challenge to America's Schools," *American Education* 5(1969):2–4.

In 1965 the passage of the far-reaching Elementary and Secondary Education Act gave the public schools of America a clear new mandate and some of the funds to carry it out. It was a mandate not just for equality of educational opportunity but for equity in results as well. In place of the old screening, sorting, and reject system that put students somewhere on a bell shaped curve stretching from A to F, the schools were asked to bring educational benefits to every young person to prepare him for a productive life. Under the new mandate the schools were expected to give every pupil the basic competence he needed, regardless of his so-called ability, interest, background, home, or income. After all, said a concerned Nation, what's the purpose of grading a basic skill like reading with A, B, C, D, or F when you can't make it at all today if you can't read?

In essence, this meant that education would be expected to develop a "zero reject system" which would guarantee quality in skill acquisition just as a similar system now guarantees the quality of industrial production. Today's diplomas are often meaningless warranties. In the words of one insistent inner-city parent, "Many diplomas aren't worth the ink they're written in." We know, for example, that there are some 30,000 functional illiterates—people with less than fifth grade reading ability—in the country today who hold diplomas. And untold more are uncovered each day as manpower training and job programs bring increasing numbers of hardcore unemployed into the labor market.

Instead of certifying that a student has spent so much time in school or taken so many courses, the schools should be certifying that he is able to perform specific tasks.

Just as a warranty certifies the quality performance of a car, a diploma should certify a youngster's performance as a reader, a writer, a driver, and so on.

If, then, the new objective of education is to have zero rejects through basic competence for all, how can the educational establishment retool to respond to this new challenge? Developing a system of quality assurance can help provide the way.

The first step toward such a system is to draw up an overall educational redevelopment plan. Such a plan must first translate the general goal of competence for all students into a school district's specific objectives. These objectives must be formulated in terms of programs, courses, buildings, curriculums, materials, hardware, personnel, and budgets. The plan must incorporate a timetable of priorities for one year, for five years, 10 years, and perhaps even for 20 years. Such a plan should be based on "market research," that is, an investigation of the needs of the students in each particular school. It should also be based on research and development to facilitate constant updating of specifications to meet these needs. Through the plan the school district would be able to measure its own output against the way its students actually perform. It would be able to see exactly what results flow from the dollars it has invested.

The purpose of the educational redevelopment plan, of course, is to provide a systematic approach for making the changes in educational organization and practice necessitated by the new demands on the education system. To assure that the plan will provide quality, it should use a mix of measurements that are relevant, reliable, objective, easily assessable, and that produce data in a form that can be processed by modern-day technology. As a further guarantee of quality, teams of school administrators, teachers, and modern educational and technical specialists competent to interpret the results should be available. The plan should also spell out a clear relationship between results and goals, thus providing for accountability.

In reality, this educational plan is only a piece of paper—a set of ideals and a set of step-by-step progressions which schools and districts can approximate. But it does provide a blueprint for the educational managers of the district—the superintendent, teachers, principals, and school boards—who must provide the leadership and the understanding to carry out educational change.

To be effective and to assure that its specifications remain valid, an educational redevelopment plan must set aside dollars for research and development. The Committee for Economic Development in last summer's report revealed that less than one percent of our total national education investment goes into research and development. "No major industry," the report said, "would expect to progress satisfactorily unless it invested many times that amount in research and development." Many private companies plow as much as 15 per cent of their own funds back into research and development.

If one percent of the yearly budget for education was set aside for research and development, we would have a national educational research and development fund of roughly $500 million. Such money could attract new services, new energies, new partnerships to education. And they would inspire competition that would spur rapid educational development. This research and development money could be used to buy

technical assistance, drawing on the expertise of private industry, the nonprofit organizations, the universities, the professions, and the arts. The administrative functions of a school system—construction, purchasing, disbursement, personnel, payroll—also demand business and management skills.

Why not draw on business for technical assistance or actual management in these areas? Or for that matter, in formulating the educational redevelopment plan itself? The final step in setting up a quality assurance system is providing for accountability of both the educational process and its products, the students. Do pupils meet the overall objectives and the performance specifications that the school considers essential? Can Johnny read, write, figure? Can he also reason? Can he figure out where to find a given piece of information not necessarily stored in his head? Does he understand enough about himself and our society to have pride in his culture, a sureness about his own personal goals and identity, as well as an understanding of his responsibilities to society? Does he have the various cognitive and social skills to enter a wide range of beginning jobs and advance in the job market?

The accountability of process, of classroom practice, is somewhat harder to get at. At the risk of mixing it up with ideas about educational hardware, we might call it the technology of teaching. To find out a little about it, we might start by asking whether things are being done differently today in a particular classroom than they were done in the past.

A host of disenchanted teachers and others—from Bel Kaufman in her *Up the Down Staircase* to Jonathan Kozol in *Death at an Early Age*—have been telling us over the past few years what has up to now been happening in many classrooms in America. In *The Way It Spozed To Be,* James Herndon, a California schoolteacher, describes one kind of advice he got from experienced teachers during his first year in an inner-city school: "This advice was a conglomeration of dodges, tricks, gimmicks to get the kids to do what they were spozed to do. . . . It really involved gerrymandering of the group—promises, favors, warnings, threats . . . A's, plusses, stars. . . . The purpose of all these methods was to get and keep an aspect of order . . . so that 'learning could take place. . . .'"

Today, teachers often try to teach order, responsibility, citizenship, punctuality, while believing that they are in fact teaching reading or French or gym. If Johnny forgets his pencil, for example, he actually may not be permitted to take the French quiz and might get an F—presumably for forgetfulness, certainly not for French, for the grade does not reflect Johnny's competence in French.

In one state's schools, girls' physical education regularly chalks up far more F's than any other course. A study of the reasons indicated that gym teachers actually were attempting to measure citizenship by tallying whether Jane kept a dirty locker or failed to take a shower. The grade hardly reflected her competence in physical education. Requirements such as punctuality, neatness, order, and time served, ought not to be used to reflect school subject mastery.

Despite considerable evidence to the contrary, many schools and teachers are still grouping youngsters as good or bad raw material. What can you do with bad raw material? some teachers ask, much as some doctors once asked about the mentally ill.

What we are searching for in place of a "demonology" of teaching is sensitive and sensible classroom practice—a practice that treats every child as a person and uses a variety of pleasurable techniques to improve his performance in anticipated and replicable ways. We are not sure this will result in more learning—though we think it will—but we do know that sensitive and sensible classroom practice is good in itself. As such it will pay off in human ways, even if it doesn't pay off in learning.

As teachers' salaries rise and their demands for rights and benefits are rightfully met by the communities they serve, those communities can expect that teacher responsibility will also grow. In fact, they can insist on it. They can insist that better pay, more rights, and more status bring with them better standard practice in the schools and classrooms. They can insist that teachers become accountable for relating process and procedures to results. And pupil accomplishment, though it may reflect some new hardware and construction, by and large reflects teacher and administrator growth and development. This is the true meaning of a new technology of teaching.

Thus the changes that result when the redevelopment plan has been carried out must be demonstrably apparent in terms of both teacher and pupil progress. In order to measure how these actual results compare to the detailed objectives of the plan, it makes sense to call for an outside educational audit, much like the outside fiscal audit required of every school system today. The school system could request an audit either of its overall program or of specific parts of that program.

This new approach could conceivably lead to the establishment of a new category of certified educational auditors whose principal job would be to visit school districts, on invitation, to help determine the success of local program planning in achieving pre-stated goals. One expert suggests that an educational audit need take only 10 school days a year for a single school system. His idea is to send a completely equipped and staffed mobile educational audit van to visit about 20 school systems a year.

Educators should also be encouraged to describe and measure the behavior expected of each student upon completion of programs funded from Federal sources. To reinforce accountability for results, contracts for Federal funds might be written as performance agreements. Thus a proposal for funds to back a reading program might stipulate that 90 per cent of the participating students would be able to satisfy criteria by demonstrating they had achieved a particular advance in grade level in the time proposed.

Furthermore, special financial incentives based on meeting performance criteria might be specified in these contracts. For example, a certain amount of dollars might be awarded to a school for each student who achieves a high school diploma (defined as a verification that 16 credits have been attained in specific subjects with a credit defined as 72 hours of successful classroom study). Or a school might be given monetary awards for each student who has been employed for a year after leaving the institution.

Lest the idea of performance contracts strike anyone as novel or bordering upon the impossible, it should be pointed out that they have been formulated and applied with great success by both industry and the armed services for years. The fact that many results of education are subjective and not subject to audit should not stop us from dealing precisely with those aspects that do lend themselves to definition and assessment.

Most directors of ESEA projects should have more training in how to manage large sums of money than they have had in the past. Anyone who knows business knows you don't run half-million and million-dollar programs without considerable expertise in management. Obviously, managers of these projects need technical assistance if they are to manage in the best and most modern sense. For example, there should be technical reviews of all successful programs, practices, and materials used in embryo experimental projects. Educational objectives should be translated into a clearer framework for the purposes of reporting, evaluation, and feedback. In most cases, schools would need outside technical assistance to carry out either of these tasks.

Greater educational management competence is also needed in an area that might be called "educational logistics." Many projects don't get off the ground because the equipment, personnel, and training they depend upon are not properly coordinated. The notion of staging, for example, to bring together all the elements that are necessary for a project to achieve performance, is very important. Virtually the only time you see this, in education in general as well as in ESEA projects, is in the school drama programs or on the athletic field.

Today formal education is the chief path to full citizenship. School credits and diplomas and licenses are milestones on that path. Schooling is literally the bridge—or the barrier—between a man and his ability to earn his bread. Without it a citizen is condemned to economic obsolescence almost before he begins to work.

If we accept competence for all as one of the major goals of education today, then we must devise a system of accountability that relates education's vast budget to results. It is a paradox that while our technologically oriented society is a masterful producer of the artifacts our civilization needs, it seems incapable of applying that technology to educating our young citizens.

We can change the way our educational system performs so that the desired result —a competently trained young citizenry— becomes the focus of the entire process. In the same way that planning, market studies, research and development, and performance warranties determine industrial production and its worth to consumers, so should we be able to engineer, organize, refine, and manage the educational system to prepare students to contribute to the most complex and exciting country on earth.

The Learning Process

Section III is concerned with the learning process and basic to this process is the learner. There are many different kinds of learners; differing, for example, in age, intelligence, background and purposes. In fact, no two individuals are exactly alike. By the same token it is doubtful that they learn in the same way. Teachers, and others who work in education, find that knowledge about human growth and development, variability, and motivation, is valuable knowledge to have.

A second important part of the learning process is the curriculum. In most basic terminology the curriculum consists of "what is taught, or perhaps, what is learned." While experts might disagree on the technical definitions of curriculum, for purposes of this book it is defined as consisting of three parts: (1) *goals,* or what students should learn, (2) *methodology,* or how they are going to learn it, and (3) *evaluation,* or how well students have learned. The teacher as a front line person interacting daily with students can be a valuable resource person in developing curriculum.

In the past decade tremendous strides have been made in the area of instructional resources. Chapter nine is devoted to this pertinent and important topic. Multi-media resources, while frequently used by one teacher or one learner, are also often used with para-professional help. Many of the resources are helpful in individualizing instruction.

The learning process is both fascinating and frustrating. When learning occurs, teaching can be a most gratifying profession. When learning does not occur, teaching can be challenging and frustrating. Teachers exist to facilitate the learning process.

CHAPTER 7

The Nature of Learners

I TAUGHT THEM ALL

I have taught in high school for ten years. During that time I have given assignments, among others, to a murderer, an evangelist, a pugilist, a thief, and an imbecile.

The murderer was a quiet little boy who sat on the front seat and regarded me with pale blue eyes; the evangelist, easily the most popular boy in the school, had the lead in the junior play; the pugilist lounged by the window and let loose at intervals a raucous laugh that startled even the geraniums; the thief was a gay-hearted Lothario with a song on his lips; and the imbecile, a soft-eyed little animal seeking the shadows.

The murderer awaits death in the state penitentiary; the evangelist has lain a year now in the village churchyard; the pugilist lost an eye in a brawl in Hong Kong; the thief, by standing on tiptoe, can see the windows of my room from the county jail; and the once gentle-eyed little moron beats his head against a padded wall in the state asylum.

All of these pupils once sat in my room, sat and looked at me gravely across worn brown desks. I must have been a great help to those pupils—I taught them the rhyming scheme of the Elizabethan sonnet and how to diagram a complex sentence.[1]

The primary responsibility of a teacher is leading learning activities. While the teaching task is for the most part centered around a group of learners, the teacher must be sensitive to the uniqueness of each learner within his group. The brief quote above suggests that the function of teaching may be so subject-centered as to not be meaningful or relevant for individual learners within the classroom setting.

Teachers sometimes tend to minimize the fact that learning is natural. Children do not

1. N.J.W. "I Taught Them All," *The Clearing House,* November, 1937.

have to be forced to learn; they have to be forcibly restrained to prevent them from learning something. But this does not mean that they will learn what we want them to learn. Teaching may be generally defined as the process by which one person helps others achieve new skills, knowledge, and attitudes. While teaching involves both the teacher and the learner, learning is an activity of the learner. Guidance for the learner is provided by good teachers who help create conditions which direct learning toward that which they do want to be learned.

Teachers at all levels need mastery of their subject-matter specialization. However, mastery of subject-matter areas is not

> Education is the leading of human souls to what is best, and making what is best out of them; and these two objects are always attainable together, and by the same means; the training which makes men happiest in themselves also makes them most serviceable to others.
>
> John Ruskin

enough. In most states, before the teaching certificate is issued prospective teachers are required to include in their study professional education courses which include educational psychology. A basic intent of educational psychology is to assist teachers in using the principles of psychology (behavior) to help students learn.

Psychology is the science that studies human and animal behavior. Psychologists are interested in understanding the needs and motives of people, their thought processes, their feelings and emotions, and how people learn. Psychology is usually classed with biology, sociology and anthropology as one of the behavioral sciences. The modern psychologist is concerned with behavior rather than skills, knowledge, and attitudes. Therefore, psychologists generally agree that learning refers to change in performance (behavior) arising from experience.

Individual Differences

There is a wide range of differences among individuals. At the approximate age of puberty individual differences in physical size among youngsters are particularly evident, including such differences as size, physical fitness, and motor coordination. As children grow and mature, sex differences become pronounced with regard to size and strength, aptitude and motivation. Age differences, socioeconomic differences, and intellectual and academic differences also exist. Schools have responded in one way to individual differences by providing programs centered around ability groups, ranging from gifted children and retarded children to many others. Generally, such attempts by our schools for dealing with individual differences have not been glowingly successful. Classroom teachers are, and have been, somewhat adept at providing for individual differences within our schools. However, this aspect of the teaching task is becoming increasingly more difficult, since increasing numbers of children of varied abilities and backgrounds are in

Our schools must be sensitive to the fact that each child is a unique individual and needs to be treated uniquely.

attendance. The contemporary teacher comes into daily contact with much larger numbers of pupils than ever before. Further, the impact of science and technology on teaching can be accompanied by a strong tendency for having teaching become more and more impersonal. Yet teachers are constantly and continually called upon to be skilled at providing for individual differences. In the future, teachers who will be the most competent at providing for individual differences will be those who continue to learn about learners. This will enable them to know how to better provide for human variability and learning within the group framework of our American public schools.

Human Variability and Learning

Any discussion regarding human variability and learning, however long or brief, brings together several theoretical assumptions which are fraught with controversy. Hardly a statement can be made regarding human variability and learning with which some psychologist or educational psychologist will not take exception to as being overly-simplified, incomplete or irrelevant. George W. Denemark cited six areas of human variability and their implications for learning which he deemed especially salient, such as: differences in perceptions, variations in types of intelligence, differences in rate of maturation, variations in societal demands, and differences in objectives.[2] Some of Denemark's discussion comments for each of these areas follow.

Differences in Perception. . . . People behave basically in terms of what seems to them to be so rather than what others think

to be true or what others might wish them to believe. Children and youth often learn very differently in circumstances which to the outside observer have many identical elements because the students' perceptions are different. . . .

Translating the matter into more conventional educational terms we might reflect on the possible differences in perception existing between a given student and the instructor in a class in world literature. A major objective of the teacher is likely to be that of instilling in each of his students a love of good literature. The impact of the experience on one or sometimes on many students may be extremely negative, a painful ordeal, leading him to the conclusion that he will never again read this sort of thing after he is free from the obligations of the class. Under such circumstances the teacher has one set of perceptions about the teaching-learning experience centering on the objectives of the course and his own aspirations while the student may have a very different perception of what is happening. The outcomes, in terms of the student's feelings, may be far different from the objectives.

Before turning to another area of human variability it would be well to note that perhaps the most important perception of all is that of self-perception—the notion which the individual has of himself. In too many instances young people have established self-quotas for failure rather than ambitious self-expectations for achievement and success. Too often they have come to view themselves as unable to do very well, having little to contribute, and inferior to most

2. Walter B. Waetjen, ed., *Human Variability and Learning,* Washington, D.C.: Association for Supervision and Curriculum Development, National Education Association, 1961, pp. 1–13. Used by permission.

everyone else around them. Unfortunately, parents and teachers sometimes lend support to such evaluations and in so doing confirm a self-perception of mediocrity that becomes a major determinant in the subsequent behavior of the child. If his own expectations and those of others demand little of him, he is unlikely to perform beyond those expectations. The devastating effects of the insensitive teacher's categorization of his students into the bright and the stupid, the industrious and the lazy, the honest and the cheaters, etc.—categorizations which are soon communicated to the individuals and the group—are hard to overstate as influences upon the performance of children and youth. Self-perceptions are extremely important in the learning process and represent a significant facet of human variability. . . .

Variations in types of intelligence. Educators must recognize that the school population represents many kinds of ability and many levels of talent. . . . we must not make the mistake of adopting a narrow or a constricting view of excellence. Our conception of excellence must embrace many kinds of achievements at many levels of performance. No single scale or simple set of categories will be adequate to measure excellence. There may be excellence in abstract intellectual activity, in art, in music, in managerial activity, in craftsmanship, in technical work, to mention but a few. Intelligence and excellence have many dimensions, many variations among children.

Differences in maturity levels. . . . Obvious and important human differences are apparent as we are here concerned with a group of nursery school children, here with a class of early adolescents, and at another point with an adult group of parents or teachers. Significant differences in attention span, small muscle coordination, capacity for self-direction and for dealing with abstractions are but a few of the many variables linked with maturation. Programs must be planned which take into account these kinds of differences. Many easy assumptions about curriculum and about teaching methods are in need of critical re-examination in the light of systematic experience and research data on maturational implications for learning behavior. For example, a favorite rationale for the organization of the elementary curriculum has been the concentric circle approach. The assumption is that the interests of the primary child are focused on himself and his immediate family. As he grows up his interests are thought to extend first to neighborhood, next to total community, then to state and nation, and finally at a much more mature age, to the world. This plan has a good deal of logical appeal, but it would seem that today's children less and less fit such a pattern. Boys and girls at many ages and stages of development demonstrate interests in problems and concerns, people and things far beyond the reach of their own neighborhood, even their own nation. As the problems of a world community press in around their families, these children display an ability to deal with these broader dimensions of human relationships in a manner that necessitates our reassessment of the pattern of the school curriculum.

Another evidence of need for rethinking about the impact of differences in maturity upon learning lies in the extent to which some of us stoutly maintain that teaching is the same for everyone—that the same approaches, techniques and procedures used for college classes and for adult groups can be employed with elementary school children—or vice versa. It is extremely important that we actively seek out the common characteristics of effective teaching and learning in all subject fields and at all levels. It is equally important that we recognize that the techniques and procedures by which we seek to implement common basic objectives must be geared to the stage of maturity represented by our students. The first grade teacher who, after a 45 minute arithmetic session with her children, dismisses them for recess with the remark, "When you return we'll continue with our arithmetic lesson"; the high school program that provides students no time for independent work and study; the college education professor who makes his mature charges wince by treating them as if they were kindergartners rather than adults—all these are illustrations of failure to understand the maturity level of the group being instructed.

Differences in rate of maturation. . . . We have just been considering some implications for learning of different maturity levels. It is also important to recognize that among individuals within the same general age group there are wide variations in rate of maturation and development. . . .

Our failure to recognize variations in the rate of development among children, to recognize the importance of the concept of readiness can cause us to devote tremendous energy to and be terribly wasteful in the educational enterprise, trying to accomplish objectives that are simply not appropriate to a child at that point. The same goals may be reached quickly and easily when the organism has developed the kinds

of physical and mental maturity necessary for them. Trying to achieve such objectives too early may not only be wasteful of the school's efforts but may leave the children with initial negative experiences in such areas that will be difficult to overcome later.

Variations in societal demands. . . . It is as important for the educator concerned with human variabilities to comprehend the demands which society makes upon individuals for such variations as it is to perceive the adjustments which society must make because of other variations. To what extent are human variabilities called for—demanded—by changes in the environmental situations to which learning is expected to apply? We live in a world of tremendously rapid change, a world in which the pace of change continues to accelerate.

In such a world, it is well to inquire as to how persons and institutions have dealt with change. To what extent have societal patterns, school programs adapted and adjusted with sufficient flexibility to meet and cope with a world of tremendously rapid change, a world characterized as a permanent explosion?

Modern education must remain sensitive to the various and changing demands today's world places upon our children and youth. Human variability cannot be merely tolerated by educators when it is being demanded by the conditions of life around the school.

Differences in objectives. . . . Both among teachers and students important differences may be seen in the objectives set for learning. Some of these variations include: (a) the objectives of general education versus specialized education; (b) the objectives linked to the development of a reasonable level of literacy over a broad range of fundamentals contrasted with the conception of developing considerable depth in one field; and (c) objectives associated with social class or other group factors. Failure to recognize that the purposes of schooling may be quite different for different individuals may cause us to draw many unwarranted conclusions about the appropriateness of certain content or teaching procedures. The sensitive teacher cannot assume that all come to school with the same objectives, or that those with purposes and interests different from those of the teacher must be remade in his image. One of the most perplexing pedagogical issues is that involving the determination of criteria to be applied to the efforts of teachers to change the behavior of students. Whose standards shall be used? The teacher's—the community's "upper class"—the parents'? Or is there some broad common denominator which can be constructed and applied? Whatever the answer, the question remains a most perplexing one for teachers. . . .

Psychology provides vast additional information which ought to be included in any discussion of human variability and learning. A continuing task of the contemporary educational psychologist is to draw from available information that which has greatest significance for the professional educators. Teacher preparation institutions are charged with the responsibility of providing relevant and meaningful experiences for prospective teachers enrolled in their programs. Certified teachers are assumed to be knowledgeable regarding the determinants of human behavior, including the concept of needs and satisfaction of needs, motives and theories of motivation, and the

effects of child rearing practices on motivation. Teachers should be competent in understanding learners as persons, with special consideration for their self-concepts.

Child Growth and Development

Growth and development are inclusive terms, each influenced by the contributions of the factors of both heredity and environment. Whether heredity or environment contributes most to one's level of development is open to speculation and disagreement. Of special interest to teachers is knowing the extent to which the behavior of pupils is the result of their inherited potential and/or the result of the influences of their environment. The influence of inherited factors upon behavior is not under the control of the teacher. The influence of environmental factors is at least partially under the control of the teacher. Teachers

At times like this during the school day, teachers become most aware of the variations among children regarding growth and development.

most effective in bringing out the potential of their pupils are those who are capable of coordinating the maturational processes with the environmental influences of their classrooms.

In their study of child growth and development prospective teachers explore specific aspects such as physical and motor development, emotional development, social development, and individual differences.

Physical and motor development. Wide variations exist among children of any given age group with regard to physical growth and motor coordination. As a group, girls mature earlier than boys. During the years of approximately eleven through fourteen, girls are superior to boys in height, weight, and motor coordination. One's sense of physical adequacy enhances one's self-concept. Motor proficiency is important in the satisfaction of various needs. Problems associated with physical and motor development, the formation of the self-concept, and the advent of sexual maturity may be relatively serious for both the early-maturing child and the late-maturing child. Schools should provide a variety of motor skill activities to satisfy the needs of children at all levels of development.

Emotional development. Human behavior encompasses nearly unlimited varieties of emotions. Emotions vary from a state of mild pleasure to intense states of anger and panic. Many body changes occur during intense emotions. Consequently, one's nervous systems and endocrine glands work to regulate intense emotions. Emotions are not readily differentiated in a child at birth; emotional differentiation is associated with maturity. Familiarity with the kinds of emo-

tions identified by the age level of the learners, along with knowledge about what constitutes emotion-producing situations, is of great significance for classroom teachers.

Social development. This involves the ability to get along with others. It is important for an individual to achieve social adequacy while attaining his individuality. Schools can make special contributions to the social development of children. Influencing factors upon one's social development are his peer groups, sex drives, friendships, and sense of security. The importance

The school "commons" area contributes to the socialization process of the school.

of group activities upon the social development of group members is great. Manifestations of various kinds of behavior can be viewed as part of the process of attaining social adequacy.

Motivation and Learning

Learning takes place best when the learner is motivated. Thus, an important aspect of the teachers' job is to help provide their pupils with motives to learn what is being taught. In addition to a desire to learn all that can be learned about learners, teachers should also desire to learn more and more about motivation and learning.

It may be said that individuals are never without motivation. Each of us continually endeavors to maintain and enhance personal adequacy. We tend to remain motivated toward those activities which provide success rather than failure. It follows that a pupil who does well and likes school will be more likely to respond to school related activities than a pupil who does poorly in school. As a consequence of this specific aspect of motivation considerable speculation and debate exists among educators as to the grading practice in schools, particularly since most grade systems include a failing grade. Some argue that if we wish learners to be continually motivated toward school activities learning experiences should not permit failure. However, if success consists of reaching a goal, somewhere along the way the determination of whether the goal has been reached must be made by the teacher. The learner must be made aware of his progress toward goals. Hopefully, teachers can provide learning situations in which realistic goals are set for each learner at his threshold of achievement and motivation

The magic of motivation turns students on in the pursuit of their learning tasks.

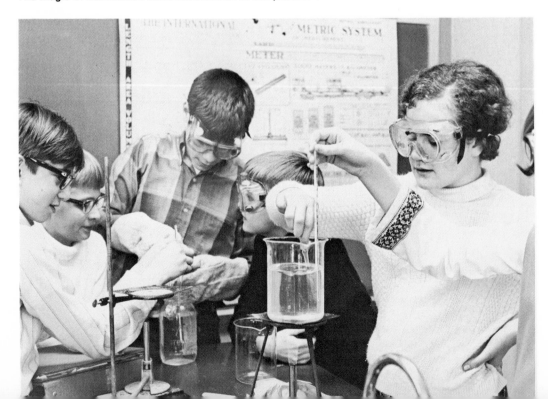

encourages each to persist until these goals are successfully reached.

Motivation is a complex phenomenon. Factors influencing motivation and learning, in addition to first hand experiences, include the learner's perception of these experiences, values ascribed to the experiences, and the self-concepts of the learners. Also, teacher and student variables, such as personality, and teacher and learner styles, are also related to motivation and learning.

Self-concept. Increasing evidence indicates close relationships between self-concept and learning. Inadequate perceptions of the self may bring about misguided motivation and student failures in school subjects. Many students who do poorly in school have learned to consider themselves incapable of being successful in academic work. Students with such low academic self-concepts also perceive others as having little faith in them and in their ability to do well in school work. A student's motivation and learning may also be closely related to his perceptions of other's expectations for him.

Teacher and learner styles. The *best* teacher style or the *best* learner style cannot be generalized. Caution must be taken to avoid the trap of judging a teaching style or a learning style as wrong just because it doesn't match one's own style or one's own belief about a learning style. Also, there is considerable overlap between the personal characteristics of teachers and teaching styles, and between the personal characteristics of learners and learner styles. A summary of research evidence reported by Don E. Hamachek[3] states that when it comes to classroom behavior, interaction patterns, and teaching styles, teachers who are superior in encouraging motivation and learning in students seem to exhibit more of the following characteristics:

1. Willingness to be flexible, to be direct or indirect, as the situation demands.
2. Capacity to perceive the world from the student's point of view.
3. Ability to "personalize" their teaching.
4. Willingness to experiment, to try out new things.
5. Skill in asking questions (as opposed to seeing self as a kind of answering service).
6. Knowledge of subject matter and related areas.
7. Skill in establishing definite examination procedures.
8. Willingness to provide definite study helps.
9. Capacity to reflect an appreciative attitude (evidenced by nods, comments, smiles, etc.).
10. Conversational manner in teaching—informal, easy style.

In addition to individual differences in personality factors, assessment of motivation must give consideration to student reactions to praise and blame, student reactions to success and failure, and student differences in learning style. In the interests of effective motivation, it is important to identify each student's learning style as quickly as possible. Hamachek's summary statement regarding student variables related to motivation and learning states:[4]

What is important for one student is not important to another; this is one reason why cook-

3. Don E. Hamachek, *Motivation in Teaching and Learning*, p. 15. Used by permission.
4. *Ibid.*, p. 21.

book formulas for good teaching are of so little value and why teaching is inevitably something of an art when it comes to motivating students and helping them learn. The choice of instructional methods makes a big difference for certain kinds of pupils, and a search for the "best" way to motivate can succeed only when student variables such as intellectual and personality differences are taken into account.

QUESTIONS FOR DISCUSSION

1. What aspect of human variability do you consider most relevant to learning? Discuss.
2. What is your opinion regarding the respective influences of the factors of heredity and the factors of environment upon maturation of children?
3. What is meant by the following statement? Learning is a matter of the formation and strengthening of associations.
4. How is the self-concept of the learner related to learning?
5. How important is the knowledge of subject matter to a teacher? In what other areas should a teacher be knowledgeable?

SUPPLEMENTARY LEARNING ACTIVITIES

1. Poll the members of your class for the purpose of listing the ways in which teachers have motivated them.
2. Assign a panel discussion of the factors of personality as related to learning.
3. Read and report on the findings of a research study related to self-concept and learning.
4. Visit a special education class. List the techniques used by the teacher to moti-

vate her pupils. Discuss the effects of those techniques.
5. Invite a school psychologist to address the class about the nature of his job. Conduct a question and answer session following the presentation.

SELECTED REFERENCES

Allport, Gordon W. *Pattern and Growth in Personality.* New York: Holt, Rinehart & Winston, Inc., 1961.

Barry, R., and B. Wolf. *Motives, Values, and Realities.* New York: Teachers College Press, Columbia University, 1965.

Cofer, C. N., and M. H. Appley. *Motivation: Theory and Research.* New York: John Wiley & Sons, Inc., 1964.

Coleman, James E. *Personality Dynamics and Effective Behavior.* Chicago: Scott, Foresman and Co., 1960.

Combs, Arthur W., and Donald Snygg. *Individual Behavior: A Perceptual Approach to Behavior.* rev. ed. New York: Harper & Row, Publishers, 1959.

Dinkmeyer, D., and R. Dreikurs. *Encouraging Children to Learn: The Encouragement Process.* Englewood Cliffs, N.J.: Prentice-Hall, Inc., 1963.

Eyesenck, H. J., ed. *Experiments in Motivation.* New York: The Macmillan Co., 1964.

Gale, Raymond F. *Developmental Behavior.* New York: The Macmillan Co., 1969.

Haber, R. N., ed. *Current Research in Motivation.* New York: Holt, Rinehart & Winston, Inc., 1966.

Hamachek, Don E. *Motivation in Teaching and Learning.* Association of Classroom Teachers of the National Education Association, 1968.

Lindgren, H. C. *The Psychology of Personal and Social Adjustment.* New York: John Wiley & Sons, Inc., 1962.

Lindgren, Henry Clay, and Don Byrne. *Psychology: An Introduction to the Study of Human Behavior.* New York: John Wiley & Sons, Inc., 1961.

Logan, F. A., and A. R. Wagner. *Reward and Punishment.* Boston: Allyn and Bacon, 1965.

Madsen, K. B. *Theories of Motivation.* Cleveland: Howard Allen, 1964.

Maslow, A. H. *Motivation and Personality.* New York: Harper & Row, Publishers, 1954.

Mouly, George J. *Psychology for Effective Teaching.* 2nd ed. New York: Holt, Rinehart, & Winston, Inc., 1968.

Prescott, Daniel. *The Child in the Educative Process.* New York: McGraw-Hill Book Co., 1957.

Severin, F. T. *Humanistic Viewpoints in Psychology.* New York: McGraw-Hill Book Co., 1965.

Teevan, R. C., and R. C. Birney, ed. *Theories of Motivation in Learning.* Princeton, N.J.: D. Van Nostrand Co., Inc., 1964.

Wilson, John A. R., Mildred C. Robeck, and William B. Michael. *Psychological Foundations of Learning and Teaching.* New York: McGraw-Hill Book Co., 1969.

Help for Spanish - Speaking Youngsters

Joseph Stocker

There are more than one and one-half million children with Spanish surnames in the schools of five Southwestern States— Arizona, California, Colorado, New Mexico, and Texas. Nearly all of them are Mexican-Americans. In scholastic attainment they lag far behind their Anglo-American schoolmates, and their dropout rate is high. The reason for their underachievement can be summed up in a single word: language.

Monroe Sweetland, Western States legislative consultant for the National Education Association (NEA), has described the school record of Mexican-American youngsters as "tragic." He said bluntly, "It constitutes the greatest single failure of our systems to provide equality of educational opportunity in this region."

The Mexican-American child comes out of a Spanish-speaking home into an English-speaking school, and from that point on it's a case of oil trying to mix with water. In many instances, says John M. Sharp, professor of modern languages at Texas Western College, El Paso, the child's parents speak little or no English, and his first significant contact with our language occurs when he begins school. "English is no less a foreign language to him than it would be to a child from Argentina or Colombia," says Dr. Sharp. "He suddenly finds himself not only with the pressing need to master what

to him is an alien tongue, but also, at the same time, to make immediate use of it in order to function as a pupil."

In many states English is prescribed by law as the language of instruction. Schools even forbid Mexican-American students to speak Spanish except in Spanish classes, the obvious theory being that if they speak only English, they will learn English. Some schools have been known to administer corporal punishment to students for lapsing into Spanish. "If you want to be American," the young Latin is told over and over again, "speak American."

These speak-English-only laws are hard to enforce. "Obviously it is impossible to make a person speak a language," says James Burton, who teaches English and speech to Mexican-American students at Jefferson High School in El Paso. "Any teacher in control of his classroom can prevent his students from speaking Spanish, but the result is likely to be a thundering silence. It is certainly no guarantee that fluent, idiomatic English will gush forth like the water from the biblical rock."

It's not only an alien language that the Mexican-American child encounters, it's an alien set of cultural standards as well. The

---

* Joseph Stocker, "Help for Spanish-Speaking Youngsters," *American Education*, May, 1967, pp. 17, 18, 24.

tempo is faster than that to which he is accustomed. The school environment lacks what one Southwestern educator has described as "the plasticity and warmth of human relationship" so often found in the Mexican-American home, however humble. Customs are strange. "Take the matter of funerals," says Florence Reynolds, principal of Pueblo High School at Tucson, Ariz. "If a member of the family dies, the Mexican-American child is likely to stay out of school as much as a week. He does so at the insistence of his parents. But we say it's wrong to stay out of school a week for a funeral. So the school is putting itself above the parents, in effect, and the youngster is caught in a dichotomy of values."

Many a Mexican-American child, therefore, suffers not only educational but psychological damage. He is being told in every conceivable way that his language and his culture are no good. He must inevitably begin to suspect that he is no good either. If he is no good, how can he succeed? And if he cannot succeed, why try? "These children," summed up a California school administrator, "are conditioned to failure in the early years of their schooling, and each passing year only serves to reinforce their feelings of failure and frustration. Is it any wonder that as soon as they are 16 or can pass for 16, they begin dropping out of school?"

Schools have tried one remedial measure or another, with no great success. Perhaps the most widely used approach has been to group all Spanish-speaking beginners in a special prefirst-grade class to teach them English, after which they are "promoted" to the first grade. But this means that little Juanito must go through his entire school career a year behind his age group, which simply confirms his feelings of inferiority.

Lately, however, a new concept has emerged that seems to hold out real hope and might even bring a dramatic breakthrough in the education of Mexican-Americans. It's the concept of bilingualism: using Spanish as a vehicle to education for the Spanish-speaking child, with English being taught as a second language.

The idea is only now catching on. In a school system here, another there, teachers and administrators have become aware that bilingualism may hold a key to the future for hundreds of thousands of Mexican-American children.

It's a spontaneous movement, with no central direction or coordination. Different schools go about it in different ways, but the results in almost all instances have been encouraging. At Laredo, Tex., in the United Consolidated Independent School District, a suburban district encompassing 2,440 square miles, bilingualism has been put to work in the primary grades. The student body is a mix of Anglo-Americans and Mexican-Americans, and instruction is carried on in both English and Spanish. The district tried it the other way, forbidding the Mexican-American children to speak Spanish, educating them solely in English. The result was frustration and failure and a heavy proportion of Mexican-American dropouts.

Then a concerned school board appointed a superintendent, Harold C. Brantley, who believed in bilingualism and wanted to build a program along such lines. In September 1964, the district launched what it called "an experimental biliteracy program" —bilingualism for both Mexican-American and Anglo-American children. It began in the first grade and was extended to the second grade in the fall of 1965 Last fall it moved to the third grade, and eventually it is to extend through all the grades, including high school.

At Tucson's Pueblo High School, Mexican-American students are offered courses in Spanish custom-tailored for them. The school had discovered that many Mexican-Americans are actually "bilingual illiterates," that is, they speak, read, and write both languages poorly. Their Spanish is often a hybrid catch-as-catch-can mixture of Spanish and English. Yet when some of these Mexican-American students enrolled in conventional Spanish courses they were bored to tears. One Latin miss said candidly to her teacher, "I came here to learn good Spanish but you haven't taught me very much." "I don't wonder they were bored," says Principal Florence Reynolds. "Imagine —teaching a Spanish-speaking youngster to say, 'Buenos días.'"

In 1959 Pueblo High offered an experimental course in Spanish for the Spanish-speaking. It was such a success that the students petitioned the faculty to provide a second year. At the end of the second year they again asked for more. Today the school conducts 14 such classes, nearly all taught by native speakers, several of whom were born in Mexico. Along with language skill, the curriculum emphasizes the cultural heritage of Spain and Mexico to help the student gain a sense of identity and pride. Attesting to the success of the program is the fact that, although English-speaking students are in the majority at Pueblo High, more Spanish-speaking than English-speaking students are enrolled in Spanish courses. Two of the program's alumni, their interest whetted by the courses, chose careers in education, got their degrees, and are now back at Pueblo High as Spanish teachers.

Some months ago the program also caught the attention of the NEA. Its staff members, impressed by what they saw at Pueblo High, heard also of similar programs springing up in other Southwestern communities. Bilingualism, they sensed, held a significant answer to the problem of educating Mexican-Americans. So the NEA set up a project, the NEA-Tucson Survey on the Teaching of Spanish to the Spanish-Speaking, to survey the five Southwestern States. Its purpose was to search out some of the more promising approaches to bilingualism, and to persuade more schools to try them now that financing was available under the Elementary and Secondary Education Act of 1965. Seven Tucson educators, all involved in one way or another with the education of Mexican-Americans, comprised the NEA's survey team. Chairman was Maria Urquides, dean of girls at Pueblo High and herself a Mexican-American.

Members of the team visited 37 schools in 21 cities. Their report, titled "The Invisible Minority . . . Pero No Vencibles" ("But Invincible"), firmly concludes that bilingualism "can be a tool—indeed the most important tool—with which to educate and motivate the Mexican-American child."

Chairman Urquides, a vigorous, exuberant, outspoken woman, intensely proud of her "Mexicanness," insisted at the outset that the survey wasn't to be just another study of the Mexican-American education problem. "The heck with a study!" she snorted when an NEA staffer first broached the idea. "We've been studied so much we're sick of it. Let's do something about it —something to strengthen the youngster's concept of being a Mexican-American, to make him proud of being a Mexican-American. The schools are doing so much now to destroy it!"

And so the NEA report doesn't just assemble recent research on the subject, as do so many similar reports. It describes in detail a number of the most promising programs in bilingualism that the survey team observed in its travels through the five States. Then it says to other schools with sizable Mexican-American enrollments and high Mexican-American dropout rates: Go thou and do likewise. A number of schools are doing just that.

There is evidence that the best bilingual teachers are those who speak Spanish natively. And this, by the nature of things, means mostly Mexican-Americans. For the teacher of Spanish to the Spanish-speaking is usually much more than just a teacher: he is a counselor, a parent-substitute, an understanding friend, even, sometimes, a father confessor.

Maria L. Vega performs just such a multiple role at Phoenix Union High School, which has a 50 per cent Mexican-American enrollment. Born in Mexico, speaking labored English even yet, Mrs. Vega started the Spanish-speaking program at Phoenix Union in 1960. There was one class that year. Last year there were 14.

"They come to us with every problem they have," she says. "Once a boy came to me. 'Mrs. Vega,' he said, 'I stole a car. Here are the keys.' I helped him, and he got another chance, and this past year he graduated. A girl comes to me and says, 'Mrs. Vega, I'm going to have a baby. What shall I do?' I say, 'Do your parents know?' And she says, 'No.' And I say, 'Let's tell them.'

"Our classes deal with human relations, with the problems of our community—drinking, TB, juvenile delinquency. School is so important to them. For a majority of them there is no other place—their homes are so small. They have no place to study.

"I teach them more than Spanish. I teach them Spanish history, geography, literature. If they know their great heritage, they can be proud. And they can *be* something, instead of just on welfare. They can be better American citizens."

What Maria Vega and all the rest are doing is what Daniel Schreiber, former director of the NEA's Project Dropout, must have had in mind when, at a Mexican-American seminar held in Phoenix in 1963, he talked of the need of young people to "achieve confident self-identity." "The youngster," he said, "whose school experience begins and ends in failure—and those of minority children too often do—having discovered that he is good at nothing, stands a strong chance of becoming good for nothing. And far too many young lives, with all the potentials and real talents and capabilities they embody, are being wasted and crushed. The challenge is to redeem them through inventiveness and energy and dedication."

Now, four years after Schreiber spoke these words, there is much activity to report. New and imaginative programs are springing up in many communities. More and more, there is the "general feeling of great urgency—of urgency for positive action," that Regina Goff, OE's Assistant Commissioner of Programs for the Disadvantaged called for at a conference last August on Federal educational programs affecting Mexican-Americans.

Action takes many forms, often innovative. Pueblo, Colo., schools and other community agencies are working on a bicultural program of art, music, literature, history, and language with financial help from title III of the Elementary and Secondary Education Act. In Alpine, Tex., where more than 60 per cent of the children speak Spanish, schools are using two-way radios for guidance and counseling, and experimenting with leased wire and voice-writers for language teaching. El Paso is beginning the first phase of its model center for teaching English and Spanish and is also planning a general culture center.

In such ways, through bilingualism, it begins to appear that the process of redemption is under way for at least one group—the "invisible minority" of the American Southwest.

CHAPTER 8

The Nature of Curriculum

Earlier in this book the societal expectations for schools were discussed. These expectations in a sense are representative of society, its problems and its ideals. They represent society as seen by its members, seen as it is and as its members want it to become. These expectations serve as one basic source of the curricula of our schools. A second basic source is the body of organized knowledge that man has accumulated over the centuries. This vast reservoir is selectively tapped to provide the elements of knowledge deemed necessary as basic material for general education. A third source resides within the needs and desires of the learners; learners that in our formal system range from the pre-elementary school child to the mature adult. From these three sources school curricula are evolved.

There have been many definitions of curriculum over the years. These various definitions have reflected both the thinking of the times and sources of curriculum as discussed previously. Historically the curriculum was thought of as the list of subjects taught in school. This definition reflects the body of knowledge or subject-centered approach. While more recent definitions tend to be broader, content is still an important part of curriculum. Foshay has concluded that the subject-centered emphasis dominated the educational philosophy of the 1890–1930's period.[1] Since the 1930's, the

> Subject matter is the medium through which the adult mind of the teacher and the immature mind of the learner find communion.
>
> Earl C. Kelley

idea of experience as proposed by John Dewey has steadily gained impetus. In terms of experience Ragan has defined curriculum "to include all of the experiences of children for which the school accepts responsibility."[2] Smith, Stanley, and Shores have stated that the curriculum is "a sequence of potential experiences set up in the school for the purpose of disciplining children and youth in group ways of think-

1. George Beauchamp, *Curriculum Theory*, p. 36.
2. William B. Ragan, *Modern Elementary Curriculum*, p. 3.

ing and acting."[3] These definitions are relatively broad with the word "experience" implying an active involvement of the learner rather than a passive receptivity. In addition to reflecting the concept of the needs of learners as serving as a source for curriculum, they also relate to the importance of learning theory as presented in chapter seven. Beauchamp has defined curriculum as "the design of a social group for the educational experiences of their children in school."[4] This definition and that of Smith, Stanley, and Shores stress the importance of society as a source for curriculum.

Goals and Objectives

School curricula, in order to be functional, must eventually be expressed in terms of specific goals and objectives. In chapter four, broad goals as expressed by various national committees and authorities were discussed, particularly as they related to the conventional graded levels of school organization. For purposes of illustration, let us examine three broad statements of objectives and translate them into specific objectives as they might appear in a curriculum guide for a local school system. The following three objectives of American education are from a 1955 White House Conference on Educational Problems:

1. The fundamental skills of communication—reading, writing, spelling, as well as other elements of effective oral and written expression; the arithmetical and mathematical skills, including problem solving.
2. Civic rights and responsibilities and knowledge of American institutions.
3. Physical and mental health.

Specific behavioral objectives that might be developed from the above for a first grade class might include:

1a. Count aloud from one to one hundred.
2a. Tell other members of the class two ways in which they think policemen are important.
3a. Wash hands before eating.

At the secondary level, the same broad objectives might yield the following specific behavioral objectives:

1b. Derive the correct algebraic equation to solve a word problem dealing with time, rate, and distance.
2b. List the steps necessary for a bill to become a law in the United States.
3b. After proper medical clearance, run one quarter mile in two minutes.

It should be noted that in this illustration the objectives are written behaviorally; that is, in terms of behavior that can be observed in the learner. The writing of objectives in this fashion facilitates evaluation.

The selected objectives also illustrate different domains of learning. Bloom has identified three domains of objectives—cognitive, affective, and psychomotor.[5] Cognitive objectives are those that are concerned with remembering, recognizing knowledge, and the development of intellectual abilities and skills. Objectives *1a* and *1b* are clearly in this category. Affective objectives are those which are concerned with interests, atti-

3. B. Othanel Smith, William O. Stanley, and J. Harlen Shores, *Fundamentals of Curriculum Development*, p. 3.
4. Beauchamp, *op. cit.*, p. 34.
5. Benjamin S. Bloom, ed., *Taxonomy of Educational Objectives*, pp. 6–8.

tudes, opinions, appreciations, values, and emotional sets. Objective *2a*, since it may elicit opinions or values, is in the affective domain. Objective *3b* is most clearly psychomotor involving large muscles.

Thus the broad objectives of American education can be specifically transformed into specific objectives for children in classrooms. Objectives, however, are only one part of the curriculum. They represent the desired goals or outcomes. After a teacher

> Education is life, not subject matter.
>
> John Dewey

has decided upon the objectives, it then becomes necessary to decide upon a method or means of achieving the objective. Thus methodology, since it provides the "experiences," is often included in the concept of curriculum. Some authorities, however, consider methodology as instruction. It is most important at this point in planning that the methodology be appropriate to the attainment of the objective. For example, if an objective for the student is to moderate a small group discussion of four people causing them to arrive at a plan for action on a current social problem, then the teaching method would most certainly include practice discussion sessions. It would probably also include an explanation by the teacher as to how discussions are led. Using other information from learning theory is also important in determining methodology. For example, in the previous illustration involving discussion leadership, the notion of having the students actually lead and participate in discussions rather than merely listen

to an instructor tell them how discussions should be led reflects the principle that active participation results in more learning than passive receptivity. Further, if one were to consider motivation as a factor, the topic for discussion would be very important. Since the objective in this case is not specifically aimed at a precise body of content, the topic of discussion could and should be one in which students are interested. Since methodology, in fact, determines the experiences that students have in achieving objectives, it is an important part of the curriculum. A third essential part of curriculum is a scheme of evaluation. Teachers, parents, school authorities, and many others need to know what progress students are making. So, in addition to decisions as to what it is students are to learn (objectives), and how they are going to learn (methodology), a curriculum must include a measure of how well students have learned (evaluation). Carefully formulated objectives assist immensely in this task, for it is practically impossible to determine students' achievement if it is not clear what objectives the students are to have achieved. As teachers develop curricula for their students, plans for evaluation which are appropriate for the objective should be included.

The Teacher and Curriculum

While national commissions write goals, academic specialists analyze content, and other experts theorize about curriculum, it is the teacher on the front line who actually makes curriculum. Each day as teachers interact with students they produce and present curriculum. Even without advance planning, as has been advocated, a teacher in doing whatever he or she does with students is in a sense implementing a curriculum.

The role of teachers in formally planning curricula is becoming increasingly important. Teachers today are asking for greater participation in educational decision-making. Perhaps the most important role they can play in decision-making is in cooperatively building curriculums. Teachers are experts in providing practical information about curricula from their experiences in working with students. They are also very often academic specialists. They should participate actively in determining goals, methodology, and evaluation techniques. Once

Active participation in learning.

these facets of curriculum have been decided for a school system or a school, the teacher must then put his talents into action in implementing the curriculum. Resourceful teachers at this point develop their own style of teaching as they bring their own uniqueness to the task of teaching.

Trends

Recent activity in the area of curriculum can be classified into three areas: (1) efforts that have to do with reorganizing or restructuring academic content, (2) efforts that have to do with reorganizing the ways in which teachers and other instructional personnel work with students, and (3) the application of advanced technology to teaching and learning. Technology is considered as a part of instructional resources in chapter nine.

Concepts in Content

It has been mentioned earlier in this text that one of the problems of selecting the content to be taught in our schools is that of deciding what shall be selected out of the tremendous amount of content available. The knowledge explosion of the last few years has caused this problem to be more complex. Scholars in the academic areas have begun to address themselves to this problem. At the risk of understating or oversimplifying their work, it can be said that academic scholars have attempted to select general concepts from their disciplines that should be taught, rather than specific factual materials. Their emphasis also tends toward process, that is, an emphasis on the methods of inquiry and discovery, rather than on the content. In practice one finds that content, concept, and process are inseparable, but the relative emphasis can be altered. For example, the emphasis in mathematics as developed by the School Mathematics Study Group and the University of Illinois Committee on School Mathematics tends more toward problem solving than it does toward basic operations. In programs such as those developed by Biological Science Curriculum Study Group, Physical Sciences Study Committee, and the Chemical Education Materials Study Group the emphasis is also placed on basic theoretical concepts rather than on facts, and on discovery through experimentation rather than presentation or perusal of textbooks. Similar activity by scholars has occurred in foreign languages, English, and social studies. Much of the monies needed to finance these curriculum efforts have come from private foundations such as Carnegie, Danforth, Ford, Kellogg, Kettering, Rockefeller and Sloan. The federal government has also participated through grants under the National Defense Education Act, and more recently under the Elementary and Secondary Education Act of 1965. The National Education Association, through its Project on Instruction, was also active in inspiring and presenting innovative practices. While these approaches seem to have merit, and do address themselves to the problem of what to teach, they have not been in actual operation for a sufficient length of time to be adequately evaluated. Also, as they are implemented they are altered. This process makes a sophisticated research design type of evaluation nearly impossible. Nevertheless, it is clear that while the programs that have been developed may not have been used precisely as they were designed or intended, they have made an impact on curricula. One

Intense individual participation toward a group goal.

decided impact has been that of causing teachers to carefully examine their objectives and methodology. This in and of itself is of value.

Organizing Students for Learning

One problem of instruction that has been mentioned in a number of places in this text is that of finding ways to individualize instruction. We know that students are different—they differ in intellectual capacity, interests, rate of achievement, and many other ways. This knowledge indicates that students should be treated and taught as individuals as much as is possible. Yet, at the same time, the United States is committed to mass education, and to accomplish this goal we have tended to group students. In chapter four it was pointed out that historically the most common grouping pattern

Active group participation in learning.

was grouping by chronological age. We have also usually assumed that one teacher can instruct thirty youngsters that are within our defined limits of normality. Under these circumstances, try as a teacher may, it is extremely difficult to teach individuals. In a general way it can be said that teachers tend to teach to what they perceive to be a composite average. Of course, there is no such individual as the "average." The problem of individualizing instruction in mass education within the limits of the public's willingness to pay still plagues our educational system.

Homogeneous Grouping

A number of ways have been attempted to bring about the individualization of instruction. One of the initial methods was

that of homogeneous grouping; that is, grouping students by some pre-determined criteria such as intelligence, reading achievement, or any number of other criteria. This does reduce the range of differences with which the teacher must work; however, it does not individualize instruction. Recently homogeneous grouping has come under attack as being discriminatory. Judge J. Skelly Wright of the U.S. Court of Appeals for the District of Columbia, sitting as a district judge, stated in his opinion in *Hobson v. Hansen* that the track system, a form of homogeneous grouping, should be eliminated. The track system was portrayed by Judge Wright as being a rigid one in which students were grouped by ability on the basis of standardized test scores, and in which it was extremely difficult to move from one track to another. While the major thrust of the *Hobson v. Hansen* case was directed toward eliminating racial segregation, Judge Wright apparently saw fit to make additional comments on the track system. These are many arguments that can be presented for and against the many ways of homogeneous grouping; yet, the available research on the topic does not indicate that a teacher can consistently achieve better results with homogeneous groups.[6] Grouping is not the complete answer to individualizing instruction.

Team Teaching and Flexible Scheduling

Team teaching and flexible scheduling are two closely related organizational schemes designed in part to enhance individualizing instruction. Both of these orga-

6. Miriam L. Goldberg, A. Harry Passow, and Joseph Justman, *The Effects of Ability Grouping*, p. 150.

nizational concepts provide opportunities for independent study which is essential for individualization. In team teaching a number of staff members cooperatively plan and carry out instruction for students. Basically, these types of instructional groupings are employed: large group (100–150 students), small group (8–15 students), and independent study. The team usually consists not only of members of the teaching staff with their specialized competencies, but also other staff members such as teacher aides, intern teachers, media specialists and clerks. The grouping used for instruction is designed to be appropriate for the expected learnings. Most often special facilities such as resource material centers, learning centers, laboratories, and libraries are made available with capable personnel on hand to guide independent study. It is the independent study phase of the team teaching plan that facilitates individualized instruction.

> The object of teaching a child is to enable him to get along without his teacher.
>
> Elbert Hubbard

The time allotted to independent study varies; however, it is generally recommended that independent study consist of thirty per cent of the student's time. Flexible scheduling, which is particularly pertinent to departmentalization, is based upon organizing the school day with shorter time periods. Typically school periods are forty-five to sixty minutes; in flexible scheduling the day is composed of twenty to thirty minute modules. The shorter modular type of programming permits greater flexibility. Student's programs could consist of some sessions being as short as twenty minutes and other sessions of various additive combinations of twenty minutes, dependent upon

A modern elementary school building, PS219, Flushing, New York.

the learning activity. Flexible scheduling enhances the potential of team teaching. Used together with a combination of special resources available for independent study, team teaching and flexible scheduling have possibilities for individualizing instruction. At the very least, through encouraging independent study, they encourage the development of students toward accepting greater responsibility for their own progress.

Nongraded Programs

Two techniques that seem to have particular merit for individualizing instruction are nongraded programs and individually prescribed instruction. Both require determining the threshold of achievement of in-

dividual learning, and as with most other innovative techniques they require a definite change in the teacher behavior. Teachers must devote more of their energies to guiding individual learners and acting as resource persons.

The nongraded school operates under the assumption that each child should progress through school at his own unique rate of development. The pupils are organized within the school to facilitate their individual development. For example, in an elementary school operating under the nongraded plan, what were originally the kindergarten, grade one, two, three, and four are likely to be called the primary school, while grades five, six, seven, and eight are likely to be called the middle school. This arrangement,

Many students today are transported to and from school.

however, in and of itself does not make a nongraded school. The distinctiveness of the nongraded school lies in the fact that youngsters progress on the basis of achieving specified learning skills, whether or not those skills are typically thought of as being affixed to a particular grade. In a sense, instead of grouping children by chronological age, they are grouped by their achievement of a specific skill. The skills are arranged sequentially in order of their difficulty. Ideally, there is much flexibility among this grouping. For example, a child who learns the elementary skills of reading is moved into another group appropriate to his reading development, or perhaps given more independent study time. It is also possible that a youngster could be placed at an advanced level in his attainment of reading skills and at the same time be placed at a lower level in arithmetic reasoning. Nongraded schools, when functioning ideally, permit flexibility. There should be less failure in the traditional sense because grade level standards have been removed. Further, the child who learns rapidly should have greater opportunity to do so because specific arrangements are made for him to progress as rapidly as he can. He is not locked into a graded grouping in which it is likely that instruction will be aimed at the "average" child. The nongraded plan attempts through grouping by developmental achievement skills, along with flexibility and the opportunity for movement between groups, to provide greater avenues for individualization. It has potential to accomplish this task. Much of its potential, however, resides in skills of teachers and administrators to assure that it does in fact promote individual development. There is a persist-

ent danger that nongraded schools based on developmental achievement grouping can become just as rigid as the traditional graded organization. While most nongraded schools are at the elementary school level, the plan is also used at the high school level. The Melbourne High School of Florida was one of the first secondary schools to implement a nongraded plan.

Individually Prescribed Instruction

Individually prescribed instruction represents a most direct and specific effort to meet the individual needs of students. The basic materials for students consist of a sequentially ordered listing of behaviorally stated instructional objectives. To date, the greatest effort in preparing objectives has been in mathematics and reading. An illustrative objective in mathematics might be to count to one hundred by tens. The objectives are organized by area and by level of difficulty. Among the areas in mathematics are: numeration, place value, addition, subtraction, multiplication, combinations of processes, fractions, money, time, systems of measurement and geometry. Some reading areas are: visual discrimination, auditory discrimination, literal comprehension, oral reading, library skills, and phonetic analysis.

The first step in implementing individually prescribed instruction is to determine each student's threshold of achievement in each area by diagnostic testing. This information then serves as a basis for prescribing the student's activities. Most often the student's activities will be in a programmed booklet, but they may involve the use of various manipulative activities. Ideally the student receives immediate feedback on his success in accomplishing the prescribed instructional objectives. The system in order to be effective requires the help of teacher aides to relieve the teachers of clerical tasks. Aides assist students in filling prescriptions and scoring their work to assure immediacy of feedback.

A distinct psychological advantage of individually prescribed instruction is that it requires a one-to-one relationship between teacher and student, and therefore the student is more likely to feel that he is an important individual and not merely another face in a sea of faces. For individually prescribed instruction to be most effective, differentiated staffing with aides is necessary. The plan is complemented by providing learning resource centers.

Individualizing instruction is a desirable process for achieving many learning outcomes. There are, however, learning outcomes which depend on group processes. Students must learn to interact with other students in order to function in society. A desirable curriculum will provide opportunities for many kinds of outcomes.

In summary, in planning curricula, educators and citizens still have much work to do in deciding what it is they want youth to be taught; expressing these objectives in behavioral terms; and determining the most effective and efficient ways of accomplishing them. For feedback to students, teachers, and parents, appropriate evaluation techniques must be devised. We are on the threshold of many breakthroughs in American education. To accomplish these breakthroughs, a commitment on the part of citizens as to their willingness to pay for education is necessary.

National Assessment of Progress

The importance of each teacher assessing the progress of his students toward achieving specified objectives has been stressed. In addition to this, it is important to know how our educational system is functioning on a broader level. In a decentralized system such as ours this is difficult to accomplish. It must, however, be done. At the suggestion of Francis Keppel, U.S. Commissioner of Education from 1962 until January, 1966, the Carnegie Corporation began to explore this problem. They created a committee headed by Ralph Tyler of the Center for Advanced Study in the Behavioral Sciences to study and set forth the purposes of such a program. In terms of purposes the committee said:

First, it would give the nation as a whole a better understanding of the strengths and weaknesses of the American educational system. Thus, it might contribute a more accurate guide than we currently possess for allocation of public and private funds, where they are needed, what they achieve, and decisions affecting education.

Second, assessment results, especially if coupled with auxiliary information on characteristics of the various regions, and would provide data necessary for research on educational problems and processes which cannot now be undertaken.

Third, when sampling and testing procedures are adequately developed, international comparisons might be possible.[7]

Their purposes seem reasonable, yet many objections were raised to national assessment. Most of these objections centered about the undesirability of comparing school districts and states. Finally a pro-

7. American Association of School Administrators, *National Educational Assessment: Pro and Con*, p. 6.

Flexible spaces for learning activities, PS219, Flushing, New York.

gram was worked out to the satisfaction of most authorities and the national assessment became a reality. The Committee on Assessing the Progress of Education (CAPE) was incorporated in 1964 as a non-profit corporation of the Regents of the state of New York. Funds to operate came from the Carnegie Corporation, Ford Foundation, and the U.S. Office of Education. On July 1, 1969, the assessment project was turned over to the Education Commission of the States. Progress is being made. De-

> Schools need not preach political doctrine to defend democracy. If they shape many capable of critical thought and trained in social attitudes, that is all that is necessary.
>
> Albert A. Einstein

tailed objectives and sub-objectives have been prepared for the subject areas of science, writing, and citizenship. A sampling of 17-year-olds in school were queried in spring 1969, and a summer assessment of 20,000 adults between 26–35 years of age and 1500–1800 out-of-school 17-year-olds was begun. Plans call for the assessment of 13 and 9-year-olds in the near future. At the same time objectives for other areas are being developed. The criteria used in developing objectives were that every objective be:

1. considered important by scholars,
2. accepted as an educational task by the school,
3. considered desirable by thoughtful lay citizens.[8]

8. Committee on Assessing the Progress of Education, "Objective Brochures," *National Assessment of Educational Progress* 2(1969):5.

The assessment project is not designed to report test results from individual students, schools, or teachers. It is designed to report on regional and nationwide educational levels. As a nation we need such information. The American people expect much of education—they deserve to know what is being accomplished.

QUESTIONS FOR DISCUSSION

1. What has been the major source of curricula in American education? Will this same source serve effectively for the future? Why?
2. How should national objectives or goals for education be developed? What individuals or groups should be involved? Why?
3. What should be the role of the teacher in developing curricula?
4. Why has it been so difficult to achieve individualization of instruction in American schools?
5. Is national assessment a legitimate and necessary procedure? Why?

SUPPLEMENTARY LEARNING ACTIVITIES

1. Invite a curriculum coordinator to your class to explain his role.
2. Prepare a list of behavioral objectives for a group of your own definition. Include objectives from the cognitive, affective, and psychomotor domains.
3. Visit a nearby school to observe their techniques for individualizing instruction.
4. Interview lay citizens and teachers to gain their impressions of what a school curriculum should be like. Report your findings to the class.

5. Interview students to ascertain their perceptions of the objectives of their instruction.

SELECTED REFERENCES

American Association of School Administrators. *National Education Assessment: Pro and Con.* Washington, D.C.: National Education Association, 1966.

Association for Supervision and Curriculum Development. *Curriculum Decisions Social Realities.* Washington, D.C.: Association for Supervision and Curriculum Development, 1968.

———. *New Curriculum Developments.* Washington, D.C.: Association for Supervision and Curriculum Development, 1965.

Beauchamp, George. *Curriculum Theory.* Wilmette, Ill.: The Kagg Press, 1961.

Bloom, Benjamin S., ed. *Taxonomy of Educational Objectives.* New York: Longmans, Green and Co., Inc., 1956.

Bruner, Jerome S. *The Process of Education.* Cambridge: Harvard University Press, 1960.

Cawelti, Gordon. "Innovative Practices in High Schools: Who Does What—and Why—and How." *Nation's Schools* 79(1967):56–60.

Clark, Leonard H., Raymond L. Klein, and John B. Burks. *The American Secondary School Curriculum.* New York: The Macmillan Co., 1965.

Conant, James Bryant. *The American High School Today.* New York: McGraw-Hill, Inc., 1959.

Goldberg, Miriam L., A. Harry Passow, and Joseph Justman. *The Effects of Ability Grouping.* New York: Teachers College Press, Columbia University, 1966.

Goodlad, John I. *The Future of Learning and Teaching.* Washington, D.C.: National Education Association, 1968.

Gwynn, J. Minor, and John B. Chase. *Curriculum Principles and Social Trends.* New York: The Macmillan Co., 1969.

Hopkins, L. Thomas. *Interaction: The Democratic Process.* Boston: D. C. Heath and Co., 1941.

Inlow, Gail M. *The Emergent in Curriculum.* New York: John Wiley & Sons, Inc., 1966.

Keith, Lowell, Paul Blake, and Sidney Tiedt. *Contemporary Curriculum in the Elementary School.* New York: Harper & Row, Publishers, 1968.

Krathwohl, David R., Benjamin S. Bloom and Bertram B. Masia. *Taxonomy of Educational Objectives.* New York: David McKay Co., Inc., 1964.

Miller, Richard I. *The Nongraded School: Analysis and Study.* New York: Harper & Row, Publishers, 1967.

National Education Association Project on the Instructional Program of the Public Schools. *Education in a Changing Society.* Washington, D.C.: National Education Association, 1964.

Ragan, William B. *Modern Elementary Curriculum.* rev. ed. New York: The Dryden Press, Inc., 1960.

Smith, B. Othanel, William O. Stanley, and J. Harlan Shores. *Fundamentals of Curriculum Development.* rev. ed. New York: Harcourt, Brace & World, Inc., 1957.

The Phantom Nongraded School

William P. McLoughlin

Few propositions for educational change have generated and sustained as much interest as the nongraded school. It is discussed at nearly every major educational conference, and symposiums on the nongraded school are increasing in popularity. Furthermore, the body of available literature is increasing rapidly; most leading professional journals have published several articles on this topic. Through these and other means, educators have learned more of the promises of the nongraded school than they have of its accomplishments.

This is understandable, for nongrading appears to be preached more than practiced and practiced more than appraised. In fact, few dependable estimates on the present status and anticipated growth of the nongraded school are currently available and sound studies on its accomplishments are even more difficult to come by. From what is available one would be hard put to determine just how many schools have nongraded their instructional programs and how many are seriously contemplating the change. If findings in these areas are obscure, the outcomes of the evaluations of existing nongraded programs are even less definitive.

The available estimates of the number of schools with nongraded programs fluctuates from 5.5 per cent[1] to 30 per cent.[2] These, it must be pointed out, are unqualified esti-

mates; they do not consider the quality of the programs purporting to be nongraded. When this element is added, estimates of the number of schools with *truly* nongraded programs shrink considerably. Goodlad, in 1955, estimated that less than one per cent of the schools in the country were nongraded[3] and in 1961 he felt there were probably fewer than 125 schools to be found with *truly* nongraded programs.[4]

If uncertainty marks present estimates of the number of schools operating nongraded programs, certainly forecasts for future growth are dubious. In 1958 the NEA reported 26.3 per cent of the respondents to its survey saying they intended to nongrade their schools.[5] Five years later, however,

* William P. McLoughlin, "The Phantom Nongraded School," *Phi Delta Kappan* 69(1968):248–250. Used by permission.

1. Lillian L. Gore and Rose E. Koury, *A Survey of Early Elementary Education in Public Schools, 1960–61.* Washington, D.C.: U.S. Department of Health, Education and Welfare, 1965.
2. National Education Association, *Nongraded Schools.* Research Memo 1965-12. Washington, D.C.: Research Division, NEA, May, 1965.
3. John I. Goodlad, "More About the Ungraded Plan," *NEA Journal*, May, 1955, pp. 295–96.
4. National Education Association, *Nongrading: A Modern Practice in Elementary School Organization.* Research Memorandum 1961-37. Washington, D.C.: Research Division, NEA, October, 1961.
5. National Education Association, *Administrative Practices in Urban School Districts, 1958–1959.* Research Report 1961-R10. Washington, D.C.: Research Division, NEA, May, 1961.

this estimate had dwindled to 3.2 per cent.[6] On the other hand, the USOE's pollings reverse this trend. Of schools queried in 1958, only 13.4 per cent expected to become nongraded,[7] but two years later this estimate doubled and 26.3 per cent of the respondents reported considering nongrading their schools.[8] With these conflicting findings it is difficult to know if the nongraded school is coming into its own or passing out of existence.

One thing seems clear from these surveys, however: nongrading is related to district size. Nearly all available surveys confirm this; the larger the district, the more likely it is to have one or more nongraded units. Here we should stress that this does not mean that nongrading is the principal organizational pattern in large school districts. It simply means a nongraded unit is operating in one or more of the district's several elementary schools.[9]

Studies of the influence of nongrading on students are rare, too, and their composite findings somewhat bewildering. Thirty-three empirical studies of the influence of nongrading on student academic achievement have been identified. Not all of these, however, consider the same variables. About half of them assess the influence of nongrading on reading achievement, while 25 per cent look at its influence on arithmetic performance. Only 11 per cent of the studies question the impact nongrading has on the student's development in language arts. Nine per cent report on the total achievement scores of children. The remaining studies are spread so thinly through the other curricular divisions that a detailed consideration of their findings is hardly profitable.[10]

Judged by these studies, the academic development of children probably does not suffer from attending a nongraded school; there is some evidence, admittedly sketchy and tentative, to indicate it may be somewhat enhanced. One thing is certain; children from graded classes seldom do better on these measures than children from nongraded classes. More commonly, children from nongraded classes excel their contemporaries from graded classes.

For example, 15 studies considered the influence of nongrading on the general reading achievement of children. Seven of these report no significant difference between children from graded and nongraded classes. In other words, nothing is lost by having children attend nongraded classes. But only two studies found children from graded classes outscoring children from nongraded classes, while six studies found the general reading attainments of children from nongraded classes superior to that of children in graded classes.

Similar though less distinct outcomes are attained when the reading subskills of comprehension and vocabulary development are examined. Again, the principal finding of 14 studies is that there are no marked differences in the accomplishments of children in these areas regardless of the type of organization in which they learn to read.

6. NEA, *Nongraded Schools, op. cit.*

7. Stuart E. Dean, *Elementary School Administration and Organization: A National Survey of Practices and Policies.* Washington, D.C.: U.S. Department of Health, Education and Welfare, 1963.

8. Gore and Koury, *op. cit.*

9. William P. McLoughlin, *The Nongraded School: A Critical Assessment.* Albany, N.Y.: The University of the State of New York, The New York State Education Department, 1967.

10. *Ibid.*

Furthermore, for every study showing greater gains for children from graded classes, there is an equal number of studies counterbalancing these findings.

The mirror image of this picture emerges when the arithmetic attainments of children from graded and nongraded classes are contrasted. Eleven studies considered the influence of nongrading on children's general arithmetic achievement, and their findings are inconclusive. Three report differences favoring children from nongraded classes, five found differences favoring children from graded classes,[11] and three found no difference.

But when the arithmetic subskills of reasoning and knowledge of fundamentals are examined, different outcomes appear. Of the 12 published studies in these areas, one reports differences favoring children from graded classes but six report differences favoring children from nongraded classes. The remaining five show no real difference in the achievement of children in these areas, regardless of the type of class organization.

In language arts, too, there is scant evidence to demonstrate that organization influences achievement. Seven of the 10 studies in this area report no true differences in the language skills developed by children from graded and nongraded classes. One reports achievement test scores of children from graded classes as superior to those of children from nongraded classes, while two studies found the observed differences in the achievement of children from nongraded classes indeed significantly superior to that of controls in the graded classes. Apparently, nongraded classes are no more effective in developing language arts skills than are graded classes.

Total achievement test scores, too, seem remarkably immune to change because of changes in organizational pattern. Half of the eight studies using them to measure the efficacy of the nongraded school found no significant differences in the achievements of children from graded and nongraded classes. The remaining studies divide equally: Two reported differences favoring children from graded classes while two found differences favoring children from nongraded classes. So here, once again, the influence of nongrading on the academic development of children is indeterminate.

Better student achievement is not the only claim put forth for the nongraded school. Its advocates maintain, implicitly or explicitly, that superior student adjustment is attained in the nongraded school. Certainly student adjustment and personality development are crucial concerns of educators and, quite reasonably, they are interested in developing learning settings which foster this goal.

Unfortunately, studies assessing the influence of nongrading on student adjustment are even more rare than studies assessing its influence on their academic achievement. Moreover, the diversity of procedures utilized in these studies to measure adjustment lessens their cumulative value. Sociograms, adjustment inventories, anxiety scales, and even school attendance records have all been used as indices of pupil adjustment. But no matter how measured, there is scant evidence to support the contention that superior student adjustment is realized in nongraded schools. On the 32 separate indices of adjustment used in these studies, the overwhelmingly majority, 26, indicate that

11. *Ibid.*

there is no significant difference in the adjustment of children from graded and nongraded classes. Only four of the measures (general adjustment, social adjustment, social maturity, and freedom from age stereotypes) showed differences favorable to children from nongraded classes, while the remaining two (social participation and freedom from defensiveness) were favorable to children from graded classes.[12]

Research, then, finds little to impel or impede practitioners interested in nongrading. Under either organization children's adjustment and achievement appear to remain remarkably constant. For those to whom the nongraded school is a magnificent obsession, these findings must come as a numbing disappointment. Taken at face value, current research on the nongraded school seems to say that its contribution to the academic, social, and emotional development of children is marginal.

But should these findings be taken at face value? It might be naive to rest the fate of the nongraded school on past research. The validity of these studies should be rigorously tested, for they depend on one tacit but critical assumption: that the experimental schools, those purporting to be nongraded, are *truly* nongraded. If this assumption is not met and the experimental schools are not nongraded, then research has told us nothing about the efficacy of the nongraded school.

Too often, on close inspection, one finds that schools credited with operating nongraded programs are not nongraded at all. Homogeneous grouping and semi-departmentalization of instruction in reading and arithmetic are frequently passed off as nongraded programs. These techniques must be recognized for what they are. They are administrative expediencies developed to make the *graded* school work. They are not nongraded instructional programs.

If these are the "nongraded" programs represented in these studies, then researching their effectiveness is an exercise in futility, for the *experimental* schools are as graded as the control schools and no experimental treatment is being tested. Research has done nothing more than contrast the performances of children from graded schools called graded schools with the performance of children from graded schools called nongraded schools. Essentially, we have simply researched the age-old question: "What's in a name?"

The nongraded school is defensible only because the graded school is indefensible. Its justification flows from its efforts to correct the instructional errors of the graded school. It is reasonably unlikely that any amount of manipulation of the physical arrangements of schools will produce discernible differences in the academic or psychosocial development of children. Every grade label can be cleansed from every classroom door in the school without influencing the school's attainments with children as long as graded instructional practices prevail behind these doors.

Nongrading begins with significant alterations in instructional, not organizational, procedures. As long as schools seek practices designed to group away differences they are *not* nongraded. The nongraded school never held this as a goal, for it is impossible. Rather, nongrading says: "Accept children as they are, with all their differences, and teach to these differences. Don't try to eradicate them!" Until educators de-

12. *Ibid.*

velop instructional programs that will meet this challenge they are not nongrading.

They are simply masking their old egg-crate schools with a new facade.

CHAPTER 9

Instructional Resources

Historically, the teacher's primary job has been that of presenting information to students in a demonstration or lecture discussion manner. Various kinds of devices, including books, have always been used by teachers as instructional resources for assisting them in reaching their pupils. Johannes Gutenberg invented the type mold during the mid-1400's which made printing from movable metallic type practical for the first time. Educational historians record this breakthrough in printing as greatly significant in that teachers have since had books and other printed materials more readily available as resources. In addition to printed materials, teachers have used such things as wax tablets, slate boards, blackboards and chalk, hornbooks, microscopes, animal cadavers, works of art, architecture, music and musical instruments, and the theatre to facilitate learning. With a relatively stable society prior to the end of World War II changes in the institutions of society were few. Thus, the development of instructional resources was slow, moving with little more than bare essential expenditures allocated from school budgets.

Schools have undergone a great deal of change since the end of World War II. Extensive building programs and experiments with modular scheduling, team teaching, and educational television were brought about by the increasing numbers of students during the 1950's. The suddenly changing world of education was spurred by the launching of the Russian satellite Sputnik in 1957. Following Sputnik, the American

A truly vigorous personal, intellectual, and social education can be created only if the teacher and the student, as they work together, have many options available to them—options which enable students to engage in a large variety of instructional activities and which assist teachers to perform a corresponding diversity of instructional roles. They need a rich laboratory of books, audiovisual media, and other technological resources . . .

National Commission on Teacher Education and Professional Standards

199

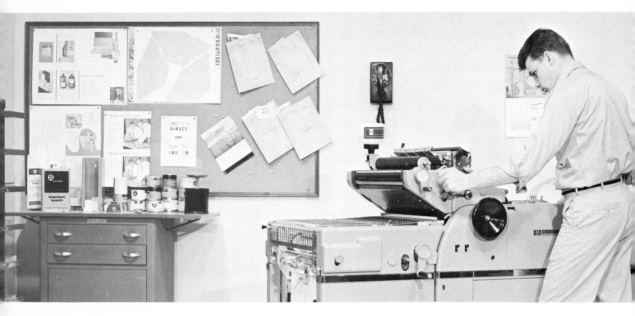

Many kinds of printed materials are often produced within the school.

public demanded improvements in school curricula. The federal government enacted the National Defense Education Act of 1958 which expanded federal financial aid to education for programs to improve instruction. This act also provided funds to develop audiovisual media services and facilities. Modifications to this act culminated in several federal programs being enacted by the Eighty-ninth Congress. Federal research funds were granted for educational media research and for library research. Big businesses jumped into the competition for this new source of federal money for education and the pace quickened in the development of many kinds of instructional resources.

The growth of knowledge during the post World War II years has provided not only an additional stimulus to the growth of educational media, but also provided one of the greatest challenges to teaching. Teachers have come more and more to understand that learning is an active rather than passive process. Information-giving pedagogy, assigning facts to be studied and memorized, is considered out of vogue in many schools today. A contemporary view of the teacher's primary task is to serve as a facilitator, planner, and director of varied active learning experiences. The teacher also serves as a diagnostician who must demonstrate his competencies for organizing instructional material and techniques geared to the achievement of teaching-learning objectives.

Mediaware

Educational media are the tools of the professional teacher. Educational media include printed, audio, visual, and real materials. Certainly, texts, graphs, pictures, newspapers, magazines, encyclopedias, and comics are educational media. Other important media include films, filmstrips, slides, overhead and opaque projectors, commercial and educational television, records, audio-tapes, radio, real things such as animal pets, insects, etc., models of real things such as skeletons and model machinery, simulation devices such as driver trainers and communication kits, as well as computers. The media list is ever increasing, as it must be, to accompany the ever increasing knowledge growth. Future teachers will be more and more media-minded as they assume their teaching tasks.

Software

Software products are those generally associated with the teacher which have been used for years. Software media include textbooks, paper and pencil learning materials, workbooks, encyclopedias, newspapers, magazines, graphs, charts, posters, maps, globes, and most recently, various kinds of programed materials. The kinds of materials found in typical school libraries are generally considered as software. Many

Paperbacks have reduced the cost of many great books.

Wall charts and maps are important aids for learning.

Audio tapes are available for several kinds and types of machines.

Elementary students use tapes to help develop listening skills.

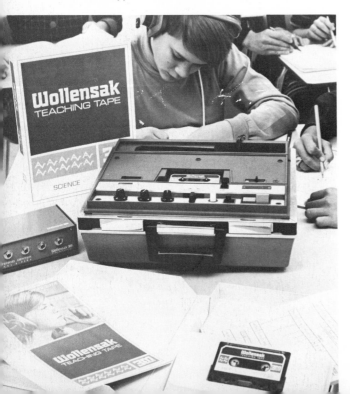

software products have been manufactured specifically for sale to the homes, such as encyclopedias, book-of-the-month publications, and school oriented papers and magazines. Software materials are very important to the teaching-learning process and continue to undergo changes in form and patterns of use.

Hardware

Only recently have we begun to make applications of technology and the products of technology to improve education. Such hardware products of technology include all kinds of mechanical and electronic devices which aid or supplement the software products. In many schools, movie projectors, filmstrip and slide projectors, record play-

ers, tape recorders, opaque projectors, overhead projectors, reading machines, and other devices of an audiovisual nature may be kept in rooms designated as audiovisual rooms. Also, many schools employ a director of audiovisual education who is responsible for the maintenance of equipment and for the coordination of teacher utilization of equipment. The concept of audiovisual (AV) programs to enhance instruction is considered the forerunner for the contemporary thrust in the applications of technology to education.

Large sums of monies have been invested by private business and by federal acts during the past few years for modifying, adapting, and producing hardware for specific classroom use. The effect of this emphasis has been the expanding and upgrading of

Tapes and texts may be coordinated for specific learning activities.

Only a small space is required for several students to use a single tape.

Taped programmed laboratory instruction can be supplemented by visuals.

A teacher prepares to change transparencies on an overhead projector during a class presentation.

Maps project brightly on blackboards in normally lighted rooms, one of the advantages derived from using overhead projectors.

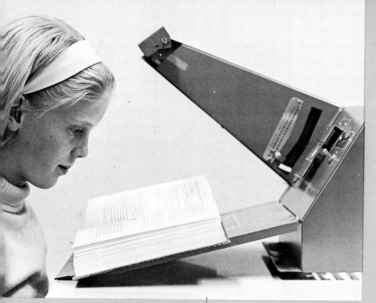

A junior high school student uses a machine to help her accelerate her reading speed.

Two young teachers preview a filmstrip before presentation in class.

Movie cameras are easy to use for filming class activities.

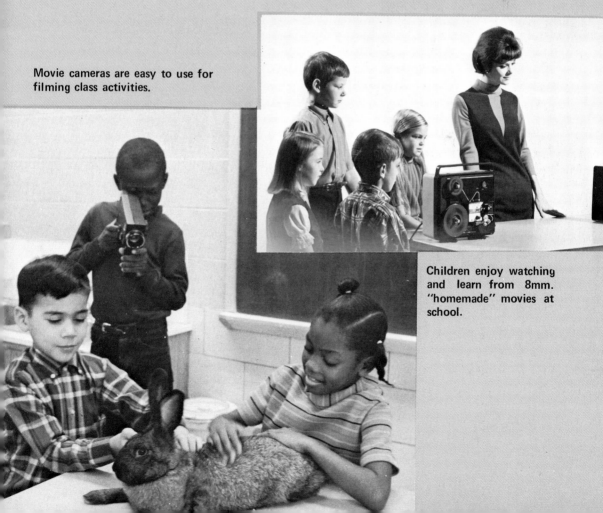

Children enjoy watching and learn from 8mm. "homemade" movies at school.

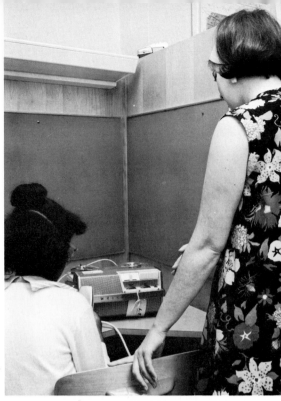

A teacher records a story for her class.

In Shaker Heights, Ohio, a volunteer mother assists a child to record a poem.

Teacher and students in a Listen-Respond type Language Laboratory.

the audiovisual program concept. The impact of software and hardware development has brought to focus the systems approach to instruction. An instructional system includes careful planning of instructional objectives, consideration of methods, facilities and people in performing various instructional activities, in addition to the valid selection of media. In effect, the systems approach to instruction brings together the audiovisual program, the school library and school personnel. Later in this chapter attention is given to the changing view with regard to future school libraries.

Title II of the Elementary and Secondary Education Act of 1965 provided to the states $100 million to improve educational quality through grants for the acquisition of school library resources. The three categories of materials eligible for acquisition under Title II included software and hardware of various kinds. The categories were school library resources (includes audiovisual materials), textbooks and other printed and published instructional materials. Most states allocated all or most of their Title II funds for school library resources, or for a combination of school library resources and

Students at San Rafael, California, learn to read from sound tapes.

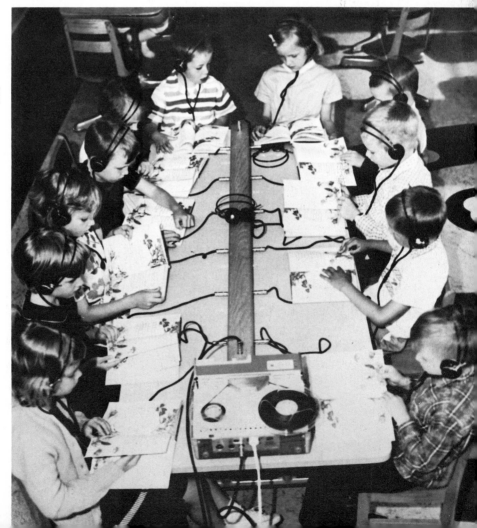

Taped instructions permit an individual student to conduct a biology experiment.

A biology class conducts experiments to taped instructions.

Students in a special education class being video taped during class.

Special education students being video taped in physical education class.

Teacher being video taped in a small studio showing camera, switcher and overhead lighting.

Two elementary students watch themselves on video tape playback.

Students in a parochial school watching program received from an Instructional Television System.

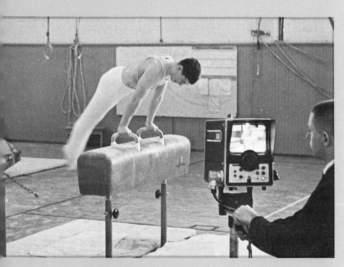

Taping Meet: A member of the University of Washington gymnastics team performs a routine on a sidehorse at the Seattle campus. His routine is picked up by a television camera and recorded on a videotape recorder as part of a meet with the University of Illinois. Each team competed on its own campus, with an impartial panel of judges viewing the video tapes of both teams to render its decision. It was the first such meet ever held. Illinois was the winner, 180.65—173.10.

Instant Replay: Coach and performer review the athlete's routine seconds after its completion. The two are watching a sidehorse routine taped at the University of Washington.

other instructional materials. The expenditure of the original Title II appropriations firmed up the trend among schools to capitalize upon the availability for new software and hardware in instruction.

Learning Resource Centers

Existing public school libraries have been criticized severely by various study groups. In 1961, the National Committee for Support of the Public Schools reported that (a) more than 10 million children go to public schools with no school libraries, and (b) more than half of all public schools have no library. Such criticism has generated renewed interest in the directions school libraries ought to be taking in order to meet the needs of today's pupils. "Beyond question, the traditional concept of a public school library, with its stiff overtones of hardback chairs and rectangular tables, is now obsolete; it has matured into a concept of a total learning resource center, which like a candy store displays what it has to offer in the most appealing way possible."[1] The trend of the future with regard to the school library concept is to arrange the various software and hardware media in a common setting which provides space specifically allocated for individual and small group usage. Individual study carrels will have individual lighting controls and electrical outlets. Small groups will have access to specific resource centers such as math and science centers. Comfortable furniture, small study desks, and carpeting will replace obsolete furnishings. The learning resource center concept demands a high level of utilization necessitating flexible schedule arrangements to permit students time to use the center.

The creation of a learning-resource center is not an attempt to do away with the school library. Instead, it attempts to utilize the typical verbal materials of the library and supplement them with additional software and hardware instructional media now available to the teacher. As children become involved in the learning process at different rates of growth they have a need to pursue learning on an individual basis and also in small group activities. The teacher may now

> But whatever they call it, and wherever they put it, public schools everywhere are going to have to find space for reducing, retaining, reproducing and displaying the incredible mountain of information that new technology now makes available. Sooner than we think, a public school without such facilities will be about as educationally effective as a log without Mark Hopkins there on the end.
>
> Aaron Cohodes, *Nation's Schools,*
> March, 1966

free the learner to go to a center where materials are provided for individual and small group learning. The center is equipped with books, programmed materials, television, tape banks with head sets and a variety of other materials which will provide auditory, visual and audiovisual learning.

This type of learning center has been more readily adopted at the elementary level but more recently has begun to move

1. Aaron Cohodes, "Put It in the Middle and Call it a Learning Center," *Nation's Schools* 77(1966): 85.

into the newer junior and senior high schools. Some of the types of materials that may be found in a learning center follow. This list is by no means all-inclusive, but only representative.

"1. *Controlled Readers.* This is a mechanical pacing device. A moving slot travels across the screen covering and uncovering reading material as it goes. Speeds of these machines range from 60 to 1000 words per minute.

2. *Tapes for Speech Patterns.* These tapes attempt to teach the child to make correctly a particular sound with his lips and teeth and teach him to become aware of the sound when he hears it.

3. *Listening Laboratories.* Listening laboratories will accommodate from one to eight students. They may be used with records or audio tapes. Currently there are some laboratories which have audiovisual facilities. These laboratories are not as fully developed as they will be in the future.

4. *Library and Reading Kits.* Multi-level reading laboratories have short stories and excerpts from great works in literature. They cover areas of poetry, history, fiction and nonfiction. A student uses these on an individual basis and it helps supplement the multi-level reading program of the school.

5. *Controlled Reader for Mathematics.* This is a mechanical device with filmstrips and headsets. Emphasis is on comprehension of basic number facts and problem-solving techniques.

6. *Elementary Science Units.* These kits include microviewers with filmstrip slides. Information is given in reading form and then strips are used to dem-

onstrate points made in the printed discussion.

7. *Video Tapes.* These tapes are prepared as teaching aids for the teacher and do not replace whole units of instruction. Students may obtain general information individually or in groups and later interact with other students and teachers in a seminar setting. The tapes are of particular value for such difficult and costly things as laboratory presentations and for specialists who otherwise could not be introduced to the learners. With the addition of color tapes this supplemental source will become even more stimulating to the learner.

8. *Computer Assisted Instruction Laboratory.* Although it is rather costly because of the hardware involved, the techniques of linear and branch programing can be utilized in a variety of ways to accommodate individual or small group (2–5) learning sessions. This type of laboratory is still in the experimental stage, but holds promise for individualizing instruction."[2]

From this type of descriptive listing it appears that the teaching task has been greatly simplified. On the contrary, the teacher must now come face to face with issues in the curriculum that have usually been reserved for administrators, supervisors and the like. The learning-resource center is little more than an administratively planned learning area and as such is not different in purpose than the classroom. Al-

2. James Johnson, et al., *Introduction to the Foundations of American Education*, pp. 412–414. Copyright Allyn and Bacon, Inc., 1969. Used with permission.

though it holds promise for the future in its potential for individualized learning, it must for the greater part be planned and developed by teachers. It should be supplied with materials that teachers have selected and developed through their experiences with children.

Recently, the nation has witnessed vast mergers of publishing companies, research bureaus and manufacturers. Seeing a growing need for all kinds of educational software and hardware, plus an economy that promises to allocate increasing funds for education, it appears that these corporations have struck a bonanza. The American businessman has traditionally operated on a profit motive and now his market research has shown a lucrative economic quest in education. Capitalizing on a national concern for increased educational output, these corporations now have the capacity to hypothesize, research, develop, produce and market an endless variety of educational software and hardware which may be used in the learning process. The knowledge explosion, increasing rates of mobility, the quest for more knowledge in a shorter time, the complex pressures of providing individualized educational opportunity for all citizens, and the educational establishment's seeming inability to direct educational change effectively have all contributed to the birth of these corporations.

This type of industrial movement has placed an ever greater responsibility on the teacher working in curriculum. Among the many splendid products on the market today there also may be found hastily developed and poorly researched materials which purport to provide the teacher with "the answer" to learning problems. As a result the teacher has the special task of discard-

ing these inferior or worthless programs and adapting those which are useful to his particular situation. Of a highly more critical nature, the teacher should, in addition to the culling of manufactured materials which may be used for the learning process, continue to develop his own new materials in light of his experience with the learner.

Resource Center Uses Showcase Technics

The library-resource center at Chicago's new South Shore High School will put its services on display through glass enclosures and functional segregation of facilities. The following diagrams, Fig. 9.1 and Fig. 9.2, of the library-resource center, were given in *Nation's Schools* by Frank Carioti.[3]

What Tomorrow's Library Will Look Like

A special report from the Bureau of School Planning, State of California Department of Education, suggested that tomorrow's library will have decentralized study areas, extensive disposable media, and electronic retrieval equipment tapping audio and video material stored at regional knowledge centers. Clair L. Eatough, supervising architectural advisor to the California Bureau of School Planning, wrote the following article for *Nation's Schools* based on suggestions made at a seminar on school libraries.[4]

3. Frank V. Carioti, "Resource Center Uses Showcase Technics," *Nation's Schools* 77(1966):91–93. Reprinted with permission from *Nation's Schools*, March, 1966. Copyright McGraw-Hill, Inc., 1966. All rights reserved.
4. Clair L. Eatough, "What Tomorrow's Library Will Look Like," *Nation's Schools* 77(1966):107–109. Reprinted with permission from *Nation's Schools*, March, 1966. Copyright McGraw-Hill, Inc., 1966. All rights reserved.

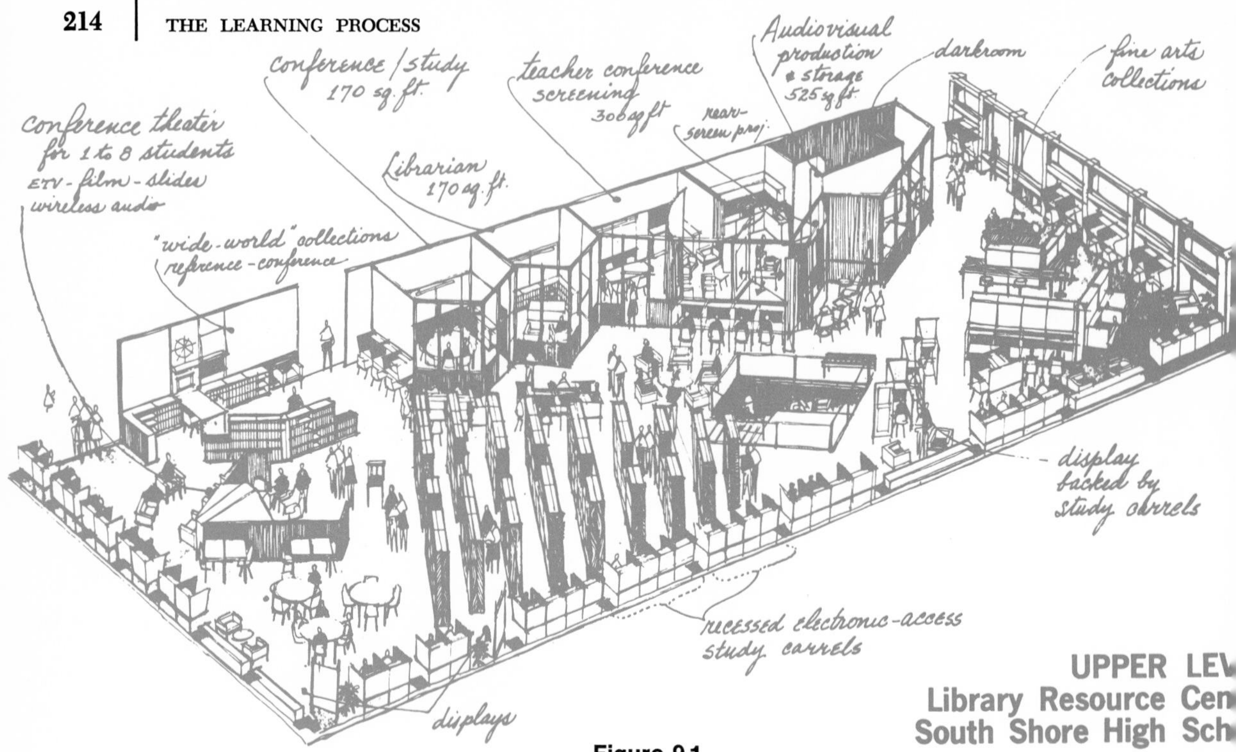

conference theater for 1 to 8 students ETV - film - slides wireless audio

"wide-world" collections reference - conference

conference / study 170 sq. ft.

Librarian 170 sq. ft.

teacher conference screening 300 sq ft

rear-screen proj.

Audiovisual production & storage 525 sq ft

darkroom

fine arts collections

display backed by study carrels

recessed electronic-access study carrels

displays

UPPER LEV
Library Resource Cen
South Shore High Sch

Figure 9.1.

The school library of the near future will be a single canopy under which all media, present and future, can be coordinated. It will have decentralized study centers, extensive paperback collections, and—most importantly—electronic retrieval systems that by the touch of a button or dial will bring televised texts, lectures, filmstrips and movies from distant knowledge centers.

The library of tomorrow will be a Knowledge Resource Center. To understand the KRC concept, school districts must think of library materials as three types of media.

Media A—Traditional material: books, films, records and so forth.

Media B—Disposable material: paperbacks, mimeographs, and so forth.

Media C—Audiovisual material: transmitted electronically.

Media A

This is the material that every librarian and every school teacher is using now. It includes: hard cover books; 35mm., 16mm., and 8mm. movie tapes; filmstrips; sound tapes; phonograph records; periodicals. It requires hand delivery from supplier to user, and schools consider it valuable and therefore catalog, file or store it and set up a staff for its control and use.

Type A media is the justification for our present library concepts. It is likely that most of this media eventually will phase out because of expense and inefficiency. Its value will be almost exclusively for specialized research. School libraries below university levels normally do not have funds to acquire and maintain sufficient quantities of esoteric material or enough advanced

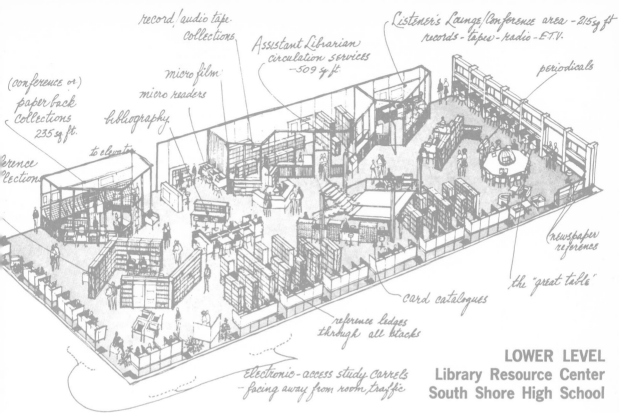

record / audio tape collections

Assistant Librarian circulation services — 509 sq ft.

Listener's Lounge / Conference area — 215 sq ft records - tapes - radio - E.T.V.

micro film

micro readers

periodicals

(conference or) paper back collections 235 sq ft.

bibliography

to elevator

reference collections

newspaper reference

the "great table"

card catalogues

reference ledges through all stacks

Electronic-access study carrels — facing away from room traffic

LOWER LEVEL
Library Resource Center
South Shore High School

Figure 9.2.

students to make the concept productive. Most schools have little to gain by the archival approach to media.

Media B

This media in whatever form is *disposable*. Proper use of this material can achieve some dramatic developments. But this depends on the recognition by educators that there is a great body of printed material that can be purchased at a price that permits it to be discarded after limited use yet still achieve a high educational return on the investment.

The paperback book; reproduction by such processes as dry photo copying; the mimeographed sheet; the blue print or ozalid are examples of common disposable material. We are assuming that in tomorrow's library the school will make available means for reproduction of Type B media to every student as well as staff.

It is a mistake to think that because disposable material in many forms is in use now it will have no more impact on tomorrow's schools than it has on today's. The *extent* of use will be new. If the school were to make full use of paperbacks, purchasing mostly books of this type, it would not need to bother with cataloging, filing, storing. Only initial dispersal to various study centers would be important. Shelves could be open, and students could be given totally free access. We could at last free ourselves of the ancient phobia that the books, rather than the knowledge they contain, are valuable and must be restricted in use.

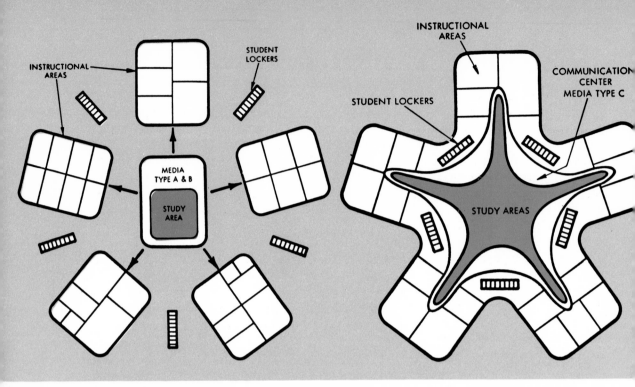

Figure 9.3. Today's library, often central in location, may separate students from materials and teachers from study areas. Tomorrow's KRC may serve 5 to 6 teaching stations, 100 to 200 students and integrate study, materials and instruction.

Ideally, librarians and instructors would evaluate this material and key the selection to the curriculum as carefully as is now done with expensive, more permanent material. Basic reference texts and encyclopedias would have to be purchased in quantity and distributed to each study center. These items must be given extensive exposure to obtain extensive use. They too should be replaced often, perhaps every year, not only because of ill treatment or loss, but because the information they contain becomes rapidly obsolete.

Disposable books and related materials permit the development of elements of a Parisian "left bank" by locating book stalls next to outdoor reading areas. These can be enhanced by snack bars and art displays.

Media C

This media is the heart of KRC. It includes any material that can be transmitted electronically to the user in audio or visual form or both. Normally the media is a cartridge loaded magnetic tape which stores both sound and picture.

Electronic retrieval systems require a centralized facility for the production and storage of programed material, and decentralized study areas. They are coupled with a network of communication channels. The receiving stations (where the students are) have instant access to the available programed material by pushing buttons or twirling a telephone dial to audio and video channels which can tap live or stored presentations.

The communication center is a great storehouse for magnetic tapes containing programed material which includes almost all texts, lectures, filmstrips and movies in all fields of knowledge. Duplication and exchange of tapes is coordinated with all other communication centers throughout the country. All indexing, filing and retrieval are computerized. The facility includes production studios and a complete staff organization for its operation. A vast electronic network links it to all schools and study centers within the geographic region which it serves. A student can then dial a number and through a telephone or television receiver listen to a lecture, view a film, read a research article from a professional journal, or take a lesson in a foreign language. When combined with independent study materials a student or teacher has all available resources at his finger tips. Catalogs are similar to telephone directories. They are designed to cover subject areas at various levels of education. School curriculum planners create and distribute special directories which are available to students. This is coordinated with the teacher's planned sequence of instruction. Thus, a sixth grade English student has the titles and numbers to dial the entire selected resource material which his teacher wishes to make available. Students working independently have more extensive directories available at major study centers. Suggested material is recommended for study by teachers and counselors so that the student is guided to available material based on his curriculum goals, state of readiness, interest and skills. This permits students to work on an individualized schedule to a degree not possible in traditional patterns.

Not only are materials containing audio-visual sequences capable of being presented to a student almost any place where desired on a campus, but eventually this service will expand beyond the confines of the school and permit a student to dial a lesson from his home in the evening. It will be possible for the student in the one-room school to have equal access and exposure to available information as the student in the large urban school. It can encompass all ages. It can serve the learner from the beginning reader in elementary school through high school and college and on through a useful adult lifetime.

KRC assumes that the student and his study centers will be dispersed throughout the campus, and eventually throughout the community. *Bringing the resources to the student rather than the student to the material* is the essence of the KRC. This requires a reappraisal of student study centers.

Students Want Study Centers

There has been much recent concern about how and where students prefer to study. The Community College Planning Center at Stanford University sent questionnaires to students. Their responses show:

— Students prefer small as against large study areas; they considered moderately sized study rooms superior to small study areas.

— Students prefer to study where there is easy access to special equipment (e.g. drafting equipment, art equipment, and so forth).

— Students expressed a strong desire to study where there is easy access to instructors.

The conclusion of the published report was, "Clearly, students generally want contact with their instructors and prefer to study in the familiar surroundings of their 'home base' classrooms, labs, practice rooms, and so forth. There seems to be a clear implication that study space should not be concentrated entirely in the library but should be available throughout the campus."

KRC study centers can be as varied as the places where people desire to study. However, a typical study center should have certain essential elements such as:

1. It is located adjacent to and perhaps as part of the instructional area of the school. (It might be a core area of a cluster type building supported directly by four or five teaching stations.)

2. It resembles an informal lounge area utilizing comfortable furniture and carpeted floors.

3. Its standards for lighting, acoustics and the thermal environment are as high as any area in the school.

4. It typically provides space and equipment for 25 to 50 students. Study areas are duplicated and distributed as required throughout the campus or building.

5. Each study center is so located that it becomes the home base for 100 to 200 students, depending on the schedule. The students' lockers (silenced by use of plastic, fibrous glass or other nonmetallic material) are located either in or immediately adjacent to his study center.

6. Each study center is equipped to supply and to use disposable media. This includes reference books, encyclopedias, dictionaries, but especially large quantities of paperbacks and other types of disposable material.

7. The study centers have a number of stations where the students dial for and receive by television monitors media from a central communications center. Directories listing the programed material are available.

8. Adjacent to most study centers are rooms or alcoves for copying machines, duplicators, silent typewriters, and so forth— all available for student and teacher use.

9. Teacher-student counseling areas and work areas are adjacent to and part of these study centers.

Many schools now in existence could be adapted to introduce some of these elements. Schools now being planned should give serious consideration to decentralizing study areas.

KRC needs a broad base for its support. Any school can implement a few of its features at little cost or effort. No single school and few school districts can create all of it by themselves. Eventually if it is to fulfill its potential of bringing available knowledge to everyone upon demand, it will require a statewide or regional organization for its operation.

The size of the central communication center would be determined by financial considerations and it is likely that one center would need a great many students to operate efficiently. California, for example, might require 5 or 10 of these centers located geographically throughout the state, probably at major colleges or universities since it could then utilize the resources from these library archives.

A museum is a typical example of a community resource which has great educational value.

California is currently installing a statewide network of computerized indexing and cataloging which will link together all state college and university libraries and the state library in Sacramento so that any item at any library can be located and transferred to the seeker. KRC could be working for these combined institutions if equipment were installed for electronic transfer of the material.

At present there are several obstacles to overcome before dial-access systems can gain wide usage. Most critical is the limited material presently available in programed form. Also lacking are trained personnel to prepare and present the material for use. Existing retrieval equipment is already more sophisticated than the staff in most schools. Money, the prime mover, will soon be available through Title II of the Elementary and Secondary Education Act of 1965. We can expect to see a greatly accelerated implementation of the electronic approach to teaching.

KRC to Dominate Instruction

KRC when implemented has the potential of alleviating today's massive problems of material logistics. Media Type A is radically reduced in quantity. Media Type B relates only to the study areas scattered throughout the campus. Media Type C is prepared, stored, indexed and distributed from a central communication center located elsewhere.

Unlike the traditional library, KRC cannot remain in a subordinate role to the instructional areas of the school, but will be-

Outdoor educational opportunities provide valuable learning experiences for these young boys.

come, through its various components, the main instructional area of the school. Proportionately more money and more space will be devoted to its requirements for space and equipment. The traditional library, along with the traditional self-contained classroom it serves, will tend to atrophy as their functions become more limited.

Community Resources

More than three-fourths of our population now live in either the central city areas or their suburbs. Improved transportation facilities have expanded the availability of community resources for school use. Students now have increased opportunities to learn about many things in their own communities. Many school boards, school administrators, and creative teachers are finding different ways in which to utilize community resources to supplement the learning activities of the schools.

Considerable educational planning is a prerequisite to the proper utilization of community resources. Educators ought to carefully develop community resource guides for the purpose of identifying and describing available educational resources, including community resource persons. Proper utilization of community resources for educational field trips requires subsequent planning which considers certain educational criteria for field trips. Finding and using resource persons, either at their place of work or in the classroom, also requires careful planning for coordinating the contributions of the resource person with the sequence of work students are doing in the classroom.

Obviously, the scope of available community resources is prescribed to a large mea-

A student teacher enjoys working with her students in an outdoor teaching experience.

sure by the nature of the community. However, every school community, large or small, has community resources at its disposal.

Outdoor Education

Programs of outdoor education are increasing in popularity, especially at the elementary level. The outdoor education program concept deals with study in an outdoor setting. In some areas outdoor education camps are maintained as a cooperative venture among school districts. In other areas the community resources of agencies such as Boy Scouts and Girl Scouts, YMCA and YWCA, churches, private clubs and various service organizations are utilized in providing outdoor facilities for educational programs sponsored by the local schools.

Teachers involved in outdoor education programs usually accompany their students on overnight expeditions to an outdoor education camp.

In summary, the laboratory concept as associated with today's schools requires the availability of many kinds of materials, equipment and facilities to assist the teacher in her work with students. The range of such needs includes the software and hardware of our technological age, classrooms constructed to best use software and hardware, library resource centers or learning centers where multi-media systems may be assembled and operationalized, and utilization of available community resources, including the use of outdoor education facilities. All of these things add to the excitement of teaching and greatly assist the teacher in meeting her daily tasks.

QUESTIONS FOR DISCUSSION

1. What is your estimate of the impact of federal aid programs in effecting specific changes and improvements in programs of instruction?
2. How could uses of new educational media aid in solving some of the school problems arising from increased enrollments, greater range of abilities and more varied backgrounds among the students?
3. What features make the overhead projector a particularly useful teaching tool?
4. How would you use educational television and commercial television as teaching resources?
5. What are the relative advantages of taking a class on a trip to a zoo or of showing them a film on the subject? Given a choice, which would you choose? Why?

Various business agencies have elaborate equipment which may be made available for educational purposes to the community.

SUPPLEMENTARY LEARNING ACTIVITIES

1. Interview the head of the audiovisual department in a nearby school. Obtain information about the kinds of services offered and the extent of their use in the classes.
2. Visit a local travel agency to obtain various materials advertising foreign countries. Arrange these materials in a display for use in classroom instruction.
3. Contact an institution which uses television as a resource tool for teaching. Obtain and record information regarding the uses of television and the results of such uses.
4. Construct a device to aid in teaching an important concept in your teaching field. Demonstrate and discuss the teaching aid which you constructed.
5. Select a desirable field trip for your teaching field in your community. Visit the location selected and develop the plans needed for the class visit.

SELECTED REFERENCES

Bright, R. Louis. "The Place of Technology in Educational Change." *Audiovisual Instruction* 12(1967):340–343.
Bruner, Jerome, ed. *Learning about Learning.* Washington, D.C.: U.S. Office of Education, 1966.
Campion, Lee. "A Department Promotes Media." *Educational Screen and Audiovisual Guide* 45(1966):32–33.
Corey, Kenneth E. "Using Local Resources in Developing Geography Concepts and Understanding." *Social Education* 30(1966):617–620.
Goodlad, John I. "Directions of Curriculum Change." *NEA Journal* 55(1966):33–37.
Greenhill, L. P., et al. *Research in Instructional Television and Film.* Washington, D.C.: Bureau of Research, U.S. Office of Education, Government Printing Office, 1967.

Johnson, James, et al. *Introduction to the Foundations of American Education.* Boston: Allyn and Bacon, Inc., 1969.

Joyce, Bruce R. *Man, Media, and Machines.* Washington, D.C.: Teacher Education and Professional Standards, National Education Association, 1967.

Keppel, Francis. "The Big Business Interest in Education." *Phi Delta Kappan* 48(1967): 187–190.

Lange, Phil C. "Technology, Learning, and Instruction." *Audiovisual Instruction* 13(1968): 226–231.

Mayer, Martin. "The Trouble with Textbooks." *Harper's Magazine* July, 1962, pp. 65–71.

McMillan, Gene, and Evelyn Stryker. "How to Survive a Field Trip." *NEA Journal* 56 (1967):58.

Miles, Matthew B., ed. *Innovation in Education.* New York: Teachers College, 1964.

Rossi, Peter H., and Bruce J. Biddle. *The New Media and Education.* Chicago: Aldine Publishing Co., 1966.

Salisbury, Gordon. *Catalog of Free Teaching Materials.* Riverside, Cal.: Gordon Salisbury, 1965.

Smith, Richard E. *The Overhead System: Production, Implementation, and Utilization.* Austin, Texas: Visual Instruction Bureau, University of Texas, 1965.

Staley, Frederick A. "Community Resources: The Forgotten World of Knowledge." *Educational Screen and Audio-Visual Guide* 44(1965):27–30.

Vandermeer, A. W. "Systems Analysis and Media: A Perspective." *Audio-Visual Communication Review* 12(1964):292–301.

Winn, Ira U. "Rafferty and the Sterile Textbook Adoption Struggle." *Phi Delta Kappan* 49(1967):37–41.

Wyman, Raymond. "The Instructional Materials Center: Whose Empire?" *Audiovisual Instruction* 12(1967):114–115.

The Time Is Now

R. Louis Bright

We are rapidly becoming a computer-assisted society. Few areas of our lives are not affected by these amazing machines which appeared less than 20 years ago. Already they schedule vast steel mills, train leaders of business, check income tax returns, and guide rockets to Venus. College students are even using them for the most personal of matters—to find dates for themselves.

What does this mean for educators? It means that unless high schools and colleges start telling their students how their lives and work will be changed by computers they are selling them short. A report from the President's Office of Science and Technology on use of computers in higher education asserts that any four-year liberal arts college that does not give students experience in data processing techniques has severely cheated its graduates educationally. I would carry this one step further. The high school which ignores the impact of computers is just as obsolete.

Some computerized techniques are within reach of the average high school and college right now. A study supported by the Office of Education's Bureau of Research shows that if several schools use the same computer facility, it would cost an average school district no more than one per cent of its total budget to take advantage of several important computer applications. For example, figures indicate that to service 120,000 elementary pupils, 40,000 secondary schoolers, and 2,000 college students, the cost of equipment, personnel, and supplies would run about $800,000 per year. For a district with 486,000 students, the cost would be about $1.7 million annually. These amazingly low figures were drawn from a study of the cost of servicing 50 high schools and junior colleges with a central computer facility.

This is no vague, futuristic supposition; it is a very practical system that conceivably could be operating within two years. The secret of its success is the regional approach. One computer would serve school districts for one hundred miles around. The computer would give these schools three things for their money: it would provide routine administrative services, offer instructional support for computer job training, and give every student in those schools the opportunity to learn how to use modern data processing techniques.

This computer would help both the elementary and high schools with administrative tasks—recordkeeping, testing, and even scheduling. Certainly, this would save time and money for the school system but the

* Louis R. Bright, "The Time is Now," *American Education*, November, 1967, pp. 12–14.

greatest benefits would fall to the students, largely to those in the secondary grades. Through remote terminals, either teletype machines or fast card readers, students could be taught data processing skills. They could learn the symbolic languages that must be fed into the machines and experiment with high-level programing.

Vocational students could learn these skills in greater depth along with the related skills of business systems analysis, file manipulations, etc. Public education can perform one of its greatest services for the disadvantaged by training them in computer jobs. Few of these jobs require more than a high school education. Industry hires college graduates for its computer training programs not because the positions demand this higher education but because college graduates are usually easier to train.

Regardless of their career plans, all the students would have some contact with the computer system. For instance, they could feed math, physics, and statistical problems into the machine and get rapid-fire solutions. With this kind of a start, students will think of using the computer to solve realistic problems all their lives.

This is extremely important for future professionals who may find their jobs in the process of transformation as soon as they graduate from college. Computers have already made drastic changes in management and engineering, and soon they will be affecting law, medicine, science, architecture, and education. It's hard to imagine a field which won't be nudged by the computer. Students have to be prepared to face this challenge. It is an enormous task; no university is even close to meeting it.

But computers will touch far more of the average citizen's life than his job. It is up to the schools to make him feel comfortable with these ubiquitous machines. There is a psychological barrier here. At an eastern junior college last year, the computer's advent led to angry strikes by students who objected to the impersonalization of just becoming numbers in a strange machine somewhere in the basement of the administration building. They were probably mistaken; computer scheduling systems can actually counter impersonalization in today's large institutions. A computerized scheduling system at Purdue University, for instance, gives each student a chance to pick the professor he wants for every course. Consequently, students get their first choice of professors about 78 per cent of the time, against about 22 per cent under the old manual system.

Students should be given enough realistic information about computers to separate fact from fantasy. They should be able to overcome fear of the unknown—the fear that makes people resist some of the most valuable computer applications. On the other hand, they should know enough to spot the danger in case technology is misapplied. Students who have daily contact with computer techniques in their high schools and colleges will probably learn most of this by osmosis.

Until now we have just been experimenting with computers in education. With the regional approach described in the feasibility study, however, it should be possible to provide high powered computer services to the schools in the very near future. Judging from the number of schools experimenting with such methods even before they were economical, I'd predict this system will be in a large number of schools in the early 1970's.

This feasibility study indicates one of the greatest contributions research can make to education today. It will help schoolmen determine from the vast amount of educational technology available what is economically sensible and what is just educationally nice to have, at least at this point. Now we know that some computer services can be made available to schools at a price they can afford: still in the offing are computer-assisted instruction and numerous other applications of technology that will eventually be within reach of the school system.

Nevertheless, educators should keep an eye on some of the more exotic computer applications because these, too, may be economically feasible in the next decade. On the administrative scene, computers may alter our entire concept of the classroom with their fantastic ability to reschedule classes. New flexible scheduling systems make it possible to reschedule an entire high school every two weeks, so that every student is almost always in a "class" that suits his individual needs.

Purdue University uses the computer to plan new buildings. It takes various proposed building layout options on the basis of projected number of teachers and students for each course and juggles them to design the most effective facilities. Purdue claims the system has saved about $30 million over the past five years. The same principle should work just as well for high schools.

Computers will be shaping what goes on in the classroom as well as the building where learning takes place. They will be grading papers, giving tests, and in many cases, actually teaching the students. One of the most time-consuming tasks in professional education, the grading of English papers, may be taken over by these instruments. Imaginative researchers at the University of Connecticut have come up with the surprising but well-confirmed result that a computer's grading and comments on essays are indistinguishable statistically from those of the English professors. (I have not fully resolved in my own mind whether this is a comment on the computer or the professors.)

In the realm of testing, the computer has two great advantages: it can make standardized tests truly standardized—each child receives test instructions in the same tone of voice—and it can skip large blocks of questions that are clearly too easy or too difficult for the student. The machine automatically selects question areas which point up the student's weak points and prescribes study materials he needs. This has special value in testing students with diverse backgrounds—first graders, high school remedial groups, and adults.

The New York Institute of Technology has been using a system that points up the computer's possibilities in instruction management. Each student pursues self-study in a standardized college text and takes a multiple-choice quiz over each unit. He feeds his answer sheet into a computer which does three things: It keeps his record current, indicating missed questions and correlating them with past errors to detect a pattern that may guide his adviser. It provides data for updating the curriculum by analyzing the responses to the questions to determine whether some are giving unexpected difficulty to certain types of students. And last, it hands the student a list of questions he missed, naming three extra tests and the page numbers where the same material is presented by a different author. If he scored 85 or better, he gets a new assignment; otherwise, he must look up the references and retake the test.

Such computer uses will give teachers more time to help each student individually in ways that are inconceivable in traditional classrooms. Freed from routine chores like recordkeeping, grading, and drill and practice exercises, the teachers will have more time to teach. They'll do things the machine can't do: teach students to speak effectively, to express their ideas, to communicate with others.

Perhaps the computer's "human" qualities stand out best in computer-assisted instruction, where the machine can tailor instruction to the needs of each individual. In teaching reading, for instance, the machine can help each student form sounds or recognize letters. Through audio and pictorial messages, it can reach children who have never seen the alphabet or the number system. And the computer never loses its temper—a characteristic that is extremely valuable for teaching young children.

Computers are also effective teachers for illiterate adults who may feel too humiliated to take advantage of what educational opportunities they have. The computer can't embarrass them; it deals with them individually with no critical human eye to watch their performance. The machine also acts as a "contingency reinforcer"; it can reward a student immediately for work well done. If the lesson is too tough for him, it prescribes material where he can be successful. This instantaneous reward technique shows striking results in motivating both adults and school age students from disadvantaged families. It can boost confidence and utterly change personality in children who have rarely experienced even the smallest success or received a reward for academic work.

School libraries will be feeling the effects of computers soon. Eventually students may not even have to leaf through books to get information. A West Coast organization has already placed an entire child's encyclopedia in a computer so that the youngster can ply the computer with questions like "What do birds eat?" and get a patient answer. A little further in the future, local libraries may be completely transformed. There will probably be a few centralized information centers with vast collections of information on specific subjects. These would be hooked up to the "local libraries" —computerized facilities throughout the country where the borrower would simply request any material he wanted. No matter how obscure, the material would be located, and would travel electronically from the central facility to the local one. Information retrieval would be instantaneous and completely automatic.

In research, the sheer computing capacity of these machines enables investigators to follow many avenues that were blocked when they were restricted to the old desk calculator techniques. The impact is felt in every quarter of social and education research through new possibilities for vast statistical correlations. But computers can do far more for researchers than handle data. They are sharp detectives of the many obscure, elusive processes that are a part of learning.

Thanks to the computer, physiological research is beginning to unfold much hidden information about the learning process. Continuous monitoring of eye movements may reveal unsuspected reading difficulties. Eye dilation seems to be a measure of comprehension and blood pressure may indicate how much effort a student has to put into learning. All these movements can best be traced by computer.

I believe the computer has real potential for teaching art and music. In addition to teaching the rules and structure of harmony, it could teach the discriminations basic to the recognition of pictorial composition and musical themes. And who knows, it might even teach perfect pitch!

The machines can simulate many situations, either by imitating real life or by games. They can mimic the inside of an aircraft, a complex laboratory, or the 16th century mercantile system. Students get a realistic feel for the subject by being involved in it.

In educating the handicapped, the machine can make its communication with the blind entirely verbal; with the deaf, entirely visual. There are psychological advantages: experiments dramatically show that some emotionally disturbed students who reject humans will relate to hardware.

The computer is already an extremely effective teacher of mechanical skills, and experiments indicate that it may soon be a right-hand man to the vocational counselor as well.

I have sketched an exhilarating future for education, where the computer is a mainstay in the classroom, the business office, the library, and the laboratory. While the computer is ready to go to work in many areas, there are still questions that research must answer. What characteristics of the machines are most valuable in the classroom? What special language will enable curriculum people to insert course material into the machines with ease and retrieve data on student performance? What will the teacher's role be like in the computerized classroom? What problems would arise from vast information retrieval networks concerning copyrights, privacy, and regulatory necessities? Such questions will undoubtedly be the subject of careful study.

In the meantime, however, there is no point in concentrating on the problems while opportunities for using computers slip by. Universities with computerized research facilities tend to do just that; they press for glamorous new developments and ignore the practical services—accounting, data processing, vocational training, and even computer-assisted instruction—that could be offered right now. When they try to do both functions, one or the other usually suffers. Such institutions may have to utilize two types of facilities, one to supply the institution's operating needs and the other to pursue research.

The Bureau of Research is currently supporting studies in nearly every area where computers touch education. In California and Iowa, the Bureau has supported State efforts to standardize information retrieval systems. There are more than 30 library studies under way under the Bureau's new Library Science and Information Program. With Federal support, computers are being developed for almost every phase of administrative management and they're already teaching children in a number of classrooms throughout the Nation.

Thus, on all education fronts computers are beginning to have powerful impact. I am firmly convinced that within the next decade we will see these remarkable instruments bring about revolution in the classroom and the entire educational process equivalent to the one already wrought by computers in industry.

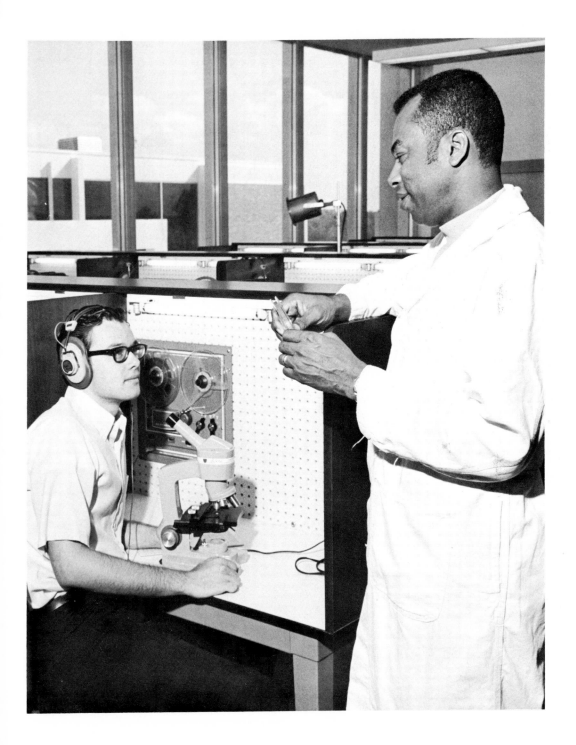

The Teaching Profession

This section explores the following major aspects of the teaching profession: the importance of teaching, the role of the teacher, the process of becoming a teacher, other careers in the field of education, teachers' organizations, and the rewards of teaching. Together these six areas tell the contemporary story of the teaching profession. This story is one of both sacrifice and reward. Sacrifice because, to become a teacher, one must work long and hard to successfully complete a teacher education program and to become a fully certified teacher. After becoming a teacher, there is the further sacrifice of having to devote long, difficult hours to one's profession. In a sense, a teacher actually sacrifices a part of himself to his students and to the profession. By the same token, while teaching requires sacrifice from the educator, it also rewards him handsomely. The financial rewards of the teaching profession have improved in recent years to the point at which educators can now look forward to a life of financial security. Yet another reward that teachers receive from their profession is the knowledge that they are making an extremely valuable contribution to our society—helping to produce the enlightened citizenry essential to our democratic way of life. But perhaps the greatest reward of all is that warm, glowing feeling that one gets from giving to and receiving from our country's youth.

> "The Nation's strength depends upon the minds of its people as surely as it does upon their arms. The education of young Americans is our first line of defense, and a broad highway to greater opportunity. Congratulations to those who have dedicated their lives and talents in the teaching profession."
>
> Dwight D. Eisenhower

CHAPTER 10

The Importance of Teaching

Teaching Is A Profession

You will notice that the title of this section of the book is "The Teaching Profession." Just as medicine, dentistry, and law are professions, so is teaching a true profession. A minority of people suggest that teaching is only a "trade" and that teachers do not really deserve to be considered "professionals." Let's consider the validity of this claim by analyzing some of the facts about teaching. One of the criteria by which an area of work is judged to be a profession or not is the amount of formal education required of the people who work in that area. As will be pointed out later in the chapter entitled "Becoming A Teacher," nearly all states now require that a teacher possess at least a bachelor's degree to be certified as a teacher. An increasing number of states even require a masters' degree for permanent certification. It will also be pointed out that a high per cent of the elementary and secondary teachers in the United States now possess a masters' degree. At the higher education level, nearly all teachers possess a

Perhaps the greatest reward of teaching is the knowledge that one is making a lasting contribution to American youth.

masters' degree and a great number have earned the doctorate, which requires a minimum of seven years of study. So, from the standpoint of formal education, at least, there can be little doubt that teaching deserves to be called a profession.

The Prestige of Teaching

Another of the characteristics of a profession is that the service being rendered is considered to be very important by the society in which this service is performed. The prestige of the teaching profession has risen sharply in the past decade. This fact is substantiated by a survey recently conducted by Louis Harris and Associates in which a random sample of 2000 Americans throughout the country were asked which professions have the most "prestige." The ranking of the professions with the highest prestige scores, as determined by the opinions of these 2000

> A teacher affects eternity; he can never tell where his influence stops.
>
> Henry Adams

Doctors	74%
Bankers	70%
Scientists	66%
Military leaders	65%
Educators	62%
Corporate heads	58%
Psychiatrists	57%
U.S. Supreme Court Justices ...	54%
Local retailers	50%
Clergy	45%
Congressmen	44%
Federal government leaders	44%
Reporters, publishers	30%
Television executives	26%
Arts	24%
Labor leaders	24%
Advertising men	22%

Figure 10.1 Prestige of Various Professions.

citizens from all walks of life, is shown in Figure 10.1.

It is interesting to note that, in the Harris survey, educators were awarded more prestige than were corporate heads, psychiatrists, U.S. Supreme Court Justices, local retailers, clergy, congressmen, federal government leaders, reporters-publishers, television executives, people in the arts, labor leaders, and advertising men. It is equally interesting to note that only doctors, bankers, scientists, and military leaders were awarded more prestige than educators.

Testimonials for Teaching

Perhaps the best single indication of the high regard that people generally have for teachers and for the importance of the teaching profession can be found in comments that individual citizens make about this subject. A number of such testimonials can be found in an excellent book entitled

A teacher is a highly educated, thoroughly prepared professional who is well respected in the American society.

Why Teach? which was edited by Professor D. Louise Sharp. Several of these comments about the teaching profession are reproduced here.

Mrs. Alice K. Leopold, who served as Assistant to the Secretary of Labor for Women's Affairs during President Eisenhower's administration, had this to say about the importance of teaching:[1]

Everyone who works at a job he likes and does well contributes to the well-being of all of

1. D. Louise Sharp, ed. *Why Teach?* p. 129. Used with permission.

us. But some jobs are indispensable to our very survival. Teaching, like nursing, is one of these.

Unless our children learn how to read, write, and calculate they cannot live without constant help from others. Unless they learn how to develop their talents and overcome their handicaps, they cannot work effectively and harmoniously with others for the common good. Unless they learn from the preceding generation the heritage of the past, they cannot add to our progress.

Teachers share with parents and religious leaders the main responsibility for this large educational task. They accept the lion's share of the responsibility for seeing that young people acquire the knowledge, skills, attitudes, and habits they will need as adults. Although all teachers are alike in this responsibility, there is infinite variety in the personality and background each brings to her task. This variety enriches our children, offering countless opportunities to each child for challenge and stimulation along the lines of his particular abilities and interests.

All of us remember at least one teacher who struck some spark in us—a spark never extinguished, but likely to kindle a spark in someone else. It is this never-ending quality of teaching that has kept many of our best teachers in the classroom, in spite of attractive opportunities elsewhere. But these opportunities elsewhere are ever increasing at the same time that the need for teaching is multiplying. Never before in the history of our country have we been so critically short of well-qualified teachers. Never before has the quality as well as the quantity of the education we offer our children been so threatened.

So concerned are we in the Labor Department over this shortage that we are working with the U.S. Office of Education as well as educational and civic groups throughout the country to draw into our classrooms mature women college graduates, many of whom have raised their families and are able and willing to take the training necessary to become teachers.

Every one of us can help, each in his own way, in this national crisis—as a parent, as a

2. *Ibid.,* pp. 25–26.

citizen, as a teacher, if we are qualified or can become so. As Horace Mann wrote in the early days of our nation's history: "In a government like ours, each individual must think of the welfare of all as the welfare of his own family, and therefore of the children of others as well as of his own."

Mary Ellen Chase—teacher and award winning author—has the following to say about teachers and teaching.[2]

I have always been more than a little suspicious of those who go into the teaching profession from missionary zeal, or even of those who remain in it for the same insufficient, if not dangerous reason. In my experience, lofty purposes alone do not often make good teachers. Teaching is, without doubt, a serious business; but overseriousness in a teacher is fatal. It is excitement in teaching, the sheer fun of it, the sharing of knowledge and enthusiasm, the opportunity to go on learning, which make teaching, at its best, not only the highest of the arts, in my opinion, but the most exhilarating of occupations.

The increasing prestige of the teaching profession is due not only to the increasing importance of education in our society, but also to the increasing competence of teachers.

As a matter of sober fact and as all honest, first-class teachers will acknowledge, the histrionic qualities of the teachers are of more value than the mere didactic, however noble their aim. For in the best teachers lies always something of the actor, of that creative gift of so entering into one's subject that the subject, whatever it is, is reborn, reclothed, reenacted.

I am also skeptical as to the value of that patience, without which the teacher is presumably doomed to failure. When I look back upon the few really great teachers I have known, it is their sublime impatience which is most memorable; impatience with mediocre or sloppy work; with laziness, lack of taste or of moral sense; righteous rage against apathy and dullness. To me, patience per se in the teacher is a perilous virtue, prophetic of little except indifference both in himself and in his students.

Each teacher must utilize his or her own personality and particular talents to develop a challenging and stimulating school program for each student.

> He who governs well, leads the ignorant; he who teaches well, trains them to govern themselves in justice, mercy, and peace.
>
> Alexander G. Ruthven

I began to teach not because I felt in any sense a vocation or calling, but merely because at the time it seemed the most sensible, perhaps even selfish, thing to do in order to continue to enjoy my love of books and to earn a necessary and respectable living. It just happened to suit me admirably. I have never known a dull moment in nearly fifty years at it, whether in a Maine country school where I began my work, in public and private high schools, in classes in adult education, or in college. I have taught or, more accurately, studied with, Maine coast children, midwestern and western high school students, taxi drivers, plumbers, streetcar conductors, housewives, and Smith College girls. I am extremely doubtful of any so-called "good" which I may have given them, but entirely certain that they have given me the best life anyone could have.

My advice to those who are now considering teaching, in these days when the young ponder more about their callings than they did in my youth, is similar to that given by someone or other about marriage: "Don't go into it unless you can't help yourself!"

Yet another famous author, Norman Cousins, gives the following testimonial about the importance of teaching.[3]

A good teacher is first of all a good human being—someone who in personality, character, and attitudes exercises a wholesome and <u>inspiring</u> influence on young people. I underline the word "inspiring" because I believe that of all the many qualities that go into the making of a good teacher, the ability to inspire is perhaps paramount. The names that come to mind

3. *Ibid.,* pp. 30–31.

A good deal of a teacher's time is devoted to getting to know each student as an individual.

in any discussion of great American teachers—names such as Horace Mann, Mark Hopkins, Charles Eliot, John Dewey—are the names of inspired teachers.

By inspiration I have in mind the quality of teaching that somehow strikes a spark deep inside the student, raising his level of awareness in life, enlarging rather than satisfying his natural curiosity, opening up a sense of individual capacity and responsibility, holding up before the student an ideal worth pursuing and realizing as a person. The factual content of education may fall away from the individual over the years, or it may become obsolete; what is not lost, however, is the deep influence of a great and inspiring teacher, someone whose general approach to knowledge and life serves as a practical guide for the individual in the world beyond the school.

Obviously, inspiration is a quality not easily come by, whether with respect to teaching or any other branch of public service. Nor is it easy to devise means for measuring a teacher's ability to inspire. But the importance of this intangible quality is so great that it should be recognized

in principle as the prime essential of a good teacher.

Lastly, Rabbi Morris Silverman, who, among other things, has received much acclaim for his work in the field of civil rights, has the following to say about the importance of teaching:[4]

Who does not recall the influence of dedicated teachers upon his life? My love of good music can be traced back nearly half a century to the principal of a public school in Brockton, Massachusetts. I remember him vividly, a colorful personality, bearded, riding to school on his bicycle. I can still hear his pitch pipe as he taught our class once a week and explained classical music.

I can still quote hundreds of lines of poetry because of a high school teacher in Utica, New York, who made English literature a fascinating subject. My present interest in a projected history of the local Jewish community goes back to

4. *Ibid.*, pp. 197–198.

A teacher influences hundreds of lives and has an opportunity to help children become good citizens, earn good livings, and live full, rich lives.

the inspiration and guidance of a college instructor at Ohio State University who was later called to teach at Harvard. All can recall similar experiences.

I come from a people who stressed learning as a cardinal principle, education as a lifelong process, and that accords the greatest honor and respect to teachers and scholars. The very title "Rabbi" means "my teacher." "The guardians of a city are not its military but its consecrated teachers." This is one of the many sayings in our ancient literature that emphasizes the position of teachers.

Although preaching is a form of teaching, I find among my varied activities that the most rewarding, stimulating, and satisfying is the actual teaching of two classes—one of teen-agers, the other adults.

The genius of Sir Isaac Newton would have been lost to the world were it not for a teacher by the name of Mr. Stokes who recognized the talent in the student and persuaded his mother to let him continue his education.

The teaching profession offers a great opportunity for influencing the lives of hundreds of people and of guiding them not only to earn a living; but to live a good life.

Great Teachers of the Past

One of the reasons that teaching is now a respected profession and that contemporary educators occupy a prestigious place in our society is that there have been many great teachers in the past. All of us can recall teachers that we have had who were influential in the shaping of our lives.

History is full of educators who have come to be recognized as making great contributions to mankind. Space permits mentioning only a few at this time.

Socrates (470–399 B.C.) is often mentioned as one of the world's first truly great teachers. This man, who lived in the Greek city state of Athens, devoted his life to teaching the students who followed him wherever he went. His main method of teaching consisted of asking leading questions which helped the student to discover the answer for himself. In fact, this technique has been so closely identified with Socrates that it has come to be known as the "Socratic Method" of teaching. Socrates was eventually put to

> Knowledge is virtue.
>
> Socrates

death for inciting the people against the government in his relentless search for truth. His dedication to teaching, knowledge and truth inspired many of his students to become renowned educators in their own right. Plato became one of Socrates' most famous students.

> The very spring and root of honesty and virtue lie in good education.
>
> Plutarch

Relics of a Roman school from a wall painting now found in a museum at Naples. The left hand case contains 3 styli for writing; the upper right is a capsa containing rolls or books. Leaning against it is a book. At the bottom a capsa is open showing the scrolls. Leaning against it on the left is a writing tablet.

Another famous teacher of his day was Quintilian (A.D. 35–95), a Roman educator. Quintilian, also a prolific educational writer, exhibited a perceptive understanding of students far in advance of his time when he wrote:

I am by no means in favor of whipping boys, though I know it to be a general practice. In the first place, whipping is unseemly, and if you suppose the boys to be somewhat grown up, it is an affront in the highest degree. In the next

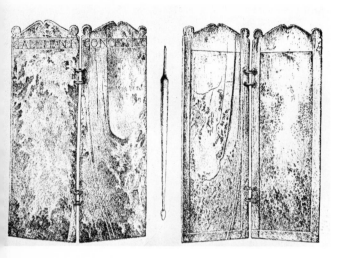

Dipticha, **or Roman wax tablet with stili. These were found on the Esquiline Hill, Rome, and are preserved in the local museum. The tablets were covered with wax and were used for accounting or in schools by writing on the wax with the stilus. The name on the upper end of the left illustration, Galleri Concessi, shows its owner to have been a man of some importance.**

The lower schoolroom of Eton College founded in 1440. The wood from which these benches were made, as well as the wainscoting and timbers in the room, was taken from the wrecked vessels of the Spanish Armada. This was one of the means by which patriotic ideals were instilled in the English boys.

place, if a boy's ability is so poor as to be proof against reproach he will, like a worthless slave, become insensible to blows. Lastly, if a teacher is assiduous and careful, there is no need to use force. I shall observe further that while a boy is under the rod he experiences pain and fear. The shame of this experience dejects and discourages many pupils, makes them shun being seen, and may even weary them of their lives.

One of the most famous teachers of the Dark Ages was an Englishman by the name of Alcuin. Alcuin became Charlemagne's educational advisor and established the Palace School at Frankland which Charlemagne himself frequently attended.

There were many famous educators during the Renaissance and Reformation periods, including Erasmus (1466–1536), Melanchthon (1497–1560), Ignatius of Loyola

(1491–1556), Jean Baptiste de la Salle (1651–1719) and Johann Amos Comenius (1592–1670). Comenius authored a great number of textbooks. Comenius' textbooks were some of the very first to contain pictures. Comenius was also among the first to recommend that a series of schools should be established. Concerning this point he wrote, "There should be a maternal school in each family; an elementary school in each district; a gymnasium in each city; an academy in each kingdom, or even in each considerable province."[5]

There were a countless number of great educators during the 18th and 19th centu-

5. G. Compayre (translated by W. H. Payne). *History of Pedagogy.* Boston: D. C. Heath and Co., 1885, p. 128.

ries. Some of the famous American educators from this period, such as Benjamin Franklin, Horace Mann, Henry Barnard, and Samuel Hall, were already mentioned in chapter three. There were also a number of famous European educators during this time whose work greatly influenced American education. These included, among others, Jean Jacques Rousseau (1712–1778), Johann Friedrich Herbart (1776–1841), Friedrich Froebel (1782–1852), and Johann Heinrich Pestalozzi (1746–1827). Of these, Pestalozzi, a Swiss educator, stands out as one who gained a great deal of fame as the founder of two schools—one at Burgdorf (1800–1804) and another at Yverdun (1805–1825).

It was at these schools that Pestalozzi put into practice his educational beliefs that children should be treated with love, respect, understanding and patience (a belief that was in contradiction to the prevailing religiously inspired view that children were

6. *Ibid.*, p. 425.

born full of sin and inherently bad). This belief is reflected by Pestalozzi when he wrote:

I was convinced that my heart would change the condition of my children just as promptly as the sun of spring would reanimate the earth benumbed by the winter. . . . It was necessary that my children should observe, from dawn to evening, at every moment of the day, upon my brow and on my lips, that my affections were fixed on them, that their happiness was my happiness, and that their pleasures were my pleasures. . . .

I was everything to my children. I was alone with them from morning till night. . . . Their hands were in my hands. Their eyes were fixed on my eyes.[6]

The direction in which education starts a man will determine his future life.

Plato

Pestalozzi also believed that teachers should use objects and games to help students learn. In fact, he developed a series of teaching materials which were very advanced for their time. A number of American educators visited Pestalozzi's schools

The library of the University of Leyden in the 16th century. By this time, the library had become an important part of the university. The books are chained to the shelves so they could not be stolen—an indication of their scarcity and value. It is interesting to note how the books were classified. Leyden was founded in 1575, and for over a century was the center of advanced thought and instruction.

Pestalozzi's first teaching experience was at Stans in 1798. There he took charge of a group of children orphaned by one of the massacres of the French Revolution. There were no teaching aids so Pestalozzi taught by using objects. This illustration is from an early 19th century woodcut.

Pestalozzi eventually moved to Yverdun where at this castle, he conducted an experimental school for 20 years. Educators came from all around the world to visit and study the teaching methods and materials he developed here.

A page from the early edition of one of Comenius' books, *Orbis Pictus,* published in 1657. Comenius' textbooks were among the first to use pictures. On this page, the idea was to have the child learn the sound of each letter in the alphabet through some sound in nature with which he was familiar. Hence, the illustration of the wind, the goose, the cricket, etc.

and brought many of his ideas back to the United States where they were put into practice.

The number of Americans who have earned a reputation as outstanding educators is great indeed. In fact, to list them would be an impossible task. Perhaps it will suffice to say that educators such as Horace Mann, Henry Barnard, Samuel Hall, Cyrus Pierce, John Griscom, Noah Webster, Edward Sheldon, David Camp, William Phelps, Charles and Frank McMurry, Francis Parker, John Dewey, George Counts and many, many others far too numerous to mention, have made very significant contributions to our society through their various educational works. Many contemporary educators are also among our leading statesmen, scientists, artists, civil rights leaders, Nobel prize winners, civic leaders, authors, researchers and philosophers. In fact, many educators can be found in all of the most important walks of life in our American society.

The Increasing Importance of the Teacher in Today's Society

Contemporary teachers are in a position to make an even greater contribution to society than were their historical counterparts. This is true mainly because education is a much more important commodity today than it has been in the past. Whereas in the past a young person could earn a good living and have a productive career with relatively little formal education, the vast majority of today's youth simply must acquire an extensive educational background to become successful, productive, self-fulfilling citizens. This means that the work of the

> The future of America is written on school blackboards and in student notebooks. The quality of thought in our classrooms today will determine the quality of our lives a generation hence.
>
> Lyndon B. Johnson

teacher has become more crucial and important in our society.

Many authorities further feel that education is the only long-range solution to many of our major social problems (poverty, race relations, delinquency and crime, etc.). This truism also helps to document the fact that a teacher now has an excellent opportunity to live a meaningful and socially significant life—an opportunity afforded by few other careers.

In conclusion, it is hoped that this brief chapter has pointed out that teaching is a true profession, is highly regarded by Amer-

> A world whose schools are unreformed is an unreformed world.
>
> H. G. Wells

cans, and is one of the most important and worthy professions in our society.

QUESTIONS FOR DISCUSSION

1. Do you believe that teaching is a true profession? What evidence do you have to support your viewpoint?

2. How do you feel teaching ranks in importance with other professions? Substantiate your position on this question.

3. How much prestige do you believe contemporary teachers have in the eyes of the general public? What indications do you base your answer to this question on?

4. You and three others (not teachers) are playing bridge. One of the others asks you, "I understand that Sally Jones is a student in one of your classes. She strikes me as being a rather dull girl. Do you know what her I.Q. is?" What would you say?

5. What has attracted you to the teaching profession thus far?

SUPPLEMENTARY LEARNING ACTIVITIES

1. Invite representatives of the National Education Association and the American Federation of Teachers (a staff member or a member teacher) to your class to discuss the philosophy of their respective organizations.

2. Have each member of your class write a brief description of the characteristics of the best teacher they ever had. Compare these qualities listed by the class members.

3. React to the following hypothetical letter that a superintendent has written to one of his teachers:

It is my duty to inform you that you will not be offered another contract to teach in our school system after the conclusion of the present school year. This decision is based upon an unsatisfactory performance during this, your first year on the faculty. Following are the major reasons that your performance has been judged unsatisfactory:

1. You have been late to your classes on a number of occasions and have been absent from school an excessive number of times.

2. A number of students have informally complained about the general quality of your classes.

3. On a number of occasions parents have registered formal complaints about your behavior outside of the classroom. A number of these complaints have centered around your use of alcoholic beverages.

4. You have generally not shown a very cooperative attitude in your relationships with other teachers and with the administration.

Sincerely yours,

4. You and nine other teachers are having coffee in the teachers' lounge. One of them says, "I sure don't know what to do with that stupid trouble-maker, Billy Fisher. With an I.Q. of 85, he must be one of the dumbest kids in our school. This morning in class he was goofing off again. I sure wish I could get him out of my class." If you were one of the teachers in that room, what would you say?

5. Invite a member of another profession (medicine, law, engineering, etc.) to speak to your class on the subject of the importance of teaching.

SELECTED REFERENCES

Alexander, William M. *Are You a Good Teacher?* New York: Holt, Rinehart & Winston, 1959.

Classroom Teachers Speak on Teaching as a Profession. Washington, D.C.: Department of Classroom Teachers, National Education Association, 1960.

Economic Status of Teachers. Washington, D.C.: Research Division, National Education Association, 1969.

Gross, E. "Sociological Aspects of Professional Salaries in Education." *Educational Record* 41(1960):130–37.

Haskew, Laurence D., and Jonathon C. McLendon. *This Is Teaching*. rev. ed. Chicago: Scott, Foresman and Co., 1962 (chapters 1, 5, 11).

"How Good Are Our Teachers?" *Changing Times* 17(1963):25–31.

Lillywhite, Ray L. "Trends in Teacher Retirement." *NEA Journal* 50(1961):45–46.

Lindsey, Margaret, ed. *New Horizons for the Teaching Profession*. Washington, D.C.: National Commission on Teacher Education and Professional Standards, National Education Association, 1961.

Mason, Ward S. *The Beginning Teacher: Status and Career Orientations*. Washington, D.C.: U.S. Office of Education, Circular 644, 1961.

"Merit Pay for Teachers." *Saturday Review,* December 16, 1961.

Michael-Smith, Harold. "It takes Self-Understanding." *NEA Journal* 49(1960):37–40.

Peterson, Houston, ed. *Great Teachers*. New York: Vintage Books, 1946.

Ragan, William B. *Teaching America's Children*. New York: Holt, Rinehart & Winston, 1961 (chapter 1).

Richey, Robert W. *Planning for Teaching*. 3d ed. New York: McGraw-Hill Book Co., 1963 (chapters 1, 2, 4).

Sharp, Louise D. *Why Teach?* New York: Henry Holt & Co., 1957.

"Teacher Supply and Demand in Public Schools." *Research Report*. Washington, D.C.: Research Division, National Education Association, 1969.

Thomas, Lawrence G., et al. *Perspective on Teaching*. Englewood Cliffs, N.J.: Prentice-Hall, 1961 (chapters 13-15).

Wasson, Margaret. *Teaching Is Exciting*. Washington: Association for Childhood Education International, Bulletin No. 88, 1951.

"What Is a Well Educated Man?" *NEA Journal* 51(1962):22–25.

Who's a Good Teacher? Washington, D.C.: American Association of School Administrators, National Education Association, 1961.

High on Teaching

Myrtle Bonn

It was the end of August. It was also the end of a trip that got a select group of bright, achieving teenagers high on careers in education. No drugs were involved. What turned them on was a summer workshop at the National College of Education in Evanston, Ill. For three weeks, 168 high school students were exposed to the kind of mind-expanding experiences that sharpened their sensitivities, built their confidence, and freed them of stereotyped notions of what could and should go on in a school.

It was the kind of experience that led 16-year-old Mike Doty, now a senior at Walters Junior-Senior High School in Walters, Okla., to say: "The educational system as I know it, I wouldn't even consider going into. But education as it will be—as we've seen it here at the workshop—it's going to be a fantastic industry and something I'd like to be a part of."

This year's workshop was a kind of dream-come-true for Joan Smutny, chairman of the Department of Communications at the College of Education, director of the workshop, and the woman behind the whole idea. A red-haired dynamo who in the three-week period somehow got to know almost all the youngsters intimately, Mrs. Smutny has some very definite ideas about recruiting for the education professions, and she admits she sometimes "runs out of saliva" communicating them.

"Almost all of the status professions—medicine, law, dentistry, even the theatre and journalism—put out tremendous efforts to attract outstanding, alive, creative young people," she says. "But not education. For young people, education has always been stereotyped. They see it often in terms of the worst kind of teaching, and almost always in terms of the most traditional kind of teaching."

As one of the workshop students said in examining her own school experience, "Something's got to change!"

The kind of change Mrs. Smutny would like to see is for high school students to associate education with "the new dimensions of the 70's and 80's." But she adds, "There's seldom a correlation between education and the creative."

Linking education with the creative and with new commitments to society is what the workshop is all about, and to do it successfully Mrs. Smutny thinks there must be an "electric" program. That is precisely what she has developed along with a staff of some 50 handpicked teachers, counselors, and community resource persons.

Many of the students came to the workshop predisposed toward careers in education, though they could envision nothing beyond what they were already familiar

* Myrtle Bonn, "High on Teaching," *American Education*, November, 1969, pp. 5–7. .

with. They had no idea of what is happening on educational frontiers: a hierarchy of professions with aides, assistant teachers, associate teachers, master teachers; teachers who develop their own curriculums, media specialists, school-community coordinators, careers in early childhood education, special education, school psychology, school social work, or school public relations. These possibilities did not enter their thinking.

At the workshop what the students get is exposure to what education careers can be like as opposed to what they have been like. They get it through teachers who are also exciting as people, who sample life outside of teaching, who think that kids are worth their time out of class as well as in class. They get it through seminars in critical thinking where they analyze editorials, poetry, speeches, radio, and TV—always probing into the feelings and attitudes and motives and intentions of the writers and the speakers.

They get it through role-playing that gives them an opportunity to examine their own attitudes and values. They get it through "talk-back" seminars with guest speakers, such as the prominent Chicago architect who helped them probe into why cities need rebuilding. They get it through opportunities to learn about television—not talking about its intricacies, but writing scripts, manipulating the college's TV equipment, putting on programs, and seeing the results. They get it through spontaneous talk sessions in the cafeteria, in lounges, in the dorms—sometimes into the wee hours. The workshop schedule offers academic, professional, and social activities in favorable proportion as is evident in the guidance and counseling program, in the

seminars, in the visits to community projects, such as Operation Breadbasket run by the Southern Christian Leadership Conference in nearby Chicago.

The idea is to sensitize the students to the many dimensions of education—not only the need for knowledge and expertise in subject matter, but also the desire to understand people and their wants. As the students soon realize, this means personal involvement, and so they find out what it is like to take over a classroom, to communicate knowledge. In afternoon sessions they have a chance to work with elementary youngsters from the community and get the feel of teaching them, while professional and fellow potential teachers watch and evaluate their efforts.

It also means getting away from "the insulation of belonging to one little high school in one little community in one part of the country," says Mrs. Smutny. "We try to encourage the kids to think sensitively and intelligently in learning about other kinds of situations and schools."

The workshop provided a perfect setting for breaking down that sort of insulation. When it was over, it was difficult to believe that only three weeks earlier these students had been strangers and all somewhat apprehensive of what awaited them. Most were middle class from the Chicago area and able to afford the $240 for board and tuition, activity fees, and books. Forty received Federal stipends as part of a special projects grant under the Education Professions Development Act. The grant made it possible for the first time to bring in youngsters from outside the Chicago area and those from a variety of ethnic groups who were unable to pay their own way—Indians from Oklahoma, kids of Chinese and Japanese ancestry from the West Coast, Puerto Ricans, Mexican-Americans, blacks from inner cities.

Early in the workshop, some white students confessed they had never before talked openly and frankly with a black person. Some had never seen an Indian outside of the movies or TV. One young black man admitted he had never had a real conversation with a white.

Apprehension even showed in application forms as some of the students set up very restricted requirements about whom they would like to room with. One specified: "Someone that lives in poverty or is in a lower income status. One who enjoys living with a messy, unorganized, low-income-bracket Chinese student." Another wrote he'd prefer to room with another stipend recipient, someone who "likes lower-middle-class people."

Counselors took great pains in matching roommates, but as workshop Assistant Director Doug Paul, a teacher at Lake Forest High School and a former workshop student himself, put it: "These kids were so eager to learn about one another that, in no time at all, it would have been simple to bunk any of the girls together or any of the boys together with full confidence that they would be compatible."

Doug elaborated on what the workshop stresses—"sensitivity to people and ideas and places and concepts . . . but most of all understanding of people's different points of view and attitudes based on background, education, beliefs. These qualities are especially important for teachers."

The staff is charged with the evaluation of the various components of the workshop. This is carried out through conferences between Joan Smutny and other staff members, as well as through talks between staff members and students. The kids are asked to evaluate instructors, courses, the program, and counselors. And they're candid about problems in the dorms, for instance, or whether they feel comfortable going to counselors for personal advice, or whether they find the seminars interesting and helpful.

As might be expected, teachers and teaching form a common ground for discussion. Students air their gripes freely. Listen to Scott Phillips of the Blake School in Hopkins, Minn.: "When a teacher just wants you to memorize facts so you'll know them when the next test comes along, then you have a breakdown in student-teacher relationships. Here, when we learn facts, we are expected to use them. It's a two way thing between the student and the teacher. Education has to be that way."

Other gripes have to do with learning to read but not evaluate, teachers who don't really seem to care, being lectured at but not involved in the learning process, the lack of opportunity to develop a personal sense of responsibility for learning.

The ratio of boys to girls was roughly one to four, but the instructors had a rationale for that. First of all, boys are conditioned to think that preparation for teaching is a feminine pursuit and teaching was stressed in recruiting. Secondly, many more boys than girls work during the summer and some have to be at school for football practice during the period when the workshop is taking place.

That doesn't stop Joan Smutny's efforts to get more men into education. In fact, it's one of the reasons she brought Cleve Williams, a local basketball hero and athletic coach into the program as an instructor. A graduate of Mississippi's Tougaloo College, and a teacher of high school history, science, and biology in Chicago, Cleve has a special interest in seeing more men teachers because he thinks a male child needs a male model.

For eight and a half years he's worked with inner-city children and he's come in contact with a lot of potential teachers. When he thinks that the kids he's met at the workshop will be the teachers of tomorrow, he wears a satisfied smile. He likes their maturity and commitment and dedication. "With these kinds of kids," he says, "education is not going to suffer."

Cleve substantiates what Doug Paul had said about the metamorphosis of this summer's group. At first, he said, those of each particular culture sought out their own kind for friendship. After about the third day, things changed. Each student looked upon others as friends and didn't see cultural or racial differences as barriers.

In his seminars, Cleve goes in for a lot of role playing. For instance, with an ethnically mixed group, he will insist, "Today we are all white." The next day, "We are all black." Each student is hungry to learn other points of view and attitudes and how he identifies with other people.

No one at the workshop—instructors, counselors, directors—expects that all of the teenagers who participated are going to wind up in education jobs. One girl wants to be a nurse, and thinks she can serve humanity better in that capacity. Another wants to be a social worker, but is vacillating. "If you are a social worker," she says, "you work with people after the damage is done. If you are a teacher, you can prevent the damage."

A survey taken at the end of the workshop indicated that for 114 of the students, the experience strengthened their interest in education and teaching to a "great extent." Thirty-nine responded that it did so to a "moderate extent." The questionnaire also showed that the students overwhelmingly felt their individual growth had been stimulated and that they developed good insights into the innovative and creative aspects of teaching.

What of the remaining young people who were not attracted to teaching? Was the workshop for them a failure? Both the instructors and the students thought that what they learned about education will make them more sensitive to education's needs— as voters, as members of the community, and eventually as parents.

There is no question that Joan Smutny and her staff are pleased with this year's workshop. If they were weary after working 20 hours a day for three weeks, including weekends, they showed no signs of it. In September they were tooling up for next year's recruitment drive—preparing brochures, setting up speaking schedules, and making appointments to confer with school administrators. No member of the staff will be completely satisfied until he sees indications that this type of recruitment program is spreading.

In the meantime Joan Smutny continues to work with a missionary zeal. "I've come to realize," she says, "that we don't need to attract only students with outstanding grades. We are living in an era when there is more awareness of human needs than ever before. And I think education ought to capitalize on this awareness. It's important that we go after kids who are sensitive, who can communicate their feelings, who are ready to step into a new developing world."

Most of all, Mrs. Smutny wants to see education go after youngsters when they are still in high school—when they can be inspired, when they are altruistic, when they are highly motivated. She doesn't want recruits who look upon education as something to fall back on. She wants them to look at it as something they can go forward with.

CHAPTER 11

The Role
of the Teacher

It has already been mentioned in the opening remarks of this section of the book that a teacher must be willing to sacrifice many long and hard hours of work to his profession. This fact was born out in a recent study completed by the Research Division of the National Education Association in which a large number of teachers

> Education is a painful, continual and difficult work to be done by kindness, by watching, by warning, by precept, and by praise, but above all—by example.
>
> John Ruskin

were asked how they spend their working week. The results of this study are shown in Figure 11.1. This figure shows that the average teacher in this study devoted a total of approximately forty-eight hours per week to his job as a teacher. Of this total time, he spends 29.8 hours actually working with pupils; 6.8 hours performing other duties (such as planning, faculty meetings, clerical work, and preparing teaching materials) during the school day; and 10.8 hours doing

school-related work outside of the school day (such as correcting papers, writing reports, scoring tests, preparing lesson plans, and attending professional meetings). It is obvious that teaching requires many long hours of hard work—and is not a job that would appeal to "clock watchers."

A Day, A Week, A Year

A teacher wears many hats in the course of a school day, a school week, and a school year. For example, he must be a lesson planner, purveyor of knowledge, motivator, disciplinarian, counselor, confidant, mediator, curriculum planner, worker for his profes-

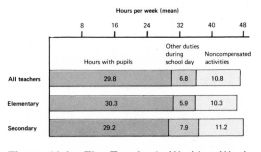

Figure 11.1. The Teacher's Working Week.

Source: NEA Research Division, *The American Public School Teacher.* Research Report 1967-R4, 1967, p. 27. Used with permission.

sional organization, human relations expert, and record keeper. Truly, a teacher must have a multitude of talents and be competent in many different roles if he is to be successful. In this chapter we will examine some of the more specific tasks included in the role of the teacher.

Keeping School

One of the tasks that has historically consumed much of a teacher's time is that traditionally called "keeping school." School keeping involves such "chores" as ordering supplies, keeping the classroom tidy and clean (even though most schools now hire competent custodians to do all the major cleaning, a teacher still has a good deal of

Today's teacher devotes many hours to the preparation of teaching materials.

Teaching is a demanding task requiring many long hours of planning.

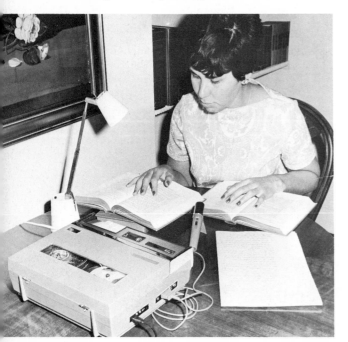

minor house cleaning chores to perform), keeping attendance records, checking books in and out, collecting lunch money, putting up bulletin boards and displays of various sorts, and filling out forms and reports that the school may require. While school keeping chores such as these are important and must be done, they have historically consumed too much of a teacher's valuable time—time that could be better spent working with students. Fortunately, in recent years schools have found ways to relieve the teacher of many of these "school keeping" chores. Many schools have developed simplified methods of record keeping which require very little time on the part of the teachers. Also, some schools now employ "para-professional" help to do these school keeping chores, thereby freeing the teacher to spend more time working with students.

A discussion of the important role and function of these para-professionals will be provided in chapter thirteen.

Planning

One of the most important roles that a teacher plays is that of "planner." A teacher is given a great deal of freedom and autonomy in planning what will take place in his or her classroom. This is as it should be, because today's teacher is a highly trained, competent professional who is the best qualified to determine what each student needs in his classroom. In some instances, a teacher will be given a broad planning document such as a curriculum guide that may originate at the state, county or school district level. Such documents, however, are only general guidelines and each individual teacher must still plan the specific day-to-day program. An increasing amount of the

An increasing amount of educational planning is being done by groups or teams of teachers.

planning task is being done cooperatively by groups of teachers, in conjunction with team teaching or in summer efforts to prepare various types of units and other curricular materials. More and more, school districts are realizing the value that can accrue from hiring teachers during the summer to do such cooperative planning.

The success of a school program for a given student will be dependent, in a large amount, upon the quality of planning that went into that student's program. By the same token, the success of the educational program of an entire school system will be determined by the planning that goes into that program. The same thing is true, incidentally, for the entire American educational system—its success is largely dependent upon the quality of the planning that goes into it.

There are a number of different levels of planning that a teacher must do. These levels are shown in Figure 11.2. As this figure shows, a teacher begins with a very general long-range yearly lesson plan for each subject that he teaches. This yearly lesson plan must be very flexible so that changes can be made in the plan during the year as the need arises. Figure 11.2 further shows that

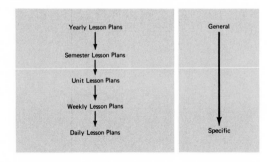

Figure 11.2. Levels of Lesson Planning.

a teacher must also make semester plans (or quarter plans, depending upon how the school year may be divided). Like the yearly plan, these semester plans must be very general and very flexible. One of the many values of long-range plans (such as those a teacher makes for an entire school year or for a semester) is that they permit the teacher to gather more and better instructional materials (some of which may be difficult to obtain) by the time they are needed. Long range planning also permits a teacher to think through what he really wants the students to learn over a long period of time.

Perhaps the single most important and valuable type of planning that a teacher does is what is commonly known as the unit lesson plan. The unit plan is one that is done for a rather discrete segment of the year's work in a given subject. Units can vary greatly in size; however, most of them range between a week and a month in length. Units can also vary greatly in scope, depending upon the grade level and subject. Examples of typical units are: finger painting in first grade art, the American Indian in third grade social studies, poetry in fifth grade English, the digestive system in seventh grade science, squares and square roots in tenth grade mathematics, forms of mental illness in twelfth grade psychology, or the role of the teacher in a college introduction to teaching course.

A unit may be defined as an organization of learning activities and experiences around a central theme, developed cooperatively by a group of pupils under a teacher's leadership. The essential features implied by this definition are that (1) learning takes place through many types of experiences rather than through a single activity such as reading and reciting; (2) the activities are unified around a central theme, problem, or purpose; (3) the unit provides opportunities for socialization of pupils by means of cooperative group planning; and (4) the role of the teacher is that of a leader rather than a task master.

There are a variety of different approaches that a teacher can take in planning a unit. For instance, a teacher can plan what is essentially a "subject-matter unit." A subject matter unit is a selection of subject matter materials, and of educative experiences centering upon subject matter materials, which are arranged around a central core found within the subject matter itself. The core may be a generalization, a concept, a topic, or a theme. The unit is to be studied by pupils for the purpose of achieving learning outcomes derivable from experiences with subject matter.

Or a teacher may plan what is essentially an "experience unit." This is a series of educative experiences organized around a pupil purpose, problem or need, utilizing socially useful subject matter and materials, resulting in the achievement of the purpose and in the achievement of learning outcomes inherent in the process.

In reality all units use both experience and subject matter. The difference is primarily one of emphasis. It should be understood that in actual practice the terminology used is not the important consideration. What is important is that the teacher must be concerned with providing rich and varied learning experiences for each student.

Yet a third type of unit plan is that commonly referred to as a "resource unit." A resource unit is not ordinarily planned as a single teaching unit. It is usually developed by a committee of teachers with little or no pupil assistance. Hence, it becomes a "resource *of* units." Frequently they are not developed with any particular group of children in mind; in fact, the materials may be used in several grades; they cover broad areas of content and always contain more information and many more suggestions than could be used with any one class. A resource unit on conservation might include materials to be used in teaching several units on recreation, public health, lumbering, fishing, mining, and flood control.

In preparing a unit plan, it is recommended that a teacher:

Part of the task of preparing a unit plan is locating and developing the teaching resources to be used in the unit.

a. State clearly the purposes (*objectives* or *goals*, as they are often called) in teaching the unit. In other words, what changes does the teacher want to make in the child in terms of knowledge, skills, habits, attitudes, and appreciations? These stated purposes of the unit should be expressed in "behavioral" terms, or, in other words, in terms of student behavior that will be exhibited when the purposes of the unit have been accomplished. When stated this way, a teacher can measure the success of the unit.

b. Look up references on the subject, read them, and write a content outline of the material. List your references.

c. List the materials to be used in the unit. This will include such items as pictures, slides, movies, models, and construction materials.

d. List the ways the teacher will lead the children into the unit of work; these are called *possible approaches.*

e. List the activities that will help the children attain the purposes or outcomes of the unit.

f. List the ways which you will use in the evaluation of the unit. If a written test is considered, include at least a rough draft of the test in your unit.

Many schools ask teachers to make very brief weekly lesson plans so that if in the event a regular teacher becomes ill, a substitute teacher would have an idea of what was planned each day for each class. These weekly lesson plans are usually extremely brief and are frequently written on special forms prepared for this purpose.

The most specific planning that a teacher does is that done for a specific lesson on a specific day. Daily lesson planning is relatively simple providing the teacher has already made adequate unit lesson plans. Excellent unit plans will have permitted the teacher to gather all of the necessary learning resources ahead of time and to have thought through clearly the general objectives for the unit. The final detail and specific objectives necessary in a daily lesson plan flow naturally and quite easily out of a well done unit lesson plan. The lesson plan is designed simply as a means to good instruction. It has no magic value in and of itself and cannot be justified simply as an elaborate masterpiece. The lesson plan is simply a means to an an end—a device to help the teacher be well prepared to teach.

Lesson plans may take numerous forms. There is no one best way to prepare lesson plans; however, most teachers find it desirable to follow some structured format and to do much of this planning on paper. One lesson plan format that has been found useful by many educators is that found in Figure 11.3. This format can serve for all the

A. Objectives (Stated in behavioral terms that can be measured):
B. Materials Needed:
C. Procedure:
    1. Teacher Activity
    2. Student Activity
D. Provisions for Measuring Extent to Which Stated Objectives Were Achieved:

Figure 11.3. A Suggested Lesson Plan Format.

levels of planning that a teacher must do, whether they be yearly plans, semester plans, unit plans, weekly plans, or daily plans. As Figure 11.3 shows, the first task that a teacher has in planning is that of determining the objectives of the plan involved. Objectives become the road map of the lesson—they indicate the purposes of the lesson and the desired learning outcomes for the students. As has already been suggested, educational objectives should always be stated in terms of student behavior that can be measured. This is necessary so that after the lesson is completed, the teacher can determine whether or not each student has achieved the desired outcomes. Objectives thus stated are frequently called *behavioral objectives.*

Figure 11.3 also shows that in planning a lesson, a teacher must determine what materials will be needed for the lesson. As was indicated in chapter nine, a wealth of instruction materials is now available to educators. A teacher must not only be familiar with these teaching materials but must also know which is the most effective material to use in a given situation.

Figure 11.3 further indicates that a teacher must thoroughly plan the procedure for each lesson. To effectively do this, he

No nation can remain free which does not recognize the importance of education. Our public schools are the backbone of American life and character. We must recognize their importance and stand firmly against any groups which oppose popular education.

Liberty can never flourish in any nation where there is no popular education.

Samuel M. Lindsay

must have a thorough understanding of the nature of the learner—a topic discussed in chapter seven. He must also be familiar with a wide variety of teaching techniques.

Lastly, Figure 11.3 shows that a teacher must make provisions for measuring the extent to which the stated objectives for each lesson are achieved. This provides the teacher with a measure of the overall success of the lesson and also helps him to determine which students have learned the contents of the lesson and which students need additional instruction.

One last important point concerning the planning role of a teacher deals with the need to individualize the learning experiences for each student in so far as it is humanly possible to do so. Unfortunately, since a typical elementary school teacher has between twenty and thirty students, and a typical secondary teacher may have as many as 150 students each day, it is simply not humanly possible for a teacher to make a specific lesson plan for each student. At best, a teacher can hope to modify a single lesson plan to fit the individual needs of each specific student. There is an indication that some of the newer innovations in education, such as individually prescribed instruction, modular scheduling, computer-assisted instruction, independent study, team teaching, and a differentiated teaching staff—all of which are discussed in some detail elsewhere in this book—will make it possible for teachers to do a much better job of tailoring an educational program for each individual student.

Helping Students to Learn

Historically, the role of the teacher has been viewed mainly as that of a "dispenser

Effective lesson planning incorporates a maximum amount of active student participation in the learning process.

of knowledge." Today's teacher can better be characterized as one who "helps students to learn." This new "helping" role of the contemporary teacher is exemplified by a teacher assisting a group of students as they plan a small group project; circulating in a science laboratory giving help to individual students; listening to an individual student who has a reading problem read aloud; or counseling with a student who has a personal problem. The following factors have helped to bring about this new relationship that the teacher has with the learner:

> I have never let my schooling interfere with my education.
>
> Mark Twain

1. Whereas a colonial school teacher had very few tools to use, except a few poorly written textbooks and his own knowledge of the subject matter he was attempting to teach, the contemporary educator has a wealth of teaching aids at his disposal. These instructional devices now make it

possible for a teacher to help students learn much more efficiently and effectively than was possible when teachers had to "dispense" whatever knowledge the students were to learn.

2. An increased understanding of the learning process has also helped educators to assume their present "helping" relationship with learners. Since the turn of the century, thanks to the pioneering efforts of the child study movement and the continued refinement of the discipline of educational psychology, an ever increasing knowledge of the manner in which learning takes place has been made available to teachers. One of the tasks of the teacher is to mold this knowledge of the learning act into excellent learning experiences for each of his students.

The colonial school master had very little knowledge of the learning act at his disposal and consequently cannot be blamed for his ignorance of the fact that students tend to quickly forget rotely memorized facts, learn best from first hand experiences rather than being lectured to, and learn more quickly and permanently that which they are highly motivated to learn—all of which are examples of important principles of learning that have grown from an increased understanding of the learning processes, those processes which guide the work of contemporary educators.

Early lesson planning allows sufficient time for the development of a variety of teaching materials. This student is putting audio tapes on a dial access retrieval system which allows individual students to listen to pre-recorded learning materials by using headphones and simply dialing the lesson they wish to hear.

Historically, students have generally been treated badly in schools. A variety of frightening and ingenious punishments have been devised by teachers in the past. This illustration of a German school during the late 19th century shows examples of punishment then employed. These included the hanging of various marks of disapproval around the offender's neck, wearing of a dunce cap, hanging of a boy in a basket to the ceiling, tying a boy to a stationary ring, and frequent whippings.

3. Yet another factor that has contributed to the view that teachers should help students learn rather than dispense knowledge has been the changes that have taken place in educational philosophy down through the ages. There was a time, for instance, when children were viewed by the church, most parents, and most teachers to be basically bad and full of original sin which somehow must be beaten from them. And "beat," literally, many school masters did, in their misguided efforts to teach and discipline their students.

Fortunately, most contemporary educators agree with Jean Jacques Rousseau (1712–1778)—the great French philosopher who deserves at least part of the credit for bringing about this change in the way youth are viewed—that children are born basically good and become bad only in the hands of man. This change in the philosophical view of the nature of a child has had a profound influence on the relationship between teacher and student.

4. Another change that has contributed to the idea that teachers should help children learn rather than dispense knowledge has been the gradual infusion and acceptance of the concept of democracy into many education philosophies. Most American educators strongly believe that the relationship between a teacher and students should be a democratic one; that is, one in which students have a voice and are respected as individuals. Students who participate in such a classroom are likely to enjoy school more, learn more, and become better citizens in our democratic society.

Evaluating

In addition to school keeping, planning, and helping students to learn, a teacher

A teacher participates in a small group discussion with members of a creative writing class.

A contemporary teacher's role can best be characterized as "helping students learn" rather than "dispensing knowledge."

> Evaluation, as contrasted with measurement, embraces a wider range of technique and evidence.
>
> Paul L. Dressel
> Lewis B. Mayhew

must also be an evaluator. For it is through a well planned program of evaluation that a teacher is able to determine the abilities and achievements of each student. This knowledge is essential for the teacher to plan an appropriate program for each student. In his role as an "evaluator" the teacher is continually assessing each student's abilities, interests, accomplishments, and needs. To help him gather data to accomplish evaluation, an educator employs standardized tests, teacher-made tests, and subjective observations.

A standardized test is one which has been constructed using carefully prescribed techniques; and one for which norms have been established. There are literally hundreds of commercially prepared standardized tests available for teachers to use. These tests are available to measure different dimensions of student aptitude, achievement, and interest. Most school districts now have rather well developed standardized testing programs which supply the teacher with a wide variety of data to use in his role as an evaluator.

Teacher-made tests, as the name implies, are those which the teacher himself constructs. These tests are usually designed to measure student achievement in the various subjects. Constructing good teacher-made tests is a time-consuming task and requires a thorough knowledge of the principles of test construction on the part of the teacher.

Examples of the vast array of technical aids now available for use in schools.

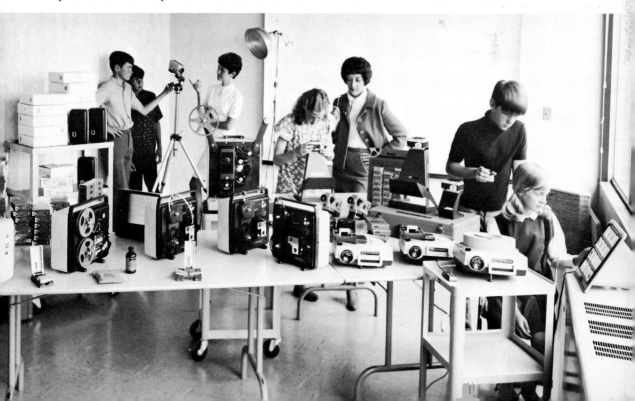

In addition to the data obtained from standardized tests and teacher-made tests, a teacher can obtain useful evaluation information by simply observing students. The skilled educator can learn a good deal about a student's abilities, achievements, interests, and needs through careful observation.

A record of the evaluative data accumulated on each student is usually kept by a school district. It becomes part of a record called a "cumulative record" and contains standardized test scores, grades, health information, and other background information about the student. A sample cumulative record card for a pupil is shown in Figure 11.4.

Reporting

A role of the teacher that is closely connected with evaluating is that of "report-

Figure 11.4. A Sample Cumulative Record.

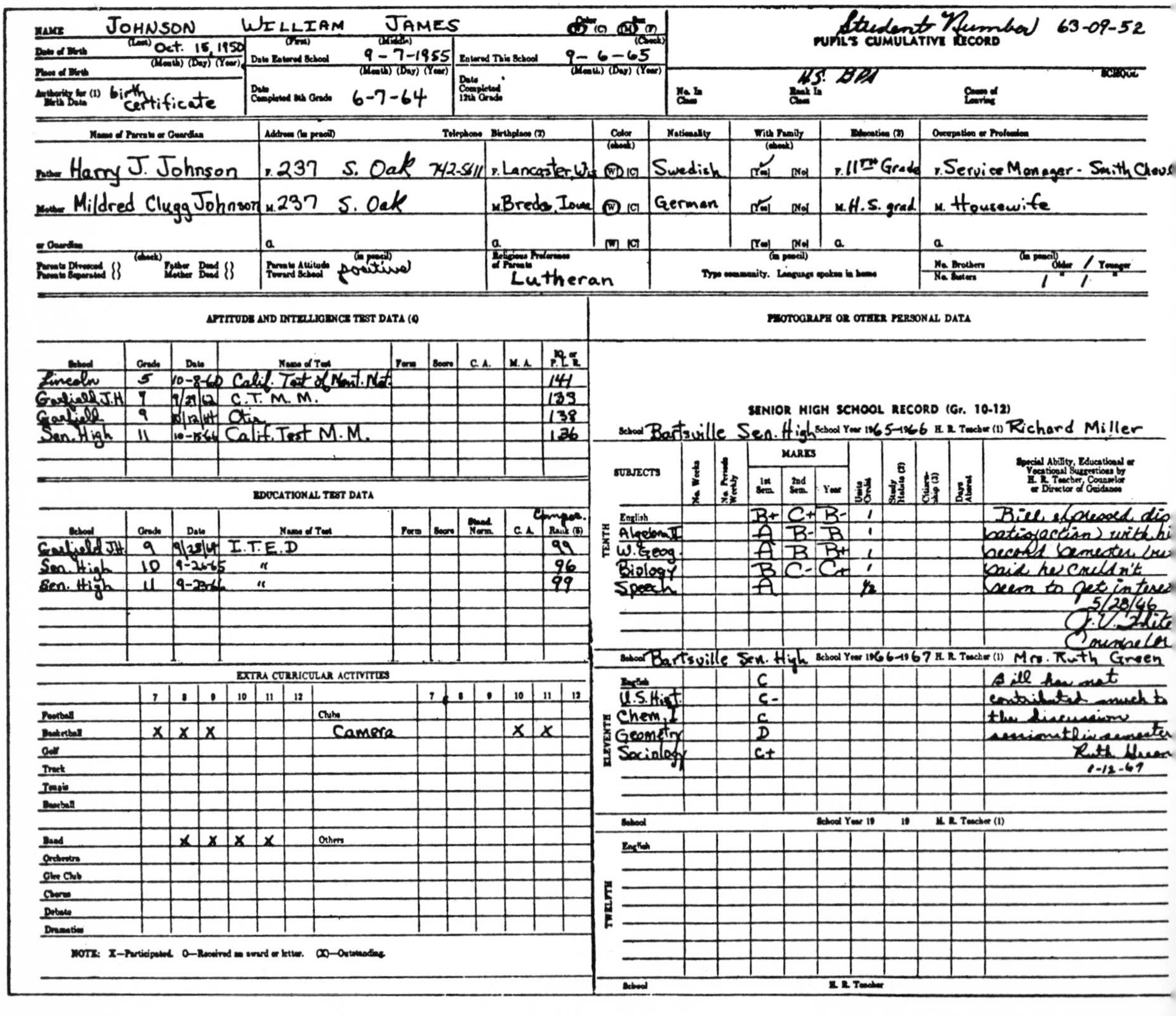

PUPIL'S CUMULATIVE RECORD — Student Number 63-09-52

NAME: JOHNSON (Last) WILLIAM (First) JAMES (Middle)

Date of Birth: Oct. 15, 1950 (Month) (Day) (Year)

Date Entered School: 9-7-1955 (Month) (Day) (Year) — Entered This School: 9-6-65 (Month) (Day) (Year)

Place of Birth

Authority for (1) Birth Data: birth certificate — Date Completed 8th Grade: 6-7-64 — Date Completed 12th Grade

No. In Class — Rank In Class — Cause of Leaving — SCHOOL: H.S. BPA

Name of Parents or Guardian	Address (in pencil)	Telephone	Birthplace (2)	Color (check)	Nationality	With Family (check)	Education (2)	Occupation or Profession
Father Harry J. Johnson	F. 237 S. Oak	742-5611	F. Lancaster, Wis.	(W) (C)	Swedish	Yes / No	F. 11th Grade	F. Service Manager - Smith Chevrolet
Mother Mildred Clugg Johnson	M. 237 S. Oak		M. Bredo, Iowa	(W) (C)	German	Yes / No	M. H.S. grad.	M. Housewife
or Guardian	G.		G.	(W) (C)		(Yes) (No)	G.	G.

Parents Divorced {} Parents Separated {} (check) — Father Dead {} Mother Dead {} — Parents Attitude Toward School (in pencil): positive — Religious Preference of Parents: Lutheran — Type community. Language spoken in home (in pencil) — No. Brothers (in pencil) Older / Younger: / — No. Sisters: 1 / 1

APTITUDE AND INTELLIGENCE TEST DATA (4)

School	Grade	Date	Name of Test	Form	Score	C. A.	M. A.	IQ or P. L. R.
Lincoln	5	10-8-60	Calif. Test of Ment. Mat.					141
Garfield J.H.	7	9/21/62	C.T.M.M.					133
Garfield	9	10/12/64	Otis					138
Sen. High	11	10-15-66	Calif. Test M.M.					136

EDUCATIONAL TEST DATA

School	Grade	Date	Name of Test	Form	Score	Stand. Norm.	C. A.	Compos. Rank (5)
Garfield J.H.	9	9/23/64	I.T.E.D					99
Sen. High	10	9-26-65	"					96
Sen. High	11	9-23-66	"					99

EXTRA CURRICULAR ACTIVITIES

	7	8	9	10	11	12	Clubs	7	8	9	10	11	12
Football													
Basketball	X	X	X				Camera				X	X	
Golf													
Track													
Tennis													
Baseball													
Band		X	X	X	X		Others						
Orchestra													
Glee Club													
Chorus													
Debate													
Dramatics													

NOTE: X—Participated. O—Received an award or letter. (X)—Outstanding.

PHOTOGRAPH OR OTHER PERSONAL DATA

SENIOR HIGH SCHOOL RECORD (Gr. 10-12)

TENTH — School: Bartsville Sen. High — School Year 1965-1966 — H. R. Teacher (1): Richard Miller

SUBJECTS	No. Weeks	No. Periods Weekly	1st Sem.	2nd Sem.	Year	Units Credit	Study Habits (2)	Citizenship (3)	Days Absent	Special Ability, Educational or Vocational Suggestions by H. R. Teacher, Counselor or Director of Guidance
English			B+	C+	B-	1				Bill expressed dissatisfaction with his second semester, he said he couldn't seem to get interested. 5/28/66 J.V. White Counselor
Algebra II			A	B-	B	1				
W. Geog.			A	B	B+	1				
Biology			B	C-	C+	1				
Speech			A			½				

ELEVENTH — School: Bartsville Sen. High — School Year 1966-1967 — H. R. Teacher (1): Mrs. Ruth Green

SUBJECTS	1st Sem.	Suggestions
English	C	Bill has not contributed much to the discussions this semester. Ruth Green 1-12-67
U.S. Hist.	C-	
Chem. I	C	
Geometry	D	
Sociology	C+	

TWELFTH — School — School Year 19 19 — H. R. Teacher (1)

English

School — H. R. Teacher

ing." Reporting basically involves communicating to the parents about their child's progress in school. This is usually accomplished in two ways: in writing, on one of the many different forms that have been created by schools for this purpose, and in person, during a conference.

There are a great variety of forms used by various schools in their efforts to report to parents. In fact, most schools create their own report card forms. An example of such a form is shown in Figure 11.5.

The role of "reporter" requires that a teacher possess not only a thorough knowledge of the progress of each student, but also the communication and human relations skills necessary to effectively pass this information along to parents.

Figure 11.5. A Sample Report Card.

STUDENT *Sue Stone* ENGLISH *III*

ADVISOR *Mrs. Anderson* TEACHER *Mrs. Anderson*

EVALUATION

	Quarters	Superior	Above average	School average	Below average	Decidedly below average
EFFORT	1				✓	
	2				✓	
	3					✓
	4					✓
ACHIEVEMENT	1	✓				
	2	✓				
	3		✓			
	4		✓			

ANALYSIS OF EVALUATION

	Strength 1 2 3 4	Weakness 1 2 3 4
Conduct		✓ ✓ ✓ ✓
Work habits in class		✓ ✓ ✓ ✓
Homework		✓ ✓ ✓ ✓
Skills		
Oral activities	✓ ✓	
Reading	✓ ✓	
Written work	✓ ✓ ✓	
Content	✓ ✓	
Mechanics	✓ ✓	
Punctuation	✓ ✓ ✓	
Grammar	✓ ✓	
Spelling	✓ ✓	
Penmanship	✓ ✓ ✓ ✓	

A teacher must possess good human relations skills to develop the type of relationship with pupils that is essential for the development of good learning experiences.

Understanding and Getting Along with People

One of the very most important general tasks of a teacher is that of understanding and getting along with the many different people with which he must deal. He must possess good human relations skills and, in a sense, must be a public relations expert. The teacher who is not able to successfully fulfill this role is destined to failure.

There are many different groups of people with whom the teacher must relate. Obviously, the group that the teacher spends the most time with is the students. It may seem redundant to suggest that a teacher must be able to understand and get along with students; however, there are a number of teachers who do have difficulty in these areas. For instance, the teacher who continually has discipline problems in his classroom quite likely does not understand students and obviously can't get along very well with them.

Parents constitute yet another group which a teacher must understand and get along with. Most parents are extremely interested in, and in many instances rather emotional about, their child's progress in school. Furthermore, it is difficult for many parents to be objective about their child's success and/or behavior in school. It requires a good deal of understanding and human relations skill on the part of the teacher, for instance, to tell a mother and father that their child has been behaving badly and/or is not achieving academically.

Lastly, a teacher must understand and get along with his colleagues—fellow teachers, supervisors, and administrators. This is more true today than it has ever been before due to the fact that education is now a very

A teacher must be able to work well with other faculty members.

complex undertaking and teachers often work in teams, do joint planning, have the help of specialists and para-professionals, and generally work more closely together than has traditionally been the case (the one room country school teacher had no colleagues, for instance). Some teachers understand and get along with students but find it difficult to relate to their colleagues. The teacher who finds himself in this situation is doomed to failure just as surely as the one who cannot relate to students.

In order to understand people a teacher must develop insight into human motivations, needs, fears, hopes, weaknesses, prejudices, and desires. A teacher's ability to get along with people is largely dependent upon his own personality, attitudes, and values, as well as the extent to which he basically likes and respects people in spite of the fact that they may be different and

may possess weaknesses. The person who is considering entering the teaching profession should carefully assess his human relations skills and decide whether or not his personality, attitudes, and values will enable him to get along effectively with the many people with whom he will have to deal as a teacher.

Keeping Up To Date

American education, both the task and the teacher, are rapidly changing. Teachers must not only keep pace with these changes, but must actually bring some of them about through devising improved teaching methods, developing educational innovations, and helping to expand the body of knowledge within their disciplines. This means that a teacher must keep up to date on all aspects of his work—advances in knowl-

Attending a variety of different kinds of conventions, conferences, and other professional meetings is one way that educators keep up to date.

edge in the subject matter, improved teaching techniques (including discovering some of his own), changes in our social system, changes in our youth, and changes on the national and international political scene. Then too, a teacher must keep up on research findings in education and put into practice those findings that are of use to his particular work. In fact, a teacher in order to be most effective must become a student of teaching, constantly studying and experimenting with learning and constantly improving his work as an educator.

This means that a teacher must spend a good deal of time reading professional literature; must attend professional conventions, conferences, and workshops; take an active part in in-service training programs; go back to a college or university and take graduate courses and possibly work on an advanced degree; and in general seek out ways of keeping up to date.

In conclusion, the role of the contemporary teacher is a many-faceted one. This

> Education is an admirable thing, but it is well to remember from time to time that nothing that is worth knowing can be taught.
>
> Oscar Wilde

A teacher must also be able to relate effectively to parents.

One of the ways that teachers can keep up-to-date in their subject matter specialty is by enrolling in graduate courses, workshops, or institutes dealing with their specialty.

chapter has mentioned but a few of the major tasks that a successful teacher must be capable of performing. Perhaps the most important concept presented in this chapter is the fact that today's teacher is no longer merely a dispenser of knowledge, but rather helps arrange learning experiences for the student—in a real sense, he is a co-learner with the students. Students learn—teachers assist them.

Questions for Discussion

1. How did the role of the teacher in colonial America differ with that of contemporary educators?
2. In what ways might "school keeping" chores be minimized so that teachers might spend more time working with students?
3. What are the functions and values of educational planning?

Micro-teaching (teaching short lessons to small groups of students) is one technique that teachers can use to improve their teaching methods. These micro lessons are usually videotaped. Here a group of teachers view and discuss the playback of a videotaped micro lesson in an effort to learn more about the teaching process and to improve their teaching.

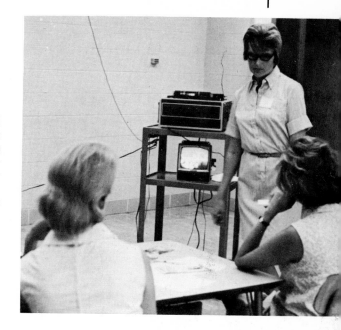

4. What factors have helped to bring about the idea that teachers, rather than dispensing knowledge, should help students to learn?
5. What qualities must a teacher possess in order to have good human relations skills?

SUPPLEMENTARY LEARNING ACTIVITIES

1. Plan a hypothetical lesson using the suggestions presented in this chapter.
2. Analyze the pupil's cumulative record presented in Figure 11.4. What does this record tell you about William James Johnson?
3. Interview a teacher concerning his or her role as an educator.
4. Study the report card in Figure 11.5. What does it tell you about Sue Stone? How could this type of report card form be improved?

5. Role-play several situations in which a teacher displays poor human relations skills. Also role-play some situations in which a teacher exhibits good human relations skills.

SELECTED REFERENCES

Abraham, Willard. *A Handbook for the New Teacher.* New York: Holt, Rinehart & Winston, Inc., 1960.

Adams, Beatrice. "The Magic Ingredient." *NEA Journal* 47(1958):571.

American Association of School Administrators. *The High School in a Changing World.* Washington: National Education Association 1958 Yearbook, 1958.

Deuel, Leo, ed. *The Teacher's Treasure Chest.* Englewood Cliffs, N.J.: Prentice-Hall, Inc., 1956.

Eckel, Howard. "How Can We Get Quality Teaching?" *The School Executive* 77(1958):19–21.

Evans, Eva Knox. *So You're Going to Teach.* New York: Hinds, Hayden & Eldridge, 1948.

Filbin, Robert L., and Stefan Vogel. *So You're Going to be a Teacher.* Great Neck, N.Y.: Barron's Educational Series Inc., 1962.

Highet, Gilbert. *The Art of Teaching.* New York: Alfred P. Knopf, Inc., 1950.

Hodenfield, G. K. "Nobody Asked Me, But . . ." *Saturday Review* 45(1962):51–52.

Holman, Mary V. *How It Feels to be a Teacher.* New York: Teachers College, Columbia University Press, 1950.

Jersild, Arthur T. *When Teachers Face Themselves.* 2nd ed. New York: Bureau of Publications, Teachers College, Columbia University, 1957.

Lambert, Sam M. "Angry Young Men in Teaching." *NEA Journal* 52(1963):17–20.

Leonard, George B., Jr. "What Is A Teacher?" *Look,* (21 February, 1956), pp. 29–39.

Lynham, Adria B. "Teachers Are People." *NEA Journal* 47:503–504.

Mayer, Martin. "The Trouble with Textbooks." *Harper Magazine,* July 1962, pp. 65–71.

Peters, Herman J., et al. *Introduction to Teaching.* New York: The Macmillan Co., 1963.

Russell, William F. "Should You Be a Teacher?" *Career Opportunities.* New York: New York Life Insurance Co., 1958.

Snow, Robert H. "Anxieties and Discontents in Teaching." *Phi Delta Kappan* 44(1963):318–321.

Stroh, M. Margaret. *Find Your Own Frontier.* Austin, Texas: Delta Kappa Gamma, 1948.

Wilson, Charles H. *A Teacher Is A Person.* New York: Holt, Rinehart & Winston, Inc., 1956.

Towards a Differentiated
Teaching Staff

M. John Rand and Fenwick English

The acute shortage of teachers [in some geographical areas and at some levels or in certain subjects] and the growing movement toward teacher professionalization are placing unbearable strains upon the present organizational structure in education. The shortage is worst in the nation's largest metropolitan areas, where organizational structures are most rigid and inner-city children in greatest need of good education. In suburban districts there is growing constituent dissatisfaction. Taxpayers are balking at increasing education costs without some proof that the pudding will be better.

Rising militancy and mass "resignations" last fall are signs that teachers are dissatisfied with their roles as mere implementers of administrative decision. Their demands are certainly more inclusive than simply a raise in pay. Teachers are telling us something we should have known or predicted long ago. When a group of people increase their technical competence close to that of the top members of the hierarchy, lines of authority become blurred. The subordinate position begins to rest more upon arbitrary and traditional distinctions than upon competence to perform the job.

Teachers are demanding inclusion in the decision-making process in education. As Corwin says,[1] professionalism is associated positively with militancy. Rather than arouse hostility in administrators and lay boards, it should be welcomed as one sign that the teaching profession is coming of age.

Increasing teacher specialization and competence mean that roles within the present educational structure are in the process of change. Teachers are recognizing that to break out of the ceilings imposed by the single salary schedule they must reexamine the assumptions which support it. The increasing need for high specialization and advanced training means that some teachers should be paid between $20,000 and $25,000 per year, as are specialists in other fields. So long as we have the single salary schedule, however, no one will get this amount. The money simply cannot be raised without a complete (and in the short run completely impossible) overhaul of tax structures, school financing, and public value systems.

Hence the dissolution of the single salary schedule is a must if the teaching profession is to advance. Teachers will generally admit that not all of them possess the same abilities or strengths. They reject the onus of "merit pay," however, as "unprofessional"

* M. John Rand, and Fenwick English, "Towards a Differentiated Teaching Staff," *Phi Delta Kappan,* January, 1968, pp. 264–268. Used by permission.
1. Ronald G. Corwin, "Militant Professionalism, Initiative and Compliance in Public Education," *Sociology of Education* 38(1965):310–331.

or otherwise undesirable. Merit pay plans offer the advantage of dissolving the single salary schedule, but ordinarily make no distinction in job responsibilities of teachers. Added pay is for "merit," not for added responsibility. As long as teaching is considered an art, one man's "superior" teacher is another's "average" teacher. Judgment of teaching "excellence" must be based on careful research just beginning to emerge at some universities. We have a long way to go before we can specify on the basis of empirical evidence what teaching excellence consists of. Hence we do not have the foundation for merit pay.

The Temple City plan approaches the problem from a different perspective. Teachers are not treated the same. They may receive additional remuneration for increased professional responsibilities, which means change in their roles as teachers. These new responsibilities imply increased training and time on the job, and implicit in the concept of advancement is professional competence as a teacher, however it is measured. Teachers are not chosen to be paid more simply for continuing to perform their same functions; they are paid more for assuming increased responsibilities in the instructional program. They are selected on the basis of their experience and qualifications for the job by a professional panel and are retained only as they are able to perform adequately in their capacities. The Temple City Differentiated Staffing Plan, almost wholly designed by teachers, offers a way for teachers to receive remuneration of $20,000 per year by differentiating teaching roles and systematically enlarging their authority and decision-making powers to shape the instructional program.

The Temple City plan is not a brand new idea. Aspects of the plan have been espoused by Myron Lieberman,[2] J. Lloyd Trump,[3] and Robert Bush and Dwight Allen[4] at Stanford University. Allen was instrumental in developing the Temple City project, funded by the Charles F. Kettering Foundation of Denver, Colorado, for an 18-month study. The TEPS program of the NEA has also been active in proposing differentiated roles for professional personnel. The strength of the Temple City concept of differentiated staffing resides in a high degree of staff participation in its development. Indeed, the process of development is every bit as important as the product, i.e., an acceptable organizational design to implement the ideas of the professional staff.

The original model of differentiated staffing was developed by Allen and presented to the California State Board of Education in April of 1966 (see Figure 11.6). Later it was altered in the work done by Temple City Teachers (see Figure 11.7, p. 278). At the present, this model is undergoing further revision as a result of financial studies and further staff feedback. A brief sketch of the job descriptions follows.

Teaching Research Associate

The teaching research associate (TRA) is the "self-renewal" unit of the organization. His primary function is to introduce new concepts and ideas into the schools. He is well versed in research methodology and evaluation of instruction. The TRA may

2. Myron Lieberman, *The Future of Public Education.* Chicago: University of Chicago Press, 1960.
3. J. Lloyd Trump and Dorsey Baynham, *Guide to Better Schools.* Chicago: Rand McNally & Co., 1961.
4. Dwight Allen and Robert Bush, *A New Design for High School Education.* New York: McGraw-Hill Book Co., 1964.

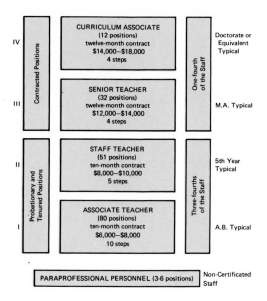

Figure 11.6. The Proposed Teacher Hierarchy Based on Differentiated Compensation and Responsibilities.

conduct field studies, but his major purpose is to translate research into instructional probes at the school level. The TRA functions in the present structure as a classroom teacher, as do all of the other personnel in the differentiated staffing plan, although in a limited capacity. In this way he does not lose sight of the receivers of his efforts. The TRA represents the apex of professional advancement for the aspiring teacher.

The teaching research associate meets all of Rogers'[5] criteria for initiating planned change in education. These are: 1) base the topics investigated on felt needs of practitioners; 2) create an educational structure to facilitate change; 3) raise the practitioners' ability to utilize the research results. Part of the TRA's responsibilities are implied in the third criterion mentioned by Rogers. Much of his liaison work with staff

and current research will be to increase the sophistication level of teachers and help them use it in practice and evaluate its effectiveness.

Teaching Curriculum Associate

The teaching curriculum associate (TCA) also must possess knowledge of research methodology, except that his knowledge is more applicable to curriculum theory, construction, and evaluation. In addition, the TCA would be adept at modifying national curriculum studies to meet local needs and local teacher proclivities.

The TCA also works at raising the level of teacher specialization in specific subject areas. He is more of a communications specialist than the TRA. However, due to the overlap in some functions, and because it is difficult to separate research from curriculum and instructional improvement studies, these two functions will probably be combined into one position: the Teaching Research-Curriculum Associate.

The Senior Teacher

The senior teacher is primarily responsible for the application of curriculum and instructional innovations to the classroom. The senior teacher is an acknowledged master practitioner, a learning engineer, a skilled diagnostician of the learning process. He is the teacher's teacher.

The senior teacher as an instructional advisor heads a subject group and represents

5. Everett M. Rogers, "Developing a Strategy for Planned Change," paper presented at a Symposium on the Application of System Analysis and Management Techniques to Educational Planning in California, Orange, California, June, 1967.

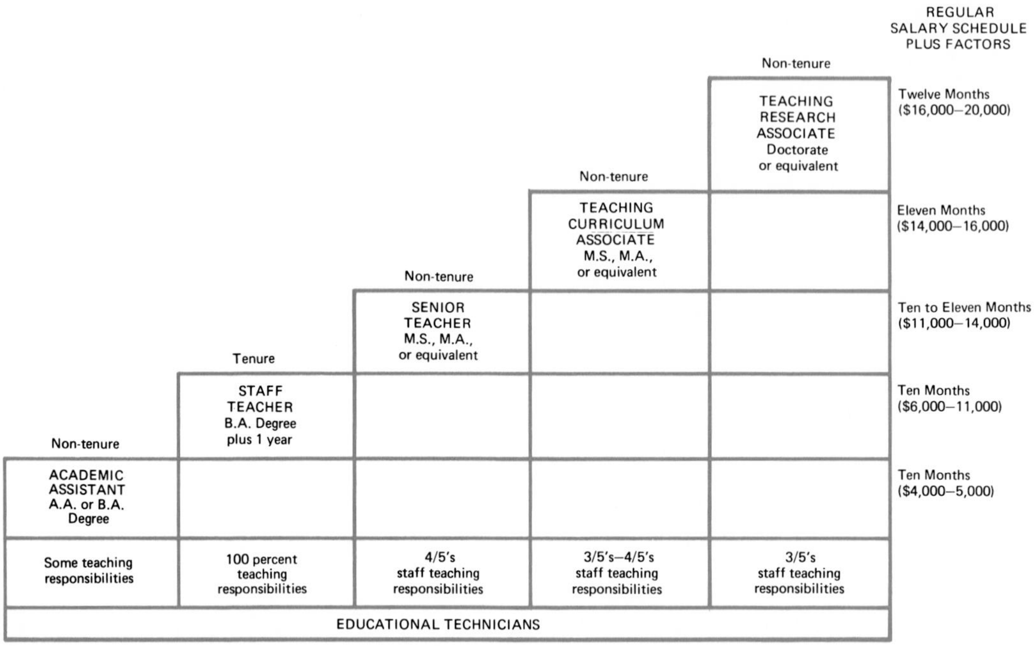

					REGULAR SALARY SCHEDULE PLUS FACTORS
				Non-tenure	
				TEACHING RESEARCH ASSOCIATE Doctorate or equivalent	Twelve Months ($16,000–20,000)
			Non-tenure		
			TEACHING CURRICULUM ASSOCIATE M.S., M.A., or equivalent		Eleven Months ($14,000–16,000)
		Non-tenure			
		SENIOR TEACHER M.S., M.A., or equivalent			Ten to Eleven Months ($11,000–14,000)
	Tenure				
	STAFF TEACHER B.A. Degree plus 1 year				Ten Months ($6,000–11,000)
Non-tenure					
ACADEMIC ASSISTANT A.A. or B.A. Degree					Ten Months ($4,000–5,000)
Some teaching responsibilities	100 percent teaching responsibilities	4/5's staff teaching responsibilities	3/5's–4/5's staff teaching responsibilities	3/5's staff teaching responsibilities	
EDUCATIONAL TECHNICIANS					

Figure 11.7. Temple City Unified School District: A Model of Differentiated Staffing.

This model of differentiated staffing was developed by Temple City Teachers. The model is currently being revised to combine the TRA-TCA functions. Salary figures are tentative.

this area on the school academic senate. He shares with the school principal the selection, performance, and evaluation of his colleagues in that subject specialty. In a team teaching situation, the senior teacher would function as a team leader. At least one-half of this teacher's day would be with students.

The Staff Teacher

In a sense, all teachers in the differentiated staffing plan are staff teachers. A full-time staff teacher spends his school hours with students. He performs the same professional functions as most teachers in typical school districts. In a differentiated staffing plan the staff teacher is relieved of

semi-professional and clerical duties by employment of the following assistants:

The Academic Assistant

The academic assistant is a skilled para-professional, or a teacher intern (associate teacher) from a nearby college or university. He works with students and may instruct in special or skilled areas. He may also maintain physical materials, grade papers, and supervise resource center activities or student study.

The Educational Technician

The educational technician assumes many of the clerical and housekeeping tasks that consume so much professional time in the present organization. The technician keeps records, duplicates material, types, supervises student movement on campus, takes attendance, etc. The technician has little, if any, instructional responsibilities.

The Academic Senate

Teachers are formally involved in school decision making through the organization of an academic senate on each campus. One of the responsibilities of senior teachers is to represent the staff in the establishment of school policies relating to the educational program and its improvement.

The School Manager

In addition, the principal's role is differentiated by establishing a position called school manager. The school manager assumes responsibility for most of the business functions of school operation and thus relieves the principal for attention to the instructional program. It is hoped that eventually the principal will also refurbish his image as a teacher by assuming some direct teaching responsibilities with students. Most principals would find this impossible now, since they too are overburdened with paperwork and administrivia.

This combination of teacher specialists and administrator generalists would provide the school with the best judgments of all the professionals occupied with shaping a dynamic instructional program. School leadership is clearly enhanced with teachers exercising judgment as to how the instructional program should be improved. The principal's role is strengthened, since he can count on the specialized expertise of his senior teachers in the hiring and evaluation of the instructional staff. Teachers are intimately involved in professionalizing and disciplining their own ranks through the academic senate. This is crucial for full-fledged maturity; effective professional regulation can only occur when teachers assume responsibility for each other's performance. Administrators should welcome this desire for more responsibilities and assist their staffs in learning how to develop and exercise the leadership concomitants to fulfill this important professional role.

A discussion of differentiated staffing would not be complete without mentioning some of the problems the district has encountered in studying this concept. Differentiated staffing challenges a basic assumption inherent in the organizational structure of education. The myth that all teachers are equal exercises a powerful influence upon our thinking. The present organizational structure which assumes that one teacher can be all things to all students is a barrier of the first magnitude, especially at the elementary level.

One way of avoiding change and protecting oneself is for the teacher to shut his door and isolate himself with his 30 children. The position of the teacher in his classroom fortress is easier and more secure without the scrutiny of his colleagues. To differentiate teacher roles is contrary to the standard organizational pattern of elementary education for the last 100 years. When teachers perform different functions and assume new responsibilities they cannot be with children all day long. They must have time during the school day to plan with colleagues and conduct studies or meet with individual students. This implies some type of flexible scheduling, plus dual use of instructional models and resource facilities. This in turn means that teachers must delegate to paraprofessionals many nonprofessional responsibilities that do not demand a high degree of skill and training.

We have found a greater resistance at the elementary level to concepts of differentiated staffing than at the secondary. Some teachers fear that team teaching, use of paraprofessionals, resource centers, and flexible scheduling will permanently "damage" their children. They fail to recall that the present organizational structure established in 1870 at the Quincy Grammar School was organized for administrative convenience and that critics pointed out even then that it rather callously ignored the needs of continuous educational progress for each individual student.

Also we noted that a greater proportion of women than men object to teachers assuming a professional disciplinary role with their colleagues. This is especially true at the primary level, where a traditionally protective environment shields both students and teachers from decision making and colleague interaction.

At the secondary level, the idea of differentiated staffing was received more warmly. Here more teachers are men and the tradition of subject area specialization and leadership through department chairmen has been well established. However, some teachers at the secondary level are just as immobilized in their six-period day, self-contained classrooms as their elementary counterparts.

Some administrators will be uncomfortable in sharing the decision-making process with their staffs. Fear of losing status is an important consideration when proposing new roles for teachers. One must remember that almost all other roles in a school district hinge upon that of the teacher. If the teacher base is expanded upward, a shift is required in functions all the way to the superintendent. This means that in the Temple City plan teachers (teaching research associates) will sit with principals in an academic coordinating council headed by the superintendent. This district-wide group plans and anticipates district movement. Teachers (teaching curriculum associates) will also be a part of the curriculum coordinating council headed by the assistant superintendent. This group articulates curriculum development through the grades. Teacher specialists form an integral part of the decision-making machinery with the administrators of the district.

The Temple City plan of differentiated staffing offers a way to emancipate the teacher. It changes and enlarges the roles of teachers, increases their autonomy and decision-making powers, offers career advancement, and places them in a position to assume a regulatory function of their own profession. From the point of the administrator it enhances the leadership potential of his staff and builds in some guarantee that the instructional program will indeed remain vital and strong in all areas. A board of education and community should be encouraged when their teachers are willing to assume a corporate responsibility for the quality of education in their schools. The fact that teachers are disciplining themselves, are constantly in the self-renewal process, and have the freedom to rise as teachers to the top of their abilities and willingness to work means that the collective human resources which lie fallow in every organization are more fully tapped. In the short time our project has been operative we have been amazed at the talent which has emerged from our staff.

The most difficult barrier of all is not physical or financial but the subtle limitations in our vision, attitudes, and expectations, conditioned by one organizational structure for over 100 years. The validity of this structure may have been eroded, but its form has been firmly implanted in our psyches. The ability to rise above our own conditioning and previous expectancy levels is the most difficult problem, for solutions cannot be devised until problems are accurately perceived. Perception is limited when assumptions cannot be questioned. Our inability to see that some of our frustrations stem from traditional assumptions is a tragic dilemma. Differentiated staffing is a concept which challenges a whole host of notions about how American education should be organized and operated. At the moment it may be heresy; in a decade it may be practice.

CHAPTER 12

Becoming a Teacher

My warmest congratulations go out to each of you for the decision you have made to follow a teaching career.

Today—as never before—we rest our hopes for America on the teachers of America. We know that our future is being forged in the classrooms and campuses of our nation. We see the wisdom of an uncompromising commitment to educational excellence and expansion.

So you have chosen well. And America will be richer for your dedication to a task that holds the promise of a better tomorrow.

I wish you Godspeed as our nation's custodians of opportunity for the children who will inherit the precious heritage we share.

Lyndon B. Johnson[1]

Yesterday

The teacher in America has historically been a rather ambivalent character in the eyes of his fellow citizens. In the past, a teacher has often been depicted as an untalented, poor undesirable who could make a living no other way. Examples of this characterization include the following:

Built like a scarecrow, a gangling, pinheaded, flat-topped oaf. But what would anyone expect? He was just a teacher.

(Washington Irving's Ichabod Crane)

A ridiculous figure, his bald head covered with an ill-fitting wig . . . a man who had aspired to be a doctor but who had been forced by poverty to be nothing more than a schoolmaster.

(Mark Twain's description of "Old Dobbins")

Their teacher was a gaunt, red-faced spinster, with fierce, glaring eyes.

(A teacher in Thomas Wolfe's *Look Homeward, Angel*)

Those who can, do: those who can't, teach.

(Attributed to George Bernard Shaw)

1. ASCUS *Teaching Opportunities for You.* Hershey, Penn.: Association for School and University Staffing, 1968, p. 3.

One can understand why teachers were viewed this way by briefly examining the history of teacher education. We might first postulate that teaching may well be one of the world's oldest tasks. Certainly early man spent much time instructing his young in the intricacies of hunting and gathering food, knowledge of the world as he knew it, and the secret rituals of early social life. But it was not until the development of symbolic language that formal education took place outside the structure of the family in what might be called schools. These first schools probably came into existence about 2000 B.C. The teachers in these first schools were probably religious men whose aim it was to pass on religious values and attitudes.

While schools have existed for approximately 4,000 years, specific efforts to train teachers are less than 300 years old. One of the early training schools was established in 1685 by Jean Baptiste de la Salle (1651–1719) at Rheims, France.[2] The first known teacher training school in the United States was that established in 1823 by Samuel Hall at Concord, Vermont. Despite these early humble efforts to train teachers, it may be said that until the twentieth century, most teachers had very little, if any, specific training for the work they did.

Teacher Certification

One of the main reasons that teachers have historically commanded little respect and prestige is that until quite recently, there were no standards governing the preparation of teachers. Anyone could be a teacher simply by declaring himself so. It was not until quite recently that states passed teacher certification laws governing the training of teachers.

An excellent account of the history of teacher certification in the United States is the following:[3]

Since there was very little in the way of teacher education in the colonial days—at least as we think of it today—there was little in the way of certification. Each community solved its educational needs in its own way. In areas where church influence was strong, a teaching license—if required at all—stressed moral character, religious zeal, and conformity to church doctrine. The first loyalty oath was demanded by the governor of New Jersey, in a proclamation requiring teachers to swear they would not engage in subversive activities against the British Crown. This was also required in other colonies and quite often was more important than anything else in the license. In general, however, the basic requirement of a colonial teacher was the ability to keep order in the classroom; not too much attention was given the question of whether he knew anything at all about the Three R's. There was mobility of teachers in those days, too. A teacher dismissed by one community as drunk, disorderly, dishonest and immoral, or maybe just plain ignorant, had only to hike to the next community to get another job.

Changes in teacher certification were slow to come after America won its independence (although the loyalty oath to the British Crown was followed by one to the

----

2. G. Compayre (translated by W. H. Payne). *History of Pedagogy.* Boston: D. C. Heath and Co., 1885, p. 261.
3. G. K. Hodenfield and T. M. Stinnett. *The Education of Teachers.* Englewood Cliffs, N.J.: Prentice-Hall, Inc., 1961, pp. 101–103. Used with permission.

United States). Gradually there came a movement toward state supervision of public schools, a movement that began when the states began bearing part of the cost, but it was not until after the Civil War that the authority to issue a certificate began to move slowly from local and county authorities to the states. Really, not until the early 1900's did this shift get underway in earnest. State certificates were issued on the basis of written examinations, usually without regard to the prospective teacher's own education. Even after the turn of the twentieth century the typical examination did not require education beyond the tenth grade, and it was not until 1907 that Indiana became the first state to require a high-school diploma as a condition for all teachers' certificates.

The explosive expansion of American education after 1910 brought new rules and regulations in certification. Before 1900, most states issued a blanket certificate that was good for any subject at any grade level. Only six of the states required a different certificate for elementary- and secondary-school teaching. Gradually there was a move toward special certificates for special teaching assignments. The standards were tightened and graduation from college became more important, even though it was some time before courses in professional education were required.

World War I reversed the trend toward insistence on better teachers and better education. A survey by the National Education Association in 1918 showed that half of the teaching force of 600,000 persons had no special professional education, and 100,000 of the total had less than two years of education beyond the eighth grade. In 1921 there were thirty states which had no definite scholarship requirements for a certificate, but by 1926 this number had dropped to fifteen.

With the Depression and general unemployment of the 1930's, there came a surplus of teachers and a continuing rise in minimum standards. It was during this period that the first major demands were made for a five-year college program for teachers. Even so, it is shocking to realize that as recently as 1931 nearly half the states would issue a certificate to a high-school graduate. These graduates—and many of them from poor high schools at that—were given teaching jobs in elementary schools and it is impossible to calculate the damage they were able to do.

Whatever improvements were made during the Depression were virtually wiped out by the effects of World War II. Teachers flocked to war industries and the number of students enrolled in teacher education programs dropped off. A teacher shortage developed. . . . Because somebody had to be in the classroom, emergency or substandard certificates became the order of the day. At the height of the teacher shortage it was estimated that as many as 140,000 teachers held emergency certificates. By 1948 the number was about 101,000 and by 1959 it was 95,700.

But during these postwar years the total number of teachers increased tremendously and there is hope in the fact that while one out of ten teachers held an emergency certificate in the 1949–50 school year, by 1958–59 the ratio had dropped to one out of thirteen. It should be pointed out again that there is no precise or universal definition of an "emergency certificate"; some are better than others, and some are even better than a few standard certificates.

Any history of teacher certification in this country has to be a chronicle of chaos. The situation is better now than ever before, but there is still considerable room for improvement. All the states require a bachelor's degree for a secondary-school certificate. Forty-two of the states require the bachelor's degree for elementary-school teachers, and Missouri adopted the degree minimum effective in the fall of 1961.

One hurdle, more irritating than real, to the free flow of teachers across state lines is the requirement of nine states of special courses which usually can be secured only in an institution within the states. The states, and the special requirements are as follows (as of 1961):

Arizona, "Constitutions of the United States and Arizona"

Louisiana, "Louisiana History" for upper elementary-grade teachers only

Nevada, "Nevada Constitution and State Law"

Oklahoma, "Oklahoma History"

Rhode Island, "Rhode Island Education," which must be completed within three years after the teacher begins teaching in the state

Texas, "Texas and Federal Governments"

Washington, "Washington School Law, History and Government"

Wisconsin, cooperatives and conservation for certain teachers only

Wyoming, "Wyoming Constitution"

The number of such special courses has been declining steadily in recent years, and even where they still exist the regulations have been eased somewhat. For instance, in Nevada, Oklahoma, and Wyoming, the applicant for a certificate is allowed to demon-

Getting to know your advisor and other college instructors and having an opportunity to work individually with them is a valuable part of the formal teacher education program.

strate his competence in the special fields by examination instead of being required to take a formal credit course.

In 1959 the states issued a total of 630 different certificates, ranging from one in West Virginia (with one or more forms) to 65 in New Jersey. Of the total, 88 are issued on preparation below the bachelor's degree, 312 require the bachelor's degree, 45 require more than the bachelor's degree but less than five years of college work, 161 require the master's degree, 8 require more than five but less than six years, 10 require six years, and 6 require the doctor's degree.

Current certification requirements differ considerably from state to state. Nearly all states require at least a bachelor's degree for permanent certification at the elementary or secondary level. Most states also require a sequence of special courses in psychology and education, plus a series of supervised clinical experiences such as observation, participation, micro-teaching, student-teaching, simulation and internship, as well as extensive study in the subject matter to be taught. A secondary school teacher needs a major in whatever subject he wishes to teach (such as English, history, mathematics, biology, chemistry, business education, industrial education, home economics, physical education, art, or music). An elementary school teacher needs a major in elementary education, which typically includes a study of the materials and methods for teaching language arts, science, social studies, mathematics, art, music, etc. —all of the areas included in the elementary school curriculum.

A summary of the minimum requirements for the lowest regular teaching certificate for each state is presented in Figure 12.1. Of course, the specific certification requirements for each state are much more elaborate and detailed than the brief summary data presented in Figure 12.1.

The first two years of a teacher education program are devoted largely to general and liberal arts education courses.

	Elementary School			Secondary School		
State	Degree or Number of Semester Hours Required	Professional Education Required, Semester Hours (Total)	Directed Teaching Required, Semester Hours (Included in Column 3)	Degree or Number of Semester Hours Required	Professional Education Required, Semester Hours (Total)	Directed Teaching Required, Semester Hours (Included in Column 6)
1	2	3	4	5	6	7
Alabama	B	27	6	B	21	6
Alaska	B	24	C	B	18	C
Arizona	5[a]	24	6	5[a]	22	6
Arkansas	B	18	6	B	18	6
California	B[b]	AC[b]	AC[b]	B[b]	AC[b]	AC[b]
Colorado	B	AC	AC	B	AC	AC
Connecticut	B	30	6	B	18	6
Delaware	B	30	6	B	18	6
District	B[c]	15	C	5[c]	15	C
Florida	B	20	6	B	20	6
Georgia	B	18	6	B	18	6
Hawaii	B	18	AC[d]	B	18	AC[d]
Idaho	B	24	6	B	20	6
Illinois	B	16	5	B	16	5
Indiana	B	27	8	B	18	6
Iowa	B	20	5	B	20	5
Kansas	B	24	5	B	20	5
Kentucky	B	24	8[e]	B	17	8[e]
Louisiana	B	24	4	B	18	4
Maine	B	30	6	B	18	6
Maryland	B	26	8	B	18	6
Massachusetts	B[f]	18	2	B[f]	12	2
Michigan	B	20	5[g]	B	20	5[g]
Minnesota	B	30	6	B	18	4
Mississippi	B	36	6	B	18	6
Missouri	B	18	5	B	18	5
Montana	B	AC	AC	B	16	AC
Nebraska	60[h]	8	3	B	AC	AC
Nevada	B[i]	18[j]	6	B	20	6
New Hampshire	B	30	6	B	18	6
New Jersey	B	30	6[k]	B	21	6[k]
New Mexico	B	24	6	B	18	6
New York	B	24	C[l]	B	12	C[l]
North Carolina	B	24	6	B	18	6
North Dakota	B	16	3	B	16	3
Ohio	B	28	6	B	17	6
Oklahoma	B	21[m]	6	B	21[m]	6
Oregon	B	20	—[n]	B[c]	14	—[n]
Pennsylvania	B	AC	6–12[p]	B	AC	6–12[p]
Puerto Rico	68[q]	53[q]	6[q]	B[q]	29[q]	5[q]
Rhode Island	B	30	6	B	18	6
South Carolina	B	21	6	B	18	6
South Dakota	60[r]	15	3	B	20	6
Tennessee	B	24	4	B	24	4
Texas	B	18	6	B	18	6
Utah	B	26	8	B	21	8
Vermont	90	18	6	B	18	6
Virginia	B	18	6	B	15	6
Washington	B[s]	AC	AC	B[s]	AC	AC
West Virginia	B	20	6	B	20	6
Wisconsin	64[t]	26	5	B	18	5
Wyoming	B	23	C	B	20	C

LEGEND: — means not reported. AC means approved curriculum; B means a bachelor's degree of specified preparation; 5 means a bachelor's degree plus a fifth year of appropriate preparation, not necessarily completion of the master's degree; C means a course.

* Professional requirements listed are the basic requirements for degree or lowest regular certificates. Some variations from the professional requirements as stated in this table may be found in the requirements for specific certificates listed for the respective states.

[a] Standard certificates: master's degree or 30 semester hours (s.h.) of graduate credit. Temporary certificates: bachelor's degree and completion of an approved program; valid for five years only.

[b] Under the approved-program approach for elementary and secondary teacher certification, California will accept the number of semester hours for the major, minor, professional education, directed teaching, and general education as required by the preparing institution for the completion of its approved teacher education curriculum. However, professional education is not acceptable for a credential major or minor. Four years of preparation (bachelor's degree) is the minimum requirement for initial elementary or secondary certification; a fifth year is required for the permanent certificate.

[c] Bachelor's degree for elementary and junior high school; master's degree for senior and vocational high.

[d] Not included in Columns 3 and 6.

[e] A teacher who has taught successfully for four or more years is required to take only 4 s.h. of practice teaching or a seminar of 4. A teacher who has had two years of successful experience may take a seminar dealing with professional problems instead of the 8 s.h. in practice teaching.

[f] Completion of the bachelor's degree or graduation from an approved four-year normal school.

[g] Total of 8 s.h. of laboratory experience, 5 of which must be student teaching.

[h] Provisional teaching certificates are issued for specifically endorsed grades, subjects, fields, and areas in designated classes of school districts upon evidence of partial completion of an approved teacher education program, generally at least 60 s.h., including specified amounts of general and professional education. Effective September 1, 1972, elementary teachers in accredited schools must hold a certificate based on degree preparation.

[i] A temporary certificate will be issued on completion of 96 hours in a program leading to the bachelor's degree.

[j] For a five-year nonrenewable certificate. Must establish eligibility for regular five-year certificate, the requirement for which is 30 s.h.

[k] The practice-teaching requirement is 150 clock hours, 90 of which must be in actual classroom teaching.

[l] One-year of paid full-time satisfactory teaching experience on the level for which certification is sought may be accepted in lieu of college supervised student teaching, but only when such experience carries recommendation of the employing school district administrator.

[m] For the standard certificate; for the temporary certificate the requirement is 12 s.h.

[n] Required, but there is no specific hours requirement.

[o] Provisional certificate only; for standard certification, a fifth year must be completed within five years after provisional certification.

[p] Minimum 6, maximum 12.

[q] Puerto Rico did not report for 1970. Requirements shown are carried over from the 1967 edition.

[r] All teachers in independent school districts must have a certificate based on a bachelor's degree. The 60-hour certificate has very limited validity. It will seldom be used after July 1, 1970; none will be issued after July 1, 1972.

[s] Provisional certificate only; for standard certification, a fifth year must be completed within six years after provisional certification.

[t] Bachelor's degree must be completed within seven years. Apparently issued only to graduates of two- or three-year programs in state or county colleges. Will not be issued after 1971–72. Effective with the 1972–73 school year, the bachelor's degree will be the minimum requirement for initial certification.

Figure 12.1. Minimum Certification Requirements for Lowest Regular Teaching Certificates for Each State.

Source: T. M. Stinnett, *A Manual on Certification Requirements for School Personnel in the United States.* Washington: National Commission on Teacher Education and Professional Standards, 1970. Used with permission.

As one can see by Figure 12.1, teacher certification is very complex. Furthermore, certification requirements differ from state to state. Space does not permit the inclusion of the complete certification requirements for each state; however, abbreviated examples of the 1969 certification requirements in a sampling of other states are as follows:[4]

1. To be an elementary school teacher in the state of Washington, one must obtain a "Classroom Teaching Certificate." This certificate is based upon a broad state pattern adopted by the State Board of Education effective July 10, 1961. The pattern provides for: Provisional Certificate valid for 3 years, two years of teaching experience following pre-service education, and a fifth year of teacher education at the graduate level prior to issuance of a standard certificate. Content pattern for the pre-service program of four years: 35 per cent undergraduate study in broad education in liberal arts and sciences, 35 per cent in fields or areas of learning applicable to public schools, 20 per cent in professional education, 10 per cent in electives. Provisional Certificate may be renewed once on successful experience and 8 semester hours earned during period covered by certificate.

2. To be an elementary school teacher in Florida requires a bachelor's degree from an accredited institution of higher learning. Academic requirements—General Preparation 45: Communication Arts 6–12; Human Adjustment 6–12; Biological and Physical Science (may include Math) 6–12; Social Studies 6–12; Humanities and Applied Arts 6–12. Professional Requirements 20: Foundations of Education (Psychological and Sociological) 6; Teaching in the Elementary and/or Secondary School—at least 3 at elementary level, 6; Methods of Teaching Reading 2; Observation and Practice Teaching or an approved internship program, 6, or three years teaching experience, or 3 hours in observation and practice teaching plus 2 years of teaching experience. Specialization in each of the following elementary subjects 21: Materials; Science or Nature Study; Social Studies or Geography; Health and/or Physical Education; Art; Music; Arithmetic 6 hours or 3 years of teaching experience in the past 5 years.

3. The requirements for teaching secondary school (grades 6–12) in Illinois (excluding Chicago) are as follows: Possession of a bachelor's degree. General education requirements 42: Language Arts 8; Science and/or Mathematics 6; Social Studies (including a course in American History and/or Government) 6; Humanities 6; Health and Physical Education 3; Additional work in above fields and/or Psychology (except Educational Psychology) to total 42. Professional Requirements 16: Educational Psychology (including Human Growth and Development) 2; Methods and Technology (Secondary) 2; History and/or Philosophy of Education 2; Student teaching in grades 6–12, 5; Electives to total 16. Specialization requirements: single major 32 or 3 minor areas of 16–18–20–24 each 48–72: Electives 0–30. Total Hours 120.

It must be kept in mind that certification requirements change frequently as states pass new certification laws. Because these laws change frequently and vary from state to state, the only sure way of obtaining the current certification requirements for a par-

4. Philip C. Wells, Verl M. Short, and Howard D. Sims, *U.S. Teacher Certification Map.* 105 Thornbrook Road, DeKalb, Ill. 1969.

A future teacher learns much about child development by working with individual students.

Future teachers should capitalize upon every opportunity to work with children whether it be in regular classrooms, recreation programs, social welfare agencies, or church activities.

ticular state is by contacting the State Office of Education, usually located in the capital city of that state.

In recent years there has been some effort made to develop reciprocity agreements between states so that a teacher certified in one state could be automatically certified in another state. One reciprocity plan that has gained some support involves the automatic certification of any graduate of an NCATE (National Council for Accreditation of Teacher Education) accredited teacher education program, regardless of which state that program may be located in. In other words, if a person graduates from a college in Florida that has been accredited by NCATE, other states would automatically certify that person as a teacher. As of 1966, variations of this type of reciprocity, based on NCATE accreditation, had been adopted by approximately one-half of the states. Once again, the only sure means of checking on the current reciprocity agreements for any one specific state is by contacting the State Office of Education, which is usually located in the capital city of each state.

Teacher Education Programs Today

State certification laws specify the minimum legal requirements for becoming a teacher in each state. As one might expect, the formal teacher education programs found in colleges and universities are designed to meet at least the minimum certification requirements in the respective states. In fact, most teacher education programs provide more than the minimum certification requirements in their efforts to prepare teachers.

The young person deciding to enter the teaching profession today has a broad field of choices as to the specific program which

College students preparing for educational careers also take courses dealing with various aspects of teaching such as educational psychology, foundations of education, and teaching methods. Closed circuit television is often used in such courses to facilitate the study of learners and of teaching.

he may wish to pursue. He must decide what age range of students and what subject or subjects he wishes to teach. This wide choice of educational careers is examined in considerable detail in chapters four and thirteen of this book.

The specific educational career that a student selects determines the nature of the training to be undertaken. The future elementary teacher, for instance, is schooled in a broad variety of subjects because many subjects are taught in each elementary classroom. Mathematics, science, grammar, phonics, spelling, geography, history—are all part and parcel of the elementary teach-er's preparation. In addition, the prospective elementary teacher delves deeply into the psychology of the developing child. He must know what to expect from the child at each stage of growth and how to identify that which might be atypical in the individual child, so that problems might be identified early and unusual capabilities might be developed.

The specific courses required for a major in elementary education differ from college to college; however, the following requirements listed in the catalog of a midwestern university are rather typical of those found throughout the country:

Major in Elementary Education (with the degree Bachelor of Science in Education)

This is a comprehensive major for those who plan to teach in the kindergarten and grades 1–8.

Required of all majors*
Professional Education courses:

Educ. 275	Human Development & Learning (Prerequisite: Psych. 102 Introduction to Psychology—3)	(6)
Educ. 375	Elementary School Curriculum & Instruction	(10)
Educ. 476	Seminar in Elementary Education	(4)
Educ. 477	Problems of the Beginning Teacher (Elementary)	(2)
Educ. 478	Tests & Measurements (Elementary)	(2)
Educ. 496	Student Teaching (Elementary)	(7)
	and one additional course to be approved by adviser	
	Group total	(34)

Related courses in other departments:

Art 383	Teaching Art in Elementary Schools	(3)
Math 402	Teaching Practices in Arithmetic	(3)
Music 209	Fundamentals, Principles & Practices in Elementary Music	(4)
PE-W 302	Elementary School Physical Education	(2)
	Group total	(12)

Additional requirements: A 15-hour area of concentration in a field outside Education .... (15)

Total for major .... (61)

* An outdoor education experience is required for three days during the junior block and five days during the senior block Education courses. The student will be required to stay overnight and assume his share of the responsibility for additional costs which may be incurred as a result of this off-campus assignment.

Future teachers must also become familiar with and proficient in using all of the tools of teaching.

The person who chooses to teach junior or senior high school undergoes a somewhat similar program of training. The primary difference is that at this level the training concentrates less on breadth of subject matter preparation and more on depth. For example, if one wishes to become an English teacher, he will make an extensive study of that subject in his college program. He, too, undertakes considerable study in the psychology of the adolescent, learning perhaps most importantly that he is teaching *children* subject matter, rather than teaching *subject matter* to children. This distinction is essential.

While programs vary considerably from college to college, the following requirements listed in the catalog of a midwestern university for a program leading to certification as a junior high school teacher are rather typical of other programs throughout the country:

Major in Junior High School Education (to meet secondary school certification requirements with the degree Bachelor of Science in Education).

Students wishing to specialize in teaching at the junior high school level may choose one of the several subject matter patterns which may be incorporated into the following program. A student may wish to elect a particular major and minor combination such as English-History or Mathematics-Science. This program is intended to meet the needs of junior high schools whose curricula are organized in terms of such a dual approach. Students in this program shall have advisers in each subject area involved.

    Required of all majors:
1. University General Education requirements.
2. A major and a minor. Each student's program must be approved by the Junior High School advisers in the major and minor departments.
3. Professional Education Courses:

Educ. 302   Human Development & Learning (Secondary) .... (6)
Educ. 486   Foundations & Evaluation of Secondary Education .... (5)
Educ. 495   Student Teaching (Secondary) .... (7)
Method Course(s) in the subject matter Major & Minor Areas .... (2, 2)
        Group total .... (22)

Near the end of the teacher education program the future teacher participates in student teaching. During this time he gradually assumes the role of a teacher under the close supervision of a regular teacher. The student teacher is often video-taped so he can see himself in action and improve his performance.

There are many challenges for the student teacher, one of which is being able to work effectively with a large group of students.

This same university lists the following requirements for a major in secondary education:

Major in Secondary Education (with the degree Bachelor of Science in Education)

Students preparing to teach in the high school should have two teaching areas (two majors, or a major and a minor). In addition to meeting "General Education Requirements" these students must take the following sequence of courses:

Professional Education Requirements—20–25 Semester Hours

Educ. 302 Human Development and Learning (Secondary) .... (6)
Human Growth and Development—Birth Through Adolescence
Educational Psychology
Guidance Function of the Teacher

Educ. 486* Foundations and Evaluation of Secondary Education .... (5)
History and Philosophy of Education
Curriculum Patterns and Construction
Organization and Administration in Secondary Education
Educational Measurement: basic statistics, construction of teacher-made tests, and other evaluative techniques and instruments.

Educ. 495* Student Teaching .... (7)**
Nine weeks full-time student teaching routinely taken in the same semester as Education 486.

A course or courses in the Methods of Teaching a particular secondary school subject, offered by the respective subject-matter department (2–7), is required of students preparing to teach in the secondary school. In the event the special methods course for their major is not offered, they may substitute Education 424 Methods and Materials in the Secondary School.

* Nine-week courses are blocked together or alternate.
** Required of majors in some of these fields, such as Art, Home Economics, Industrial Arts, Music, or Physical Education, Education 493 Student Teaching (Elementary, Special Subjects) (1–3).

For the young person who feels himself capable of extreme patience and dedication, there is yet another field, special education. It is the special education teacher who undertakes to educate the handicapped —those unable for reasons of physical or mental shortcomings to participate in a normal classroom environment. The special education teacher may have the most rewarding job of all, but it is equally true that working with special education students can be very frustrating. Becoming a special education teacher requires a very specialized form of training. Sign language, braille, lip reading, the natures and limitations of the various forms of physical and mental disability—all are within the purview of special education. Careers in special education are discussed more fully in chapter thirteen.

If one wishes to teach at a junior or community college or university, he must obtain advanced degrees (at least a master's, but usually also a doctor's degree). Most master's degrees require a total of five or six years of study (including the bachelor's degree), while most doctor's degrees require a

Student teachers soon discover that students learn best by having an opportunity to actively participate in the classroom activity.

total of approximately eight years of study (including the bachelor's and master's degrees). Of course, these advanced degrees must be in the subject that one wishes to teach at the college or university level.

In addition to teaching there are a host of other careers in the education field available at the elementary, secondary, and higher education level. These other careers in education are discussed in chapter thirteen.

Personal Qualifications Needed for Teaching

No matter what choice the individual may make as to the age level of students and/or the subject matter he wishes to teach, cer-

A teacher must be concerned.

tain personal qualifications are essential for all teachers.

Many groups and individuals have created lists of the desirable personal traits for a teacher to possess. For instance, in a pamphlet prepared by the New York State Education Department,[5] it is suggested that a teacher should possess the following traits:

T — thoughtfulness
R — reliability
A — ability in leadership
I — integrity
T — tact
S — sense of humor

O — objectivity
F — fluency

A — ability to do creditable college work

G — gregariousness
O — open-mindedness
O — originality
D — discernment

T — tidiness
E — enthusiasm
A — adaptability
C — cooperativeness
H — health
E — efficiency
R — resourcefulness

Obviously, no one person can hope to possess all of these traits to a liberal degree; however, unless one possesses a fair number of these qualities he probably should not pursue a career in the teaching profession.

A very creative and insightful discussion of the qualities necessary to be an effective teacher appeared in a recent issue of *Today's Education*.[6] This essay, authored by Richard Calisch, entitled "So You Want to be a Real Teacher?" states:

Over the years, literally thousands of young people have neglected to write and ask my advice as to whether they were making a mistake in preparing to be teachers. By now, hundreds and hundreds of them (many no longer quite so young, of course) are moving about in the world of the classroom. With more brashness than modesty, I have finally decided to speak out to them, and to all teachers and would-be teachers everywhere. Although I'd run for cover if anyone started deciding just how qualified I am to be a career teacher, I'm prepared to list what I think those qualifications ought to be. Many people will undoubtedly disagree with one or several items on my list, but here goes, anyway.

In the first place, if you're not a brainy, top-level, creative student, consider doing something else. Good teaching is done by good students, by people who themselves are compulsive about learning. It takes intelligence; it takes the ability to read and to write well.

Good teaching takes the kind of person who wants to know just about all there is to know about his subject and who tops everything off with a strong desire to help his students acquire knowledge. You can't be content to keep just a few pages ahead of them. You must really know the field, whether it be mathematics or physical education, literature or cooking. (This calls for even

5. Bureau of Guidance, *Looking Ahead at Teaching*. Albany, New York: State Education Department, April, 1952.
6. Richard Calisch, "So You Want to be a Real Teacher," *Today's Education*, November, 1969, pp. 49–51. Used with permission.

greater emphasis on subject matter courses in college.) You need to be an expert, a specialist, a scholar, a consistent learner, in order to be a teacher. Teaching is, after all, primarily an intellectual art.

Being an intelligent specialist isn't enough, however. You must also have a wide range of adult knowledge and interests. It goes without saying that a teacher of any subject should be well-versed in the literature, music, art, and history of his world, as well as alert to the newest of the new. He should be hip to the world around his eyes and ears—knowledgeable about the latest cars, movies, fashions, books. You may not be able to answer all your students' questions

A special education student teacher discovers that teaching is an exciting, stimulating experience—an opportunity to put into practice all that she has learned in her teacher education program.

A teacher must be adaptable.

or participate in all their discussions, but at least you should know the terms they use. A teacher who can't rap with the guys on their ground isn't going to educate them on his.

But—and this is important—never forget that you are there to bring young people up the educational ladder, not to bring yourself down.

A teacher must understand students' likes and dislikes, hopes and fears, but at the same time, he must teach as an adult. Sometimes it takes courage to tell a youngster he is wrong; but when he *is*, pretending he *is not* is a grave sin, in my mind. I guess what I am saying here is that I wholeheartedly endorse the client concept of education, in which the teacher has the obligation to know his subject and much more besides; in which the student comes to the teacher as a client to absorb what he can, to learn what the teacher has to teach.

Your responsibility is to make your teaching relevant to your students, but you must not succumb to the pressure to tell them only what they want to hear because that way is easier.

Treating children childishly produces childish grown-ups. To avoid doing this, you must use all of the intelligence, knowledge, and expertise that you possess. You must be in command, and this takes that added combination of confidence, wit, maturity, and strength of character. If you lack these attributes or are satisfied with your present attainment of them, there is another occupation for you.

I have stressed the teacher's need to have knowledge and intelligence. Hand in hand with these attributes go two others: creativity and imagination. A teacher needs to be an idea person. You must be able to make use of any idea, from any source, and turn it to a thought-producing teaching technique.

When Georgy asks, "Why?" when Suzy says, "What for?" when Mary says, "Are you kidding?" you've got to be able to come up with answers, and they aren't always in the book. Answering a question, such as "What good is this ever going to do me?" from a belligerent, bored, boorish troublemaker is going to take creativity and imagination, as well as a conviction on your part that whatever it is *will* do him some good. This conviction can arise only if you yourself are an expert in whatever field you teach.

In summary, a teacher, first and foremost, must be intelligent, knowledgeable, creative, and imaginative. I know that's not the standard definition, but if Mr. Binet doesn't complain, I won't knock his test. Score yourself one point each for intelligence, expertise in your subject matter, creativity, and imagination. If you don't have four points now, quit here.

My next bit of advice will seem strange, but take it anyway. Sometime when you're feeling up to par, find a quiet, secluded room with no books, no TV, no transistor radio, no cokes, no tasty snacks. Go in, sit down, and stay for an hour. Ask a friend to let you know when the time is up. If the hour seems like a year or if you fall asleep, forget about teaching.

If your inner resources are not enough to keep you interested in yourself for one class period, imagine how you will affect your students. Your subject matter is only subject matter until you add the vital ingredient to it—you. And if your *you* isn't enough to make that hour of solitude pleasant and interesting, it is going to be hell for the 30 or so squirming students who have just straggled in after an hour's ordeal with some other dull pedagogue.

That hour you spend alone in the empty room may be the most eye-opening hour of your life. You'll find out whether someone

A teacher must be open-minded.

A teacher must be efficient.

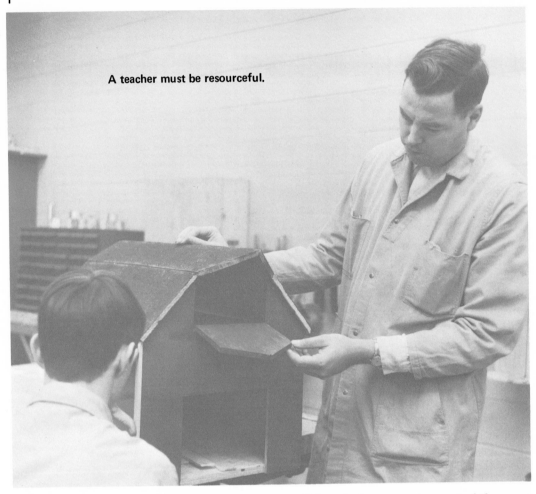

A teacher must be resourceful.

could possibly spend 60 minutes in your company without going out of his mind from simple boredom.

If you've read this far and still think you want to teach, test your weirdo quotient. Every good teacher has in him the confidence and self-reliance to be a weirdo. From Socrates to "Sock it to me!" the memorable lessons have been taught by showmen who knew the value of a vivid performance. The classroom is a stage and the teacher is the player: hero, villain, clown,

and the whole supporting cast of the greatest long-run, hit show ever to play off Broadway or on. And it's a show whose script changes daily, without notice, and usually without consultation with the cast.

In every good classroom personality, there is some of P. T. Barnum, John Barrymore, Ringo Starr, and Houdini. Are you afraid to stand up and sing with a wastebasket over your head, to demonstrate the various qualities of sound? Can you be King Richard bawling "A horse! A horse! My kingdom for a horse!" or act out photosynthesis, playing all parts yourself?

Think back to your own teachers. From which did you learn the most? Certainly not from the sit-behind-the-desk mumblers who read their lectures from neatly typed notes. Teaching involves a great deal of showmanship and salesmanship, and the great teaching personalities are those that are not afraid to be different, unusual, or what the current jargon styles "weirdo." Classroom spontaneity and showmanship take confidence and a degree of cool that the average person doesn't possess; but, then, a teacher isn't an average person.

Have you ever tried to talk a died-in-the-wool Democrat into voting for a Republican, or a vegetarian into eating meat, or a Card fan into cheering for the Cubs? How did it come out? Probably it produced a humdinger of an argument—one with sparks, flames, daggers, and music played by the brasses. Or else the person you were talking to just turned you off, wouldn't even listen.

Those two responses to persuasion are most typical, because people just don't like to have their cherished beliefs challenged and will protect them from attack in any way they can. Yet teaching involves challenging the sacred beliefs of the student and asking him, forcing him if necessary, to examine them.

Each student brings to the classroom a whole complex of his own folk beliefs about those aspects of life of which he is ignorant. Typically, his attitude will be that if he has never heard of it, it either isn't true or is unimportant. He will cling to his preconceptions like the proverbial drowning man to the proverbial log. Your job is to push him off the log and see that he stays afloat. Don't

expect him to be overjoyed about it. Don't expect him to love you for it. If he learns from you, if he matures and gains confidence under your direction, then you have achieved success. If you also want love, get married.

I tell my pupils that if I can't send them home muttering darkly at least once a week, I've failed. And I mean that. An exasperated student will think, ask, read, search for answers—and that is education. Even though he may come up with answers that disagree with your beliefs, you have done your job as a teacher if he has arrived at those answers through intelligent thought.

What students need is some answers and a lot of needling questions. So I agree with Socrates that a teacher must try to be the most irritating person for miles around. (You can expect hemlock as your reward.)

Most books I've read about teaching indicate that the prime requisite for a teacher is a "love of children." Hogwash! That bit of misinformation has probably steered more softhearted and softheaded Mr. Peeperses and Miss Brookses into our art than any other deception ever practiced on the mind of man. What you must love is the vision of the well-informed, responsible adult you can help the child become.

Your job as a teacher is to help the child realize who he is, what his potential is, what his strengths are. You can help him learn to love himself—or the man he soon will be. With that kind of understanding self-love, the student doesn't need any of your sentimentality. What he needs is your brains, and enabling him to profit from them calls for decisive firmness. "I must be cruel only to be kind," say Hamlet and many a good teacher. Discipline and firm guidance are often called meanness by those subjected to

A teacher must be enthusiastic.

them, but in my experience they are the kind of loving care most likely to produce intelligent, knowledgeable, perceptive adults who can do a better job of coping with the problems of the world than did those who taught them.

The fact that real teaching is an art is too often pooh-poohed. Some critics place teaching in the same category as baby-sitting; and far too many people enter the field because it seems like an easy way to earn a fair living. Girls may look on it as a pleasant way of biding their time until they capture husbands.

But the kind of teacher I have been talking about is a dedicated person who plans to stay in teaching despite its drawbacks. He looks upon his work with individual children as an art to which he brings his talent, his craftsmanship, his experience, learning,

intelligence, and that indefinable something called inspiration.

I hope, prospective teachers, that as you take an honest, searching look at yourselves you can sense that you have the potential for being this kind of teacher.

One of the characteristics that is vital for the teacher needs emphasizing—the desire to be a continuing scholar. Most school boards require that a teacher continue his academic work past the bachelor's degree at a certain rate in order for advancement, and in some cases to retain his position. The required number of courses within a specific time period varies with the level at which the teacher is employed and from school district to school district. Some high schools, for instance, require that the master's degree be earned within six years after the beginning of employment. But many teachers pursue graduate work at a rate far beyond the minimum required. These people may be attempting to qualify for a position such as a school administrator, but many are

A teacher must be reliable.

seeking to improve their skills as teachers. They realize that becoming a teacher is a lifelong process—one never to be fully realized. Teaching is a process that is constantly dynamic, never reaching consummation. Change's in the weather, the moods of students, moods of the teacher himself, the changing body of knowledge which he seeks to impart—all are variables from day to day and even hour to hour. The teacher must seek to gain knowledge even more ardently than he seeks to impart it.

Further insight into some of the personality traits that teachers should possess can be gleaned from a recent research study which asked a large number of teachers to state the main reason they selected teaching as a career. The results of this study are shown in Figure 12.2. As this figure indicates, the main reason listed by the 2,316

teachers participating in this study for entering the teaching profession was a desire to work with young people. The second most frequently listed reason was "opportunity for rendering important service." These two qualities, a desire to work with young people and an interest in rendering service, are perhaps the two very most important traits for a person to possess before entering a teaching career.

The person who is considering becoming a teacher must seriously examine his own personal qualifications for this kind of work. If you are considering entering the teaching profession you might consider—with your parents, teachers, counselors or fellow students—some of the following points:

1. Do you have the personal qualifications necessary to become a successful teacher?

Consideration in Choosing Teaching as Career	All Reporting	Men	Women	Elementary	Secondary	Secondary Men	Secondary Women
Number of teachers reporting	2,316	723	1,593	1,218	1,098	600	498
Desire to work with young people	34.4%	33.2%	34.9%	39.1%	29.1%	32.3%	25.3%
Opportunity for rendering important service	27.6	24.6	28.9	31.7	23.0	23.0	23.1
Interest in a subject-matter field	13.6	18.9	11.1	4.7	23.4	21.2	26.1
A tradition in my family	6.4	2.9	8.0	7.5	5.3	3.2	7.8
Example set by a favorite teacher	6.0	5.3	6.3	5.4	6.6	5.8	7.4
Job security	5.8	7.7	5.0	5.6	6.1	7.7	4.2
Financial rewards	1.6	0.6	2.1	1.9	1.3	0.7	2.0
Easiest preparation program in college	1.1	1.8	0.8	1.2	0.9	1.0	0.8
Unsuccessful in another line of work	0.4	1.0	0.1	0.1	0.7	1.2	0.2
Stop-gap until marriage	0.3	...	0.4	0.3	0.3	...	0.6
Other reason	2.9	4.0	2.4	2.5	3.3	4.0	2.4
	100.0%	100.0%	100.0%	100.0%	100.0%	100.0%	99.9%

Figure 12.2. Why Teachers Become Teachers.

Source: National Education Association, *The American Public School Teacher.* Research Report 1967-R4, Research Division of the NEA, 1967, p. 59. Used by permission.

A teacher must be a leader.

2. Do you really want to devote your life to working with students?
3. What age group of students do you wish to work with?
4. What subjects do you wish to teach?
5. Do you wish to be a master teacher, a para-professional, or some other kind of specialist such as a media specialist, supervisor or administrator?
6. Should you attempt to obtain experience as a teacher aide as part of your training for a career as a teacher?
7. How can you obtain the best possible preparation for teaching?

Obtaining A Position

For those who are nearing the successful completion of a formal teacher education program, obtaining a teaching position becomes an important task. The following discussion entitled "Selecting the First Teach-

ing Position" contains excellent suggestions about this important task.[7]

You have a big question to answer—where do I want to start this exciting career? The mind whirls and dreams of making your own money, owning your own car, being master of your own destiny push out all else and the exciting possibilities of taking a position in far-off places further stir the imagination. Hawaii, California, New England, Alaska, English-speaking schools in the Far East, Europe, Central or South America—all are real and exciting possibilities. The opportunities are so great for the new teacher of today that you can truly say, "The world's my oyster which I with 'learning' will open."

Stop a moment, though, before your thoughts go too far afield. The first basic decision you must make which definitely affects how you go about selecting a teaching position is determined by looking inward. Considering you—yourself—honestly, dispassionately, objectively, you ask yourself the question, "Am I looking for a position where there is the greatest need for help, where I can do the greatest good for society, where my abilities will be challenged to the utmost by difficult situations or am I looking for a position which will be most beneficial to me—gives me the greatest opportunity to travel, pays the highest salary, contains the pleasantest environment, commands the strongest resources, and includes the most stylish and compatible faculty? Your choice is a very personal one and to be happy and successful in your first professional experience it must be fought through with yourself honestly and dispas-

7. William H. Roe and Rose M. Verdi, "Selecting the First Teaching Position," pp. 19-20. Used by permission.

sionately for the good of your own mental health and the goodness of society. Dedicated, superior teachers are needed desperately in the slums, ghettos, in poverty-stricken outlying areas and in developing countries—but what we don't need is more frustrated, unhappy and inept teachers who may do more harm than good. Nor do we need the "do-gooder" who is impervious and unconscious to the real problem.

You must face yourself honestly in regard to this question and not feel guilty for the direction you choose. There are many legitimate reasons why you should not seek out trouble in your first experience. One important consideration is that in the safe sanctity of the suburb you may find opportunity to gain needed experience before facing more difficult teaching experiences.

Now that you have faced the more personal and philosophical question of how far you are ready to go in helping society, the next step of decision-making is simpler in terms of establishing an objective list of pros and cons.

Selecting implies choosing, making comparisons, evaluating and carefully arriving at a final decision. While you can make this next phase of the selection process quite simple and mechanical, it does take time. You should not relegate it to a last-minute activity during your senior year. The task is too crucial. Do not think you are just choosing a job for one year but rather you are beginning a career.

To keep the choice of the first teaching position from becoming a near-perfunctory one, you might ask significant questions such as the following:

What do I look for in the school system with which I wish to be associated?

How important are working conditions?

What are the opportunities for professional growth?

What are the provisions for orientation and induction of new teachers?

Can I make a contribution to this school and community?

Is recognition given to staff achievement and contributions?

How will I be evaluated?

Many of the answers to questions like these can be secured by early and persistent investigation of numerous and various sources of information available to you. Talk with teachers already employed in school systems in which you are interested. Talk with your college and university instructors and the people in the placement bureaus about the local schools or schools in another state. Even more valuable would be visits to these schools during semester breaks. These visits would permit you to see and appraise first-hand the physical facilities, variety of instructional materials and methods, and also sense the climate of the school and community.

If you are interested in teaching in another state, you could secure additional information about the schools and communities by writing to the state departments of education, the superintendents of the various school systems or to the chambers of commerce. State educational associations and state departments of education very often publish comparative fact sheets about the schools of their states which would assist you in analyzing a school system. Most school systems publish brochures, pamphlets or handbooks containing information on the school program, salary schedules and prerequisites, teaching and special services staff, policies pertaining to supervision and tenure, opportunities for professional growth, professional associations, and the history of the community. Some schools publish separate and special materials for new teachers which include very detailed orientation information on daily teaching schedule, classroom discipline, policies regarding homework, procedures for fire drills, location and distribution of instructional materials and resources, samples of forms for reporting pupil progress, checklists of duties and suggested teaching plans for the first few days of school.

A critical examination of all the information you receive through informal discussions or printed materials will enable you to eliminate from future consideration those teaching situations which are least promising or attractive to you. The personal visits that you make to schools and communities recommended by teachers in service or by college staff will reveal whether you can adjust to the situation, and, more important, be stimulated to grow as a member of the profession. Analysis of the content of the printed materials you receive can also help you in selecting the most promising teaching situation. These materials often contain statements about "meeting the needs of pupils of varying interests and abilities," or "providing for the gifted, the mentally retarded and the emotionally disturbed." Are there supportive statements regarding special services personnel, flexibility in the educational program and descriptions of special programs? Take a careful look at the sample report card or reporting form which the school system uses in communicating to parents the growth of the progress of the child. Many educators agree that the pupil reporting forms reflect the operating philosophy of the school, the curriculum and the organizational pattern. Does the report form set forth a list of subject matter areas and a letter or numerical grade for each area? Can this type of reporting be reconciled with statements about "full partnership in evaluating each child's growth," "attainment and uniqueness of each child" or "learning is personal, unique, unstandardized"? Examine the statements concerning supervision and evaluation of probationary teachers. Who is involved in evaluation? Are written records kept? Are these records available to you? What new media or procedures are being used for appraising performance? What support, cooperation and assistance will be given during your beginning years of service? Those school systems which you feel are presenting the most positive or desirable practices in these areas should be included on the list of school systems to which you would apply for your first teaching position.

The personnel in the placement office in your college or university can give you much help in obtaining a teaching position. There are many forms to be completed and records to be filed. Great care should be given to the preparation of these materials. You will also need to write a letter of application. It, too, should be carefully written. Specific suggestions about the form and content of these letters are usually presented by the college director or coordinator of student teaching. Sample letters may be found in publications such as student teacher handbooks or professional texts dealing with the student teaching program. Your letter should include a statement regarding arrangements for an interview.

For most students the interview experience is a strained one. They often report that they were tense, nervous and uncomfortable. However, if you devoted the necessary time and thought in visiting and inquiring about many schools, and applied only in selected schools, your interview should be an exhilarating experience. The background of information that you will already have about the school system will not only allow you to ask pertinent and meaningful questions but will also facilitate communicating your own dedication to teaching and your sincere interest in the particular teaching position. It will also permit you to respond to questions with confidence and clarity, and serve you well in decisions you will have to make.

The decision regarding the particular position to accept is often a troublesome one, especially when accompanied by a deadline date for acceptance. However, your preliminary research should make your decision an easy one. Since you have applied only in selected systems, any offer should be immediately desirable to you.

When you have signed the contract, you should inform your college placement office that you have accepted a position. It is also in good taste to notify at least the school systems which interviewed you and include some expression of gratitude or appreciation for any consideration they may have given to your application.

This chapter has attempted to briefly introduce some of the important concepts related to the subject of "becoming a teacher." Teacher certification, the nature of teacher education programs today, personal qualifications needed for teaching, and the task of obtaining a teaching position—all vital topics for one contemplating a career in teaching—have been briefly discussed. It is hoped that this brief discussion will stimulate the reader to seriously contemplate and further explore these important topics.

Questions for Discussion

1. What personal qualifications do you believe a teacher should possess?
2. If you were asked by the state superintendent of public schools to recommend an ideal teacher certification law for your state, what would your recommendations be?
3. Try to recall the best teacher that you have ever had. What age level and subject(s) did he/she teach? What qualities did this teacher possess? What made him/her such a good teacher?
4. What do you feel most hiring officials look for when interviewing prospective teachers?
5. What steps do you believe a teacher should take after beginning teaching to keep up on his subject matter and on the latest teaching techniques?

Supplementary Learning Activities

1. Conduct an informal poll of teachers to see what qualities they believe one should possess before entering a teacher education program.
2. Interview a director of a teacher placement bureau regarding teacher employment opportunities, letters of application, interviews, etc.
3. Invite the superintendent of a school to your class to discuss what he looks for when hiring new teachers.

4. Arrange a field trip to visit a nearby school. While there, try to visit with a variety of school personnel, talk with students, and observe different aspects of the school operation.

5. Arrange a panel discussion on the general topic of "Becoming A Teacher." Invite a college teacher, high school teacher, elementary school teacher, a student teacher, and a school administrator to participate on the panel.

SELECTED REFERENCES

Alexander, William M. *Are You a Good Teacher?* New York: Holt, Rinehart & Winston, Inc., 1959.

American Association of School Administrators, Department of Classroom Teachers, and National School Boards Association. *Who's a Good Teacher?* Washington: National Education Association, 1961.

Armstrong, W. Earl, and T. M. Stinnett. *A Manual on Certification Requirements for School Personnel in the United States.* Washington: National Commission on Teacher Education and Professional Standards, National Education Association, 1971.

Biddle, Bruce J., and William J. Ellena, eds. *Contemporary Research on Teacher Effectiveness.* New York: Holt, Rinehart & Winston, 1964.

Bruce, William F., and A. John Holden, Jr. *The Teacher's Personal Development.* New York: Holt, Rinehart & Winston, Inc., 1957.

Highet, Gilbert. *The Art of Teaching.* New York: Alfred A. Knopf, Inc., 1950.

Hughes, Marie. "What is Teaching? One Viewpoint." *Educational Leadership* 19(1962): 251–259.

Lang, Carroll L. "Success Begins With The Employment Interview." *1969 ASCUS.* Hershey, Pennsylvania: ASCUS Communication and Services Center, Inc., 1969.

McGrath, Earl J. "The Ideal Education for the Professional Man." In *Education for the Profession,* ed., Nelson B. Henry, pp. 281–301. The Sixty-first Yearbook of the National Society for the Study of Education, Part II. Chicago: University of Chicago Press, 1962.

Mason, Ward S. *The Beginning Teacher: Status and Career Orientations.* Washington: U.S. Office of Education Circular 644, 1961.

Massey, Harold W., and Edwin E. Vineyard. *The Profession of Teaching.* New York: The Odyssey Press, Inc., 1961.

Michal-Smith, Harold. "It Takes Self-Understanding." *NEA Journal* 49(1960):37–40.

National Education Association. *Teaching Career Fact Book.* Washington, D.C.: The Association, 1966.

——. *Who's a Good Teacher?* Washington, D.C.: The Association, 1961.

Ragan, William B. *Teaching America's Children.* New York: Holt, Rinehart & Winston, 1961 (chapter 2).

Roe, William H., and Rose M. Verdi. "Selecting the First Teaching Position." *1969 ASCUS.* Hershey, Pennsylvania: ASCUS Communication and Services Center, Inc., 1969.

Turner, Richard L., and Nicholas A. Fattu. "Skill in Teaching, Assessed on the Criterion of Problem Solving." *Bulletin of the School of Education.* Bloomington, Indiana: Indiana University, May, 1961.

Van Til, William. *The Making of a Modern Educator.* Indianapolis: The Bobbs-Merrill Co., Inc., 1961.

Wiles, Kimball. *Teaching for Better Schools.* Englewood Cliffs, N.J.: Prentice-Hall, Inc., 1959.

Wynn, Richard. *Careers in Education.* New York: McGraw-Hill Book Co., Inc., 1960.

Points of Emphasis for Teacher Education

Milton S. Eisenhower

The novelist James Hilton, who created that winsome portrayal of an English schoolmaster, *Goodbye, Mr. Chips,* once said that if a son of his were entering upon a career as a teacher, he would say farewell to him as though he were departing for war.

By this, Mr. Hilton certainly meant to stress the spirit of dedication which motivates the true teacher and the vital importance of his function in society. The soldier-like aspects of the profession of teaching are all too apparent in these times, to teachers and to those engaged in educating teachers, at any rate. As one crisis is piled on another —social, economic, and political—*education* is continually being called from the barracks to man the ramparts and save our way of life, even to preserve civilization itself.

The fact is that education must do these very things, if they are to be done at all, for in our day there is no other single agency that can do them. The danger is that those who work in education, like the villagers in the story of the boy who cried, "Wolf!" will become satiated with alarms and will relax their vigilance, or become perfunctory in their responses to the challenges of the times.

It requires no argument to demonstrate that most Americans live today under pressures which less than a generation ago were exerted on the comparatively few.

Today, not only is the world council table in the family living room, but so are the witness stand, the political forum, and the battlefield itself. The sights and sounds of human affairs, at all levels from the personal and local to the international and global, are interwoven with the fabric of family daily living, and their impact is supplemented by numberless ubiquitous spoken and written opinions, commentaries, and exhortations.

There was a time not so long ago, when the progress of a war, for instance, could be judged by the considered reports of the movements of entire armies, by the comparatively slow daily progress of a black line on a newspaper map. The grist of a thousand-and-one front-line and headquarters reports had been ground, and the man or woman at home received a condensed, largely predigested body of information on which to form his judgments, usually some time after the event.

Today, John and Mary Doe *and their children* are, in effect, omnipresent in the whole area of intellectual, political, and physical conflict. Out of a welter of the personal, eye-witness accounts of the experiences of individual soldiers, the press releases of commanding generals, the arguments of

* Milton S. Eisenhower, "Points of Emphasis for Teacher Education," *Journal of Teacher Education,* June, 1951, pp. 88–89. Used by permission.

congressmen, the debates of national representatives, and the impressions and opinions of reporters and commentators—presented with little, if any, delay as they are expressed—out of this continuous bombardment of ideas by the press, radio, television, and motion pictures, the ordinary American must attempt to form his own comprehensive evaluation of the world in which he lives.

On the domestic scene the same conditions prevail; judgments on moral, intellectual, social, economic issues of great import must be made on evidence conglomerate enough to bewilder a Solomon.

One of two eventualities will occur: either the American people will develop and strengthen their individual abilities to discriminate between truth and falsehood, between the trivial and the important, and between right and wrong, or they will erect a psychological barrier of idea-deafness and become apathetic to the significance of factors that affect the integrity of our civilization. Education must bear the greater share of the responsibility for bringing about the former result and preventing the latter.

A truly perceptive college president recently stated that the real purpose of the liberal-arts college is to educate people to grasp the "main idea." Is not this the essential of *all* educational effort, not only the liberal-arts college but of all teaching from the level of the nursery school through the graduate university: to help boys and girls, and men and women, to discern shades of difference, to weigh values, to judge critically, and to form valid conclusions—in other words, to grasp the main idea?

Grasping the main idea is certainly the heart of the solution of any physical or biological problem, whether it involves the simplest carpentry or the most complex medical diagnosis. Discernment and judgment are no less vital factors in the solution of the less-tangible problems which make up our individual and common lives, the problems involving economic forces, social relationships, and moral values.

By force of circumstances, the individual American must form judgments, if only subconsciously, on such complicated and varied issues as price and wage control versus uncontrolled economy, character assassination versus legitimate investigation of subversion, and underworld influence versus good government and clean sports. The quality of the judgments arrived at by the ordinary, everyday American is a vital factor in the shaping of our future.

The task of educating people to think critically and judge intelligently requires teachers who themselves have developed their critical faculties, who themselves have been trained to discern, to analyze, to weigh, and to evaluate through rational processes. This is the challenge for all those who educate teachers. It is a challenge that must be met.

There is no pat formula by which young men and women can be made into teachers adequate for the task which faces them. But in view of the importance in modern life of the ability to make value-judgments, added emphasis might well be placed on the following elements in the education of teachers:

(1) The acquisition of a broad background in history, economics, sociology, psychology, and philosophy, for knowledge of social man precedes the understanding of human affairs and relationships. Considerable depth as well as breadth in this intellectual background also contributes to the

teacher's own ability to grasp the "main idea."

(2) Practice in critical thinking. Precision in the analysis and evaluation of ideas can best be achieved through active, disciplined exercise of the critical faculties.

(3) Intensified training and practice in communication—in reading, listening, writing, and speaking. The teacher, now as never before, must himself be able to read and listen accurately and with comprehension, and to express himself with clarity and precision on paper and in speech.

(4) The development through contemplation and association of a *personal philosophy of living equal to the teacher's voca-tion*—a philosophy which, as Sir Richard Livingstone put it, will serve "for shaping conduct, for reference in doubt, for challenge, stimulus, and driving power." This is perhaps the essential factor in the transformation of an individual into an effective teacher.

(5) The achievement by every teacher of a genuine and abiding commitment to the democratic way—a commitment based upon a thorough understanding of the sources and cardinal principles of democracy and of the principles underlying other forms of social endeavor, ancient and modern. This commitment must be the framework within which all other critical thinking proceeds and value-judgments develop.

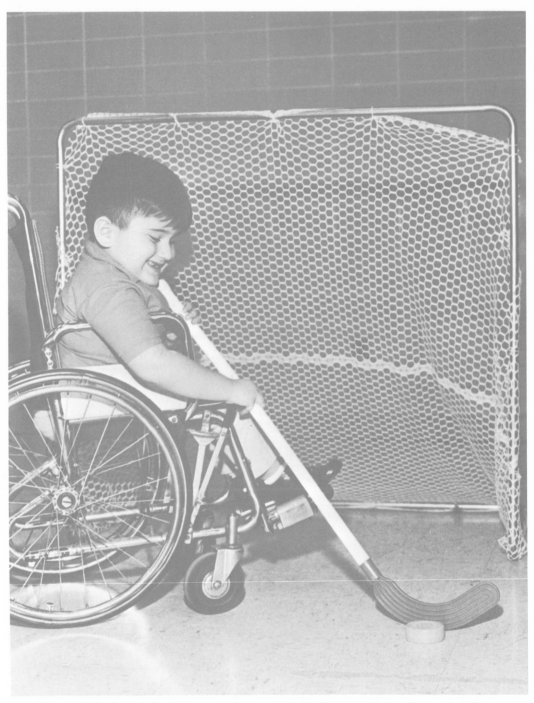

A great deal of specialized equipment is now available for use with handicapped students.

CHAPTER 13

Other Careers in Education

I congratulate all of you who have chosen teaching as a profession. You bear a heavy responsibility. For the future of this nation will be what its schools make it. And it is the skill and dedication of our teachers that will shape our schools.

This is a challenging time to be teaching. The United States is exploring horizons in space, under the seas, and in medical and other sciences that were thought impossible a generation ago. We are learning more about how our society works, and we are exploring new dimensions of the human personality. Children are quick to sense the fast pace of change in our society, and young men and women are anxious to influence it. In some cases their reach exceeds their capacity. All of this makes the teachers' role more vital than ever.

Sophisticated technology has recently come to the aid of the teacher. Educators are continually combining new equipment, new materials, and new methods with their own creative energies to make schools more responsive to our changing society and to the students' individual needs.

I know you will find teaching a career that is very demanding and rewarding. On behalf of your country, I thank you for your decision and wish you every success.

Richard Nixon[1]

The previous chapter dealt with various aspects of the history, training, and qualifications of the regular classroom teacher. There are, of course, a number of other important related careers that are available to those who are considering a career in American education. This chapter will explore some of these alternatives.

Special Education

Over the past several decades, an increasing number of students with special learning problems of various sorts have been pro-

1. ASCUS. *Teaching Opportunities for You.* Hershey, Penn.: Association for School and University Staffing, 1970, p. 3.

With proper help, facilities, and equipment, special education students can participate in nearly all of the learning activities that normal students take part in.

vided with special educational programs by the American public school system. Chapter twelve pointed out that the special education teacher must possess great patience and dedication to be effective working with students who have special learning problems.

It is sometimes difficult for a school to distinguish between students with special learning problems and the so-called normal student. In fact, in a real sense all students have special learning problems of one sort or another. However, in most school systems the special education student is defined as

"one who deviates intellectually, physically, socially, or emotionally so markedly from what is considered to be normal growth and development that he cannot receive maximum benefit from a regular school program and requires a special class or supplementary instruction and services."[2]

There are four different broad categories of special education students. These include the intellectually handicapped, the physically handicapped, the emotionally handicapped, and the multi-handicapped.

The intellectually handicapped student is essentially one whose native intelligence is sufficiently lower than the average student as to require a special class or supplementary instruction and services. Intellectually handicapped children can be roughly classified as "trainable" (having I.Q.'s ranging roughly from 25 to 50), and the "educable" (having I.Q.'s ranging roughly from 50 to 80). Students with I.Q.'s in the 80 to 95 range are often referred to as "slow learners." One must keep in mind, however, that the I.Q. scores obtained from even the best intelligence tests available today are still only rough estimates of a student's native intelligence. In fact, some authorities feel that most intelligence tests really reflect a student's environmental exposure to learning opportunities more than his native intelligence, and therefore should not be used at all to classify students.

It is estimated that .3% of the population fall in the trainable category. The schools can hope only to train students in this category to take care of their own immediate personal needs (dressing, eating, using the bathroom, personal hygiene, how to get

2. William M. Cruickshank and G. Orville Johnson, *Education of Exceptional Children and Youth*, pp. 3–4.

along with others, etc.) Trainables require care and supervision throughout their life. The school's objective with trainable students is to help make their life as comfortable and useful as possible.

It is estimated that approximately 3 per cent of the student population falls in the "educable" category. Some schools place these students in special classes and other schools attempt to provide these educable mentally retarded students with supplemental help while leaving them in the regular classes with other so-called normal students. The typical educable student, with special help, can learn to be a productive self-sufficient adult. The school's objective for these students is to provide them with this special educational help.

It is estimated that roughly 15 per cent of the school population falls in the "slow learner" category (I.Q.'s roughly from 80 to 95). Nearly all school systems allow the slow learners to remain in the regular classroom. Unfortunately, most schools do not supply the slow learner with much special help other than that which the regular teacher is able to provide.

The physically handicapped student, as the name implies, is one who has a physical disability extensive enough to require a special class or supplementary instruction and services. Special education students in this category may be blind, partially sighted, deaf, hard of hearing, may have speech defects such as stuttering or that caused by a cleft palate, or may have had any one of a number of crippling diseases such as cerebral palsy, or poliomyelitis. Children with some forms of brain damage also fall in this category.

The emotionally handicapped student is one who is so socially maladjusted or emo-

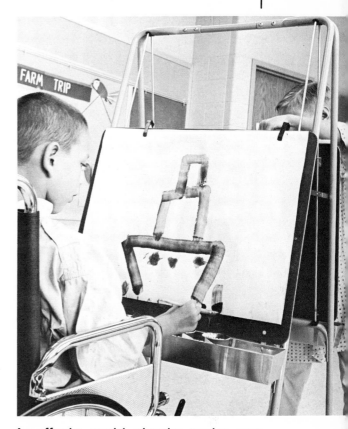

An effective special education teacher must possess a good deal of understanding and patience.

tionally disturbed that he requires a special class or supplemental instruction and services. Estimates of the number of students in the United States that fall in this category range all the way from one to four million. It is often difficult to identify the emotionally handicapped student due to the fact that all children from time to time exhibit neurotic behavior. Unfortunately, many emotionally disturbed children go undetected, especially those who are quite shy and withdrawn, and never receive the special help they so badly need.

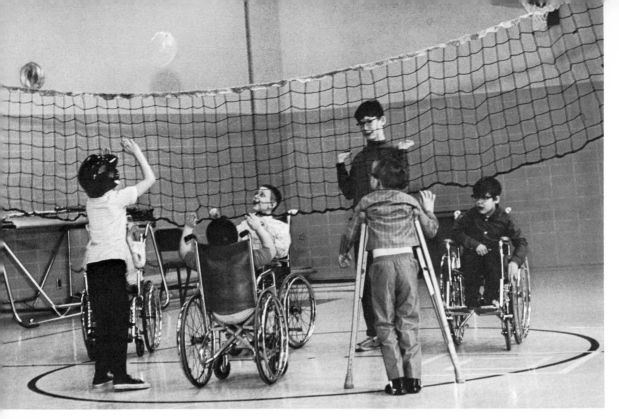

Our schools have the responsibility of providing a good education for each child in our society.

The multi-handicapped child is, as the name implies, one who has a combination of the handicaps just discussed. For instance, it is quite common to find children who are both mentally retarded and physically handicapped. It is also rather common to find children who, due to their mental retardation, also have rather severe emotional problems. This problem is frequently caused, at least in part, by normal students making fun of the slow learner.

Becoming qualified to work in any one of these many special education areas requires a great deal of special training in addition to regular teacher training. Not all colleges and universities offer training in special education and, therefore, people contemplating entering such a training program must seek out a college or university that offers specialized training in special education. Each state has its own certification requirements for becoming a special education teacher. A bachelor's degree with a

> Education is leading human souls to what is best, and no crime can destroy, no enemy can alienate, no despotism can enslave. At home a friend, abroad an introduction, in solitude a solace, and in society an ornament. It chastens vice, it guides virtue, it gives at once grace and government to genius. Without it, what is man? A splendid slave, a reasoning savage.
>
> Joseph Addison

major in special education is the most common requirement; however, the specific requirements for each state can be obtained by writing to the State Superintendent of Schools in the capital city of each respective state.

One can gleen from Figure 13.1 an indication of the employment opportunities in special education. This figure also shows estimates of the number of elementary and secondary school children affected by each of the different types of handicaps. Figure 13.1 clearly points out that there is a serious shortage of qualified teachers and specialists in the area of special education.

People considering entering one of the special education fields should possess a sincere desire to work with and help handicapped children as well as a great deal of patience, understanding, and human relations skill in working with such students.

> To reshape reality by means of ideas is the business of man, his proper earthly task; and nothing can be impossible to a will confident of itself and of its aim.
>
> Frederich Paulsen

Such work is very taxing and requires a great deal of dedication.

Counseling

A school counselor spends most of his time working in a one to one relationship

Special education programs are growing rapidly and there is currently a great demand for well-qualified teachers to staff these programs.

Area of Handicapped	Estimated Children of Elementary and Secondary School Age	Number of Additional Teachers and Specialists Needed
Speech Handicapped	1,833,230	12,733
Emotionally Disturbed	1,047,560	121,791
Mental Retardation	1,204,694	58,406
Specific Learning Disabilities	523,780	22,564
Hard of Hearing	261,890	12,100
Crippled and Other Health Disorders	261,890	5,674
Visually Handicapped	52,378	2,877
Deaf	39,283	823
TOTAL	5,224,705	236,968

Figure 13.1. Manpower Needs to Educate the Handicapped.

Source: The Council for Exceptional Children, NEA.

with individual students. These students may need vocational or college information, help in selecting elective courses, someone to talk with concerning a girl or boy friend, help with peer or parental conflict, or assistance with any one of a variety of different kinds of emotional and psychological problems. A school counselor does not, however, attempt to provide therapy for stu-

The school social worker visits the homes of students in an effort to help parents maximize the learning experiences of their children.

dents with severe problems, but rather refers such cases to appropriate specialists such as a clinical psychologist or psychiatrist. The long-term goal of a counselor is not to solve problems for the students, but rather to help students solve their own problems. To do this a counselor must himself: be well adjusted, have a good understanding of human psychology, be familiar with and proficient in using a wide variety of counseling techniques, highly respect the dignity and worth of individual students, and possess a sincere desire to understand and help his fellow man.

In most states, to be certified as a counselor requires that a person have some teaching experience and possess a master's degree with a major in school counseling. There are some states, however, that do not require prior teaching experience to be certified as a school counselor.

School Social Worker

An educational career closely related to that of a school counselor is that of a school social worker, the distinction being that a social worker goes out into the community and into the home to work with students and parents. For instance, if a school counselor, in working with an individual student, suspects that the student's problem may be caused by conditions in the home, he may refer the case to the school social worker. The social worker will then call at the home and may work closely with members of the family in an attempt to bring about a solution to the problem.

Of course, not all schools have a school social worker on the staff. In some school systems this function is carried on by a school counselor and in other schools the teacher does whatever work in the home with parents that needs to be done. An increasing number of school systems, however, are finding it advantageous to have a school social worker on the staff who is specifically trained to do this kind of work.

A school social worker typically possesses a masters' degree with a major in school social work.

Media Specialists

Chapter nine discussed the general topic of instructional resources that are now available for use by teachers. More and more school systems are now employing specialists who have been trained in media and whose sole job it is to help teachers create and utilize a wide variety of different kinds of media in their teaching. These media specialists must, of course, be familiar with all of the different kinds of audiovisual equipment available for use in schools. Such equipment includes, for example, movie projectors, film strip projectors, 35 mm. slide projectors, opaque projectors, overhead projectors, audio tape recorders, video tape recorders, record players, overhead transparency makers, photo copy machines, cameras —the list gets longer each year as more and more such hardware is developed and made available for use in schools.

The media specialist, in some schools, also does minor repair work on audiovisual equipment; however, the main function of the media specialist so far as media hardware is concerned is to advise the school system on what hardware to buy and help teachers use such equipment.

A media specialist should have had prior teaching experience and have a masters' degree with a major in educational media.

The school counselor is a valuable member of the educational staff—helping individuals or small groups of students with a wide variety of problems.

The educational media specialist must be familiar with all of the educational hardware now available for use in the schools.

An important function of the media specialist is that of helping teachers develop and prepare teaching materials.

Educational Administration and Supervision

There are many different kinds of specific educational administration careers that one may pursue. These include, for example: general superintendent (in charge of an entire school system), assistant superintendent (assisting the general superintendent with the operation of part of the school operation, such as curriculum, personnel, business, elementary education, or secondary education), principal (in charge of a single elementary or secondary school building), and assistant principal (assisting the principal with specific parts of the operation of a single school building). The size and philosophy of each school district determines the number and type of administrative positions that school district will have.

Many school systems also employ a number of different kinds of supervisors. Whereas an administrator typically has a certain amount of "authority" over the area in which he administers, a school supervisor frequently does not actually have authority over teachers. Rather, a supervisor plays more of a "consultant" role. For example, an elementary music supervisor would help the regular elementary teachers do a better job of teaching music. She might do this by occasionally teaching the music class in each of the elementary classrooms and/or by helping the regular classroom teacher do a better job of teaching her own music lessons. Common supervisory positions are those in elementary music, elementary art, elementary physical education, elementary reading, and some schools even have supervisors who have broad responsibility supervising one subject, such as science, for instance, in all grades starting at kindergarten and continuing through the twelfth grade. In many of the larger junior and senior high schools, department heads will have supervisory responsibility for their respective departments.

It is difficult to generalize about administrative and supervisory positions in American schools because the number and nature of such positions vary a great deal from school to school. However, there are a considerable number of such positions existing in the American public school system. For

> Small boy scowling over report card to Dad: "Naturally I seem stupid to my teacher; she's a college graduate."
>
> Dallas Morning News

instance, in 1967 it was estimated that there were 13,481 superintendents of schools and 105,007 principals and supervisors in public elementary and secondary schools in this country.[3] To pursue a career in educational administration and/or supervision one must obtain a good deal of successful teaching experience and at least a masters' degree which is related to that kind of work.

Librarians

A school librarian is, in one sense, really a teacher whose classroom is the library. Some people erroneously think of a school librarian as one who only takes care of books and periodicals. Much to the contrary, a good librarian can be one of the very most effective teachers in an entire school. One of the major goals of American public education is to help each student become capable of learning on his own without the help of the classroom teacher. The library contains many of the resources necessary for independent study and the task of the librarian is to help each student learn how to use these resources. To do this effectively, a librarian must not only be able to order, classify, catalog, and shelve books, but also must be able to work effectively with individuals and groups of students.

Almost all of the junior and senior high schools in this country have libraries and, therefore, librarians. It has been only recently that elementary schools have begun to have libraries in many schools. The library has been expanded into "learning resource centers" where a wide range of learning materials such as books, periodicals, learning machines, programmed self-teaching materials, film strips, single con-

> I love to teach as a painter loves to paint, as a musician loves to play, as a singer loves to sing, as a strong man rejoices to run a race. Teaching is an art—an art so great and so difficult to master that a man or a woman can spend a long life at it, without realizing much more than his limitations and mistakes, and his distance from the ideal.
>
> William Lyon Phelps

cept films, records, audio tapes, and dial access materials are made available for students to use. Schools of the future are destined to put a greater emphasis on learning centers and with this emphasis will come an increased demand for well-trained librarians and directors of learning centers.

Para-Professionals

One of the newer educational careers is that known as a para-professional (also often called a teacher aide). A para-professional assists the regular classroom teacher, or in some cases a number of teachers, with many aspects of teaching that have traditionally taken up much valuable time from

> The direction in which education starts a man will determine his future life.
>
> Plato

3. "The Magnitude of the American Educational Establishment 1966–1967," *Saturday Review* 50 (1967):67.

The library or learning resource center is one of the most essential parts of a contemporary school. A good librarian can be one of the most effective teachers on a school staff.

A supervisor's main task is that of helping each teacher become a more effective educator. Here, a supervisor helps a beginning teacher analyze a video tape of a lesson she has just taught.

the teacher. The following is a partial list of the kinds of duties typically performed by a para-professional:[4]

Tutorial activities:
—help children in their search for materials such as charts, pictures, and articles
—help children organize games and sports
—play with children and help them to use toys and playthings, and assist in supervising at recess
—assist teachers in the use of equipment such as projectors, viewers, and tape recorders
—help teachers with emotionally upset children by giving them personal attention
—serve as laboratory assistants
—help the teacher in reading and evaluating pupil work
—assist the teacher with children who have learning difficulties in reading and number work
—help the teacher with problem cases by working with the child outside of the class in activities he is interested in
—assist with instructional activities in art, music, on field trips.

Clerical activities:
—help the teacher with files of materials such as pictures, stories, and articles
—help with making and preparing materials of instruction, and type and duplicate instructional materials
—help teachers with examinations and records.

Housekeeping activities:
—keep order in cafeteria and hallways
—help in the library
—help in class with the distribution of materials
—supervise clean-up activities.

As one can see from this list of activities, a para-professional is an important member of the teaching team.

The qualifications necessary for becoming a para-professional vary greatly from state to state and from school district to school district. Most states do not yet issue certificates for para-professionals—however, there seems to be a trend in this direction—which means that the qualifications are determined by each local school district. Some school districts hire mothers of school age children—regardless of how much formal education they may have had—to assist elementary teachers. This practice has been particularly popular and successful in inner city schools. Other school districts require a minimum of two years of college for para-professional work. A small but increasing number of junior colleges and community colleges are developing specific two year training programs for para-professionals.

One can gleen from the following comments of a third grade teacher the importance of a para-professional in today's school:[5]

Click, click, click, click! The sound echoes in an empty hallway. It probably means nothing to the average American citizen, but to three third-grade teachers at Douglas School in Freeport it is the welcome sound of our teacher's aide tripping gaily down the hall.

"Good morning," she calls in a cheery voice; and we know immediately that it is a good morning, for at last we have someone to help us with the numerous tasks that confront us each day—tasks that are neces-

4. B. Othanel Smith, et. al., "The Role of Teacher Aides," *Teachers for the Real World*. Washington, D.C.: American Association of Colleges for Teacher Education, 1969, p. 35. Used with permission.
5. Vera E. Johansen, "A is for Aide," *Illinois Education*, December, 1968, p. 149. Used by permission.

sary and demanding, yet the kind that can be done by a non-professional.

We teachers are busy, so she checks her folder which contains the day's schedule and an outline of the work that is to be done. She checks papers and workbooks (objective tests only), records grades, and calls attention to children who are having difficulties that will require special help from the teacher. She gives vocabulary and arithmetic flash card drills, which are necessary for some children. This she can do as efficiently as a teacher. Her listening ear is welcomed by children who need an audience plus a little help while reading a library book or a story from a reader. She cares for the room library and assists in selection of books.

The aide "listens in" on small-group planning. She makes master copies of ditto work and arranges material for free-time activities. She weighs and measures children and records the information on the health cards. She folds and puts on book covers (nearly 500 of them), makes numerous trips to the office, picks up mail, prepares supplies for art and science, cleans up after a painting session, orders films that we want to use from the central office, gets all audio-visual equipment, and sees that everything is ready to do.

Bulletin boards are wonderful teaching aids, but in the primary grades the teacher is largely responsible for preparing them and putting them up. Now we give our helper the ideas and materials and our bulletin boards take shape as if by magic!

But the days are never long enough to accomplish all we have set out to do, and our minds are still full of valuable ways to use an aide. A teacher's aide must contrib-ute to the achievement of goals which teachers see to be those of the school program, and this we feel she has done. Elementary education, particularly at the primary level, is committed to the development of children educationally, emotionally, and physically. This commitment is one that is almost impossible for a teacher to fulfill to the best of her ability when there are innumerable routine tasks to be accomplished in addition to teaching an average of 35 children. When a teacher is relieved of some of these duties there is more time for careful planning, more time for individualized instruction, and more time for guidance. A full-time teacher's aide would mean that at least a teacher could become a full-time teacher. Wouldn't that be wonderful?

Click, click, click, click! For three teachers at Douglas School that is music to our ears. We hear a cheery "Good morning" and we know that every morning is a good morning because a teacher's aide has come to our rescue.

Closely associated with the development of the para-professional position is the concept of "differential teaching staff." This concept involves the idea that our schools should be staffed with a wide variety of different types of educators, each of whom

> What can only be taught by the rod and with blows will not lead to much good; they will not remain pious longer than the rod is behind them.
>
> Martin Luther

Many schools select, as para-professionals and teacher aides, mothers who have school age children. Para-professionals are becoming an increasingly important member of the teaching team.

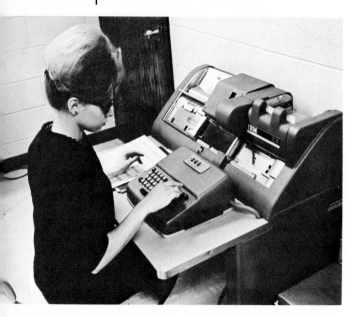

Other schools employ people who have a minimum of two years of college to perform a wide variety of para-professional tasks.

would play a slightly different role in the education process. Such a differential staff, for example, might include the following categories of personnel.[6]

1. *Teacher Aide.* This might be a person who could not certify for standard or provisional credentials; a person who is willing to devote only a part-time effort to education; a person unable to decide upon education as a career; or a person using education as a background for another field.

2. *Assistant Teacher.* This might be a person who is provisionally qualified or minimally qualified for a standard certificate; a person who views teaching as a means of second income, exerting minimal time and effort; a person who is merely "exploring" before trying to move elsewhere in education, or a person who is using teaching as a

transition position before moving into another endeavor, such as business, marriage, the military, etc.

3. *Regular Teacher.* This might be a beginner with a master's degree along with a great deal of preparation beyond certification requirements; a person of several years of otherwise successful experience, who does not wish to exert much more than a "40-hour week" in teaching, or who is an adequate teacher of several years of experience who does not exert real effort to improve.

4. *Senior Teacher.* This may be a person with a few years of highly successful experience who is well beyond certification requirements and exerts "extra effort" beyond regular school hours and days, or a good teacher who has taught dozens of years and operated as a "professional" in all respects.

5. *Master Teacher.* This might be a teacher with several outstanding years of teaching and service to the profession, who continually makes outstanding or unique contributions to some phase of education, or a teacher who puts to good use an outstanding degree of expertise gained from experiences or preparation.

While educational staff differentiation schemes such as this are not yet widely used in school systems, they are becoming more common and will undoubtedly become even more so in the future as schools search for more effective ways to utilize a staff.

In conclusion, this chapter has attempted to briefly discuss some of the careers, other than classroom teaching, that exist in American public education. All of these different kinds of educational careers are essential in

6. Wade N. Patterson, "Teacher-Ranking: A Step Toward Professionalism," *Educational Forum*, January, 1969, p. 172.

the American educational task. A career in any one of these educational careers can be rewarding and enable a person to make a significant contribution to the education of American youth.

> Knowledge is power.
>
> Francis Bacon

QUESTIONS FOR DISCUSSION

1. What do you believe the function and the role of a superintendent should be in a public school system today? A principal?
2. What do you believe would be some of the characteristics of a successful school administrator?
3. Discuss the advantages and disadvantages of putting exceptional children into special classes as opposed to attempting to provide for their special needs while leaving them in the regular classroom.
4. Discuss the advantages and disadvantages of some of the different types of careers in American public education.
5. What are your views concerning the role of counselors in our educational system? What qualities do you believe a counselor should possess?

SUPPLEMENTARY LEARNING ACTIVITIES

1. Invite a public school administrator to your class to discuss his or her work.
2. Visit a relatively large school and interview the various types of educational personnel you find there.
3. Describe what you believe would be an ideal staff (in terms of number and types of positions) for an elementary school; a junior high school; a senior high school.
4. Select one of the educational careers discussed in this chapter and make arrangements to spend one full day following in the footsteps of someone now serving in that career.
5. Make arrangements for a school librarian or learning center director to discuss his or her work with your class.

SELECTED REFERENCES

Association for Supervision and Curriculum Development. *Leadership for Improving Instruction.* Washington, D.C.: National Education Association, 1960.

Auxiliary School Personnel. Washington, D.C.: National Commission on Teacher Education and Professional Standards, 1967.

"The Business Official." *Overview* 2(1961):43–46.

"Children with Problems: What Does the Social Worker Do?" *NEA Journal* 51(1962):55–57.

Cruickshank, William M. and Orville G. Johnson, eds. *Education of Exceptional Children and Youth.* 2nd ed. Englewood Cliffs, N.J.: Prentice-Hall, 1967.

Eiserer, Paul E. *The School Psychologist.* Washington D.C.: The Center for Applied Research in Education, Inc., 1963.

Goldman, Samuel. *The School Principal.* New York: The Center for Applied Research in Education, Inc., 1966.

Green, John A. *Fields of Teaching and Educational Services.* New York: Harper & Row, Publishers, 1966.

Griffiths, Daniel E. *The School Superintendent.* New York: The Center for Applied Research in Education, Inc., 1966.

Hildreth, Gertrude H. *Introduction to the Gifted.* New York: McGraw-Hill Book Co., 1966.

Johnson, G. Orville. *Education for the Slow Learners.* Englewood Cliffs, N.J.: Prentice-Hall, Inc., 1963.

Johnson, Wendell, and Dorothy Moeller, eds. *Speech Handicapped School Children.* 3rd ed. New York: Harper & Row, Publishers, 1967.

"Lay Readers of English Papers." *School and Society* 90(1962):102.

National Education Association. *Teaching Career Fact Book.* Washington, D.C.: The Association, 1966.

Riessman, Frank. *The Culturally Deprived Child.* New York: Harper & Row, Publishers, 1962.

Roeber, Edward C. *The School Counselor.* Washington D.C.: The Center for Applied Research in Education, Inc., 1963.

Shadick, R. G. "School Librarian: A Key to Curriculum Development." *Elementary School Journal* 62(1962):298–303.

Turney, D. T. "Secretarial Help for Classroom Teachers." *Education Digest* 28(1962):24–26.

U.S. Office of Education. *Employment Outlook for Teachers.* Washington, D.C.: Government Printing Office, 1967.

Zirbes, Laura. *Spurs to Creative Teaching.* New York: G. P. Putnam's Sons, 1959.

Teaching the Handicapped Child

Carl H. Hanson

At our school, where all of the children are physically handicapped, both the teaching techniques we employ and the way we arrange the classrooms are designed to provide the optimum learning climate for children with physical impairments. I believe that teachers of regular classes that include one or more physically handicapped children might improve the learning opportunity they offer those children by borrowing some of the features of our special classes.

Turn the lights on, feed the goldfish, open the window, greet the parakeet, arrange the materials, check lesson plans, and then watch the children come rushing into the room. Any classroom? Yes, even a classroom for physically handicapped children.

The day starts with a sharing period that encourages language development and provides the opportunity for the teacher to become better acquainted with the students, and the students, with one another. "What do you have to share this morning?" may bring responses like: "I have a worm," ". . . a frog," ". . . a butterfly." The teacher, of course, must remain calm, cool, and collected, even if strange beasts are deposited in his hand or are scuttling around the room.

After the sharing and baring of secrets is over, we turn to classwork. We approach the three *R's* in many different ways, and the variety makes for interest. "Where's my ball?" may sound like a strange question for a child to ask during the writing session, but our classwork comes to a halt momentarily as a bouncing ball—a strange looking one with a pencil pushed through it—is retrieved. We call the ball a writing aid for those who have difficulty holding the pencil. We make other writing aids from such unlikely materials as bleach bottle handles, curler sponges, twisted wire, and rubber tubing.

The solution to a particular problem may be so obvious that we tend to overlook it. For example, one boy who was left-handed and had tonic neck reflexes and a condition known as athetosis that caused his fingers to move involuntarily could only pull toward his body. He wrote quite well, but the writing was upside down. The solution for his problem was to turn his paper upside down while he wrote, then reverse it. The procedure wasn't according to the rules of penmanship, but not everybody can write upside down, either.

The electric typewriter on the floor may cause some concern to the visitor, but when somebody has a tonic neck reflex, the floor is the easiest place to manage those fighting muscles. "Wham" goes the boy's hand. He is not fighting the typewriter; he is just putting his hand on the keyboard so that he

* Carl H. Hanson, "Teaching the Handicapped Child," *Today's Education*, December, 1969, pp. 46–47. Used by permission.

can write. A special guard on a typewriter enables another boy, an athetoid, to produce a legible paper instead of causing the keys to jump out of the machine.

Many times the students themselves come up with the answer to a particular problem. One girl couldn't write on the board because she couldn't get her wheelchair close enough. It seemed hopeless until she asked, "Can you put the board on the floor and take me out of the wheelchair?" Indeed we could, and lying on her stomach enabled her to write on that fascinating blackboard.

At other times, finding the solution to problems is my responsibility. When someone says, "What did you say? I can't hear you," it is the signal for me to say, "This seat near me is just your size. Won't you come up and try it?" In order to avoid hearing, "Teacher, don't turn your back," I use the overhead projector instead of writing on the board. In this way, I can present a full face to the acoustically handicapped.

The auditory trainer is a real boon to those who need extra sound volume and fewer distractions in order to become involved in the intricacies of reading and other classwork. By tuning in with their earphones, the children can hear stories and music coming from tape recorder or record player.

Little dramas are acted out in my classes every day. For example, one day a book came sailing from a boy's outstretched hand directly at my head. A quick duck foiled a direct hit, and the blackboard took the punishment. Instead of disciplining the boy, I put the book into the wastebasket (to be retrieved after school). As the boy explained why he didn't like that book, he relaxed. It seems that it had been forced on him at an-

other school. After several months, during which he read out of a notebook that contained stories based on his personal experience, studied a basic vocabulary, did kinesthetic tracing of letters, and received love and care, he was able to return to the basic reading series.

When one boy was told that he was doing fine work, he got up, bowed deeply to the rest of the class, and said, "I love you, Teacher." The teacher responded with a quick hug; after all, it is a joy to be loved.

Every day for several days a boy who was badly disturbed emotionally would huddle under my desk whenever he came into the room. I sat at the desk acting as if he weren't there. After several days, he began a form of communication by untying my shoes, taking the laces out, and waiting to be disciplined. When I didn't get upset, he communicated further by crawling into my lap. Finally, he talked to me. When I suggested that the desk near me was empty and had his name on it, he was able to make the giant step away from his secluded sanctuary. I assured him that he could return to the kneehole of my desk at any time.

When the many activities going on in the classroom bring a feeling of frustration to some of the students, I provide a quiet place away from the confusion where they can concentrate on the work at hand. A "private office" created by placing two folding screens around a desk was very handy for one little boy who was determined to get his arithmetic done. When I was walking about helping various individuals, I stopped to peer over the screens and asked, "How are you doing?" He answered, "Please don't bother me. Can't you see that I'm busy?" He was, and he made a perfect score. When the need for them was over, we put the screens away to use another time.

Initially, the interns, student teachers, work-aid personnel, volunteers, and observers in my room are tense and undecided about what to do when working with various handicaps. They show this by the questions they ask during counseling sessions, questions like "What do you do when a child falls down?" My response is, "Check to see if anything is broken, namely, the floor." I go on to say that a quick survey will reveal whether anything serious has happened and that a cuddle can soothe a minor hurt. I assure them that the handicapped child usually knows how to fall and should be encouraged to get himself up.

It is important for interns to become acquainted with the child as a person. For this reason, I urge them to observe the children's play activities. Playacting, for example, brings out the experience backgrounds of the children. Their play makes it evident that they are no strangers to hospitals, nurses, doctors, therapists, and teachers. It isn't uncommon for pupils to have dolls that are bandaged all over or equipped with braces and special devices for eating and sleeping.

Visitors who come to the room with the idea that they will witness misery and the unnatural are surprised to find the children working diligently, with one purpose, to get the assignment done in the allotted time. Their first concern in the classroom is about learning, not about their handicaps.

During one visit, a sympathetic lady was clucking over a little girl who, face screwed up, tongue out of one corner of her mouth, was working with a pencil holder. The visitor said, "Oh, you poor little girl, having to use that thing for writing." The little girl looked up and with a bright smile said, "Yes, and I have cerebral palsy, too." The lady was shocked. I hastily assured her that all the children knew what their problems were, had ceased to worry about them, and now worked to solve them. Then each of the youngsters told her about his particular handicap.

I feel that fear of the unknown can cause failure. When we know the reason for a handicap, we cease to think about it and instead watch the child grow in spirit and in body. This was illustrated early one spring when the usual yard work was under way around the various homes at the Center. A hemiplegic boy came into the room moaning and groaning, with his good hand to his back.

"What's the matter? Are you crippled?" someone asked. "I sure am, from all that raking and work in the yard," he answered.

Instead of thinking about the side of his body that was paralyzed, this boy was concentrating on the hard work he had been able to do and feeling proud about it.

Concentrating on the child and what he can do rather than on his handicap and what he *cannot* do will go further than anything else a teacher can do to help a physically impaired child to realize his potential. Sometimes, however, it is helpful to make concessions to the handicap by making minor changes in the equipment and arrangement of the classroom.

Crutches on the floor can cause quite a problem, for they seem to sneak out from under a desk just in time to trip someone. Small hangers attached to the side of a desk end this hazard.

Trikes are helpful when the schedule

demands that classes change in a certain span of time. The trike is certainly quieter than crutches and often speedier, and the handlebars make a great place to prop a book in the classroom.

• A pathway for wheelchairs on the perimeter of the room makes it possible for the wheelchair-bound to come to the classroom, get to the library corner or to the teacher's desk, and go back to home base. Home base is usually located near the door, so that wheelchairs have a head start at recess time and at noon.

CHAPTER 14

Teacher Organizations

During the process of socialization we strive to identify ourselves as acceptable members of groups in our social milieu. Most of us want to "belong" and, in order to belong, we often do what others expect of us. Sometimes we do not do what we would personally like to do, but that which will win for us the approval and acceptance of others. As a member of a group, one has a sense of belonging that is further enhanced by conforming to group norms.

Membership in teacher organizations may also be considered as an important determinant of social success, and even physical survival in certain situations. Organizations are prized by some members in terms of what the organization can do for them. Often the pressures of special interest groups, such as teacher organizations, have a significant influence on the operations of school government. In this way teacher organizations are effective agents in dealing with teacher concerns.

Teachers are solicited for membership in numerous and varied types of organizations. The most popular types of organizations are those which bring members of an occupational group together for the advancement of their mutual purposes. The two major teacher organizations are the American Federation of Teachers, a union affiliated with the American Federation of Labor–Congress of Industrial Organizations, and the National Education Association, a non-union group which claims to be the professional organization. Speaking in terms of sociological stratification that affects the specialized lower echelon employees in a large scale industry, Fred M. Smith suggests the following for teachers:

Teachers in smaller areas work under conditions and live in a social milieu similar to professionals and develop attitudes similar to professionals. Working conditions and social milieu of the metropolitan teacher are similar to those of lower level employees of mass industry.

Therefore, teacher unions will be perceived by metropolitan teachers as the best means of attaining those things which are important to them, and teachers not in metropolitan centers or in areas characterized by metropolitan conditions will perceive the professional association as the best means of attaining those things which are important to them.[1]

1. Fred M. Smith, "The Teachers' Union vs. the Professional Associations," pp. 439–440.

The largest teacher organization in the United States is the National Education Association with over one million members located in large metropolitan schools, suburban schools and rural schools. The second largest teacher organization is the American Federation of Teachers, with most of its 170,000 membership found in the large metropolitan schools.

National Education Association (NEA)

The NEA was originally founded in 1857 as the National Teachers Association. In 1870 a merger was effected with the National Association of School Superintendents and the American Normal School Association to form the National Education Association (NEA). The two purposes stated in the charter are "to elevate the character and advance the interests of the profession of teaching and to promote the cause of education in the United States."

The Association is governed by the annual Representative Assembly composed of over 7,000 delegates from affiliated state and local associations. This body develops policy resolutions which are interpreted by the Board of Directors, of which each state has one member for every 20,000 NEA members, and the Executive Committee, made up of the officers and four elected members.

Tied into the Association are a number of departments. While a part of the parent NEA, these department associations often represent the major organizational affiliation for the teachers. These department associations are self-governing groups within the profession, some serving general interests, such as the Association of Classroom Teachers (ACT), others representing separate disciplines, such as the Department of Art Education. Created by the Representative Assembly and financed by the Association, a number of national commissions also develop their own programs. Typical of these are the National Commission on Professional Rights and Responsibilities (PR&R) and the National Commission on Teacher Education and Professional Standards (TEPS). The Association also organizes a number of standing committees which are charged with developing specific programs in such areas as Citizenship and Ethics. The organization chart of the NEA, as outlined in Figure 14.1, shows the various departments, institutes, divisions, commissions, committees and councils within the NEA.

The income of the Association is derived almost entirely from membership dues with a small amount returning from the sale of publications. In 1967–68 budgeted expenditures totaled $11.25 million.

Headed by the Executive Secretary, who is chosen by the Executive Committee, a staff of approximately 600 individuals serves in the NEA Center (1201 Sixteenth St., N.W., Washington, D.C. 20036) and in eleven regional offices. The staff is organized into divisions whose directors serve under a cabinet of one deputy, two associates, and six assistant executive secretaries. Employees of the departments housed in the NEA Center bring the total staff to more than 1,000 individuals.

The Association is an affiliate of the World Confederation of Organizations of the Teaching Profession (WCOTP) which includes national teacher organizations in practically every country of the free world.

A pamphlet published by the National Education Association entitled *Your Future*

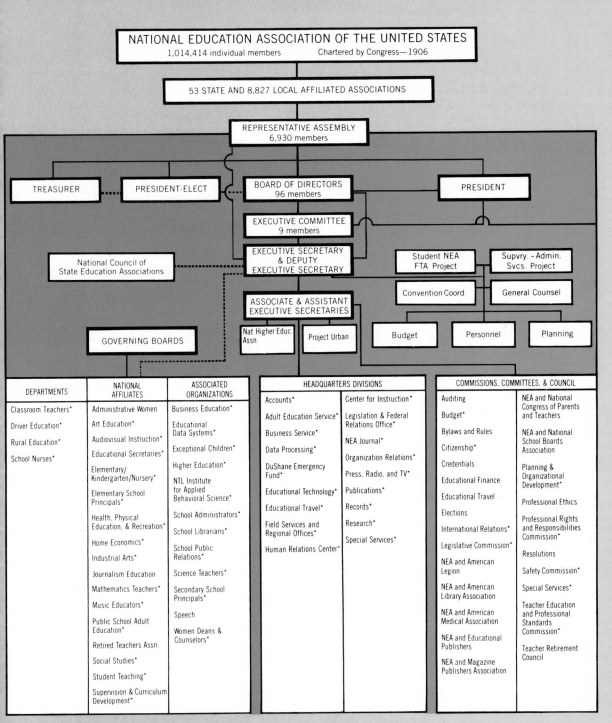

Figure 14.1. Organization Chart of the National Education Association of the United States.

Source: National Education Association, 12-1 Sixteenth Street, N.W., Washington, D.C. 20036. August, 1969. Used with permission.

in a Great Profession lists a few close-up looks at professional cooperation at work on three levels—local, state, and national—as follows:

Each year . . .

The NEA produces several half-hour films designed to acquaint Americans with the problems, purposes, and progress of education in this country . . .

The state associations cooperate in planning the films and arrange bookings for them on TV stations throughout the state . . .

The local associations promote and publicize the TV film programs and often arrange for supplementary showings to PTA, civic, business, and other community groups . . .

Continuously . . .

The NEA represents you and the nation's teachers before Congress and Federal Agencies . . .

The state association represents you and the teachers of your state before the State Legislature and State Department of Education . . .

The local association represents you before the School Board and often before other local legislative bodies . . .

Cooperatively . . .

The local, the state, and the NEA conduct instructional and professional welfare workshops, institutes, conferences, conventions, exhibits, and demonstrations—local, statewide, or on a regional or national scale . . . and publish the world's outstanding professional journals, newsletters, instructional materials, and classroom aids . . .

The NEA, in the same publication, suggests that the organizational benefits are not automatic. Things which the members need to do at the local, state, and national level are:

LOCALLY

Meet your faculty representative at once. He is your faculty's professional leader and will introduce you to professional members and friends. He will help you, or secure help for you, during those hectic first weeks of school. . . . He is your source of information about your professional associations.

Read the newsletters published by your local association and become familiar with events and issues which concern you.

Attend meetings. Meet your fellow teachers who serve as association officers and chairmen. Become acquainted with your professional co-workers who volunteer to work for you. Conscientiously use your influence and vote.

Learn about the activities of committees and meet the committee members who are working voluntarily to improve your salary, and gain other welfare benefits for you.

Volunteer to work in your local education association in some capacity. Take full advantage of your local association's services, savings, and social events.

STATEWISE

Read your state journals. Inform yourself about educational and professional affairs in your state. They concern you.

Learn about special state association services such as insurance programs and others. Plan to make full use of them.

Attend state institutes, conferences, conventions, and workshops.

Plan to meet association officers and leaders who serve and represent you on the state level.

Keep informed about, and do your part to support, state legislative campaigns.

NATIONALLY

Read *Today's Education*—mailed to members monthly. Take full advantage of its professional articles, classroom aids, guides to publications, instructional tools, and many other special features. Read, also, the NEA Reporter which will keep you up-to-date on NEA accomplishments and plans.

Secure a copy of NEA's Publications Catalog, arranged by subject matter and available to members on request. NEA is the world's largest publisher of professional materials. Obtain and use them to meet your needs.

Write to the NEA for information or resources that will help you to meet your classroom needs, improve your relations with parents, help you function well in local association activities, or guide you in your advanced studies.

Plan to spend a day at the NEA Center when you visit Washington, D.C. At the NEA Center you will meet staff employees who work for you on the national level: produce your publications, represent you before Congress; maintain contacts with the press and with national lay organizations; provide many kinds of information and service.

Plan to attend an NEA Convention, held annually during the summer in some large city. At NEA conventions about 20,000 members of your profession and visitors from every state and many foreign countries meet, exchange ideas, share experiences, and learn. Some 7,000 delegates from local and state affiliated associations vote to determine NEA's program of activities for the coming year.

Take full advantage of NEA materials to help you to participate effectively in NEA-originated events such as American Education Week.

Learn to use NEA's many special services, such as NEA's field representatives; NEA's salary and negotiation consultants; NEA's consultants in instruction; NEA's research in all areas of educational practice and teacher welfare; NEA's publications and aids with such classroom problems as discipline and the use of TV and teaching machines; NEA's regional instructional conferences in basic and in special subject matter areas.

Avail yourself of savings and advantages made possible by NEA, such as NEA's Life Insurance programs; NEA Accidental Death program; NEA tours—U.S. and foreign— some with opportunities to earn college credits enroute; NEA-secured deductions on your federal income taxes for your advanced-educational expenses; quantity discounts for NEA's professional publications.

American Federation of Teachers (AFT)

The American Federation of Teachers is not a new organization. It was organized on April 15, 1916, affiliated with the American Federation of Labor May 9, 1916, and has grown in membership and influence every year since. While the AFT is the largest teachers' union in the United States, the general membership of 163,000 members as of May 1, 1968 is small as compared to the one million members of the NEA. However, the AFT functions as the dominant teachers' organization in some of our largest cities.

In the fall of 1961, an election was held among New York City teachers to elect an agent to bargain with the Board of Education. In the election, the United Federation of Teachers (AFL-CIO) defeated the Teacher's Bargaining Organization which was supported by the National Education Association. This election has been referred to as the opening skirmish of what has grown to be a noisy battle for the loyalties of American teachers.[2] The New York election is cited as a major factor in the rise of the AFT to a position of national prominence.

A pamphlet entitled *Questions and Answers about AFT* published by the AFT provides information regarding organizational structure and affiliation with organized labor. The American Federation of Teachers comprises more than 650 local unions of teachers in the United States, the Canal Zone, Guam, and in Armed Forces Overseas Dependents Schools. State federations of teachers exist in a majority of the states, and are active in legislative and or-

2. Stanley Elam, "Who's Ahead and Why: The NEA-AFT Rivalry," *Phi Delta Kappan*, September, 1964, p. 12.

ganizational work. The national headquarters of the AFT is located at 1012 14th St. N.W., Washington D.C. 20005. The president, secretary-treasurer, and administrative and office staffs, from here, supply organizational, membership, and other aid to local unions and members as requested.

The general offices include those of the president, secretary-treasurer, administrative staff, and the following departments: financial, organizational, legal, research, publications, public relations and publicity, civil rights, state federations, colleges and universities, membership, and mailing.

The annual convention functions as the AFT's governing body. Delegates to this convention are elected by local union members. Each affiliated local is entitled to one delegate for 25 or fewer members; one delegate for each 25 additional members up to 500; an additional delegate for each 50 members beyond 500 and up to 2,500, and one more for each 100 beyond 2,500.

The interim governing and administrative body is the Executive Council of 16 vice-presidents, and the president, who is a full-time officer. The president and vice-presidents are subject to election every two years. Vice-presidents, who are assigned to specific geographical areas, serve without remuneration (see Fig. 14.2).

Organized labor was a major instrumentality in establishing our system of free public schools, and has actively backed every practical public school improvement at local, state, and national levels. The objectives of the American Federation of Teachers coincide with labor philosophy on the importance of public education.

Labor affiliation gives the AFT and its members the support of the more than 14 million members of unions in the AFL-CIO.

Local and state teachers' federations can rely on the support of state and local central labor bodies. AFT local unions have often won better salaries and other benefits for teachers with the aid and support of local labor trades and labor councils, after teachers' organizations outside the labor movement failed to accomplish these objectives.

Labor affiliation does not impose any obligations on union teachers which would deter them from the best professional service they can render, and the highest professional ethics they can command. Labor affiliation, by emphasizing the dignity of the teaching profession, makes it easier for teachers to act, on the job, as the professionals they are. Figure 14.3 (page 342) outlines the relationship of American Federation of Teachers to the American Federation of Labor—Congress of Industrial Organizations.

Membership in the AFT includes principals, supervisors, department heads and teachers, but does not permit superintendents to join on the grounds that superintendents represent the interests of the employer. As with the NEA, a Student Federation of Teachers may be chartered in any college or university under the auspices of the parent AFT.

The AFT boasts that John Dewey held Membership Card Number 1 in the American Federation of Teachers. Dr. Dewey, who died in 1952 at the age of 93, was professor of philosophy at Teachers College, Columbia University. In an address by Dr. Dewey, published in the *American Teacher*, publication of the AFT, January, 1928, he said:

The very existence of teachers' unions does a great deal more than protect and aid those who

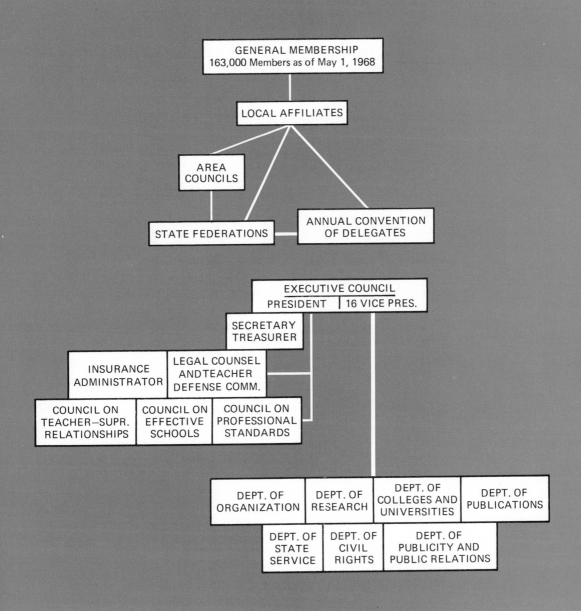

Figure 14.2. Organization Chart of the American Federation of Teachers.

Source: American Federation of Teachers AFL-CIO, 1012 14th Street N.W., Washington, D.C. 20005. Used with permission.

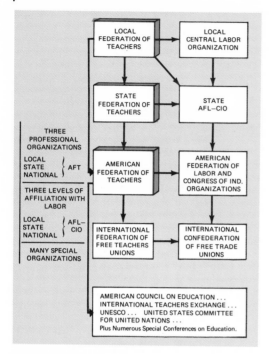

Figure 14.3. Relationship of American Federation of Teachers to AFL-CIO.

Source: American Federation of Teachers AFL-CIO, 1012 14th Street N.W., Washington, D.C. 20005. Used by permission.

are members of it; and that, by the way, is one reason the teachers' union is not larger. It is because there are so many teachers outside of it who rely and depend upon the protection and support which the existence and the activities of the union give them, that they are willing to shelter behind the organization without coming forward and taking an active part in it.

And if there are teachers . . . who are not members of the union, I should like to beg them to surrender the, shall I call it, cowardly position, and come forward and actively unite themselves with those who are doing this great and important work for the profession and teaching.

Total membership in the AFT at the time of Dr. Dewey's address (1928) was approximately 5000. The steady rise in membership had reached approximately 60,000 at the time of the 1961 New York City teacher election won by the United Federation of Teachers supported by the AFL–CIO labor union. From the fall of 1961 to May 1, 1968 the membership in the teachers' unions affiliated with AFL–CIO rose to 163,000 which represented a gain of approximately 103,000 during a seven year span. While the rivalry for membership continues strongly between the NEA and the AFT the total membership of the two organizations combined represents only slightly over fifty per cent of all teachers. Therefore, many teachers elect to join local teacher groups or do not join any teacher organizations.

NEA vs. AFT

During the past decade the tactics and behaviors of the AFT have greatly influenced the tactics and behaviors of the NEA and vice versa. While the two organizations have differences, such differences are becoming less and less obvious. Figure 14.4 illustrates that so far as stated objectives of the AFT and the NEA the two organizations are not in basic conflict. In view of the general similarities of purposes which continue to evolve, considerable speculation also evolves regarding the possible merger of the AFT and NEA to form a singular, more representative organization for all teachers in the United States. David Selden was elected president of the AFT in August, 1968 on a "merger" platform. On October 4, 1968 the AFT extended an invitation to the NEA to enter into discussions of merger. On October 11, 1968 the NEA Executive Committee declined the AFT invitation to discuss merger prospects.

Even though this initial invitation to discuss merger did not materialize, there are indications that local actions may open again merger discussions between the AFT and NEA. On February 1, 1970 teachers in the Los Angeles school district merged their two rival professional organizations into a single teachers' group. The new teachers' unit, to be called United Teachers–Los Angeles, was approved on a 8,999–5,042 vote by members of the Association of Classroom Teachers, local 121, AFL–CIO. The merger is the first ever of major urban locals of the rival National Education Association and the American Federation of Teachers. The only other merger occurred in October, 1969, in Flint, Michigan, where 1,800 teachers joined together. The Los Angeles merger

A.F.T. Objectives	N.E.A. Objectives
1. To bring associations of teachers into relations of mutual assistance and cooperation.	1. Educational opportunity for every individual to develop his full potential for responsible and useful citizenship and for intellectual and spiritual growth.
2. To obtain for them all the rights to which they are entitled.	2. Balanced educational programs to provide for the varied needs and talents of individual students and for the strength and progress of the nation.
3. To raise the standard of the teaching profession by securing the conditions essential to the best professional service.	3. The services of a professionally prepared and competent educator in every professional position.
4. To promote such a democratization of the schools as will enable them better to equip their pupils to take their places in the industrial, social and political life of the community.	4. School plant, equipment, and instructional materials appropriate to the educational needs of all learners.
5. To promote the welfare of the childhood of the nation by providing progressively better educational opportunities for all.	5. Effective organization, controls, administration, and financial support of public education in every state.
	6. A local-state-federal partnership in the financial support of public education with control of education residing in the states.
	7. Public understanding and appreciation of the vital role of education in our American democracy.
	8. Understanding and support of the teacher's right to participate fully in public affairs.
	9. Fair standards of professional welfare for teachers.
	10. Professional associations that evoke the active participation of all educators in working toward the highest goals for education.

Figure 14.4. AFT and NEA Objectives.

Source: *Constitution of the American Federation of Teachers*, Article II. National Education Association, *NEA Handbook*, "The Platform of the National Education Association" (Washington, D.C.: The Association, 1961), pp. 50–53.

is regarded as a major breakthrough and may be the harbinger of a single national teachers' group.

National, State and Local Affiliation

In the early years of the sixties decade, the NEA was viewed philosophically and operationally as the national organization which served as an umbrella under which the state and local associations were sheltered. Each of the three levels of affiliation could remain as autonomous as desired by their respective memberships. Individual teachers could pay membership dues for local membership only, for both state and local membership, or for all three of the national, state and local memberships. This mutually autonomous organizational structure and membership dues arrangement was espoused as a desirable feature in membership recruitment announcements by the NEA and state affiliates. During the mid-sixties teacher militancy increased sharply lending to the new concept of teacher power, discussed briefly in chapter five. Concomitant with the expansion of teacher power was a new need for unification of the three levels of affiliation. Local associations sought increased support from state associations, and state associations sought increased national unity. The need for unity across state and local levels of membership to build teacher power prompted an alteration in the NEA point of view regarding the independent organizational and dues structures. The later years of the sixties found the NEA espousing the desirability of a unified dues approach in which members would pay a single membership fee to cover all three levels of association affiliation. Several state associations have taken direct uni-

fication steps by amending their bylaws so that their dues include membership fees for both the state and national associations. The National Education Association has taken indirect steps toward unified membership by requiring both state and national association membership as criteria for eligibility for various fringe benefit programs, such as insurance programs, which are NEA sponsored. The AFT has always had a single dues arrangement whereby AFT members were automatically members at the local, state and national levels.

Yearly dues paid by the classroom teacher vary from approximately thirty ($30.00) dollars to seventy ($70.00) dollars for membership at the national, state and local levels. Most of the state affiliates of the NEA have utilized a sliding dues scale whereby the lowest paid teachers pay the least membership dues for state affiliation. The 1969–70 dues for NEA membership exclusive of state and local dues is fifteen ($15.00) dollars. Local association dues are set by the local group with a set minimum fee for each member (typically $2.00 per member) paid to the state association for affiliation. Under the NEA unified dues approach, a teacher in a given association would pay set yearly dues which would cover national, state and local costs. As indicated earlier, the AFT has always had a unified dues arrangement.

The Local Association and Teacher Power

As stated in chapter five, teacher power is manifested at the local school district level by the use of a local organization to press for negotiations. Since the local school district is the quasi-municipal governing agency, the decisions of the local board of education are the decisions which directly affect the teachers. Thus, the most powerful voice for teachers to use regarding the decision making process which affects them is the collective voice of a strong teacher association. The state Education Associations and the state Federation of Teachers provide organizational assistance to the local teacher groups ranging from formalized procedural information, printed materials, and consultant services to legal services. Generally, the local teacher organizations in the rural and small town school districts are affiliated exclusively with the state affiliate of the National Education Association. The National Education Association also has considerable strength through suburban and large city local chapters. The strength of the American Federation of Teachers is mostly associated with local affiliates in suburban and large city schools. In a few districts, strong local teacher associations exist independent of affiliation with either the NEA or the AFT.

The primary objective of a local association, whatever the state affiliation, is to vie for direct negotiation rights with the local board of education. In many school districts, two or more local organizations exist, each competing to become the sole negotiations agent for the district. Both the NEA and AFT recognize that a single negotiating agent gives maximum power to the local teachers. In school districts which have more than one strong local teacher association, elections are usually held to determine which organization will be the negotiations agency to meet with the local board of education.

After the negotiation process has been affirmed, the local teacher associations exercise their teacher power through the kinds of matters which they negotiate with the local boards. In addition to salary, negotiation items range to include curriculum matters, textbooks, teacher assignments, class size, in-service training, student teaching programs, faculty participation in the retention and selection of personnel, academic freedom and fringe benefits.

Teacher Strikes

Teacher strikes occur when negotiations between a local teacher's organization and the local board of education do not produce acceptable resolutions to the teachers' demands. The use of the strike by teachers became the vehicle of teacher power in the later part of the sixties decade. A summary of teacher strikes for the 1967–68 school year stated that a total of 114 work stoppages (strikes) occurred, which was considered a "veritable explosion in teacher strikes."[3] These 114 strikes accounted for over one-third of the number of teacher strikes since 1940.

An overview of teacher militancy around the nation covering the same period (1967–68) follows:[4]

The equinoctial storms of teacher militancy raged from Florida, where 25,000 teachers left their classrooms for three weeks, to New Mexico, where a one-week strike by teachers in the capital threatened to spread across the state; from Pittsburgh, where high schools were closed by teachers demanding an election as a prelude to negotiations, to San Francisco, where a juris-

3. "Teacher Strikes in Perspective," *NEA Research Bulletin*, December, 1968, p. 113.
4. D.W.R., "Teacher Militancy Around the Nation," *Phi Delta Kappan*, June, 1968, p. 554. Used with permission.

dictional dispute closed schools for a day. A strike was barely averted in Oakland, California. In St. Paul, Minnesota, an impasse was reached when the teachers' association charged the board with "bad faith bargaining." Oklahoma teachers staged a one-day walkout and voted to maintain a sanctions alert. The Colorado Education Association voted sanctions in the form of notifying colleges and universities nationwide that unsatisfactory educational conditions exist in that state. Many other warning notes have been sounded, like the advice South Dakota teachers were given by their association to sign contracts for only one semester of 1968–69.

The targets of most spring strikes were not local school boards, even where the walkouts were limited to a single city, but state legislatures. The Florida and New Mexico protests were aimed at pressuring the governors and legislatures of those states to approve substantially increased support programs for the schools. The AFT-inspired strikes in Pittsburgh and San Francisco were intended to prod the legislatures of California and Pennsylvania into passing new negotiation legislation more favorable to the union.

Nearly every stoppage ended with sufficient gains that teachers could call the effort successful, even though the success was in no case complete. Florida teachers did get a revenue bill, but a smaller one than they had demanded. In some Florida counties school boards took teacher resignations at face value and refused to rehire in some cases. And the AFT stepped in with a statewide recruiting campaign, hoping to capitalize on teacher unhappiness with results of the walkout. The Pittsburgh walkout won

a negotiation election in which neither the union nor the association won a majority, but no negotiations will follow unless the legislature passes a law authorizing it. Since then the Pennsylvania State Teachers Association has voted to apply state-wide sanctions and to censure the governor. The strike called by the AFT in San Francisco did result in an election, but the AFT lost the election and there is no evidence yet that the desired changes in the Winton Act will be forthcoming. In both cities union leaders figure they cannot lose. This time they have won the right to an election; next time they expect to win the election. The New Mexico militancy led to appointment of a task force that has recommended convening a special session of the legislature, a move rejected earlier by the governor.

What lies behind the militancy? Are conditions in the affected states really substandard, or have the strikes resulted more from inter-organizational rivalry and jurisdictional disputes than from an accurate perception of genuine grievances?

If five selected criteria of state-wide educational performance are applied to the nine states cited for March work stoppages, four of these states fall below the national mean in four of the five measures. In these four states—Colorado, Florida, Oklahoma, and South Dakota—the case for educational delinquency by the state seems pretty clear. In the other states the picture is less clear, though the specific deficiency attacked by the strikers may be very real.

The five criteria selected for comparison are:

1. Average salaries of all teachers in public schools, 1967–68.

2. Percent increase in instructional staff

salaries, 1957–58 to 1967–68.

3. Percent of revenue for public schools from state government, 1967–68.

4. Per capita state expenditures for all education, 1966.

5. Current expenditures for public elementary and secondary education per pupil in ADA, 1967–68.

South Dakota falls below the national norm in all five measures, ranking 49, 33, 48, 34, and 33.

On only one measure do all nine states rank below the national average, the percent of increase in salaries during the past decade. This suggests the positive relationship between failure to maintain relative salary gains and presence of teacher militancy. In no other category did more than

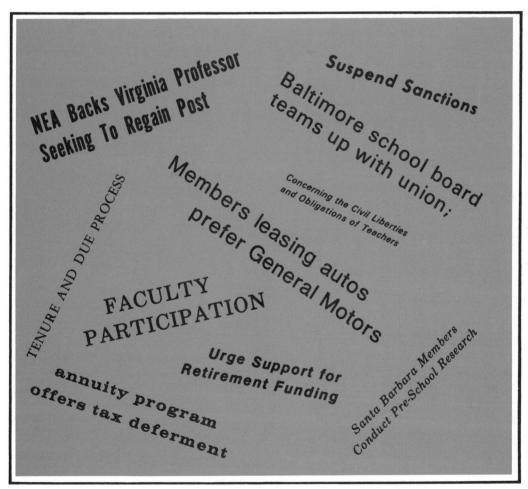

Figure 14.5. Mutual Concerns of the AFT and NEA.

five states fall below the median, though six of the nine were beneath the mean in average salaries paid this year. The influence of salary in motivating militancy is apparent, even where other factors are present. Obviously, other conditions than low salaries must be present before militancy becomes operative. Nine of the ten lowest states in average salaries paid are *not* among those states experiencing strikes. It may be significant that all but one of the nine states in which there were strikes (Florida) have a higher percentage of men in the teaching force than the national average.

Only one of the nine states experiencing a significant spring teacher strike (California) currently has a negotiations law, and in that state the major goal of the strike was to achieve revision of that law.

The fact that teacher discontent seems to center chiefly in the cities reflects not only the well-known axiom that urban dwellers are politically more active than their rural colleagues; even more, it mirrors the genuine crisis of the city schools. The teacher strikes are storm signals to state and federal officials that the cities need more attention—which means more money.

As usual, observers see a variety of possible patterns emerging from the wave of strikes. Some see the decline of the NEA, which has accepted the strike tactic recently and reluctantly, and the further strengthening of the union, for whom the strike is a natural weapon. Some analysts predict a wave of state-wide teacher strikes, while others proclaim that the lesson of Florida is that a state-wide walkout jeopardizes the positions of the teachers in the most vulnerable spots. A better tactic, they say, is pressure applied on state authorities by strikes in key urban areas where the strike is most likely to succeed.

Fringe Benefits and Support Programs

The NEA and the AFT differ in degree in their approaches to specific benefits or programs, but in general terms each organization strives to offer similar benefits to its members. Figure 14.5 illustrates the kinds of fringe benefits and support programs which are mutual concerns of both organizations.

Affiliate publications come to the members of the teacher associations. These usually consist of national journals and state journals, newsletters, handbooks, research studies, and various booklets and reports.

The benefits of research services come to members in the form of reports such as salary studies, estimates of school statistics, negotiations information, summaries of court decisions, leaves of absence and fringe benefit programs which exist.

Each of the parent associations have legislative committees at both the state and national levels. These legislative committees work on improving certification standards and improving the laws which relate to teaching.

Teacher welfare is an area of prime importance to the parent associations. Many kinds of programs which focus on advancing and protecting the welfare of members are sponsored by the parent organizations. The NEA and her state affiliates have considerably outdistanced the AFT in this area. Consequently, many teachers have been members of both organizations simultaneously in order to be eligible for teacher welfare oriented programs. The AFT is steadily increasing research services, publications, printed materials, insurance programs, and consultant services for their members. Among the state educational association teacher welfare programs are included teacher placement services, investment programs, retirement benefits, insurance programs, liability protection, auto leasing programs and regional service centers. Similar programs are sponsored by the NEA, but to be eligible for their programs the teacher must also belong to the state association. The requirement of state membership is consistent with the unified dues emphasis of the NEA and prevents the teacher from paying only the national dues in order to profit from the nationally sponsored NEA welfare programs.

A Summary View

Myron Lieberman, professor of education, is considered an authority on the growth of teacher power. Lieberman has reviewed the issues that divide the two organizations, the possible advantages of merger, and whether NEA–AFT peace would slow down growth of the collective negotiation movement in an article written for the Phi Delta Kappan journal.[5] The following quote from Professor Lieberman's article expresses his view of the future relationship between the NEA and the AFT.

A merger of the National Education Association and American Federation of Teachers will probably be negotiated in the near future. Such a move will have far-reaching national implications for teacher militancy. Perhaps because very few educators realize how imminent merger is, our professional literature is virtually devoid of any consideration of the likely conditions and consequences of merger. Inasmuch as organizational rivalry plays such an important role in teacher militancy, it would be unrealistic to consider the dynamics of teacher militancy without serious attention to the effects of merger upon it. . . .

Without question, the organizational rivalry between the NEA and AFT has been an important stimulus to teacher militancy. At all levels, the two organizations and their state and local affiliates have come under much more pressure to achieve benefits than would be the case if there were only one organization. A representation election almost invariably causes the competing organizations to adopt a more militant stance in order to demonstrate their effectiveness in achieving teacher goals. For the same reason, any failure to press vigorously for teacher objectives becomes a threat to organizational survival. State and national support are poured into local elections and negotiation sessions in order to protect the interests of the state and national affiliates. Thus at the local level organizational rivalry has led to a vastly greater organizational effort to advance teacher objectives. This development is consistent with the experience of competing organizations in other fields.

The crucial importance of the NEA–AFT rivalry in stimulating teacher militancy raises the question of whether the merger of the two organizations will reduce such militancy. Probably, the merger will simultaneously encourage some tendencies toward greater teacher militancy and some toward less militancy; the overall outcome

5. Myron Lieberman, "Implications of the Coming NEA-AFT Merger," pp. 139–144. Used by permission.

is likely to vary widely from district to district and time to time. . . .

Code of Ethics—Bill of Rights

The philosophical statements of the two major national teacher associations are expressed in the form of The Code of Ethics of the Education Profession (NEA) and the Bill of Rights (AFT). The two statements are included here in their entirety.[6]

THE CODE OF ETHICS OF THE EDUCATION PROFESSION THE NATIONAL EDUCATION ASSOCIATION OF THE UNITED STATES

PREAMBLE

THE EDUCATOR BELIEVES IN THE worth and dignity of man. He recognizes the supreme importance of the pursuit of truth, devotion to excellence, and the nurture of democratic citizenship. He regards as essential to these goals the protection of freedom to learn and to teach and the guarantee of equal educational opportunity for all. The educator accepts his responsibility to practice his profession according to the highest ethical standards.

The educator recognizes the magnitude of the responsibility he has accepted in choosing a career in education, and engages himself, individually and collectively with other educators, to judge his colleagues, and to be judged by them, in accordance with the provisions of this code.

PRINCIPLE I

Commitment to the Student. The educator measures his success by the progress of each student toward realization of his potential as a worthy and effective citizen. The educator therefore works to stimulate the spirit of inquiry, the acquisition of knowledge and under-

standing, and the thoughtful formulation of worthy goals.

In fulfilling his obligation to the student, the educator—

1. Shall not without just cause restrain the student from independent action in his pursuit of learning, and shall not without just cause deny the student access to varying points of view.

2. Shall not deliberately suppress or distort subject matter for which he bears responsibility.

3. Shall make reasonable effort to protect the student from conditions harmful to learning or to health and safety.

4. Shall conduct professional business in such a way that he does not expose the student to unnecessary embarrassment or disparagement.

5. Shall not on the ground of race, color, creed, or national origin exclude any student from participation in or deny him benefits under any program, nor grant any discriminatory consideration or advantage.

6. Shall not use professional relationships with students for private advantage.

7. Shall keep in confidence information that has been obtained in the course of professional service, unless disclosure serves professional purposes or is required by law.

8. Shall not tutor for remuneration students assigned to his classes, unless no other qualified teacher is reasonably available.

PRINCIPLE II

Commitment to the Public. The educator believes that patriotism in its highest form requires dedication to the principles of our democratic heritage. He shares with all other citizens the responsibility for the development of sound public policy and assumes full political and citizenship responsibilities. The educator bears particular responsibility for the development of policy relating to the extension of educational opportunities for all and for interpreting educational programs and policies to the public.

In fulfilling his obligation to the public, the educator—

6. National Education Association, *The Code of Ethics of the Education Profession.* Washington, D.C.: The National Education Association of the United States, 1968. Used by permission.

1. Shall not misrepresent an institution or organization with which he is affiliated, and shall take adequate precautions to distinguish between his personal and institutional or organizational views.

2. Shall not knowingly distort or misrepresent the facts concerning educational matters in direct and indirect public expressions.

3. Shall not interfere with a colleague's exercise of political and citizenship rights and responsibilities.

4. Shall not use institutional privileges for private gain or to promote political candidates or partisan political activities.

5. Shall accept no gratuities, gifts, or favors that might impair or appear to impair professional judgment, nor offer any favor, service, or thing of value to obtain special advantage.

PRINCIPLE III

Commitment to the Profession. The educator believes that the quality of the services of the education profession directly influences the nation and its citizens. He therefore exerts every effort to raise professional standards, to improve his service, to promote a climate in which the exercise of professional judgment is encouraged, and to achieve conditions which attract persons worthy of the trust to careers in education. Aware of the value of united effort, he contributes actively to the support, planning, and programs of professional organizations.

In fulfilling his obligation to the profession, the educator—

1. Shall not discriminate on grounds of race, color, creed, or national origin for membership in professional organizations, nor interfere with the free participation of colleagues in the affairs of their association.

2. Shall accord just and equitable treatment to all members of the profession in the exercise of their professional rights and responsibilities.

3. Shall not use coercive means or promise special treatment in order to influence professional decisions of colleagues.

4. Shall withhold and safeguard information acquired about colleagues in the course of em-

ployment, unless disclosure serves professional purposes.

5. Shall not refuse to participate in a professional inquiry when requested by an appropriate professional association.

6. Shall provide upon the request of the aggrieved party a written statement of specific reason for recommendations that lead to the denial of increments, significant changes in employment, or termination of employment.

7. Shall not misrepresent his professional qualifications.

8. Shall not knowingly distort evaluations of colleagues.

PRINCIPLE IV

Commitment to Professional Employment Practices. The educator regards the employment agreement as a pledge to be executed both in spirit and in fact in a manner consistent with the highest ideals of professional service. He believes that sound professional personnel relationships with governing boards are built upon personal integrity, dignity, and mutual respect. The educator discourages the practice of his profession by unqualified persons.

In fulfilling his obligation to professional employment practices, the educator—

1. Shall apply for, accept, offer, or assign a position or responsibility on the basis of professional preparation and legal qualifications.

2. Shall apply for a specific position only when it is known to be vacant, and shall refrain from underbidding or commenting adversely about other candidates.

3. Shall not knowingly withhold information regarding a position from an applicant, or misrepresent an assignment or conditions of employment.

4. Shall give prompt notice to the employing agency of any change in availability of service, and the employing agent shall give prompt notice of change in availability or nature of a position.

5. Shall not accept a position when so requested by the appropriate professional organization.

6. Shall adhere to the terms of a contract or

appointment, unless these terms have been legally terminated, falsely represented, or substantially altered by unilateral action of the employing agency.

7. Shall conduct professional business through channels, when available, that have been jointly approved by the professional organization and the employing agency.

8. Shall not delegate assigned tasks to unqualified personnel.

9. Shall permit no commercial exploitation of his professional position.

10. Shall use time granted for the purpose for which it is intended.

BILL OF RIGHTS[7]
AMERICAN FEDERATION OF TEACHERS

The teacher is entitled to a life of dignity equal to the high standard of service that is justly demanded of that profession. Therefore, we hold these truths to be self-evident:

I

Teachers have the right to think freely and to express themselves openly and without fear. This includes the right to hold views contrary to the majority.

II

They shall be entitled to the free exercise of their religion. No restraint shall be put upon them in the manner, time or place of their worship.

III

They shall have the right to take part in social, civil, and political affairs. They shall have the right, outside the classroom, to participate in political campaigns and to hold office. They may assemble peaceably and may petition any government agency, including their employers, for a redress of grievances. They shall have the same freedom in all things as other citizens.

IV

The right of teachers to live in places of their own choosing, to be free of restraints in their mode of living and the use of their leisure time shall not be abridged.

V

Teaching is a profession, the right to practice which is not subject to the surrender of other human rights. No one shall be deprived of professional status, or the right to practice it, or the practice thereof in any particular position, without due process of law.

VI

The right of teachers to be secure in their jobs, free from political influence or public clamor, shall be established by law. The right to teach after qualification in the manner prescribed by law, is a property right, based upon the inalienable rights of life, liberty, and the pursuit of happiness.

VII

In all cases affecting the teacher's employment or professional status a full hearing by an impartial tribunal shall be afforded with the right to full judicial review. No teacher shall be deprived of employment or professional status but for specific causes established by law having a clear relation to the competence or qualification to teach proved by the weight of the evidence. In all such cases the teacher shall enjoy the right to a speedy and public trial, to be informed of the nature and cause of the accusation; to be confronted with the accusing witnesses, to subpoena witnesses and papers, and the assistance of counsel. No teacher shall be called upon to answer any charge affecting his employment or professional status but upon probable cause, supported by oath or affirmation.

VIII

It shall be the duty of the employer to provide culturally adequate salaries, security in illness and adequate retirement income. The teacher has the right to such a salary as will: a) Afford a family standard of living comparable to that enjoyed by other professional people in the community b) To make possible freely chosen professional study c) Afford the

---

7. American Federation of Teachers, *Bill of Rights*. Washington, D.C.: American Federation of Teachers. Used by permission.

opportunity for leisure and recreation common to our heritage.

IX

No teacher shall be required under penalty of reduction of salary to pursue studies beyond those required to obtain professional status. After serving a reasonable probationary period a teacher shall be entitled to permanent tenure terminable only for just cause. They shall be free as in other professions in the use of their own time. They shall not be required to perform extracurricular work against their will or without added compensation.

X

To equip people for modern life requires the most advanced educational methods. Therefore, the teacher is entitled to good classrooms, adequate teaching materials, teachable class size and administrative protection and assistance in maintaining discipline.

XI

These rights are based upon the proposition that the culture of a people can rise only as its teachers improve. A teaching force accorded the highest possible professional dignity is the surest guarantee that blessings of liberty will be preserved. Therefore, the possession of these rights impose the challenge to be worthy of their enjoyment.

XII

Since teachers must be free in order to teach freedom, the right to be members of organizations of their own choosing must be guaranteed. In all matters pertaining to their salaries and working conditions they shall be entitled to bargain collectively through representatives of their own choosing. They are entitled to have the schools administered by superintendents, boards or committees which function in a democratic manner.

QUESTIONS FOR DISCUSSION

1. What is an operational difference between the NEA and AFT?

2. What is the AFT position regarding teacher strikes?

3. What is meant by a "sanction" against a school system?

4. Would a merger of the AFT and NEA be advantageous or not? Discuss.

5. In what way does teacher militancy do a dis-service to the teaching profession? Discuss.

SUPPLEMENTARY LEARNING ACTIVITIES

1. Invite representatives of the state affiliates of the NEA and the AFT to class sessions to discuss their organizations.

2. Interview the officers of a local teacher association regarding their relationships with their board of education.

3. Read and evaluate various collective bargaining agreements.

4. Invite a school administrator to a class session to discuss his views regarding the role of teacher organizations.

5. Invite an elected political figure to a class session to discuss his views regarding the role of teacher organizations.

SELECTED REFERENCES

American Civil Liberties Union. *Academic Freedom, Academic Responsibility, Academic Due Process.* New York: American Civil Liberties Union, 1966.

American Federation of Teachers AFL-CIO. *Constitution of the American Federation of Teachers.* Washington, D.C.: American Federation of Teachers AFL-CIO, 1965.

Bishop, Leslie J. *Collective Negotiation in Curriculum and Instruction: Questions and Answers.* Washington, D.C.: National Education Association, 1967.

Chaffee, John Jr. "First Manpower Assessment." *American Education* 5(1969):11–12.

Corey, Arthur F. "Educational Power and the Teaching Profession." *Phi Delta Kappan* 49(1968):331–334.

Degnan, James. "California's Militant Professors." *Changing Education,* AFT Journal, Winter, 1967.

Goodlad, John I. *The Future of Learning and Teaching.* Washington, D.C.: National Education Association, 1968.

Henry, David D. *What Priority for Education?* Champaign, Ill.: University of Illinois Press, 1961.

Johnson, James, et al. *Introduction to the Foundations of American Education.* Boston: Allyn and Bacon, Inc., 1969.

Lieberman, Myron. "Implications of the Coming NEA-AFT Merger." *Phi Delta Kappan* 50(1968):139–144.

Lieberman, Myron, and Michael H. Moskow. *Collective Negotiations for Teachers: An Approach to School Administration.* Chicago: Rand McNally & Co., 1966.

———. "Teacher Strikes: Acceptable Strategy?" *Phi Delta Kappan* 46(1965):237–240.

———. *The Future of Public Education.* Chicago: University of Chicago Press, 1960.

Moskow, Michael, "Recent Legislation Affecting Collective Negotiations for Teachers." *Phi Delta Kappan* 47(1965):136–141.

National Education Association. *Guidelines for Professional Negotiations.* Washington, D.C.: Office of Professional Development and Welfare, National Education Association, 1965.

Smith, Fred M. "The Teacher's Union Versus the Professional Associations." *School and Society,* 5 December 1962, pp. 439–440.

Stinnett, T. M., Jack H. Kleinmann, and Martha L. Ware. *Professional Negotiation in Public Education.* New York: The Macmillan Co., 1966.

Strom, Robert D. *The Inner-City Classroom: Teacher Behavior.* Columbus, Ohio: Charles E. Merrill Books, Inc., 1966.

Tanner, Daniel. *Schools for Youth.* New York: The Macmillan Co., 1965.

Zeluck, Stephen. "The UFT Strike: Will It Destroy the AFT?" *Phi Delta Kappan* 50(1969):250–255.

Educational Power and the Teaching Profession

Arthur F. Corey

The constant use of the term "black power" has given a new connotation to a word which has in the past usually derived its meaning from the context in which it was used. Yesterday one might have asked, "What kind of power?" Today the word "power" is defined as the organization and implementation of the activities and influence of a somewhat homogeneous group in an attempt to gain conscious and desirable ends.

We often find illustration or parallel for human relations in mechanical principles. In the physical world, raw force is usually disorganized and uncoordinated energy. A tornado, an earthquake, or a huge waterfall exerts unbelievable amounts of energy. They possess great force, but in a mechanical sense they develop no power. Natural sources of energy—that is, natural forces—must be concentrated and organized and channeled to accomplish desired ends before they can accurately be called "power."

In human relations, individuals have influence. Personal influence is social energy; it is tremendous force. When personal influence is so organized and concentrated and directed that it affects other people it can rightfully be called "power." Good teachers have unique opportunity to exert such power over their students. If children are significantly different because of the influence of a teacher, then that teacher is truly "powerful." This is what Thomas Jefferson meant in ascribing to William Small, one of his teachers at the College of William and Mary, a "powerful" effect on all his later life.

Teachers have opportunity for "power" in all their personal relations. They can affect the opinions and attitudes of their family, neighbors, friends, tradesmen, and parents of their pupils. They may even have acquaintances within the power structure of the community. They can, if they will, have influence with a congressman, a state legislator, a city councilman, or a school board member. In all these relationships there is the possibility of "power." One of the negative aspects of today's larger school districts is the fact that personal relationships are less intimate—more tenuous and fragile—and therefore personal "power" is more difficult to establish and maintain.

It is not to deprecate the challenging possibilities of the influence of the individual teacher to accept the fact that the profession cannot be effective in directing changes in the schools unless these "units" of individual influence are organized, concentrated, and directed to desired ends.

The term "pressure group" is an epithet which has no definite meaning, usually applied to a group with which one disagrees

* Arthur F. Corey, "Educational Power and the Teaching Profession," *Phi Delta Kappan*, February, 1968, pp. 331–334. Used by permission.

and which one wishes to castigate. Most organized groups have common interests to advance and protect, and so long as their activities are honest there is nothing inimical or unethical in group activity. It must be expected that evil men will get together to further their nefarious ends. Edmund Burke once said, "When bad men combine, the good must associate." In fact, the political chicanery of certain economic groups was rampant until thwarted by the emergence of other groups strong and courageous enough to thwart them. Pure democracy in which every man as a unit speaks his own mind and controls his own destiny is a political ideal never yet approximated, and more and more difficult of realization as society becomes more complex. The play of group against group is the process of modern democracy. There is little profit in re-crying this condition. We must be interested in making it more effective for the common good.

The only possible cure for the evils of organized pressure is more and better organization among honest and intelligent men and women of good will. We can be sure that economic interests will continue to organize for pressure and we accept their right to do so. Professional groups have also learned to organize to accomplish their cherished objectives. The real danger in American life is that large segments of our people will continue to be unorganized, and will have no effective voice in government and public affairs. The man who has no share in organized "power" is certainly not independent of it. He is consistently the victim of the organized pressures which shape his way of life. The teacher who wishes to have real influence must get himself into an effective group and work in it.

Tyranny, in modern times, begins by exploiting the unorganized mass and then uses this instrument to destroy all other organizations. The strongest guarantee against authoritarianism is the presence in society of many strong, voluntary organizations. The most corrupt political machines usually have developed where the unorganized mass is largest. Huey Long's reign in Louisiana is an excellent example. The decline in the power of Tammany Hall resulted from the development of many voluntary pressure groups which could not easily be exploited. Organization which is voluntarily supported by its members, and whose program is co-operatively developed by those members, is the only thing in modern life which we can justly call self-government. Self-government is the essence of individual liberty.

The professional not only knows his field; he applies his knowledge to the control and direction of some aspects of the lives of others. In short, the conception of a profession, when expressed in terms of its function as it bears on others in a society, implies that, in relating thought to action, power is exercised in a certain way in that society.

If in more and more areas of life today people are discovering that they can get more dependably what they most basically want by forging more effective power structures, the profession of teaching should develop, with some clarity, ideas about where its weight is to be felt.

Despite some recognition in our literature that the work of a profession involves the use of power, the analysis of power as it is related to the knowledge and service of the professions, especially the teaching profession, has been neglected. This neglect has meant that efforts to professionalize teaching have had no theory of power to support and guide them. They have had no theoretical analysis sufficient to discriminate between the functions of power in different contexts and no analysis to identify its uses and abuses.

Power obviously presents awkward problems for a community which abhors its existence and disavows its possession but values its exercise. Despite this convention of reticence and understatement, which seems to outlaw ostensible pursuit of power and which leads to a constant search for euphemisms to disguise its possession, there is no indication that, as a profession, we are averse to power. On the contrary, few things are more valued and more jealously guarded by their possessors in our society.

Teachers, like other Americans, are in fact very eager for power. They enjoy its possession, but would prefer to wield it quietly behind the scenes. This reticence has a basis in the fact that many teachers have a somewhat uneasy conscience based upon the assumption that organized power and democracy are not compatible. The truth is that democracy cannot function without organized power. Our political parties, the foundation stones of our representative government, are in themselves examples of organized power.

Many teachers seem to assume a scarcity theory about power. This theory is not dissimilar to the now outmoded scarcity theory of wealth. It was long thought that the only way in which one man or one social segment could improve his or its economic status was to lower the economic status of someone else in society. Just so, the scarcity theory of power unconsciously held by many assumes that the amount of power in society is a fixed quantity and therefore, when it is assumed by one group, it is *ipso*

facto removed from some other group.

With obeisance toward these complexities, we shall take "power" to refer to organized and sustained social influence or control exerted by persons or groups on the decisions and actions of others. It relates to effectiveness in influencing action, decision, and policy in the entire range of human association. However, it is with the political aspect of power that this statement addresses itself.

America probably faces a generation of unprecedented political turmoil. The great issues will have to do with educational and social objectives and increasingly the people will begin to see that the kind of society they are to have is inescapably linked with the kind of education offered. America is heavily committed to more and more education for more of its people, but there is little consensus about what kind and quality of education this is to be.

Alvin Toffler[1] in a recent article calls the years between now and the turn of the century "The Age of Transience." Says he, "Rapid change will characterize every aspect of life. Time and space will collapse." People and things will come and go—in and out of one's life—at a faster rate than ever before. Man must learn to live with impermanence. There is ample evidence that even our ideas about goodness and badness—our sense of values—will change along with our environment. Impermanence will be further accelerated as science and technology advance and transience will permeate every aspect of life. The significant thing for us today is that in 1968 this acceleration is just barely beginning. The next third of a century will almost certainly be marked by sci-

1. Alvin Toffler, "Can We Cope with Tomorrow?," *Redbook Magazine,* Jan., 1966.

entific and social changes so severe that we must virtually abandon our habitual ways of thinking and doing and feeling. When society changes, education must inevitably change, and it will require great quantities of "educational power" to win this race with catastrophe. If teachers are to lead educational change, or even influence it, they will do it through political power.

Teachers have been distressingly naive in their insistence that "schools must be kept out of politics." It may be that such people tend to confuse "politics" with patronage. Politics is the science of determining *who* gets *what* and *when*. No segment of American government is so thoroughly political as the public schools.

There is nothing inherently unethical in political power if it is broadly based, consistent, and responsible. The insistence that group power must be broadly based leads many into erroneous conclusions. Not every member of a large group can vote on every issue but all must still be involved in decision making. Power, to be effective, must be applied speedily and effectively and by responsible leaders, but must be based upon generalizations which have been picked in advance with the broadest possible group participation. The platform of an organization, broad-based and democratically determined, should be comprehensive enough to guide the on-the-spot decisions which must be made by its leaders.

Politics is the process through which organized power is, in the final analysis, applied in a free society. The effective methods for group political action have drastically changed in California in recent years. There was probably never a teachers' organization in America which enjoyed the political power possessed by the California

Teachers Association (CTA) a generation ago. However, exactly the same methods would today be completely ineffective. The abolition of cross-filing, the sharp increase in the number of voters in legislative constituencies, and the unbelievable rise in campaign costs have combined to force groups which aspire to operate within the power structure to share the high campaign costs which otherwise keep all but the rich from running for legislative office. Time was when a pleasant letter praising a legislator for his support of public education was appreciated and was accepted as support. Those times are gone. Political support of public education is often measured in dollars, and if teachers are to stay in the game they must play the game under the new rules. This is the practical condition which gives rise to professional political action arms. Political forces are in flux. Labor and agriculture are gradually losing dominant places they once held in American politics. The present moment is indeed auspicious for the expansion and refinement of "educational power."

The expansion of educational power must be viewed and defended in terms of its objectives. Such power seeks to improve the quality of the educational experiences offered to American children. The ultimate end must always be improvement in the school program. Politicians instinctively respect that which they fear. They respect "power."

In the past the state teachers associations have generally been considered to be among the most effective groups in the legislative field. California has been no exception. The Golden State may also be typical of new conditions and new factors which must be faced if educational power is to be effective enough to give the profession some voice in educational decisions which may determine the nation's future.[2]

The unity which characterized professional legislative programs during the last decade is no longer so evident to legislators and to the public. The teachers union has been more disruptive to these programs than have the activities of organizations which have traditionally opposed public education. Although notoriously unsuccessful in attaining its own legislative objectives, the union has given legislatures the image of a house divided against itself and the excuse to defeat programs favored by a large majority of teachers. The schism between teachers and administrators, with the latter often maintaining independent representation at the capitol, has also tarnished the image of the united profession. In spite of these negative factors, the legislative record of state teachers associations has remained dramatically successful in the fields of school finance and teacher welfare.

The sad truth is that money for schools and economic security for teachers will not be enough in themselves to create the kind of schools which America now needs. These factors are basic and necessary, but well-financed schools with well-paid, secure teachers can still be woefully inadequate.

Educational power demands not only unity but commitment. Legislators have learned by experience that teachers really care about their own welfare, but lawmakers are not yet convinced that teachers are deeply motivated toward educational innovation and instructional improvement. This was painfully evident in the 1961 session of the California legislature.

Senator Fisher, and the Democratic Party which he represented, had no reason to believe that the members of the California Teachers Association would be vitally interested in a bill which sought to revolutionize the preparation of teachers. Assemblyman Casey had no reason to believe that the profession would be angered by his legislation, which mandated curricular detail. In opposing these bills, the CTA was operating outside its traditional sphere and legislators simply didn't take the opposition seriously. If these bills had attempted to weaken tenure, reduce retirement allowances, or cut state aid, they would have been killed in committee or never given a hearing. The politicians couldn't believe that the teachers back home really cared about certification or curricular detail. The fact that Senator Fisher, by his own admission, was defeated for re-election by angry teachers and that Assemblyman Casey is no longer in the legislature may be some slight assistance in correcting such legislative miscalculation in the future. However, educational power cannot be built by the occasional defeat of a recalcitrant legislator. The commitment of teachers to educational improvement must become traditional and hence accepted.

In an age of transience, society cannot permit a lag of a generation between important social and economic change and the resultant adjustment in education. The teaching profession must, through its organizational structure, be far more active in leading, or if necessary pushing, the reorganization of educational objectives, curriculum content, and teaching method.

With the collapse of space and time, we

2. Corey and Strickland, "Legislative Policies and Procedures Used by State Teachers Associations," an unpublished dissertation, University of Southern California, 1956.

must give relatively more importance to the future than the past. The traditional argument that one learns to understand the future by knowing about the past has lost much of its validity. There is little precedent in the past for what our children face in the future. This fact is profoundly disturbing to many people and gives rise to the irrational demand from the far right that we continue to educate for life in a kind of world which has ceased to exist. It will require educational power to counter these misguided pressures.

The most important change in professional association programs in the immediate future must be increased involvement in the improvement of instruction. This responsibility has long been recognized, but it must be given high priority in teacher association budgets and hence in program emphasis. No group can develop or maintain professional status when its right or competence to have a voice in basic decisions regarding its own work is challenged or denied.

The teaching profession must assert that education in America is too important to leave in the hands of the prejudiced or the uninformed. It is a specialized field, the details of which are far too complex to leave to the average citizen. When professional organizations show as much interest in improving instruction as they now do in improving salaries, the public will be more willing to accord the profession a voice in determining educational policy. This is to say that if professional organizations really assert themselves in stimulating innovation and improving instruction, this very activity will be self-serving in that it will go far in developing the professional power to secure acceptance of their proposals.

CHAPTER 15

Rewards and Frustrations of Teaching

There are various economic, as well as intangible, rewards and problems associated with any vocation. Historically, the teaching profession has been somewhat "Pollyannish" in that disproportionate worth has been ascribed to the intangible rewards of teaching, i.e., community status and rapport among teachers, as opposed to such tangible rewards as salary and fringe benefits. One of the factors identified with the rise of teacher militancy through strong organizations is the demand by teachers that increased attention be given to the economic rewards of teaching. The most attractive professions are those which provide challenges to problems and a proportionate balance of tangible and intangible rewards to the professional who satisfactorily meets those challenges. Teaching as a vocation is presently an attractive profession and has the potential of becoming increasingly more attractive.

Economic Rewards of Teaching

Salary is the prime economic aspect of teaching. A major reason for the post-World War II teacher shortage was that both private business and government jobs provided higher salaries. While the salary gap has narrowed, teaching has not as yet caught up to all the private business and government agencies. Figure 15.1 compares teachers' salaries with wage and salary workers, manufacturing employees, and civilian employees of the federal government. Teacher's salaries permanently surpassed wage and salary workers in 1949 and manufacturing employees in 1961. Teacher's salaries had not caught up with government civilian employees at the end of 1966.

In comparing starting salaries of teachers to private industry, teachers' salaries still fall significantly behind for both men and women. Figure 15.2 for men and Figure 15.3 for women show that in 1968–69, both men and women were behind the starting salaries of all other bachelor degree starting employees except that female teachers did start at a little over $100 per year more than secretaries. The widest gap was between starting male teachers, who earned about $3400 a year less than starting male engineers with similar bachelor's degrees. Fig-

Calendar year	Average annual earnings				Index: instructional staff			
	Instructional staff (calendar year)[a]	Wage and salary workers—all industries	Employees in manufacturing	Civilian employees of federal government	Instructional staff (calendar year)	Wage and salary workers—all industries	Employees in manufacturing	Civilian employees of federal government
1	2	3	4	5	6	7	8	9
1946	2,080	2,356	2,517	2,736	100.0	113.3	121.0	131.5
1947	2,380	2,589	2,793	3,074	100.0	108.8	117.4	129.2
1948	2,710	2,795	3,040	3,168	100.0	103.1	112.2	116.9
1949	2,900	2,851	3,092	3,361	100.0	98.3	106.6	115.9
1950	3,050	3,008	3,300	3,503	100.0	98.6	108.2	114.9
1951	3,235	3,231	3,606	3,777	100.0	99.9	111.5	116.8
1952	3,485	3,414	3,828	4,034	100.0	98.0	109.8	115.8
1953	3,645	3,587	4,049	4,226	100.0	98.4	111.1	115.9
1954	3,867	3,670	4,116	4,320	100.0	94.9	106.4	111.7
1955	4,019	3,847	4,351	4,595	100.0	95.7	108.3	114.3
1956	4,221	4,036	4,584	4,808	100.0	95.6	108.6	113.9
1957	4,467	4,205	4,781	4,971	100.0	94.1	107.0	111.3
1958	4,781	4,346	4,939	5,514	100.0	90.9	103.3	115.3
1959	5,017	4,558	5,215	5,682	100.0	90.9	103.9	113.3
1960	5,266	4,707	5,342	5,946	100.0	89.4	101.4	112.9
1961	5,533	4,843	5,509	6,285	100.0	87.5	99.6	113.6
1962	5,754	5,065	5,730	6,450	100.0	87.7	99.2	111.7
1963	6,015	5,243	5,920	6,792	100.0	87.2	98.4	112.9
1964	6,315	5,503	6,196	7,267	100.0	87.1	98.1	115.1
1965	6,572	5,710	6,389	7,613	100.0	86.9	97.2	115.8
1966	7,015	5,954	6,647	7,838	100.0	84.9	94.8	111.7

[a] Rounded to the nearest $5 for 1946 through 1953.

Figure 15.1. Average Annual Earnings of Public School Instructional Staff and Certain Other Groups, 1946–1966, *Calendar-Year Basis.*

Sources: Figures for 1946 through 1955 from *U.S. Income and Output,* a supplement to the *Survey of Current Business,* 1959, Table VI-15, p. 213. Figures for 1956 through 1966 from *Survey of Current Business,* various issues. Indexes in columns 6 through 9 computed by the NEA Research Division. *Economic Status of the Teaching Profession, 1967–68.* Research Report 1968-R4, National Education Association, p. 27. Used by permission.

ure 15.3 shows the widest gap between starting female teachers and private industry was with the starting salaries of engineering-technical research females who began earning over $3700 a year more than the teachers. It is obvious that a gap remains between beginning teacher's salaries and beginning salaries offered by other fields of endeavor. However, tabled comparisons of this kind do not show that teacher salaries are usually for nine months whereas the other salaries are for twelve months. A potential for increased teacher salaries lies in the expansion of summer teaching opportunities which would permit teachers to earn from their profession on a twelve-month basis.

Teacher's salaries differ from city to city and from state to state. In comparing minimum teachers' salaries in the twelve largest cities in the United States at the end of 1968, the range, shown in Figure 15.4, was

Group	Average starting salaries, school year				
	1965–66	1966–67	1967–68	1968–69	1969–70*
BEGINNING TEACHERS WITH BACHELOR'S DEGREE (School systems with enrollments of 6,000 or more)	$4,925	$5,142	$5,519	$5,941	. . . .
MEN GRADUATES WITH BACHELOR'S DEGREE					
Engineering	7,584	8,112	8,772	9,312	$9,816
Accounting	6,732	7,128	7,776	8,424	8,844
Sales-Marketing	6,276	6,774	7,044	7,620	8,028
Business Administration	6,240	6,576	7,140	7,560	8,016
Liberal Arts	6,216	6,432	6,780	7,368	7,884
Production Management	6,816	7,176	7,584	7,980	8,580
Chemistry	7,032	7,500	8,064	8,520	9,048
Physics	7,164	7,740	8,448	8,916	9,360
Mathematics-Statistics	6,672	7,260	7,944	8,412	8,892
Economics-Finance	6,600	6,732	7,416	7,800	8,304
Other fields	6,360	7,044	7,644	7,656	8,064
Total, all fields (weighted average)	$6,792	$7,248	$7,836	$8,391	$8,929

* Average salaries are based on offers made in November 1968 to men who will graduate in June 1969.

Figure 15.2. Starting Salaries: Teachers vs. Private Industry (Men)

Source: *NEA Research Bulletin,* Volume 47, Number 1, March, 1969, p. 22. Used by permission.
NEA Research Division and annual reports from Frank S. Endicott, Director of Placement, Northwestern University. For detailed information see *Economic Status of the Teaching Profession, 1969.* Research Report in process.

Group	Average starting salaries, school year			
	1965–66	1966–67	1967–68	1968–69
BEGINNING TEACHERS WITH BACHELOR'S DEGREE (School systems with enrollments of 6,000 or more)	$4,925	$5,142	$5,519	$5,941
WOMEN COLLEGE GRADUATES WITH BACHELOR'S DEGREE				
Mathematics-Statistics	6,324	7,104	7,776	8,484
Economics-Finance	6,000	6,636	6,984	7,224
General Business	5,520	6,000	6,840	7,104
Chemistry	7,056	7,452	8,280	8,532
Accounting	6,768	6,984	7,716	8,304
Home Economics	5,664	6,276	6,660	7,056
Engineering-technical research	7,260	8,208	8,904	9,672
Secretary	4,620	5,088	5,460	5,820

Figure 15.3. Starting Salaries: Teachers vs. Private Industry (Women).

Source: *NEA Research Bulletin,* Volume 47, Number 1, March, 1969, p. 17. Used by permission.
NEA Research Division and annual reports from Frank S. Endicott, Director of Placement, Northwestern University. For detailed information see *Economic Status of the Teaching Profession, 1969.* Research Report in process.

City	Bachelor's Degree			Master's Degree		
	Min.	Max.	Years to Reach Max.	Min.	Max.	Years to Reach Max.
Chicago	$7,350	$11,025	11*	$7,770	$11,813	12*
		11,288	16*		12,075	16*
		11,550	21*		12,338	21*
		11,813	26*		12,600	26*
		12,075	31*		12,863	31*
		12,338	36*		13,125	36*
Detroit	7,500	11,200	11	8,000	11,700	11
Los Angeles	7,210	10,450	12	7,310	10,550	12
San Francisco	6,820	11,695	14	7,760	12,680	14
Milwaukee	6,800	11,010	20	7,072	11,526	20
New York	6,750	11,000	14	7,100	11,500	14
Philadelphia	6,700	10,900	11	7,000	11,400	11
Baltimore	6,500	11,700	25	7,000	12,200	25
Boston	6,500	10,700	10	7,050	11,250	10
Cleveland	6,250	10,500	36	6,350	10,850	36
St. Louis	6,200	10,540	15	6,820	11,160	15
Houston	5,616	7,994	11	6,075	8,993	11

* In Chicago, a teacher will reach the maximum salary after 36 years' experience, but salaries at other levels of service are also shown.

Figure 15.4. What Teachers Earn in 12 Biggest Cities (1968).

from $5,616 (Houston) to $7,500 (Detroit) at the bachelor degree–no experience level. Also the maximum range was from $7,994 (Houston) to $12,338 (Chicago) again with only a bachelor's degree.

The average annual salaries for both beginning and experienced teachers on a state by state basis varies greatly. Figure 15.5 illustrates the difference by states in salary levels. For the 1967–68 school year, Mississippi at $4821 and South Dakota at $5700 had the two lowest annual average salaries, while California at $9450 and Alaska at $9660 were the two highest annual average salaries.

The availability of job opportunities wherever the teacher chose to locate has been given as a strong motive for becoming a teacher. Recently, however, signs point to

the fact that the teacher shortage is no longer a general shortage. The intangible plus of job mobility is now somewhat limited. The growth in the supply of beginning teachers has been on the steady upswing since 1955. Figure 15.6 shows that over 220,000 new teachers were graduated in 1967 compared to less than 90,000 in 1954. Due to this rapid increase in the number of new teachers and the change in birth rate, shortages occur only in specific curriculum areas. As of 1968 shortages occurred (Figure 15.7) only in sciences, mathematics, and regular elementary instruction. Also, a need due to short supply was indicated for six areas: technical areas, industrial arts, special education (secondary and elementary), women's physical education, and English language arts. This general

State	1949–50	1959–60	1961–62	1963–64	1965–66	1966–67	1967–68	1968–69*
1	2	3	4	5	6	7	8	9
50 states and D.C.	$3,010	$5,174	$5,710	$6,203	$6,786	$7,129	$7,709	$ 8,194
Alabama	2,111	4,002	4,070	4,820	5,350	5,800	5,900	6,050
Alaska	...	6,859	7,350	8,233	8,598	9,392	9,660	10,887
Arizona	3,556	5,590	6,150	6,610	7,165	7,430	7,840	8,465
Arkansas	1,801	3,295	3,678	4,098	4,755	5,113	5,702	6,291
California	4,268	6,600	7,200	7,700	8,600	9,000	9,450	9,800
Colorado	2,821	4,997	4,502	5,950	6,577	6,824	7,175	7,425
Connecticut	3,558	6,008	6,471	7,021	7,562	7,959	8,450	8,900
Delaware	3,273	5,800	6,242	6,677	7,532	7,804	7,994	8,400
Florida	2,958	5,080	5,549	6,176	6,378	7,085	7,700	8,600
Georgia	1,963	3,904	4,499	4,933	5,550	6,075	6,775	7,200
Hawaii	...	5,390	5,625	6,145	7,025	7,910	8,176	8,300
Idaho	2,481	4,216	4,761	5,075	5,856	6,012	6,200	6,400
Illinois	3,458	5,184	6,350	6,707	7,225	7,525	8,800	9,300
Indiana	3,401	5,542	6,081	6,492	7,292	7,663	8,269	8,350
Iowa	2,420	4,030	5,042	5,494	6,067	6,531	7,333	8,167
Kansas	2,628	4,450	5,036	5,448	5,957	6,270	6,723	7,217
Kentucky	1,936	3,327	4,232	4,613	5,200	5,680	6,288	6,750
Louisiana	2,983	4,978	5,246	5,299	5,987	6,598	6,980	7,200
Maine	2,115	3,694	4,619	5,100	5,600	5,950	7,288	7,288
Maryland	3,594	5,557	6,021	6,557	7,105	7,547	8,315	9,269
Massachusetts	3,338	5,545	5,900	6,860	7,350	7,550	7,770	8,350
Michigan	3,420	5,654	6,295	6,703	7,200	7,650	8,475	9,492
Minnesota	3,013	5,275	5,550	6,375	6,800	7,050	7,500	8,000
Mississippi	1,416	3,314	3,623	3,931	4,327	4,707	4,821	5,912
Missouri	2,581	4,536	5,142	5,587	6,027	6,307	6,858	7,372
Montana	2,962	4,425	5,000	5,550	5,900	6,300	6,650	7,050
Nebraska	2,292	3,876	4,400	5,030	5,350	5,800	6,250	6,700
Nevada	3,209	5,693	6,181	6,480	7,322	7,786	8,491	8,739
New Hampshire	2,712	4,455	4,886	5,314	5,843	6,207	6,539	7,276
New Jersey	3,511	5,871	6,300	6,738	7,233	7,647	8,162	8,775
New Mexico	3,215	5,382	5,750	6,222	6,598	6,740	7,300	7,560
New York	3,706	6,537	7,000	7,800	8,400	8,500	9,000	9,400
North Carolina	2,688	4,178	5,087	5,205	5,523	5,869	6,494	7,041
North Dakota	2,324	3,695	4,300	4,915	5,375	5,515	6,085	6,300
Ohio	3,088	5,124	5,700	5,957	6,558	6,782	7,631	8,050
Oklahoma	2,736	4,659	5,069	5,302	5,894	6,103	6,253	6,853
Oregon	3,323	5,535	5,970	6,492	6,953	7,274	7,978	8,385
Pennsylvania	3,006	5,308	5,661	6,143	6,830	7,181	7,528	8,133
Rhode Island	3,294	5,499	5,900	6,300	6,750	6,975	7,620	8,178
South Carolina	1,891	3,450	3,865	4,318	4,847	5,421	5,816	6,025
South Dakota	2,064	3,725	3,900	4,500	4,850	5,000	5,700	6,200
Tennessee	2,302	3,929	4,151	4,770	5,217	5,755	6,146	6,520
Texas	3,122	4,708	5,375	5,539	6,080	6,075	6,774	6,794
Utah	3,103	5,096	5,283	6,106	6,525	6,780	6,935	7,400
Vermont	2,348	4,466	4,780	5,450	5,808	6,200	6,585	7,085
Virginia	2,328	4,312	4,764	5,287	5,898	6,342	6,936	7,550
Washington	3,487	5,643	6,129	6,511	7,185	7,597	8,258	8,640
West Virginia	2,425	3,952	4,432	4,730	5,433	5,917	6,335	6,600
Wisconsin	3,007	4,870	5,603	6,124	6,650	6,954	7,504	8,350
Wyoming	2,798	4,937	5,596	5,840	6,572	6,635	7,163	7,375

Sources: Columns 2 and 3 from: U.S. Department of Health, Education, and Welfare, Office of Education. *Statistics of State School Systems, 1959–60.* Circular No. 691. Washington, D.C.: Government Printing Office, 1963. p. 77–78.

Columns 4, 5, 6, 7, 8 and 9 from: National Education Association, Research Division. *Estimates of School Statistics,* various issues.

* Advance estimates.

Figure 15.5. Average Annual Salaries of Instructional Staff by State, Selected School Years, 1949–50 Through 1968–69 (in dollars).

Source: *Economic Status of the Teaching Profession, 1968–69.* Research Report 1969 R-5, National Education Association, p. 14. Used by permission.

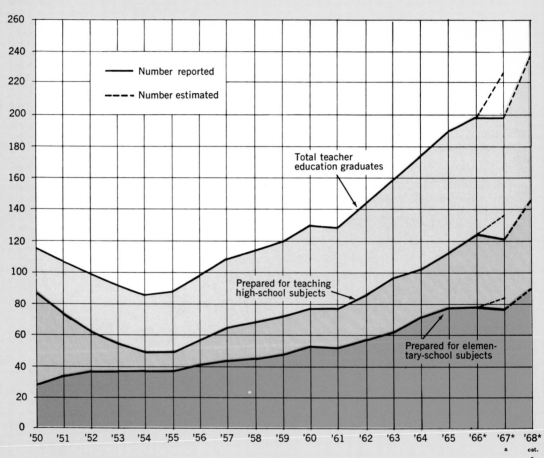

Figure 15.6.   Growth in Supply of Beginning Teachers.

Source: *Teacher Supply and Demand in Public Schools, 1968.* Research Report 1969-R4, National Education Association, p. 12. Used by permission.

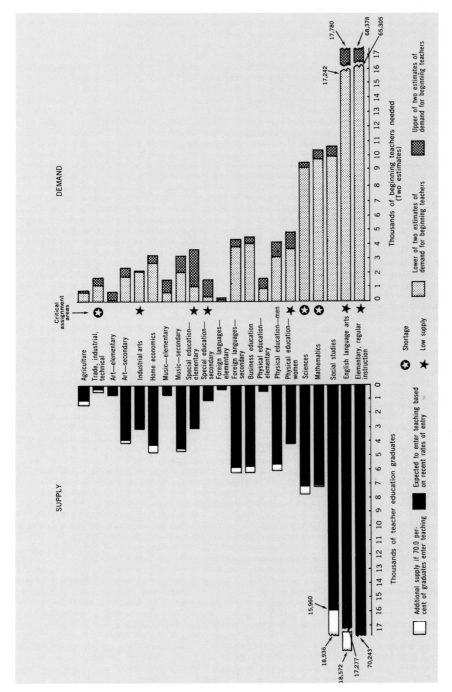

Figure 15.7. Supply and Demand for Beginning Teachers by Type of Assignment, Adjusted Trend Criterion Estimate, 1968.

Source: *Teacher Supply and Demand in Public Schools, 1968.* Research Report 1969-R4, National Education Association, p. 46. Used by permission.

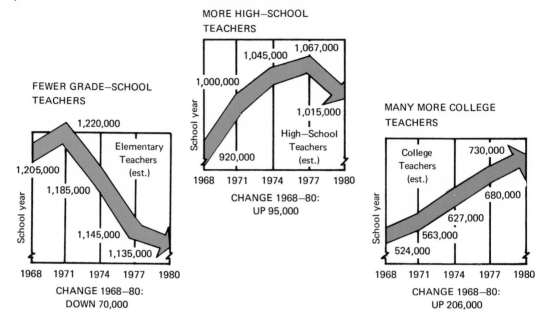

Figure 15.8. Shifting Needs for Teachers.

Sources: U.S. Census Bureau, U.S. Dept. of Health, Education and Welfare. "Impact of Changing School Enrollment," *U.S. News and World Report,* Volume LXVI, Number 23, June 9, 1969, p. 55. Used by permission.

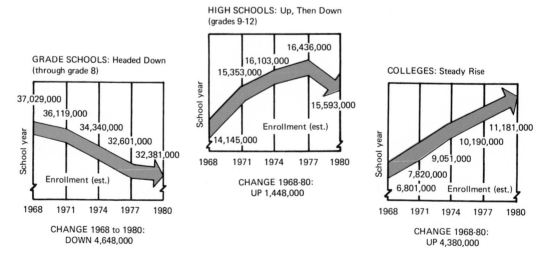

Figure 15.9. Ups and Downs in Enrollments.

Sources: U.S. Census Bureau, U.S. Dept. of Health, Education and Welfare. "Impact of Changing School Enrollment," *U.S. News and World Report.* Volume LXVI, Number 23, June 9, 1969, p. 54. Used by permission.

shifting of need for teachers is further illustrated in Figure 15.8 according to three categories: grade school, high school, and college needs. By 1980 it is possible that only college teachers will be in short supply. The shifting needs for teachers is directly related to the ups and downs in enrollments as shown in Figure 15.9.

Intangible Rewards of Teaching

Whatever the tangible problems and rewards, certain intangibles of teaching as a vocation are very much worth considering. Generally speaking, being a teacher in a community has with it reasonably high community status which is important to most professionals. Since teachers are highly motivated and well educated, various job satisfactions come about from working with such persons. Teachers benefit from assorted intangibles associated with working with youth. A kind of pride is generated within a teacher from feelings that he is contributing to the future of his nation through helping to educate the young. Only in the United States has universality of educational opportunity come to be a part of the national tradition.

All the intangibles of teaching are not so positively idealistic. Teachers are often hard pressed to produce evidence of their accomplishments. The accomplishments of teachers are not readily given to visual assessment. Therefore, teaching is accompanied by a kind of personal mental anxiety brought on by the lack of knowledge that what you are doing as a teacher is productive. Because of this aspect of teaching, the ego gratification afforded teachers through their job is at a minimum.

Thus, the rewards and problems of teaching are both tangible and intangible. Certainly, there are times when an individual teacher might feel that the problems and frustrations of teaching outweigh the rewards. However, the overall attractiveness of the teaching profession steadily improves. Tangible rewards are increasing while tangible problems are being solved. The intangible rewards continue to provide teachers with drives for professional improvement. Teaching as a vocation offers most to those who enter the profession well-prepared in their chosen area of specialty. Further, prospective teachers who orient their preparation toward those specific areas of teacher shortage can be assured of finding excellent opportunities throughout the United States.

Problems of Teaching

Teachers' problems are varied. In the spring of 1968 the NEA Research Division conducted a survey among a nationwide sample of public school classroom teachers. The questionnaire listed 17 areas of potential teacher problems and asked respondents to indicate if each one had been a major or minor problem or not a problem in their schools the past year. Results of the survey as reported in the NEA Research Bulletin, December 1968, are as follows:

Inadequate teaching conditions and insufficient compensation are the biggest problems for the greatest number of teachers. Insufficient time for rest and preparation, large classes, and insufficient clerical help top the list of items teachers rate as "major problems." Inadequate salary and inadequate fringe benefits follow closely.

The five top-ranking aspects of teaching conditions and compensation were considered major problems by more than 25 percent of the respondents. In addition, about 40 percent rated them minor problems, placing the total number of teachers who have problems in these areas in the range of 65 to 75 percent.

	Major problems	*Minor problems*
Insufficient time for rest and preparation in school day	37.6%	36.4%
Large class size	34.7	37.3
Insufficient clerical help	30.5	38.3
Inadequate salary	29.7	42.3
Inadequate fringe benefits	26.9	40.1

Less widespread are problems occurring in other areas, for the most part more specialized aspects of school activity. With one exception (ineffective faculty meetings), more than half the respondents rated the following areas either major or minor problems:

	Major problems	*Minor problems*
Inadequate assistance from specialized teachers, e.g., remedial reading, speech therapy	24.5%	34.0%
Lack of public support for schools	22.7	38.5
Ineffective grouping of students into classes	22.1	41.7
Ineffective faculty meetings	20.1	29.0
Inadequate instructional materials	18.7	40.7
Ineffective testing and guidance program	18.5	33.8
Inadequate consultative assistance with instructional problems	17.3	38.9

Lowest on the list of major problems were:

	Major problems	*Minor problems*
Ineffective administration	17.2%	28.7%
Classroom management and discipline	15.2	45.3
Ineffective local teachers association	14.4	30.5
Lack of opportunity for professional growth	11.8	30.4
Negative attitude of colleagues toward teaching	8.6	35.0

Among these, classroom management and discipline are a special case. Although not a major problem for many teachers, the large percentage of those who rate it a minor problem brings the total percentage of teachers who consider this a problem to over 60 percent. Less than 50 percent found the other items in this group either major or minor problems.

Teacher problems vary with different types of communities. Class size and discipline are major problems for a greater proportion of urban than of suburban or rural teachers. The major problem for rural teachers, as opposed to urban or suburban teachers, is inadequate assistance from specialized teachers. Rural and urban teachers, in contrast to those in suburban communities, share complaints about the inadequacy of salaries and fringe benefits, the ineffectiveness of student grouping and testing and guidance programs, and lack of public support, as major problems.

	Major Problems		
	Urban	*Suburban*	*Rural*
Large class size	40.4%	33.4%	30.6%
Classroom management and discipline	23.3	10.8	12.1
Inadequate assistance from specialized teachers	22.5	21.0	30.3
Inadequate salary	34.9	24.5	30.3
Inadequate fringe benefits	27.7	22.3	31.3
Ineffective grouping of students into classes	24.3	18.2	24.2
Lack of public support for schools	27.8	17.4	23.7
Ineffective testing and guidance program	21.1	14.2	20.8

When figures for major and minor problems are considered together, additional community differences appear. The problem of clerical help is most widespread among urban teachers; least among rural teachers. Inadequacy of instructional materials is a problem which rural teachers share with urban teachers, while lack of opportunity for professional growth is a more extensive problem among teachers in rural than in urban or suburban areas.

	Major and minor problems		
	Urban	*Suburban*	*Rural*
Insufficient clerical help	74.9%	68.4%	63.0%
Inadequate instructional materials	62.3	55.0	61.5
Lack of opportunity for professional growth	41.2	37.7	48.3

An earlier study (March, 1967) by the NEA Research Division dealt with employment status. In this study, the respondents cited the major reasons for changing location of employment as shown in Figure 15.10 (page 372).

Teaching is not without problems. Certain problems that teachers associate with teaching are also cited as major reasons for teachers changing employment from school to school. The problems of teaching also provide the challenges. Teaching as a vocation will become more attractive as school boards, administrators and teachers assist each other in solving problems.

Frustrations of Teaching

The word "frustrate" implies a depriving of effect or a rendering worthless of efforts

directed to some end. Teachers may often feel frustrated in their work. Much of this frustration comes about from the very nature of teaching. Many teachers enter the profession filled with a high degree of idealism, anxious to be doing such a socially important job. Such idealism would probably hold up strongly if each of the teacher's classes consisted of one, or at most, a very small number of pupils. However, the problem of large class size and other problems previously cited take an immediate effect. It becomes quite easy for a teacher to feel her best-meant efforts are rendered worthless and are not related to some desirable end.

Teaching is accompanied by a frustrating kind of lonesomeness also. When faced with problematical situations in the classroom, it

Major reason for change	Percent of teachers who transferred to teach in a different school				
	Elementary	Secondary	Men	Women	Total
Higher salary	20.0%	23.2%	40.0%	11.6%	22.1%
Improved working conditions	9.0	20.3	20.0	11.6	14.7
Personal reasons	11.9	15.9	8.0	17.4	14.0
Husband's work changed location	20.9	2.9	0.0	18.6	11.8
Undesirable community situation	9.0	2.9	4.0	7.0	5.9
Position eliminated	10.4	1.4	4.0	7.0	5.9
Marriage	4.5	5.8	0.0	8.1	5.1
Disagreed with school policies, administration, etc.	0.0	8.7	6.0	3.5	4.4
Termination of contract	1.5	4.3	4.0	2.3	2.9
Other	11.9	14.4	14.0	12.8	13.2
Total	100.0%	99.8%	100.0%	99.9%	100.0%
Number of persons	67	69	50	86	136

Figure 15.10. Major Reasons for Changing Location of Employment Reported by Teachers Transferring to Teach in Other Schools.

Source: *NEA Research Bulletin,* Volume 46, Number 4, December, 1968, p. 120. Used by permission.

seems logical that a teacher would seek assistance from her peer professionals. More often than not, such assistance is not meaningful to his teaching situation; often outside assistance is not available at all. Frustration results.

Evaluation of teaching effectiveness does not usually exist. Building administrators, department chairmen and teaching colleagues are reluctant to attempt to evaluate teacher effectiveness, since the criteria for evaluation are nebulous. Consequently, a teacher has little feedback regarding effectiveness and is, therefore, frustrated by this vague aspect of teaching. Most of us like to know when we are effective in our work. Jobs are less frustrating to us when we are able to know that our work is effective. The outcomes of a teacher's efforts are for the most part unknown. For those who take the frustrations as continuing challenges of the profession, the frustrations often become the driving forces for im-

provement in teacher behavior. For those whose personality disposition requires a constant reinforcement that their work is effective, the frustrations are cause enough for leaving the teaching profession.

To provide the reader with a bit of personal insight regarding the frustration dimension of teaching, a few teachers were asked to comment about their personal frustrations experienced as teachers. Some of their remarks are as follows:

I have experienced overwhelming frustration and failure in teaching and have experienced remarkable success. I have also noticed that what chafes one teacher is some other teacher's particular joyful challenge. From these observations there is a suggestion that if one is genuine in his interest in teaching and comprehends his subject there is a place he can serve educational needs with little frustration and much satisfaction. The implication of this suggestion requires realistic assessment by the teacher of himself and of the educational situation of his school.

Suburban Elementary School Teacher

My biggest frustration lies within myself. I cannot blame administrators, school boards, or anyone. This inability to reach children comes from within.

I was probably trained the way my own teachers were trained. The teacher was the authority and the students accepted and conformed. My first two classes were like this. I considered them good students because they did everything I told them to do. I felt that I was a good teacher and they were good "learners." I didn't worry too much about the two or three who weren't falling in line. I considered their borderline I.Q.'s and attributed it to this. I never considered it could be my fault.

I found that each year my two or three problem children were increasing in numbers. I found my classes generally not so accepting or conforming. I found [them] disinterested in what I was teaching and displaying an "I don't care attitude." My solution—tighten up on discipline and use threats of failure. None of this was successful. I finally began to question myself. With so many students not achieving could it be the teacher? It took me a long time to realize that perhaps it was.

Inner City Elementary School Teacher

Like all other work, teaching has its minor annoyances: clerical work such as taking the roll, filling out reports, completing rating sheets, etc.; housekeeping duties such as hall duty, lunchroom and playground supervision, cleaning transparencies and equipment; and routine classroom work such as dittoing student work sheets, grading objective-type tests, checking daily homework papers, etc. Very few schools have sub-professional help to alleviate the teacher of these time-consuming duties so that he can spend his time teaching—the activity for which he was hired and trained to do.

Many who have not had teaching experience view teaching as a thirty-hour work week. Such is far from true. What they fail to realize is that although actual teacher-student contact time may in some cases be thirty hours, the time spent in deciding upon the best method to present a certain concept or the way to handle a specific student learning or discipline deviation problem requires many, many more hours. It is

these outside-of-school hours that very much affect and are so important to the effectiveness and efficiency of the teacher during the teacher-student contact time.

As a teacher you probably associate with and have more friends among teachers than any other group of people. As a group, they are usually quite stimulating, for they are interested in the world, its events, its people, and its cultural offerings. Teachers are now far more worldly realistic in thought, and allowed to live their own lives outside of the yesteryear's rigid glass fish bowl—in short, they are human beings while still being the determiners of future society.

High School Mathematics Teacher

QUESTIONS FOR DISCUSSION

1. In what ways may teachers' salaries be considered adequate? Inadequate?
2. How would you respond to the following statement? "The most effective teachers are committed teachers."
3. What are some possible reasons for the differences in teacher's salaries from city to city and from state to state?
4. What do you consider to be the three most important problems related to inadequate teaching conditions? Why?
5. Do you feel that "teaching is accompanied by a kind of personal mental anxiety . . ."? Discuss.

SUPPLEMENTARY LEARNING ACTIVITIES

1. Let each class member report the qualities of the best teacher he has had. Formulate a list of qualities most common of "excellent teachers."
2. Conduct interviews with teachers who have a varied length of experience for the purpose of discussing the tangible and intangible rewards and problems of

teaching. Formulate a summary of the interview findings.

3. Conduct interviews with members of other vocations of varied length of experience for the purpose of discussing the tangible and intangible rewards and problems of their jobs. Formulate a summary of the interview findings.

4. Interview two or three members of a local public school board of education to obtain their views on the rewards and problems of teaching in their school district. Summarize the findings.

5. What are two or three ways in which school law affects teaching as a profession?

Selected References

Benson, Charles S. *Perspectives on the Economics of Education*. Boston: Houghton Mifflin Co., 1963.

Donovan, John C. "Implications of Manpower Training." *Phi Delta Kappan* 46(1965):366–369.

Eastmond, Jefferson N. *The Teacher and School Administration*. Boston: Houghton Mifflin Co., 1959.

Economic Status of the Teaching Profession, 1967–68. Washington, D.C.: Research Report 1968 R–4, National Education Association, 1968.

Garber, Lee O., and E. Edmund Reutter, Jr. *The Yearbook of School Law 1967*. Danville, Ill.: The Interstate Printers and Publishers, Inc., 1967.

Hamilton, Robert R., and Paul R. Mort. *The Law and Public Education*. Brooklyn, N.Y.: The Foundation Press, Inc., 1959.

Haskew, Laurence D. and Jonathon C. McLendon. *This Is Teaching*. 3rd ed. Glenview, Ill.: Scott, Foresman and Co., 1968.

"Impact of Changing School Enrollment." *U.S. News and World Report* 66(1969):54–56.

Lieberman, Myron, and Michael H. Moskow. *Collective Negotiations for Teachers: An Approach to School Administration*. Chicago: Rand McNally & Co., 1966.

———. "Teacher Strikes: Acceptable Strategy?" *Phi Delta Kappan* 46(1965):237–240.

NEA Research Bulletin, Volume 46, Number 4, December, 1968.

NEA Research Bulletin, Volume 47, Number 1, March, 1969.

"Public Funds and Parochial School Pupils." *NEA Research Bulletin* 45 (1967):43–46.

Remmlein, Madaline Kinter. *The Law of Local Public School Administration*. New York: McGraw-Hill, Inc., 1953.

Salary Schedules for Teachers, 1967–68. Washington, D.C.: Research Report 1967–R16, National Education Association, 1968.

Simon, Kenneth A., and W. Vance Grant. *Digest of Educational Statistics, 1967*. Washington, D.C.: United States Department of Health, Education, and Welfare; Office of Education, Superintendent of Documents, United States Printing Office, 1967.

State Minimum Salary Laws and Goal Schedules for Teachers, 1966–67. Washington, D.C.: Research Report 1966–R18, National Education Association, 1967.

Stinnett, T. M., Jack H. Kleinmann, and Martha L. Ware. *Professional Negotiation in Public Education*. New York: The Macmillan Co., 1966.

Teacher Supply and Demand in Public Schools, 1967. Washington, D.C.: Research Report 1967–R18, National Education Association, 1967.

United States Department of Health, Education, and Welfare, Office of Education. *Education 65, A Report to the Profession*. Washington, D.C.: Superintendent of Documents, United States Government Printing Office, 1966.

First Manpower Assessment

John Chaffee, Jr.

Those who are beginning to feel sanguine about the nation's teacher shortage will find little comfort in a comprehensive report on educational manpower soon to be published by the U.S. Office of Education. Recent studies indicate that the teacher shortage, which has plagued American education since World War II, will ease in the years ahead as declining birthrates level off elementary school enrollments and as teacher training institutions continue to produce an ever-increasing supply of persons prepared to assume classroom duties.

The Office of Education's first annual assessment of the nation's educational manpower and training needs presents a far less optimistic outlook, however. The report, which is authorized under the Education Professions Development Act, indicates that there is now and will continue to be in the foreseeable future a considerable shortage of teachers and other education personnel, professional and subprofessional, at preschool through postgraduate levels. And, while a number of examples of promising innovative training and retraining programs in both local school systems and higher education institutions are cited, the report makes it clear that education personnel training programs and practices are not sufficient, either quantitatively or qualitatively, to meet current and future needs. The disquieting conclusion: The nation's most basic educational problem is the re-

cruitment, preparation, renewal, and retention of qualified personnel to staff its schools and colleges.

Any summary of the report must begin, appropriately, with recruitment; unless the education professions can attract their fair share of qualified manpower, the quality of available training and retraining programs is academic.

More is expected of our schools and colleges today than ever before. Increased demands for services, such as individualized instruction, counseling and guidance, and special attention to the needs of the disadvantaged, require not only more and better prepared teachers but additional administrators and auxiliary and support personnel. Although the number of men and women training to enter the teaching professions is steadily increasing, nearly 30 per cent of those so trained never teach, and at least 60 per cent of those who do teach leave education during the first five years. So along with a failure to attract into education almost one of three persons specifically trained to teach, there is a teacher dropout situation as serious as the much publicized student dropout problem. One reason for this alarming predicament is that schools today are competing with other segments of a service-oriented economy for precisely those skills

* John Chaffee, Jr., "First Manpower Assessment," *American Education* 5(1969):11–12.

and communication talents possessed by good teachers. And in those other segments persons with such skills can command higher salaries and foresee greater opportunities for professional advancement than are currently available in the education professions. Thus, simply training more teachers will not guarantee an adequate supply to the schools.

The education professions must be made more attractive if we are to retain a larger proportion of those trained to teach and recruit more of those now aloof to a career in education. Probably the single factor that most discourages potential teachers is their own experience as students in schools; for students, more than any other group, are aware of the difficulties and frustrations seemingly inherent in an education career today. Rigid salary structures, lack of distinction between the duties of novice and experienced teachers, no real opportunity for meaningful and professional advancement *as a teacher,* little involvement by teachers in basic policy decision-making all contribute to the present unattractiveness of the education professions.

Finally, a major barrier to recruitment and retention is the nature of teacher training programs, for their character determines in large measure the quality of personnel entering the education professions. Prospective teachers—those currently enrolled in teacher training programs—are, in ability and performance, middle-ranking students for the most part. Most are women from middle-class families; they are "interracially inexperienced" and prefer to teach the children of white-collar families. Nearly half have spent most of their lives in their present city, town, or county.

More than 80 per cent of the nation's future teachers are being trained at institutions which are rated "C" or "D" on the American Association of University Professors' scale of faculty salaries; nearly half attend "D" level institutions. On the other hand, less than four percent are being prepared at colleges or universities rated "A" or better on the AAUP scale.

The assessment indicates that higher education has not made a substantial investment in teacher training. The cost of preparing dentists or physicians may range from $5,000 to $12,000 per student per year; the cost of training teachers averages less than $1,000 per student per year.

In addition, or perhaps as a result, teacher training institutions seem to have a penchant for producing graduates whose competence is judged solely by the successful completion of courses which too frequently bear little relationship to the realities of classroom teaching. The success of a teacher of disadvantaged children, for example, depends significantly on such inherent or acquired characteristics as openness, humanity, a capacity to love. And yet, there is no way to prevent those who lack these characteristics from entering the teaching field.

A growing number of programs across the nation enable teachers to return briefly to colleges or universities for retraining. Such programs are either remedial (efforts to correct the inadequacies of earlier training) or they are enriching (necessary because of curricular developments such as the new math). What has been missing is a commitment to regular inservice training as part of a continuous process of professional growth and renewal.

In this respect, local school districts have been negligent. They have left the burden of recruitment, training, and retraining primarily to the very colleges and universities that have demonstrated a lack of commitment to training for the education professions. Only local schools can provide contact with the students, education personnel, and community members—the vital human elements that make up the realities of the daily education scene. And only institutions of higher learning can award those with academic and research skills the necessary time for inquiry and planning that must go into development and evaluation of new programs and practices. Neither group can successfully conduct its affairs without the other. And yet, that is just what each has been trying to do.

Some possible solutions to problems of staff training and utilization may be found in two types of model programs currently being conducted on a modest scale in various kinds of universities and local school systems throughout the country: the Teacher Corps and differentiated staffing.

The Teacher Corps provides a model of the desired alliance between community, local school, and teacher training institution. Properly nurtured, such an alliance can result in a more effective means of teacher recruitment and preparation. Differentiated staffing experiments may offer answers to some basic questions: How can the duties of novice and experienced teacher be distinguished? How can teachers advance professionally and financially and still remain teachers? How can teachers become truly involved in decision making?

Teacher Corps interns are usually liberal arts graduates who receive a brief period of intensive preservice preparation at a university, followed by two years of supervised participation in the daily activities of a local school system and its community. They continue part-time graduate study during those two years. Upon completion of this program, the intern receives a master's degree in education, based upon far wider practical experience than the norm for such training. His preparation has been secured upon a widely accepted but rarely acted upon belief: The most effective training of education personnel is directly related to experience in local schools.

Differentiated staffing plans, which have been developed in such diverse communities as Temple City, Calif.; Beaverton, Ore.; Kansas City, Mo.; and Greece, N.Y., seek to create a career ladder beginning in some cases with part-time student aides and progressing through a series of pre-professional positions (aides, assistant and associate teachers, and teaching interns) and professional positions (teachers, staff teachers, senior teachers, and master teachers). Each differentiated position in such a hierarchy has its own salary schedule, and, at the highest level of the master teacher scale, it is possible for a teacher to be paid as much or more than most administrators in the school system. In addition, decisions about curriculum matters are left to senior and master teachers rather than administrators. Such staffing eliminates a number of the present barriers to recruitment and retention of quality personnel.

New alliances between schools, universities, and local communities, coupled with new means of staff utilization within the schools may eventually solve many of the most basic education personnel problems. But specific, more specialized staffing problems remain, particularly in early childhood education, vocational-technical education, school administration, and higher education.

The field of early childhood education is relatively new. Until the mid-1960's, public education by and large assumed responsibility for the child only from age six. A growing realization that by six most children have already developed a considerable part of the basic intellectual ability they will possess as adults, plus the success of Head Start, have resulted in a new emphasis on education for children aged three to eight, or from prekindergarten through grade three. However, few teacher training institutions provide programs in early childhood education. Additional training programs are needed and appropriate recruitment efforts should be undertaken.

Vocational-technical training has long been education's black sheep. Economic realities are forcing a change of attitude. The nation's economy now needs skilled workers who have both vocational or technical competence and some appreciation of the kinds of human relations and communication skills traditionally associated with an academic education. As a result, vocational-technical education programs are becoming more sophisticated. They are moving into the postsecondary school level and are, of necessity, becoming more closely tied in with academic education. But the way vocational educators are recruited, trained, and retrained remains essentially unchanged. Programs for training vocational education personnel are virtually non-existent in institutions of higher education. Business and industry—the great consumers of vocational education's products—are only slightly involved in the process of providing adequately trained professional personnel.

In school administration there is a surplus of quantity and a shortage of quality. Schools and colleges have traditionally recruited their administrators from the ranks of teachers, a pool which may be unnecessarily limited and which could be further limited if differentiated staffing practices were to become widespread. An ability in community relations is essential to a modern school administrator's success. But this is perhaps one of the most neglected aspects of administrative training programs in colleges and universities.

At the higher education level, the most critical immediate needs are for quality personnel to staff our rapidly expanding system of junior and community colleges and the developing institutions, many of which barely survive financially from year to year. The current practice of rewarding the research-scholar at the expense of the teacher-scholar has unfairly placed such institutions at a competitive disadvantage. American colleges and universities have failed to support programs for training college teachers as vigorously as they have programs for training researchers.

And so, while the teacher shortage may indeed abate somewhat as far as raw numbers are concerned, education in the United States continues to face a fundamental challenge: How to get quality personnel to satisfy the ever-increasing demands for services on a more individualized basis for more students who stay in school longer.

The answer, as outlined in the first annual assessment of the education professions, lies in more community involvement, better staff utilization, and a greater awareness by higher education of its responsibilities to all education and thus to society as a whole.

Synopsis

The tasks of education in our society are many and diverse. This textbook has attempted to depict them in terms of both societal and individual expectations. It has also attempted to briefly depict the educational milieu; the way that it was and the way that it is. The most important persons in education, with the notable exception of the learners, are the teachers.

There is little doubt that teachers are "molders and shapers"; they deal in a way with destinies. It is hoped that this textbook in some small way will help young people decide whether teaching is a career that they wish to pursue.

Index